Advances in
Clinical Child Psychology

Volume 20

ADVANCES IN CLINICAL CHILD PSYCHOLOGY

A Continuation Order Plan is available for this series. A continuation order will bring delivery of each new volume immediately upon publication. Volumes are billed only upon actual shipment. For further information please contact the publisher.

Advances in
Clinical Child Psychology

Volume 20

Edited by

THOMAS H. OLLENDICK
Virginia Polytechnic Institute and State University
Blacksburg, Virginia

and

RONALD J. PRINZ
University of South Carolina
Columbia, South Carolina

Plenum Press • New York and London

The Library of Congress cataloged the first volume of this title as follows:

Advances in clinical child psychology, v. 1—

New York, Plenum Press, ©1977—

v. ill. 24 cm.
Key title: Advances in clinical child psychology. ISSN 0149-4732

1. Clinical psychology—Collected works. 2. Child psychology—Collected works.
3. Child psychotherapy—Collected works.

RJ503.3.A37 618.9'28'9   77-643411

ISBN 0-306-45667-2

© 1998 Plenum Press, New York
A Division of Plenum Publishing Corporation
233 Spring Street, New York, N.Y. 10013

http://www.plenum.com

Printed in the United States of America

Contributors

Anne Marie Albano
Anxiety Research and Treatment Center, Department of Psychology, University of Louisville, Louisville, Kentucky 40292

Tim S. Ayers
Program for Prevention Research, Arizona State University, Tempe, Arizona 85287

Karen S. Budd
Department of Psychology, DePaul University, Chicago, Illinois 60614

Cary S. Chugh
Department of Psychology, DePaul University, Chicago, Illinois 60614

Sheila Eyberg
Department of Clinical and Health Psychology, University of Florida, Gainesville, Florida 32610

Rebecca Foote
Department of Clinical and Health Psychology, University of Florida, Gainesville, Florida 32610

Saundra Glover
School of Public Health, University of South Carolina, Columbia, South Carolina 29208

Stanley J. Huey
Department of Psychology, University of California at Los Angeles, Los Angeles, California 90095

John S. March
Departments of Psychiatry and Psychology: Social and Health Sciences, Duke University Medical Center, Durham, North Carolina 27710

Barbara Maughan
MRC Child Psychiatry Unit and Social, Genetic, and Developmental Psychiatry Research Centre, Institute of Psychiatry, DeCrespigny Park, London SE5 8AF, England

Pier J. M. Prins
Department of Clinical Psychology, University of Amsterdam, 1018 WB Amsterdam, The Netherlands

Andres J. Pumariega   *Department of Psychiatry and Behavioral Sciences, James H. Quillen College of Medicine, East Tennessee State University, Johnson City, Tennessee 36714*

Simon Rietveld   *Department of Clinical Psychology, University of Amsterdam, 1018 WB Amsterdam, The Netherlands*

Robert L. Russell   *Department of Psychology, Loyola University Chicago, Chicago, Illinois 60626*

Michael Rutter   *MRC Child Psychiatry Unit and Social, Genetic, and Developmental Psychiatry Research Centre, Institute of Psychiatry, DeCrespigny Park, London SE5 8AF, England*

Irwin N. Sandler   *Program for Prevention Research, Arizona State University, Tempe, Arizona 85287*

Elena Schuhmann   *Department of Clinical and Health Psychology, University of Florida, Gainesville, Florida 32610*

Stephen R. Shirk   *Department of Psychology, University of Denver, Denver, Colorado 80208*

Joan L. Twohey   *Program for Prevention Research, Arizona State University, Tempe, Arizona 85287*

Vanessa Robin Weersing   *Department of Psychology, University of California at Los Angeles, Los Angeles, California 90095*

John R. Weisz   *Department of Psychology, University of California at Los Angeles, Los Angeles, California 90095*

Preface

It is with both pride and sadness that we publish the twentieth and last volume of *Advances in Clinical Child Psychology*. This series has seen a long and successful run starting under the editorship of Ben Lahey and Alan Kazdin, who passed the baton to us at Volume 14. We are grateful to the many contributors over the years and to the Plenum staff for producing a quality product in a timely manner.

This volume covers a diverse array of significant topics. In the opening chapter, Maughan and Rutter explore the research literatures related to continuity and discontinuity of antisocial behavior from childhood to adulthood. Their review and conceptualization emphasize the significance of hyperactivity and inattention, early-onset conduct problems, low reactivity to stress, and poor peer relations as potentially influential variables in the persistence of antisocial behavior. Social cognitions, environmental continuities, substance abuse, cumulative chains of life events, and protective processes are considered as well.

The next two chapters address outcome and process in child and adolescent psychotherapy research. Weisz, Huey, and Weersing consider a broad range of factors connected to therapy outcome. Their conceptualization takes into account the therapies, the therapists' contributions, and the children's role in affecting outcome. A major part of this chapter addresses ethnicity and culture of treated children and their families in relation to effectiveness, matching, and contextual influences. Russell and Shirk review process research for child psychotherapy. Relative to studies of treatment outcome, psychotherapy process has been the ignored stepchild of child psychotherapy research. This chapter discusses empirical research on what actually transpires between therapist and child during their face-to-face meetings in clinical sessions. Although not yet extensive, the research is exciting and points to important relations between pathogenic processes in children and psychotherapy processes in treatment. The "match" between pathogenic and treatment processes is well articulated.

Foote, Eyberg, and Schuhmann focus on parent–child interaction approaches to the treatment of child behavior problems. By addressing family relationships, treatment gains with children for oppositional defiant disorder and early-onset conduct disorder might be sustained more readily than what can be accomplished with child-oriented approaches.

The next three chapters address pediatric issues. Rietveld and Prins analyze biomedical and psychological factors influencing children's perceptions of physical symptoms, using asthma as the primary example. Their insightful analysis has implications for conceptualization, assessment, and etiological models of psychophysiological problems that children encounter. Budd and Chugh provide a thorough review of common feeding problems in younger children. Their chapter addresses definitions of eating problems, common etiologies, assessment considerations, and management approaches. March and Albano describe new developments in assessing pediatric anxiety disorders. They evaluate self-report measures, diagnostic interviews, and behavioral assessment methods, and then discuss the role of neuroscience in emerging developmental conceptualizations related to child anxiety.

Chapter 8 by Ayers, Sandler, and Twohey is an exhaustive review regarding the conceptualization and measurement of coping in children and adolescents. Their review carefully addresses not only the wide variety of measures and assessment methods but also the extent to which situational analysis of coping is incorporated into theory and method.

The final chapter, by Pumariega and Glover, covers the emerging area of services delivery research for children, adolescents, and their families. They describe current approaches and ongoing projects, discuss anticipated developments in large system studies and in methodology, and project what the future needs and benefits will be for child mental health services research.

We want to take this opportunity to especially thank Mariclaire Cloutier and Eliot Werner at Plenum for their support over the years; however, our involvement with Plenum is far from over. We are pleased to announce that the spirit of the Advances series is being continued in a new Plenum journal, *Clinical Child and Family Psychology Review*, which begins in 1998. This new journal will publish reviews, conceptual and theoretical papers, and related work in the broad area of the behavioral sciences pertaining to infants, children, adolescents, and families. Contributions will come from many disciplines, including but not limited to psychology (clinical, community, developmental, family, school), medicine (family practice, pediatrics, psychiatry), public health, social work, and education. Topical content includes science and application, and may cover facets of etiology, assessment, description, treatment/intervention, prevention, methodology, and public policy. Contributions are by invitation only. The editors in consultation with the Editorial Board invite highly qualified authors to contribute on topics of timely interest and significance. Although solicited, all manuscripts are peer-reviewed and edited. Suggestions for topics and potential contributors are welcome and should be submitted to the editors.

THOMAS H. OLLENDICK
RONALD J. PRINZ

Contents

Chapter 3.   Child Psychotherapy Process Research   93

Robert L. Russell and Stephen R. Shirk

Chapter 4.   Parent–Child Interaction Approaches
to the Treatment of Child Behavior Problems   125

Rebecca Foote, Sheila Eyberg, and Elena Schuhmann

Chapter 5. Children's Perception of Physical Symptoms:
The Example of Asthma   153

Simon Rietveld and Pier J. M. Prins

Chapter 6. Common Feeding Problems in Young Children   183

Karen S. Budd and Cary S. Chugh

Chapter 7. New Developments in Assessing Pediatric Anxiety Disorders   213

John S. March and Anne Marie Albano

1

Continuities and Discontinuities in Antisocial Behavior from Childhood to Adult Life

BARBARA MAUGHAN AND MICHAEL RUTTER

1. Introduction

Much adult psychopathology has its roots in childhood difficulties; nowhere is that tendency more apparent than in the antisocial domain. From the time of the first long-term follow-ups (Robins, 1966, 1978) it has been clear that most severely antisocial adults have long histories of disruptive and deviant behavior reaching back to childhood. Yet these same studies also highlighted an apparent paradox: looking forward from childhood, the picture was a rather different one. Most conduct-disordered children did not grow up to be severely antisocial adults, and for many, *discontinuity*, rather than continuity, seemed the more usual course.

The identification of the mechanisms that account for these patterns constitutes a central challenge for developmental psychopathology. Which early risks or intervening processes contribute to the long-term persistence of antisocial problems in some individuals but allow an apparently more benign course in others? Do the majority of antisocial children indeed "recover" before adulthood, or do they too face continuing vulnerabilities, albeit of a less severe or possibly different kind? And can these varying developmental trajectories help us understand the underlying hetero-

BARBARA MAUGHAN AND MICHAEL RUTTER • MRC Child Psychiatry Unit and Social, Genetic, and Developmental Psychiatry Research Centre, Institute of Psychiatry, DeCrespigny Park, London SE5 8AF, England.

Advances in Clinical Child Psychology, Volume 20, edited by Thomas H. Ollendick and Ronald J. Prinz. Plenum Press, New York, 1998.

geneity within the population of antisocial children, and so illuminate classifications of childhood disorders? These questions form the main focus of this chapter.

2. Conceptual and Methodological Issues

2.1. Heterogeneity

To begin, we need to consider a number of conceptual and methodological issues. The first concerns the heterogeneity of antisocial behaviors (Rutter, 1997a; Rutter et al., in press-b). At one extreme, for example, the majority of young people are involved in occasional illegal acts; at the other, a minority show long-term, persistent difficulties that span not only criminality but also severe dysfunction in many life domains (Robins, Tipp, & Przybeck, 1991). No one doubts these variations, but opinions differ widely on their meaning. Some investigators have argued that all manifestations of antisocial behavior are best viewed in terms of a single underlying syndrome or propensity (Gottfreson & Hirschi, 1990; Jessor & Jessor, 1977). Others have dealt with the variation in terms of factorially derived dimensions involving concealing behaviors (such as theft) and confrontational/aggressive acts (Loeber & Schmaling, 1985) or the presence/absence of destructiveness (Frick et al., 1993).

Psychiatric classifications, by contrast, have sought to subdivide disruptive or antisocial behavior into discrete syndromes. Thus distinctions are drawn between oppositional defiant disorder (ODD, involving negative, hostile, and defiant behavior); conduct disorder (CD, characterized by violation of the rights of others and by bullying, cruelty, firesetting, and stealing); and hyperkinetic/attention-deficit disorder, defined in terms of hyperactivity, impulsivity, and overactivity (American Psychiatric Association, 1994; World Health Organization, 1992). Further subdivisions are made according to whether the antisocial behavior is socialized or unsocialized, or according to age at onset. The World Health Organization (WHO) system, ICD-10, also recognizes the frequent co-occurrence of conduct problems with other patterns of psychopathology by introducing separate mixed categories for conduct disorder that are associated with hyperkinetic disorder or depression. The high rates of comorbidity between disruptive disorders and a range of other diagnoses (Hinshaw, 1992; Hinshaw, Lahey, & Hart, 1993; Loeber & Keenan, 1994; Zoccolillo, 1992) raise crucial classification issues (Caron & Rutter, 1991; Nottelman & Jensen, 1995). On the one hand, they may suggest boundary problems in current diagnostic systems; on the other, co-occurring patterns of symptomatology may be of key significance for etiology and outcome. From other perspectives again, there have been proposals to classify antisocial behaviors according to age at onset (DiLalla & Gottesman, 1989; Moffitt, 1993a; Patterson & Yoerger, 1993, in press). And most recently, behavior genetic strategies have begun to identify subtypes varying in their degrees of heritable and environmental risk (Silberg et al., 1996). In the face of these contrasting models, we have not organized this review according to any specific diagnostic distinctions, but have aimed instead to consider their validity in terms of the longitudinal findings we survey.

2.2.   Categories and Dimensions

A closely related issue, still unresolved, concerns whether antisocial behaviors are best conceptualized as qualitatively distinct categories or varying admixtures of dimensional traits and risks (Cantwell & Rutter, 1994; Clark, Watson, & Reynolds, 1995; Waldman, Lilienfield, & Lahey, 1995). Although much existing literature is premised on categorical models, it is far from clear that this is in fact the most appropriate stance. Studies in both medicine and psychology suggest that behaviors can function dimensionally for some purposes but categorically for others. Clearly categorical outcomes (such as the occurrence of a heart attack) may have their origins in dimensional variables (such as cholesterol levels), and clinically important dimensions can often be identified within qualitatively distinct disease categories. Diagnostic assessments of childhood disorders show considerable overlap with dimensional syndrome scores (Gould, Bird, & Jaramillo, 1993; Jensen et al., 1996), and, as we discuss in more detail later, subclinical levels of difficulty frequently show correlates and consequences similar to those of more severe disorder categories. From a methodological perspective, dimensional approaches offer greater power, and categorical models are sensitive to threshold variations (Farrington, 1991). In some instances, however, especially when constellations of factors are examined, categorical models can have considerable force (Magnusson & Bergman, 1990). At this stage, the issue is an empirical one, and longitudinal data offer one important means of testing alternative formulations.

2.3.   Continuity and Change

Turning to questions of continuity and change, several rather different concepts need to be examined in studies of behavioral development (Kagan, 1980; Rutter, 1987). First, there is the question of *normative consistency*, or the stability of individual differences over time. In relation to antisocial behaviors, such stability is high. Olweus (1979) estimated disattentuated correlations of .60 for measures of aggression over 10-year age spans in childhood and early adulthood, with relatively stable individual differences in aggressive tendencies evident from the preschool years. This consistency extends beyond measures of phenotypically similar behaviors; *heterotypic continuity* (Kagan, 1969)—whereby differing, but conceptually coherent, indicators of antisocial tendencies are related across development—is also strong. Huesmann, Eron, Lefkowitz, and Walder (1984), for example, reported significant correlations between peer-nominated aggression at age 8 and the number and seriousness of convictions, rates of drunk driving, and harsh physical punishment of children over 20 years later. Rydelius (1988) documented markedly increased risks of violent death among previously incarcerated delinquents. Numerous other studies, using a range of different indicators, have reached similar conclusions; individual differences in antisocial and aggressive tendencies are relatively stable across development. Equally important, this is so even over developmental age periods when the overall level of antisocial behavior is rising—as in early adolescence—or falling sharply, as in early adulthood (Farrington, 1990).

These age trends form a second key part of the backdrop to studies of individual development. Probably the best-known example here is the age–crime curve. Beginning at the age of criminal responsibility, rates of recorded male crime show a gradual increase over the early teens, a sharp rise in the later teens, then an equally sharp decline in the midtwenties. Studies of offenders reveal a similar pattern. In the United Kingdom, for example, less than 5% of males are convicted of offenses in the early teens and again in the midtwenties, but some 12% of young men are likely to be involved with the criminal justice system in their late teenage years (Farrington, 1992; Home Office, 1995). Self-reports highlight a similar pattern, suggesting that illegal behaviors are so common as to be virtually normative among boys in adolescence (Elliott, Ageton, Huizinga, Knowles, & Canter, 1983). Although age trends in disruptive and antisocial disorders have been less systematically documented, they too show a marked adolescent peak. Before age 11, rates of oppositional and conduct disorders occur at around 6% in boys and 2% in girls (Offord et al., 1987). For both sexes, rates of oppositional disorders then rise to levels as high as 15–16% among 13- to 16-year-olds, with a sharp decline thereafter (Cohen et al., 1993b). Prevalence curves differ between the sexes in conduct disorder. Rates for boys fall after the early- to midteens, whereas those for girls increase to around age 16, then decline steeply. In early adulthood, some 6% of males and 0.6% of females have been reported as meeting criteria for antisocial personality disorder (Newman, Moffitt, Caspi, Magdol, & Silva,

1996); rates fall further in the later adult years (Robins et al., 1991). Drug and alcohol disorders emerge for the first time in the late teens. They too show a marked male preponderance and a decline in prevalence with age across the adult years (Anthony & Helzer, 1991; Helzer, Burnham, & McEvoy, 1991).

Individual trajectories will not, of course, necessarily follow this same pattern. Indeed, longitudinal studies of offending (Blumstein, Cohen, Roth, & Visher, 1986: Farrington, 1986a; Nagin, Farrington, & Moffitt, 1995) have highlighted the very different implications that emerge from cross-sectional and longitudinal designs. Longitudinal analyses make clear that the adolescent peak in offending is composed of at least two elements: an increase in the prevalence of *offenders*, along with an adolescent increase in rates of *offending* among those already involved in crime (Farrington & West, 1993; Nagin et al., 1995). Alongside relatively stable individual differences in antisocial behaviors, the developmental picture also gives clear evidence of important *within-individual* change.

2.4. Reports and Reporters

Research on antisocial behaviors draws on a variety of accounts: reports from parents, teachers, and peers; self-reports; and official records. Multiple informants have been seen as essential in assessing child psychopathology, yet epidemiologic studies have consistently found that agreement among them is poor (Achenbach, McConaughy, & Howell, 1987). To some extent, these differences will reflect meaningful source variations: Some behaviors are situational, and others are only known to particular reporters. In addition, each source is prey to particular types of bias. These measurement issues are of central importance in all research on child psychopathology. In the present context, three main issues need to be stressed. First, different accounts may suggest quite different patterns of stability and change in antisocial behaviors. Self-reports, for example, suggest longer-term persistence in illegal activities and antisocial lifestyles in early adulthood than is reflected in official records (Graham & Bowling, 1995; Nagin et al., 1995), and stability coefficients may differ depending on whether they are based on parent, teacher, or self-reports. Second, in longitudinal as in cross-sectional analyses, differing methods of combining reports may give rise to differing conclusions (Canino, Bird, Rubio-Stipec, & Bravo, 1995). Third, attention to measurement error and method factors is crucial in deriving appropriate estimates of effects. In principle, analyses based on observed measures could either over- or underestimate the true extent of continuity. In practice, most empirical demonstrations to date have found higher levels of continuity when measurement error has been taken into account (see, e.g., Fergusson, Horwood, & Lynskey, 1995; Zoccolillo, Pickles, Quinton, & Rutter, 1992). Latent class or latent variable models (Dunn, Everitt, & Pickles, 1993; Waldman et al., 1995) offer important advantages here, though their assumptions may not always mirror the constructs investigators are aiming to test. Advances in both measurement and analytic strategies are central to progress in understanding behavioral development.

One final reporting issue is more specific to longitudinal studies: the reliability of retrospective reports. Although prospective evidence on continuities in antisocial behaviors is expanding rapidly, large-scale retrospective studies of adult samples, such as the Epidemiologic Catchment Area studies (ECA; Robins & Regier, 1991), and the National Comorbidity Study (Kessler et al., 1994), continue to provide key data sources, especially for small or extreme groups. Direct tests of the reliability of retrospective reports of childhood problems remain limited (Maughan & Rutter, 1997). It seems likely that the presence or absence of childhood symptoms can be documented reliably in adulthood using appropriate interviewing styles (Holmshaw & Simonoff, 1996), but accuracy in the timing and dating of symptoms is much more questionable (Angold, Erkanli, Costello, & Rutter, 1996), especially when recall is for events many years in the past. Retrospective accounts typically involve some "telescoping," with events brought closer to the present, or systematically moved further into the past, than contemporaneous reports suggest (Menard & Elliott, 1990; Sudman & Bradburn, 1973). Simulations (Guiffra & Risch, 1994) have shown how relatively small tendencies to forget events in the past could mimic true cohort effects, giving rise to spurious conclusions on secular trends. Although retrospective reports continue to provide important sources of data, we have, whenever possible, sought to confirm and complement them with prospectively ascertained accounts.

2.5. Gender Differences

Male gender is perhaps the best established correlate of antisocial behavior, and many (though not all) measures of antisocial difficulties show a marked male preponderance. In principle, these consistent gender differences could provide a rich source of hypotheses about the etiology and maintenance of conduct problems in both sexes. In practice, with only a few notable exceptions, the research literature to date has concentrated almost exclusively on males. As a result, it is still unclear how far gender differences in antisocial behavior reflect biosocial influences, differences in vulnerability to environmental adversity, or variations in parental rearing and cultural expectations. The dearth of empirical data is compounded by concerns that current diagnostic criteria fail to detect behaviors relevant in assessing conduct disorder and its sequelae in girls (Zoccolillo, 1993). Loeber and Hay (1994) have charted early stages in the development of gender differences in aggression and conduct problems, and one of us (Rutter, Giller, & Hagell, in press-a) has recently summarized current evidence on the biological, social, and developmental factors that may contribute to evolving differences between the sexes in expressions of socially disapproved behaviors. In the present chapter, we have noted similarities and differences between the sexes in longer-term continuities in antisocial behavior so far as current data allow, in the hope that these will act as a stimulus to further research. At this stage, however, the important task of tracing the development of girls' antisocial behavior is only in its earliest stages.

3. Continuity and Change: Longitudinal Findings

With these issues in mind, we turn to a brief overview of existing longitudinal findings. Much early evidence centered on clinical and high-risk samples, or community samples drawn from severely disadvantaged inner urban areas (Offord & Bennett, 1994). Much of the most detailed and informative evidence still comes from studies of this kind. More recently, however, these sources have been supplemented by large-scale retrospective investigations and by prospective follow-ups of more socially representative groups. We begin by surveying evidence from "broad-range" childhood–adult studies, examining adult outcomes for groups assessed at differing points in childhood. Then, to fill in the developmental picture, we provide a brief summary of continuities over more focused age periods.

3.1. Broad-Range Childhood–Adult Studies

Diagnostic criteria for antisocial disorders have been much influenced by Robins's (1966) early findings that the central adult outcome of childhood conduct problems lies in the pattern of severe antisocial difficulties, evident across domains of functioning, typified by antisocial personality disorder (ASPD). Taking this focus, both prospective and retrospective evidence has confirmed early studies with striking consistency. In replications of her original child guidance study, Robins (1978) found that the great majority of severely antisocial adults had shown similarly severe behavior problems in childhood. "New onset" of antisocial behavior in adulthood was infrequent, occurring in only 5–12% of cases. Looking forward from childhood, persistence was much less strong; between 23% and 41% of severely antisocial children went on to become antisocial adults, but the majority, whatever the severity of their initial difficulties, seemed, on these criteria, to have "recovered."

Very similar estimates emerged from retrospective reports of childhood conduct problems collected in the ECA studies (Robins et al., 1991). Rates of ASPD rose with the number of childhood symptoms but never went above half, even among those reporting multiple childhood problems. The number of childhood problems functioned dimensionally as a predictor of later disorder and was a better predictor than any individual type of early behavior problem. The same pattern of childhood–adult continuities held for both men and women, and across different age cohorts, despite marked secular changes in overall rates of childhood difficulties. Finally, early-onset conduct problems seemed especially ominous in terms of persistence: The average age at onset of the first childhood symptom was 8–9 years, and 80% of future cases reported occurrence of at least one symptom by age 11.

Childhood conduct problems and aggression also show robust links with later offending (Farrington, Loeber, & Van Kammen, 1990a; Hämäläinen & Pulkkinen, 1996; Huesmann et al., 1984; Magnusson, 1988; Moffitt, 1994; Pulkkinen & Pitkanen, 1993; Robins, 1993; Stattin & Magnusson, 1989). Here, much of the available evidence is prospectively ascertained and based on representative samples. Modest associations with early adult offending have been reported from behavioral observations made as early as age 3 (Caspi, Moffitt, Newman, & Silva, 1996), and later in childhood, stronger links are found. Stattin and Magnusson (1989), for example, examined associations between teacher ratings of aggression at ages 10 and 13 and offending up to age 26 in a socially representative Swedish cohort. Among males, the majority of delinquents and recidivist offenders were drawn from early aggressive boys. Aggression predicted to violent crimes, damage to public property, and most strongly to diversified offense patterns, including both acquisitive and other crimes. Among females, aggression also predicted later offending, but only from age 13.

For men, offense histories paint a similar picture. In U.S. samples, between 31% and 71% of juvenile offenders have some subsequent arrests in adult life (Blumstein et al., 1986), and comparable patterns have been documented in European cohorts (Farrington & Wikström, 1994). Individual offenders vary widely in the length and seriousness of their criminal careers. As many as half of the men who come in contact with the criminal justice system do so only once; at the other end of the spectrum, all studies reaching into adulthood have also identified small groups of chronic male offenders with extended criminal "careers," who account for large proportions of recorded crime (Farrington & Wikström, 1994; Wolfgang, Figlio, & Sellin, 1972). Typically, these chronic offenders show an early onset of offending and engage in a diverse range of offenses, both violent and nonviolent.

Offense histories have been less widely documented for women, but available evidence suggests that they differ in important ways (Home Office, 1995; Krazter & Hodgins, 1996; Wikström, 1990). First, recidivist criminality is relatively unusual among women, and the great majority of those who receive official convictions receive only one. Second, ages at offending show a much less marked peak in the teens than for males, and relatively stable (though very low) proportions of women continue to receive first convictions well into their twenties. In one U.K. birth cohort, for example, the median age for first convictions among women was 22 years, and one-fourth of female offenders had their first conviction after age 28 (Home Office, 1995). In a large-scale Swedish cohort (Krazter & Hodgins, 1996), adult-onset cases accounted for the largest proportion of crimes up to age 30. Whereas adolescence-related factors seem of major importance in understanding criminality in males, female offending appears, on this evidence at least, to be less clearly age related.

In addition to these specifically antisocial outcomes, it has long been clear that childhood conduct problems are associated with later risks of much wider kinds (Robins, 1966). Some of these—most notably elevated rates of alcohol and substance use (McCord & McCord, 1960; Robins, 1966; Robins & McEvoy, 1990; Vaillant, 1983) and "dramatic" personality disorders—fall within a broadly "externalizing" spectrum of difficulties. In addition, small-scale follow-ups of referred and high-risk samples have pointed to increased risks for a range of other adult disorders (Zoccolillo, 1992). Using ECA data, Robins and Price (1991) confirmed this same picture in community samples, documenting significant relationships between childhood conduct problems (often below current thresholds for disorder) and later phobia, major depressive episode, obsessive–compulsive disorder, schizophrenia, panic disorder, manic episodes, and somatization. In general, these risks were dependent on the presence of externalizing disorders in adulthood, though there were also modest direct associations with childhood conduct problems. Some evidence (Quinton, Rutter, & Gulliver, 1990; Robins, 1986) suggests that risks of affective disorder are higher for women than for men. In addition, where depressive phenomena are associated with ASPD, they seem almost exclusively of a relatively mild kind, as judged by the type of symptomatology rather than chronicity or degree of social impairment (Rutter, Harrington, Quinton, & Pickles, 1994). Thus, bipolar disorders and unipolar disorders with marked vegetative features are rare.

Finally, other findings suggest that the legacy of childhood conduct problems extends well beyond conventional assessments of psychopathology or crime. Zoccolillo et al. (1992) assessed functioning in work, marriage, and social relationships, as well as in offending, in an early adult follow-up of a high-risk sample (children raised in group care), together with an inner-city comparison group. In addition to those meeting criteria for ASPD, the great majority of previously conduct-disordered subjects showed poor outcomes in two or more of these domains. Problems in individual role areas were not uncommon in subjects without childhood conduct problems; the characteristic feature of the outcome for conduct-disordered children, however, lay in the pervasiveness of their difficulties across domains. This pattern has since been replicated in other samples (Maughan, Pickles, & Quinton, 1995; Quinton, Pickles, Maughan, & Rutter, 1993).

These findings raise central questions about the nature of the long-term risks associated with childhood conduct problems and the mechanisms by which they are sustained. In particular, they argue that later outcomes are not confined to severe personality difficulties and criminality, but show effects on interpersonal relationships and social functioning on a much more extensive scale. It is unclear at this stage how far these problems constitute an inherent part of the conduct disorder syndrome, or secondary features, arising as a consequence of early impairments. The samples assessed in this way so far have been at high psychosocial risk, or from disadvantaged inner-city areas. In more middle-class groups, adolescent conduct problems appear to hold few implications for early adult work histories, family relationships, or friendship patterns (Jessor, Donovan, & Costa, 1991). Psychosocial adversities—all too often faced by conduct-disordered youth—may thus play a central role in the long-term persistence of poor functioning.

3.2. Assessments over More Focused Age Spans

These findings provide a broad overview of childhood–adult links but tell us little about developments over the intervening period. No prospective studies have yet provided detailed coverage of continuities across the full age span from early childhood to adult life. Follow-up data on representative samples are, however, available over more focused periods. Beginning early in childhood, these show that behavioral precursors of stable antisocial difficulties in late childhood and early adolescence can be reliably detected in the preschool years (White, Moffitt, Earls, Robins, & Silva, 1990). In epidemiologic studies, between 50% and 75% of children who meet criteria for disruptive disorders before adolescence continue to do so in their early teens, and a further proportion go on to show predominantly emotional difficulties (Esser, Schmidt, & Woerner, 1990; Graham & Rutter, 1973; Moffitt, Caspi, Dickson, Silva, & Stanton, 1996; Offord et al., 1992; Rutter, Tizard, Yule, Graham, & Whitmore, 1976). These findings may underestimate the extent of continuities (Fergusson et al., 1995). Many childhood-onset behavior problems persist; a minority, however, do appear more transitory.

Male gender, hyperactivity, aggression, poor verbal skills, low school achievements, and problems in peer relationships, along with indicators of family disruption and adverse parenting, have emerged as central risks for childhood-onset conduct problems (for reviews, see Dishion, French, & Patterson, 1993; Earls, 1994; Robins, 1991). Quite different factors appear to presage onset in adolescence. First, male–female ratios are less marked at this stage, and many adolescent-onset cases do not show aggression or learning problems, though links with family disadvantage and poor social competence remain (McGee, Feehan, Williams, & Anderson, 1992). In addition, the quality of peer relationships varies with age at onset in key ways. Early-onset delinquents frequently show marked problems in relationships with peers. Adolescent-onset offending, by contrast, is associated with sociometric popularity and relatively intense peer orientation (Stattin & Magnusson, 1995), and is heavily influenced by peer delinquency (Patterson & Yoerger, in press).

Prospective studies of epidemiologic samples are now beginning to detail developments between the late teens and early twenties. At this stage, continuities in broadly externalizing disorders are most marked among those who showed severe or aggressive conduct disorder in adolescence (Cohen, Cohen, & Brook, 1993; Feehan, McGee, & Williams, 1993). New onset of CD/ASPD (cases not showing comparable symptomatology at previous study contacts) is relatively rare, occurring in only around 10% of cases (Newman et al., 1996). Increased risks for later mood and anxiety disorders have been noted in a number of samples. In the Dunedin Multidisciplinary Health and Development Study, for example, emotional disorders at age 18 were the most common consequences of nonaggressive CD at age 15, and occurred at only slightly lower rates than in groups with internalizing disorders in the midteens (Feehan et al., 1993). Increased risks of depressive symptomatology in early adulthood have also been documented in the British National Child Development Study (Rutter, 1991; Rutter et al., in press-b). Comorbidity with other disorders is associated with increased risks for a range of aspects of later adolescent functioning. Lewinsohn, Rohde, and Seeley (1995), for example, found that whereas only 5% of adolescents with pure disruptive disorders reported suicide attempts, over one-third with comorbid disorders did so. Bardone, Moffitt,

Caspi, Dickson, and Silva (1996) provide some of the few prospective data on early adult outcomes of CD in girls. Adolescent CD exclusively predicted ASPD symptoms and substance dependence; it was also associated with increased risks for anxiety disorders and polydrug use, though not, in this sample, for depression.

Studies using empirically derived syndrome scores, rather than diagnostic categories, have reported similar findings. In a large-scale U.S. study, Achenbach, Howell, McConaughy, and Stanger (1995) found that preadult aggressive syndrome scores showed strong predictive links with aggression in early adulthood. Delinquent syndromes also showed clear specificity for males, though a wider range of earlier predictors, including small contributions from both somatic complaints and earlier attention problems, were associated with later delinquency in females. Similar patterns have been reported in Dutch samples (Ferdinand & Verhulst, 1995). In addition, whereas high scores on global measures of externalizing problems in early adulthood were only predicted by previous externalizing scores, early adult internalizing problems were predicted by both prior internalizing and externalizing scores.

3.3. Secular Change

These findings are drawn from study cohorts spanning a range of historical eras, and from retrospective data for subjects of different ages collected at particular points in time. Inevitably, each of these sources confounds effects associated with chronological age with either general historical (period) effects, or secular influences specific to individual cohorts (Rutter, 1995). The last 50 years have seen major increases in rates of conduct problems and juvenile offending in most Western societies, along with a narrowing of the sex ratio for many, though not all, types of offense (Smith, 1995). Cohort and cultural differences in rates of antisocial behaviors, and in peak ages of offending, have been documented in both retrospective and prospective studies (see, e.g., Harada, 1995; Robins et al., 1991; Tracey, Wolfgang, & Figlio, 1990), and a range of social structural factors advanced to explain them. Over such a relatively short period, increases of this magnitude must reflect changes in the environmental risks for antisocial behavior. Changes in family structure and functioning, increasing mobility and declines in the cohesiveness of local communities, along with changes in the pattern of crime opportunities, seem likely to be among the central factors involved (Smith, 1995).

The factors involved in variations in overall levels of antisocial behavior will not necessarily, of course, be the same as those affecting individual differences, though the two may overlap. Moffitt (1993a), for example, has argued that secular increases in crime rates largely reflect "adolescence-limited" behaviors and have few implications for persistent offenders whose criminality extends across the life span. Data from the ECA studies, by contrast, showed that secular changes in rates of childhood conduct problems were associated with parallel increases in adult ASPD (Robins et al., 1991), and that patterns of childhood–adult continuity were similar across all the age cohorts studied. Two different processes may thus be involved here, one influencing the proportions of adolescents expressing relatively time-limited antisocial tendencies, the second affecting expression of an underlying liability to persistent antisocial behavior of a possibly quite different kind. In addition, secular change in opportunity structures around the transition to adulthood, or the increased availability of alcohol and drugs, may also impact on risks for the persistence of conduct problems from adolescence to adult life. Though relatively little examined as yet, these issues constitute important areas for future study.

4. Accounting for Continuities and Discontinuities

As these findings make clear, any comprehensive model of continuities in antisocial behavior must account for both continuity and change, the stabilization of antisocial tendencies in some individuals, but their more temporary expression in others. A variety of models has been explored to account for these patterns. Some have focused on individual susceptibilities, others on variations in age at onset, and yet others on the role of intervening experiences in fostering or inhibiting persistence over time. We begin by examining the role of individually based risks.

4.1. Individual Susceptibilities and Their Expression

Hyperactivity/impulsivity, low autonomic reactivity, sensation seeking/risk taking, aggressivity, cognitive impairments or executive planning deficits, and problems in social cognition have all been identified as risks for persistent antisocial behavior (Stoff, Breiling, & Maser, 1997). It is unclear at this stage how far these reflect different facets of the same risk dimension, or differing routes to long-term impairment. Each is likely to include heritable elements; indeed, twin studies have shown that antisocial behavior that persists to adulthood includes a clear genetic component, whereas adolescent delinquency seems largely environmentally determined (DiLalla & Gottesman, 1989; Lyons et al., 1995; Simonoff et al., reported in Rutter et al., in press-b). In addition, however, heritable factors will depend crucially on environmental effects for their expression. Although we must await multivariate quantitative genetic studies to identify the behaviors for which genes code, several pointers to the *form* of the associations are already available. Here, adoption studies have reported gene–environment interactions for a number of antisocial outcomes (Bohman, 1996; Cadoret, Yates, Troughton, Woodworth, & Stewart, 1995; Crowe, 1974). Though neither the genetic nor the environmental influences involved here has been specified in any detail as yet, the pattern of findings points to what has been described as genetic control of sensitivity to the environment (Kendler & Eaves, 1986): The genetic factors contributing to antisocial traits depend heavily for their expression on exposure to adverse environmental circumstances. As we examine evidence of individual risks for persistent antisocial behaviors, we highlight some possible avenues for effects of this kind.

4.1.1. Hyperactivity

Hyperactivity, impulsivity, and attentional difficulties have consistently been identified as among the more important markers of poor long-term outcome for conduct problems, at least in males. When the two disorders co-occur in childhood, conduct problems appear to arise as a complication of hyperactivity. Hyperactive symptoms emerge first in comorbid groups (Barkley, Fischer, Edelbrock, & Smallish, 1990), and early hyperactivity predicts the development of conduct problems, but the reverse does not apply (Taylor, Heptinstall, Chadwick, & Danckaerts, 1996). In addition, behavior genetic analyses suggest that etiological factors for "pure" CD and the comorbid pattern differ in important ways. Comorbid groups include a strong genetic component, whereas pure CD, especially when defined in terms of adolescents' own accounts, seems largely environmental in origin (Silberg et al., 1996).

Prospective studies have now examined the specific contributions of hyperactivity and conduct problems to later outcomes at a number of stages. Kindergarten measures of restless, impulsive behavior predict early onset delinquency (Tremblay, Pihl, Vitaro, & Dobkin, 1994), and hyperactivity is associated with the persistence of CD across childhood and adolescence (August & Stewart, 1982; Schachar, Rutter, & Smith, 1981). Taylor et al. (1996) followed subgroups of boys from an epidemiologic sample over longer age spans, from early childhood to age 17. Although the threshold for conduct problems fell below diagnostic criteria for conduct disorder in this study, the findings were striking in pointing to hyperactivity as the main risk for poor later outcome. Defiant and disruptive behaviors, problems in peer relationships, and poor social adjustment at age 17 were all most strongly predicted by early hyperactivity; the only sequelae specific to conduct problems were behavior problems in school and aggression. In a similar way, Farrington et al. (1990a) found that a composite measure of hyperactivity–impulsivity–inattention, though strongly related to indicators of early conduct problems, independently predicted both early onset and chronicity of offending among males up to age 25.

These findings leave little doubt that hyperactivity constitutes a central marker for the persistence of poor global functioning. Several key questions remain to be addressed. First, it is unclear which aspects of this complex— temperamental impulsivity, motor restlessness, or inattentiveness—convey the prime risk, and whether it functions predominantly as a dimensional risk factor, a discrete diagnostic category, or as part of a wider constellation of problem behaviors. Genetic analyses (Silberg et al., 1996) suggest that the genetic effect extends beyond the small group of children who show a severe hyperkinetic syndrome. The genetically influenced risk characteristics may thus also operate more widely and depend on co-occurrence with other risks for effects on persistence. Parental emotional disorder, family discord, and negative parent–child relationships, especially negative expressed emotion toward the child (Rutter & Quinton, 1984; Rutter et al., in press-b; Taylor et al., 1996) are all known to be associated with the persistence of disruptive disorders across childhood and adolescence. Markers of this kind may provide valuable starting points in examining gene–environment interactions that may be specific to the *persistence* of antisocial behavior across development. Alongside these issues, we need to know more about the role of hyperactivity in girls and to clarify the basis for the genetic vulnerability. Although the genetic component is especially associated with hyperactivity, overactivity or inattention need not necessarily constitute the key susceptibility trait.

4.1.2. Neuropsychological Deficits, Cognitive Impairments, and School Achievements

Neuropsychological deficits (Moffitt, 1993b) offer a second possibility here. Depressed IQ scores, most marked on measures of verbal skills, have been widely documented among both juvenile and adult offenders (Hirschi & Hindelang, 1977; Wilson & Herrnstein, 1985), and modest but consistent longitudinal associations have been reported between early childhood verbal skills and criminality in adult life (Stattin & Klackenberg-Larssen, 1993). Tests of executive function have also been found to discriminate between antisocial and nonantisocial adolescents (Moffitt, 1993a). These latter deficits seem especially characteristic of comorbid CD/ attention-deficit/hyperactive disorder (ADHD), but not of CD alone (Pennington & Ozonoff, 1996).

Poor verbal skills and difficulties in executive planning might contribute in quite direct ways to the onset and persistence of antisocial behaviors. Moffitt (1993a), for example, has argued that relatively subtle neuropsychological deficits (whether genetically or environmentally mediated) may in stressed family environments initiate a chain of developments culminating in conduct problems. Early temperamental and communication problems may challenge parenting capacities and possibly also compromise attachment bonds. As the child enters school, so new environmental demands compound the process, and problems in peer relations and learning difficulties are added to an escalating pattern of risk.

Spiraling difficulties of this kind, affecting relationships and social competence in a range of domains, may cumulate across the life course. During schooling, they are likely to have particular implications for achievement. Criminological theories have posited a particular role for poor school achievement in the genesis of delinquency, running through effects on self-esteem, or reduced attachment to the school system as a support for conventional values (Hawkins & Lishner, 1987). In the most recent review of the extensive literature on academic performance and delinquency, Maguin and Loeber (1996) concluded that intelligence and attentional problems were likely common causes for both difficulties, but that academic performance made additional contributions to the prediction of delinquency when both socioeconomic status (SES) and prior conduct problems were controlled.

These models suggest rather different predictions for the persistence of antisocial behavior beyond the end of schooling. On the one hand, because verbal deficits and reading difficulties themselves persist (Maughan, Hagell, Rutter, & Yule, 1994; Rodgers, 1986), associated antisocial behaviors might also be expected to show high levels of persistence. On the other, if much of the initial impetus for delinquent activity among low achievers arises from relatively phase-specific stressors in adolescence, links between reading problems and antisocial behaviors might decline in adulthood, as other sources of accomplishment become available. In relation to reading difficulties, the limited prospective evidence available to date favors the second of these accounts. Poor-reading males in an inner-city sample showed somewhat elevated rates of offending in the teens but no excess of officially recorded crime or self-reported antisocial behaviors in adulthood (Maughan, Pickles, Hagell, Rutter, & Yule, 1996). These young men left school at a time when opportunities for skilled manual work were relatively plentiful; importantly, social outcomes for women with childhood reading problems were rather less positive (Maughan & Hagell, 1996). Contextual effects of this kind may hold important implications for later outcomes.

4.1.3. Aggressive and Other Behavioral Trajectories

Among specific manifestations of antisocial difficulties, aggression has long been canvassed as a key element in persistence (see, e.g., Stattin & Magnusson, 1989). Individ ıal differences in aggression show considerable stability from early childhood onward (Olweus, 1979), and Robins (1978) argued that in the absence of later-onset major mental disorders, violent and aggressive patterns do not appear in adults if they have not been evident earlier in life. Violence is a dominant component of antisocial personality disorder in both women and men (Robins et al., 1991), and chronic male offenders show high rates of interpersonal as well as criminal aggression (Farrington & West, 1993). Genetic influences, however, seem less marked for violent than for nonviolent crime, and specific links with aggressive outcomes have proved elusive, reflecting the strong overlaps between aggression and other indices of antisocial behavior in adult life. In general, early family risks seem similar for both violent and nonviolent crime (Farrington, 1989). Once again, the key may lie in the interplay between individual and environmental characteristics. Henry, Caspi, Moffitt, and Silva (1996), for example, found that although violent offending in the late teens showed links with temperamental lack of control in early childhood, effects were most marked in the small group where temperamental difficulties were combined with disrupted parenting. In a similar way, Moffitt et al. (in press) found that elevated serotonin levels were predominantly associated with violent convictions among young men who grew up in incohesive and conflictual families.

Behavioral trajectories might offer alternative approaches to examining variations in persistence. Building on factor-analytic findings (Loeber & Schmaling, 1985), Loeber (Loeber et al., 1993; Loeber, DeLamatre, Keenan, & Zhang, 1997) has proposed that there may be different behavioral trajectories associated with progressions in overt, confrontational behaviors; covert, concealing acts; and aspects of antisocial behavior reflecting conflict with authority. Some individuals will show escalations in all three types of deviance, whereas others may take more "exclusive" routes. Empirical tests thus far have shown that although boys showing overt, aggressive behaviors often progressed to more covert types of deviance, the reverse pattern was much less common. Hypothesized progressions within each pathway were more evident for boys with persistent difficulties than for "experimenters," and although ADHD was associated with initiation into all three types of deviance, it showed no additional links with escalating difficulties beyond that point.

To date, these models have only been applied to boys up to the midteens. From the opposite developmental perspective, a number of investigators have explored offense histories of known chronic offenders, in an effort to identify early behavioral trajectories characteristic of long-term persistence in crime. In practice, however, although chronic offenders have long been known to account for disproportionate numbers of serious and violent offenses, only a minority are convicted of any serious violent crime (Weitekamp, Kerner, Schubert, & Schindler, 1995). In the Cambridge Study in Delinquent Development, chronic offenders (all of whom had been convicted of at least nine offenses) accounted for exactly equal proportions of both serious and nonserious offenses; "the chronic offenders committed more serious offenses in total purely because they committed more offenses in total" (Farrington & West, 1993, p. 498).

Chronic offenders may nonetheless show characteristic patterns of escalation in offense seriousness. This possibility raises difficult methodological issues: Because later offenses are committed at older ages, and older offenders in general commit more serious crimes, it is important to disentangle general age-related changes from those reflecting escalation *within* individual careers. Strikingly, Weitekamp and colleagues (1995) found that the mean seriousness of early offenses committed by chronic offenders in the Philadelphia cohorts was no higher than that of early offenses committed by youth with much shorter criminal careers. In the Cambridge study, Farrington and West (1993) noted an increase in the seriousness of chronic offenders' crimes between the third and tenth offenses; after this, seriousness levels began to fall, probably reflecting changes in the types of offenses more usual at older ages. The issue is a complex one; to date, however, it has proved difficult to identify characteristic behavioral features of the criminal careers of chronic offenders.

4.1.4. Multiproblem Groupings

Hyperactivity, aggression, and cognitive deficits frequently overlap. The prime risks for poor adult outcomes might thus emanate from just one of these domains, or might lie in multiproblem subgroups showing all of these difficulties. To test these possibilities, Magnusson and Bergman (1990) advocated a different style of analysis from the usual variable-oriented approach, focusing instead on "person-oriented" clustering of problems within individuals. Using this strategy, they found strong support for a multiproblem model in a cohort of 13-year-old boys. High scores on aggressiveness, motor restlessness, lack of concentration, and low school motivation always occurred in multiproblem groupings; importantly, these groups also showed low autonomic activity. Pervasively poor outcomes in the midtwenties (including psychiatric hospitalization, as well as criminality and alcohol problems) were most strongly concentrated in the multiproblem group. Equally striking, neither poor peer relations nor early adolescent aggression showed any links with adverse later outcomes when it occurred alone. Pulkkinen (1992; Hämäläinen & Pulkkinen, 1996), clustering cases in terms of prosociality, aggression, and school achievement, confirmed a similar pattern. Constellations of individual susceptibilities, rather than individual risk traits, may thus play a key role in long-term persistence.

4.1.5. Depression, Anxiety, and Shyness/Withdrawal

Childhood conduct problems also show frequent overlaps with both anxiety and depression (Hinshaw et al., 1993; Loeber & Keenan, 1994), and, as we have seen, antisocial behavior is associated with increased risks of affective disorder in adult life. Early links between conduct problems and depression seem likely to reflect correlated or shared risks (Fergusson, Lynskey, & Horwood, 1996), and the mixed pattern appears to share more in common with pure conduct than pure emotional difficulties (Steinhausen & Reitzle, 1996). From the limited evidence available to date, comorbid depression has little effect in modifying the course of antisocial behavior. In a follow-up of a child guidance sample, Harrington, Fudge, Rutter, Pickles, and Hill (1991) found that adult outcomes for a small group showing mixed CD and depressive disorders were closely similar to those with CD alone. Both groups faced high risks of ASPD, officially recorded crime and alcohol abuse/dependence, and lower risks of major depressive disorders than subjects with a primary diagnosis of depression.

Risks for adult depression might arise in a variety of ways. Continuities from earlier mixed disorders may provide one route, though questionnaire-based data suggest that this is unlikely to be the whole story (Rutter, 1991). Antisocial adolescents showed elevated rates of emotional distress in early adulthood, independent of levels of emotional problems in the teens. Instead, effects may be dependent on later antisocial lifestyles. Robins (1978) was among the first to note that job troubles, poor marital relationships and other concomitants of ongoing antisocial difficulties could function as stressors in adult life. Champion, Goodall, and Rutter (1995) tested this directly in a follow-up of community samples in the late twenties. Childhood behavioral deviance showed strong links with severely adverse life events in adulthood, in particular those known from other studies to act as "provoking agents" for psychiatric disorder (Brown & Harris, 1978). In many instances, these were dependent on features of the young people's behavior; in addition, early deviance was also associated with increased rates of independent life events, especially those reflecting more chronic psychosocial difficulties and lack of supportive adult relationships. Both directly and indirectly, early behavior problems appeared to place individuals in adult environments carrying heightened risks for affective disorder.

Links between anxiety and antisocial behaviors have proved more complex (Lahey, McBurnett, Loeber, & Hart, 1995). Both anxious and shy children have been found to be at reduced risk for delinquency (Loeber & Keenan, 1994), and Lahey and Loeber (1991) found that prepubertal boys with comorbid CD and anxiety showed fewer symptoms of aggression than those with conduct problems alone. At the same time, Tremblay et al. (1994) found that low kindergarten anxiety showed small but positive effects in the prediction of early adolescent delinquency. The key may lie in the frequent overlap of two related but distinct aspects of anxiety/shyness: behavioral inhibition and social withdrawal. Assessing these separately, Kerr, Tremblay, Pagani, and Vitaro (1997) showed that it is behavioral inhibition that acts as a protective factor, rather than a lack of social connections with delinquent peers. In their study, inhibited–aggressive boys were protected against delinquency, while withdrawn–disruptive boys were at risk for both ongoing antisocial behaviors and depression. The poor outcomes associated with shy/withdrawn and aggressive groups in other studies (see, e.g., Fleming, Kellam, & Brown, 1982; McCord, 1988; Serbin, Moskowitz, Schwartzman, & Ledingham, 1991) may thus largely reflect patterns of this latter kind.

4.2. Age at Onset

A more explicitly developmental approach to conceptualizing variations in persistence has emerged from studies of age at onset. Early onset is among the strongest predictors of continuities in disruptive disorders across childhood (Loeber, 1982), and early onset delinquency shows similar links with persistence in adult crime (Farrington et al., 1990b). Risks for childhood- and adolescent-onset antisocial behaviors differ in systematic ways, and, as we have seen, although adult offending shows a clear heritable component, adolescent delinquency is largely attributable to shared environmental effects (DiLalla & Gottesman, 1989; Lyons et al., 1995).

Building on these observations, a number of investigators have proposed divisions according to age at onset (DiLalla & Gottesman, 1989; Hinshaw et al., 1993; Patterson & Yoerger, 1993). The most comprehensive model is Moffitt's (1993a) developmental taxonomy, which divides the overall "pool" of antisocial children into two distinct groups: a small, early-onset group showing many of the risks discussed thus far, and assumed to show strong persistence of antisocial behavior into adulthood, and a second, adolescent-onset group, accounting for the short-lived rise in prevalence rates in adolescence. These "adolescence-limited" delinquents are argued to display a much less pervasive array of early risks and difficulties; instead, their delinquent behaviors are largely prompted by status frustration during adolescence, and by social mimicry of delinquent peers. Importantly, they are also argued to be of relatively limited duration.

If confirmed, this model could provide a powerful organizing framework. Initial tests on childhood and adolescent data seem promising (Jeglum Bartush, Lynam, Moffitt, & Silva, 1997), identifying a childhood-onset factor showing the hypothesized links with childhood hyperactivity, poor verbal skills, impulsive personality traits and increased risks of violent offending, and a separate adolescent-onset factor, more strongly associated with peer delinquency. Several questions do, however, arise. First, as we have seen, by no means all childhood-onset conduct problems persist into adolescence (Moffitt et al., 1996). This suggests that early-onset cases include a separate "childhood-limited" group, not facing a severe long-term prognosis. It is unclear at this stage whether this group is characterized by less severe individual vulnerabilities, less serious or persistent environmental risks, or positive protective factors. It constitutes an important focus for future developmental studies.

Second, a main prediction of the model is that adolescence-onset groups will desist from antisocial behavior once they gain access to adult statuses and roles. Nagin et al. (1995) found only mixed support for this proposition in the Cambridge study males. By age 32, men whose official crime records were limited to the teens and early twenties had, as expected, made good adjustments in their working lives and showed little evidence of severe discord in relationships with their wives. In other respects, however, their adult functioning was by no means problem-free. Antisocial lifestyles continued, though registered crime did not. In this disadvantaged sample, a variety of factors may have contributed to this pattern. Further tests, in more diverse social groups, are needed to determine the basis for such ongoing difficulties.

Third, we need to know *why* early onset is associated with long-term risk: Does it serve primarily as a marker for other early vulnerabilities; as an index of severity; or does early onset per se affect the likelihood of persistence? The few direct tests of this last possibility have produced inconsistent findings. Nagin and Paternoster (1991), for example, found evidence for "state dependence"—prior involvement in offending itself influencing the likelihood of future involvement—in self-reports of relatively minor offending in the late teens. Over more extended age ranges, however, Nagin and Farrington (1992) found that associations between age at onset and persistent offending were almost entirely accounted for by time-stable individual differences. And Tolan and Thomas (1995) found a small but significant effect for age at onset on later involvement in offending across adolescence, most marked for persistence in serious crime; age at onset was less influential than psychosocial variables and also of rather less importance for females than for males.

Is early onset also associated with persistence in girls? Retrospective reports of age at onset were very similar—and early—for both males and females who met criteria for ASPD in the ECA samples (Robins et al., 1991), but other findings suggest a more mixed picture. Adolescent, but not childhood, aggression appears to predict offending in girls (Stattin & Magnusson, 1989), and affiliations with deviant peers only become marked for girls in adolescence (Cairns, Cairns, Neckerman, Gest, & Gariépy, 1988). As we have seen, official offense histories suggest much more diversity in the onset of criminality in women than in men (Home Office, 1995; Krazter & Hodgins, 1996), and Tolan and Thomas (1995) found age at onset a less important factor in predicting persistence of self-report offending among females in the late teens. More detailed studies, focusing specifically on antisocial women and girls, are needed to resolve these questions.

Finally, for both males and females, there is the important issue of "adult" onset. DiLalla and Gottesman (1989) proposed the inclusion of a separate group of "late bloomers" in their developmental model, and it is clear that using either diagnostic criteria or offense histories, small but nontrivial groups of individuals appear in prevalence estimates for the first time in adult life. Surprisingly little is known about these groups. Some severe antisocial behaviors are known to develop in the context of major mental disorders, or in response to trauma; new onset of pervasive antisocial behavior in adulthood may predominantly reflect influences of this kind (Hodgins, 1993). In relation to offending, alcohol- and drug-related crime may also play an important part (Kaplan, 1995), and feminist sociologists have argued for some routes into adult crime particular to women, reflecting rational responses to severe environmental pressures or demands (Daly, 1993; Heidensohn, 1994). Comprehensive developmental models need to provide a more systematic picture of these important groups.

5. Mechanisms for Stability and Change: Person–Environment Interactions

The identification of individual vulnerabilities associated with persistence, or subgroups that follow differing developmental trajectories, constitutes an important first step in understanding continuities over time. On their own, however, these approaches tell us nothing of the *mechanisms* that contribute to the stabilization of antisocial tendencies in some individuals but their more time-limited expression in others. Implicitly or explicitly, much early research from a clinical perspective assumed a relatively autonomous unfolding of pathogenic processes. Sociological accounts, by contrast, attributed continuities at the individual level to parallel consistencies in the environment. More recent evidence suggests a more complex pattern, whereby development occurs as a joint function of organismic and environmental forces, and the expression and maintenance of antisocial tendencies depends crucially on the evolving interplay between individual and environmental effects (Magnusson & Cairns, 1996). In the sections that follow, we outline some of the key processes that seem likely to be involved here.

5.1. Social Cognitions

A first route for the stabilization of behaviors may run through views of the self and others. Social psychology suggests that most effects of experience operate through cognitive transduction, and that the self is made up of an arrangement of schemas representing past experiences and personal characteristics, as well as future hopes and fears (Markus & Cross, 1990). Aggressive individuals have been found to show characteristic patterns here, believing, for example, that behaving aggressively increases self-esteem and helps avoid a negative image in the eyes of others (Slaby & Guerra, 1988). Among delinquents, Oyserman and Markus (1990) found an imbalance between fears and expectations for the future: Although young offenders feared negative outcomes such as being on drugs, many lacked the "possible selves" that could provide an organizing vision of ways to avoid such adverse outcomes.

Dodge and colleagues (Dodge, Bates, & Pettit, 1990a; Dodge, Pettit, Bates, & Valente, 1995) have explored some of the bases of such cognitions in early childhood experiences of abusive parenting. They have elaborated a general model of social information processing, positing five sequential stages in responding to social cues: encoding, interpretation, response accessing, response evaluation, and enactment. Aggressive behavior seems associated with particular biases or deficits in information processing at each stage; aggressive individuals search for fewer cues before interpreting others' actions, overattribute hostile intent in ambiguous situations, and are more likely both to select and to generate aggressive responses. Followed prospectively, abused children were at increased risk of acquiring subsets of these biased processing patterns. Importantly, social-cognitive processes mediated links between preschool abuse and risks for conduct problems some 5 years later (Dodge et al., 1995).

The longer-term role of social cognitions remains to be established. Similar cognitive biases have, however, been identified among incarcerated delinquents (Dodge, Price, Bachorowski, & Newman, 1990b), and among partners in distressed and violent marital relationships (Bradbury, Beach, Fincham, & Nelson, 1996; Holtzworth-Munrow & Anglin, 1993). Biased social cognitions, in relation to both the self and others, seem likely to be among the mechanisms that foster persistence in deviant behaviors, or militate against the possibility of change.

5.2. Accentuation Effects

A second mechanism for the stabilization of behavior reflects what Elder and Caspi (1990) have described as the *accentuation principle*: that new or challenging experiences, though often assumed to prompt change in behavioral development, may in some circumstances function to reinforce existing patterns. Previously vulnerable individuals are most susceptible to the effects of stressors (Rodgers, 1990), and in novel, uncertain, or unpredictable situations, individuals must have recourse to their own inner resources in deciding how to act (Caspi & Moffitt, 1993). For antisocial children and adolescents, new environmental demands—whether prompted by developmental transitions or situational stressors—may only go to reinforce deviant tendencies.

Effects of this kind have been noted in a range of domains (Rutter, 1994). The hostile attributions of aggressive boys are most apparent in ambiguous situations, or those lacking familiar cues. In a similar way, the increase in delinquent activities associated with unemployment is most marked for young men with previous histories of delinquency (Farrington, Gallagher, Morley, St. Ledger, & West, 1986), and the rise in norm-breaking shown by early maturing girls (Stattin & Magnusson, 1990) is most apparent for those showing behavior problems *before* the main changes of puberty occur (Caspi & Moffitt, 1993). In each case, new, challenging, or stressful life experiences have been found to accentuate pre-existing behavioral tendencies.

As these examples suggest, both the biological and the social role changes of adolescence and early adulthood hold the potential for accentuation effects of this kind. It is less clear at this stage how far they carry long-term implications. In relation to early puberty, for example, Stattin and Magnusson (1990) found that by age 15, most differences in deviance between early and later maturing girls had diminished. The most clear consequences for early adult development arose if girls had dropped out of school; then, educational attainments continued to be compromised many years in the future. As in other arenas, the effects of adverse experiences seem likely to be most marked if they close off later opportunities or trap individuals into adverse circumstances that provide few avenues for escape.

5.3. Environmental Continuities

If changed environments can contribute to the persistence of antisocial behaviors, continuities in environmental conditions also play a key role. For many antisocial children, adverse environments are likely to persist across development. Many antisocial children grow up in disadvantaged and disorganized neighborhoods, antithetical to development at any stage. The same communities that lack adequate supports for early parenting or health care of young children offer limited activities and poor supervision for adolescents, and restricted work opportunities in adult life (Caspi & Moffitt, 1995). To date, research linking macrosocial, contextual processes of this kind with more individually oriented measures is still in its infancy (see, e.g., Farrington, Sampson, & Wikström, 1993; Sampson, 1992), and there have been few direct tests of the impact of such broader ecological consistencies on the course of behavioral development. In childhood, much of the effect of neighborhood disadvantage seems mediated via family risks (Rutter et al., 1975; Sampson, 1992). In adolescence and adulthood, more direct effects may arise. As we have seen, much current evidence on the long-term outcomes of conduct problems derives from disadvantaged samples, likely to have faced ongoing difficulties of this kind. Comparative studies in less distressed groups, along with the integration of community-level indicators in individually oriented analyses, are crucial to clarify the processes involved here.

5.4. Selecting and Shaping Environments

In addition to these broader environmental consistencies, it is now clear that individual actions also play a part in selecting and shaping the environments that individuals experience. Both evocative and active person–environment interactions seem likely to be involved here (Caspi & Moffitt, 1995). Early in childhood, evocative processes may be most salient. Child characteristics are known to elicit differing reactions from caregivers (Bell & Chapman, 1986; Lytton, 1990), and early oppositional behaviors fuel spiraling cycles of coercive interchanges within the family (Patterson,

1982). Later in development, as individuals gain increasing autonomy of action, so options for more direct selection and shaping of environments increase (Scarr, 1992; Scarr & McCartney, 1983).

Behavior genetic analyses highlighted the importance of such processes for the persistence of antisocial tendencies (Kendler, 1995). As outlined earlier, genetic and unique environment effects on antisocial behavior become more salient in adult life. Importantly, however, no new genetic or familial environment risk factors appear to come "on-line" between adolescence and adulthood (Lyons et al., 1995). Instead, the increased impact of genetic influences later in development arises because they operate at that stage not only to influence behavior, but also to select individuals into interpersonal and social environments congruent with their dispositions. In some instances, processes of this kind may reflect active selection processes. In others, shaping of environments may arise in less direct but nonetheless powerful ways through the cumulating consequences of early impairments. We focus here on three main routes for effects of this kind: social selection into adolescent peer groups; the implications of conduct problems for transitions to adult roles; and assortative pairing in the selection of life partners.

5.4.1. Peer Relations

Deviant peer relationships are among the most powerful correlates of adolescent delinquency (Thornberry & Krohn, 1997). The adolescent surge in delinquent involvement is paralleled by markedly similar age trends in associations with delinquent peers (Warr, 1993); as peer influences rise and fall, so delinquency seems to follow. More debated, however, has been the causal nature of the processes involved: Does the association primarily reflect niche-picking—a social selection model—or do links with deviant peers also serve to promote and sustain antisocial development (Rowe, Woulbroun, & Gulley, 1994)? Recent evidence suggests that both processes are important and operate in reciprocal ways over time (Thornberry & Krohn, 1997).

Social selection in adolescent peer relations has been documented for many years (Kandel, 1985). Among boys, the tendency to affiliate with others showing similar levels of aggression is clear in late childhood and increases as they enter adolescence. For girls, similar processes become marked in the early teens (Cairns et al., 1988). Peer similarities in aggressive tendencies are largely independent of specific individual friendships: The membership of social groupings may change, but the quality of aggressive adolescents' networks tends to remain quite stable over time. Longitudinal analyses, taking into account individuals' prior levels of deviance, have shown that these deviant peer associations play an independent role in both the initiation (Keenan, Loeber, Zhang, Stouthamer-Loeber, & Van Kammen, 1995) and the continuity of delinquency in adolescence (Fergusson & Horwood, 1996). Earlier antisocial tendencies make it more likely that adolescents make delinquent friends, but those friendships in turn play a key role in maintaining deviant behavior.

Longer-term effects of adolescent peer relationships have been less widely studied. For some girls, however, early links with deviant peers appear to constitute a key "stepping-stone" in the progress toward cohabitation with a deviant spouse (Quinton et al., 1993). For males, Warr (1993) has argued that delinquent friendships may be especially "sticky" and themselves tend to persist over time. Strikingly, evidence from much later in development suggests that continuity in male offending in the twenties and early thirties remains strongly associated with links with deviant peers (Farrington, 1991; Graham & Bowling, 1995). For some individuals, adolescent peer relationships may mark early steps in a chain of developments that contributes, directly or indirectly, to ongoing deviance.

5.4.2. Early Adult Role Transitions

The social role transitions of adolescence and early adulthood provide other routes for shaping environments. Sociological analyses have confirmed that choices made at this period have major implications for subsequent life-chances (Hogan & Astone, 1986), and developmental studies suggest that differing transition patterns can also have powerful effects on later psychosocial development. In some circumstances, these can be positive, offering breaks from the past and escape from risk trajectories (see, e.g., Elder, 1986). In others, these same role transitions can function to reinforce and amplify earlier difficulties, cutting off opportunities, and trapping individuals in increasingly deviant, unsupportive, or stress-prone interpersonal and social worlds (e.g., Caspi, Elder, & Herbener, 1990; Kerner, Weitekamp, & Stelly, 1995; Rutter, Champion, Quinton, Maughan, & Pickles, 1995).

For many conduct-disordered adolescents, their impulsive behavioral style contributes to a pattern of accelerated early-adult role transitions that cut short education, compromise employment options, and precipitate early entry into heterosexual relationships and family formation. In the National Comorbidity Study, for example, early-onset CD was associated with a more than doubled risk of drop out from high school and showed continuing, though less marked, effects on later educational transitions (Kessler, Foster, Saunders, & Stang, 1995). Other studies suggest that these effects are not simply a function of prior associations between conduct problems and poor school achievement. Early exit from schooling is most marked for young people showing both aggressive/antisocial and academic problems, but conduct problems alone also have an effect (Cairns, Cairns, & Neckerman, 1989; Maughan, Gray, Smith, & Rutter, 1985).

Not surprisingly, depressed educational qualifications affect entry to the workforce (Stanford et al., 1994). In addition, conduct problems may influence early labor-market involvement more directly through reduced efforts at job search or problems in relationships with colleagues and employers (Caspi, Wright, Moffitt, & Silva, in press). For some young offenders, the stigmatizing effects of arrest and imprisonment will compound these difficulties, further compromising job prospects (Kerner et al., 1995; Sampson & Laub, 1993). Moffitt et al. (1996) found that both early- and adolescent-onset behavior problems were associated with increased risks of unemployment in the late teens in males; for girls, however, adolescent CD appears to have fewer implications for early labor force indicators (Bardone et al., 1996).

Patterns of early partnership and family formation may be more consequential for women. Teenage pregnancy in particular is known to be associated with a plethora of adverse consequences for both mother and child (Furstenberg, Brooks-Gunn, & Chase-Lansdale, 1989). In both clinical (Kovacs, Krol, & Voti, 1994) and epidemiologic samples (Bardone et al., 1996), conduct-disordered girls have been found at increased risk. These tendencies may be becoming more marked over time. Cohort comparisons (Maughan & Lindelow, 1997) suggest that as secular changes have favored delayed entry to parenthood, and access to contraception and abortion has become more widespread, so the groups selected into early motherhood have become more behaviorally deviant.

5.4.3. Assorting on Deviance

Early and unsupportive marital relationships may also reinforce problems in individual functioning. In the Dunedin study, girls with adolescent CD were over five times more likely than others to have entered a cohabiting relationship by age 21. Many of these relationships lacked support; by their early twenties, almost half of these girls had already received some form of physical violence from a partner. As yet, relatively little is known of the more proximal processes involved in these effects. Risks of unsupportive partnerships do, however, seem to depend in part on assorting on behavioral deviance. Quinton et al. (1993) found that girls with histories of conduct problems were much more likely than their peers to enter first cohabiting partnerships with deviant men. These relationships reflected the end point of a series of prior influences, including adolescent associations with deviant peers, lack of supportive guidance from families, early pregnancy, and the lack of a "planning" disposition among many of the girls themselves. Similar evidence of assortment on deviance is emerging in other samples (Peters, Serbin, & Schwartzman, 1996).

5.5. Alcohol and Substance Use

We cannot conclude this section without noting the strong and mutually reinforcing associations between drug and alcohol problems and antisocial behavior (see, e.g., Kaplan, 1995; Tonry & Wilson, 1990 for overviews). It is beyond the scope of this chapter to review the extensive literatures that have examined these associations. For our present purposes, just a few key links can be highlighted. First, childhood conduct problems are strong predictors of alcohol and drug use (Robins & McEvoy, 1990), and deviant adult lifestyles further increase the probability of heavy alcohol consumption (Kerner, Weitekamp, Stelly, & Thomas, 1996). The complex links between alcohol and aggression have been much debated and are likely to include pharmacological, psychological, and social effects (Fagan, 1990). In the case of drug use, U.S. data suggest that although small groups of heavy polydrug users account for a large proportion of predatory crime, in the majority of cases, links are much less apparent (Chaiken & Chaiken, 1990). Possibly as important for the persistence of antisocial behavior, heavy alcohol use also compromises many other aspects of social functioning; marital relationships and job stability are likely to be especially vulnerable (Sampson & Laub, 1993; Vaillant, 1983). As we discuss in later sections, these often play a key role in desistance from crime. In addition to their direct links with aggressive or criminal acts, alcohol and drug use may thus contribute to the maintenance of antisocial behavior in more indirect ways, through jeopardizing adult roles and relationships that themselves offer options for change.

5.6. Cumulating Consequences: Indirect Chains

Taken together, these findings clearly argue that important routes for continuities in antisocial behavior run through selection into adverse environments and the cumulating consequences of early behavior difficulties (Rutter et al., 1995). Through their characteristic patterns of peer and partnership choices, many conduct-disordered youth will enter their early adult years with limited material resources, restricted labor-force prospects, unsupportive personal relationships, and responsibilities for dependents. From a developmental perspective, the key questions concern the extent to which these patterns contribute to the persistence of poor functioning, and the extent to which, if such negative outcomes are avoided, opportunities exist for trajectories to be redirected over time.

A number of investigators have now shown that processes of this kind do indeed contribute in important ways to the persistence of antisocial behavior over time. Adverse outcomes at one stage of development elevate risks of persistence at the immediately succeeding stage, acting as "stepping-stones" into increasingly more deviant pathways. The models advanced—variously described as stepping-stone effects (Farrington, 1986b), processes of cumulative continuity (Caspi & Moffitt, 1995), indirect chain mechanisms (Rutter, 1997b; Rutter & Rutter, 1993), or, more specifically in the criminology field, processes of social exclusion and marginalization (Kerner et al., 1995)—all suggest that continuities in antisocial behavior depend not only on trait persistence, but also crucially on indirect mechanisms of this kind.

Several empirical demonstrations of these effects have now been reported. Fergusson and Horwood (1996), for example, found that affiliation with delinquent peers accounted for a substantial proportion of the continuity between childhood behavior problems and adolescent offending. Direct behavioral continuities were apparent, but peer-mediated effects accounted for up to half of the associations observed. Caspi, Elder, and Herbener (1990), tracing adult outcomes of men with early histories of temper tantrums, reported a similar pattern. Impulsive personality styles persisted to adulthood; in addition, however, progressive deteriorations in occupational status derived in part from indirect effects of truncated educational careers. In a parallel way, Kerner et al. (1995) argued for dynamic processes in the development of criminal careers, whereby the cumulating effects of behaviors, attributions, sanctions, and stigma across the life course progressively limit options for escape into nondeviant pathways and increase risks of persistence in crime. And, as we have seen, similar processes appear to contribute to girls' risks of cohabitation with a deviant spouse (Quinton et al., 1993). Lack of family support in adolescence, lack of a "planning" disposition in approaching life choices, and association with deviant peers each, in succession, increased girls' risks of achieving deviant partners. Pathways to more distal outcomes depended crucially on these intervening links.

5.7. Breaking the Chain: Turning Points in the Life Course

A key corollary of these models is, of course, that those who avoid such adverse consequences should show a much reduced likelihood of persistence in deviant behaviors. For those at greatest risk, supportive adult roles or relationships have been argued to function as turning points in the life course, offering opportunities for the redirection of more long-standing deviant trajectories (Caspi & Moffitt, 1993; Pickles & Rutter, 1991; Rutter, 1996; Sampson & Laub, 1993). Three broad categories of experience seem likely to offer the potential for turning points of this kind: those that open up new opportunities; those that result in a radical environmental change (perhaps especially in terms of close relationships); and those that have marked effects on the self-system, or on views and expectations of others (Rutter, 1996).

5.7.1.   Testing for Change

Many apparent changes in behavior represent no more than error, or random fluctuations between measurement points (Fergusson et al., 1995; Moffitt, Caspi, Harkness, & Silva, 1993). To demonstrate systematic change, several methodological steps are required. First and most basic, longitudinal, repeated measurements on the same individuals are needed both before and after the postulated turning point. Weak measures of behavior may give rise to artifactual impressions of change. Multiple indicators provide one safeguard here, along with the use of statistical techniques designed to take account of measurement error and persistent unobserved heterogeneity between individuals (Nagin & Paternoster, 1991; Sampson & Laub, 1993; Zoccolillo et al., 1992). Second, as we have seen, there is a need to explore a wide range of later outcomes, to distinguish heterotypic continuity from change (Robins, 1986; Zoccolillo et al., 1992). Third, equally careful attention is needed in delineating aspects of the experiences postulated to be involved in turning-point effects. Marriage per se, for example, may have little effect on desistance from offending (West, 1982). A more specific focus on those aspects of relationships theoretically assumed to be of importance—harmonious, supportive marriages that can foster positive social bonds—has revealed a quite different pattern (Quinton & Rutter, 1988; Sampson & Laub, 1993).

Two additional points need stressing. To detect possible turning points, analyses must focus on those segments of a study population for whom new experiences have the opportunity to have effects. In disadvantaged and deviant samples, these may be quite small; few previously deviant individuals may achieve harmonious marriages or strong attachments to work (Quinton & Rutter, 1988). Because of this, conventional tests of the proportion of sample variance explained by such experiences may suggest quite minor effects. Instead, analyses must be designed to focus on those subgroups in the population in which change may be expected (Pickles & Rutter, 1991; Zoccolillo et al., 1992). And finally, causal assumptions will be most convincing if reversal effects are also observed.

5.7.2. Positive Adult Experiences

A number of studies, including a range of checks of this kind, have now demonstrated that positive adult experiences can act as turning points out of deviant, antisocial trajectories. For both sexes, supportive marital attachments have proved central here. Especially for men, positive labor force involvement and geographical moves to new living environments also appear to play key roles. Sampson and Laub (1993), for example, found strong effects of positive marital attachment and bonds to the labor force in reducing risks of offending in adult life. The effects were similar for previously incarcerated delinquents and in a control group, and held when the effects of early heavy drinking were controlled. In addition, although the most marked changes were associated with roles and relationships formed early in adulthood, later improvements in job stability or marital attachment were also followed by later decreases in crime.

Farrington and West (1995) used additional strategies to examine the effects of marriage on offending. In samples matched for age and severity of prior offending, married men committed significantly fewer offenses in the 5 years following their marriage than those who remained single. In addition, some reversal effects were evident. Men whose marriages broke down offended at rather higher rates during periods of separation and were more likely to offend than those who remained with their wives. Focusing on women, Quinton and Rutter (1988) found that marriage to a nondeviant, supportive partner had marked protective effects against parenting problems in their sample of institutionalized women; and Zoccolillo et al. (1992) found similar positive effects of marriage on continuities between CD and problems in social functioning in these same samples. Importantly, although women's likelihood of achieving a supportive partner was influenced by dispositional protective factors, the positive effects of a supportive marriage applied even when these were not apparent.

These findings provide strong support for the role of positive adult experiences in influencing antisocial trajectories. As yet, the basis for these influences remains to be clarified: Do they emanate primarily, as Sampson and Laub (1993) have argued, from the informal social controls implicit in adult social bonds, or do the changes reflect more intrapersonal processes, arising from enhanced self-esteem or altered social cognitions? Equally important, we know very little at this stage of how far such effects generalize, or persist beyond their immediate context. Farrington and West's (1995) findings that marital separations were followed by somewhat increased levels of offending suggest that effects may be time-limited, and context-dependent. Further tests, exploring the persistence of positive turning-point experiences across subsequent life transitions, are needed here. In addition, the more extended "timetable" for the transition to adulthood in recent generations may hold important implications for the ages at which young people gain access to constructive adult involvements (Graham & Bowling, 1995), and so for secular trends in persistence in crime.

5.8. Protective Factors

To conclude, we turn briefly to the question of individual and social factors that may protect against continuance in deviant behavior or crime. Here, high-risk designs are needed to identify effects, contrasting the development of individuals at equivalent early risk who do and do not show the posited protective factors. Several demonstrations of this kind have now been undertaken.

As expected from the consistent associations of antisocial behaviors with depressed intellectual skills, IQ shows protective effects against criminality in at-risk groups (Kandel et al., 1988), and interventions designed to improve school motivation are also associated with reductions in delinquency (Yoshikawa, 1994). As we have seen, behavioral inhibition can protect against delinquency in adolescence (Kerr et al., 1997), and prosocial tendencies had important effects in moderating longer-term outcomes of childhood deviance in other samples (Hämäläinen & Pulkkinen, 1996).

In addition, an individual disposition to planfulness (Clausen, 1991) has emerged as of central importance in a number of studies. A planful, considered approach to life choices may be especially important for behaviorally deviant youth and for those in situations where family or wider social supports for life-planning are restricted. Shanahan, Elder, and Miech (1996), for example, found that planning was of greatest consequence for educational and occupational outcomes in cohorts when institutional structures were less supportive of continuance in education. Champion et al. (1995) showed that planning was associated with reduced risks of exposure to adverse life events, and Quinton and Rutter (1988; Quinton et al., 1993) found important effects of planning on later life-course developments of institution-reared girls. In this sample, planning seemed of central relevance for partnership choices, reducing the likelihood that girls from high-risk psychosocial backgrounds, or those with histories of CD, would enter unsupportive partnerships. No comparable effects were evident in a community comparison group. There, family supports, along with less deviant peer affiliations, seem likely to have offered alternative supports for partnership choices. Effects of planning were also less marked among institution-reared men (Rutter, Quinton, & Hill, 1990), reflecting their generally lower risks of gaining a deviant partner.

Finally, researchers have begun to investigate psychophysiological factors that may protect against the persistence of antisocial behaviors. Raine, Venables, and Williams (1995), for example, have reported that antisocial adolescents who desisted from crime in adulthood showed *high* autonomic arousal in the teens, exceeding levels found in a nondeviant comparison group. These first findings clearly require confirmation; if replicated, however, they may offer important clues to heterogeneity in adolescence and provide additional pointers to groups whose deviant behavior owes little to psychophysiological predispositions and most to environmental and contextual effects.

6. Conclusions

Recent years have seen major advances in our understanding of developmental continuities in antisocial behavior. It is now clear that the long-term risks extend more widely than to severely antisocial outcomes, that childhood and adolescent onset behavior problems may vary in both risks and long-term consequences, and that although progress to adult outcome depends in part on trait persistence, it also turns heavily on intervening developments, each holding the potential to maintain or redirect behavioral trajectories over time. Behavior genetic analyses have begun to illuminate the interplay between heritable and experiential risks across development, and longitudinal studies are providing an increasingly detailed picture of the complex forces that shape lives through time.

Alongside these advances, key questions remain to be resolved. We have pointed to a number of these in the course of the discussion, and we note just a few central issues in conclusion here. First, the heterogeneity of antisocial behavior continues to present major challenges. It now seems clear that long-term persistence is associated with hyperactivity/inattention, generally involves early onset, often includes low reactivity to stress, and may be dependent on poor peer relationships. How far these features reflect one or several categories, or are better considered in dimensional terms, remains obscure; answers to these questions will hold important implications for the classification of antisocial disorders.

Second, though many broad-range mechanisms for the maintenance of antisocial behavior have been described, we still know very little of the more proximal processes involved in these effects. Assortment on deviance, for example, might reflect a range of processes: active choice of deviant partners; limitations on the "field of possibles" from whom conduct disordered youth can select their mates; or residue effects, whereby antisocial individuals are effectively "deselected" by more conventional others. Comparable questions arise in almost all the areas we have surveyed. To advance theory, and for the lessons they hold for prevention, these more proximal processes are key targets for future research.

Third, we have drawn attention to the indirect causal connections through which later experiences serve to accentuate or alter earlier behavioral patterns. We have also shown how individual differences contribute in shaping and selecting later environments. But almost nothing is known about the role of individual differences in relation to responsivity to environments in later adolescence or adult life. Does a harmonious marriage, for example, have the same effects in individuals with early-onset antisocial behavior associated with hyperactivity as in individuals with less marked individual-risk characteristics? Does the shaping and selection of environments primarily affect outcome for those initially at highest risk? To date, these differing issues have in general been examined by separate groupings of investigators, each approaching developmental issues in antisocial behavior from somewhat different perspectives. The richness of research in the field attests to the value of these different approaches. At the same time, however, undoubtedly the most major advances of future years can be expected from integrations across domains, and from efforts to bring together, both conceptually and methodologically, the currently separate veins of evidence we have surveyed here.

7.   References

Achenbach, T. M., Howell, C. T., McConaughy, S. H., & Stanger, C. (1995). Six-year predictors of problems in a national sample: III. Transitions to young adult syndromes. *Journal of the American Academy of Child and Adolescent Psychiatry, 34,* 658–669.

Achenbach, T. M., McConaughy, S. H., & Howell, C. T. (1987). Child/adolescent behavioral and emotional problems: Implications of cross-informant correlations for situational specificity. *Psychological Bulletin, 101,* 213–232.

American Psychiatric Association. (1994). *Diagnostic and statistical manual of mental disorders* (4th ed.). Washington, DC: Author.

Angold, A., Erkanli, A., Costello, E. J., & Rutter, M. (1996). Precision, reliability and accuracy in the dating of symptom onsets in child and adolescent psychopathology. *Journal of Child Psychology and Psychiatry, 37,* 657–664.

Anthony, J. C., & Helzer, J. E. (1991). Syndromes of drug abuse and dependence. In L. N. Robins & D. A. Regier (Eds.), *Psychiatric disorders in America* (pp. 116–154). New York: Free Press.

August, G. J., & Stewart, M. A. (1982). Is there a syndrome of pure hyperactivity? *British Journal of Psychiatry, 140,* 305–311.

Bardone, A. M., Moffitt, T. E., Caspi, A., Dickson, N., & Silva, P. A. (1996). Adult mental health and social outcomes of adolescent girls with depression and conduct disorder. *Development and Psychopathology, 8,* 811–829.

Barkley, R. A., Fischer, M., Edelbrock, C. S., & Smallish, L. (1990). The adolescent outcome of hyperactive children diagnosed by research criteria: I. An 8-year prospective follow-up. *Journal of the American Academy of Child and Adolescent Psychiatry, 294,* 546–557.

Bell, Q., & Chapman, M. (1986). Child effects in studies using experimental or brief longitudinal approaches to socialization. *Developmental Psychology, 22,* 595–603.

Blumstein, A., Cohen, J., Roth, J. A., & Visher, C. A. (Eds.). (1986). *Criminal careers and "career criminals."* Washington, DC: National Academy Press.

Bohman, M. (1996). Predisposition to criminality: Swedish adoption studies in retrospect. In G. R. Bock & J. A. Goode (Eds.), *Genetics of criminal and antisocial behaviour. CIBA Foundation Symposium 194* (pp. 99–194). Chichester, UK: Wiley.

Bradbury, T. N., Beach, S. R. H., Fincham, F. D., & Nelson, G. M. (1996). Attributions and behavior in functional and dysfunctional marriages. *Journal of Consulting and Clinical Psychology, 64,* 569–576.

Brown, G. W., & Harris, T. O. (1978). *The social origins of depression: A study of psychiatric disorder in women.* London: Tavistock.

Cadoret, R. J., Yates, W. R., Troughton, E., Woodworth, G., & Stewart, M. A. (1995). Genetic–environmental interaction in the genesis of aggressivity and conduct disorders. *Archives of General Psychiatry, 52,* 916–924.

Cairns, R. B., Cairns, B. D., & Neckerman, H. J. (1989). Early school dropout: Configurations and determinants. *Child Development, 606,* 1437–1452.

Cairns, R. B., Cairns, B. D., Neckerman, H. J., Gest, S., & Gariepy, J.-L. (1988). Social networks and aggressive behavior: Peer support or peer rejection? *Developmental Psychology, 24,* 815–823.

Canino, G., Bird, H. R., Rubio-Stipec, M., & Bravo, M. (1995). Child psychiatric epidemiology: What we have learned and what we need to learn. *International Journal of Methods in Psychiatric Research, 5,* 79–92.

Cantwell, D. P., & Rutter, M. (1994). Classification: Conceptual issues and substantive findings. In E. Taylor, L. Hersov, & M. Rutter (Eds.), *Child and adolescent psychiatry: Modern approaches* (pp. 3–21). Oxford, UK: Blackwell Scientific Publications.

Caron, C., & Rutter, M. (1991). Comorbidity in child psychopathology: Concepts, issues and research strategies. *Journal of Child Psychology and Psychiatry, 32,* 1063–1080.

Caspi, A., & Moffitt, T. E. (1991). Individual differences are accentuated during periods of social change: The sample case of girls at puberty. *Journal of Personality and Social Psychology, 61,* 157–168.

Caspi, A., Elder, J. G. H., & Herbener, E. S. (1990). Childhood personality and the prediction of life-course patterns. In L. Robins & M. Rutter (Eds.), *Straight and devious pathways from childhood to adulthood* (pp. 13–55). New York: Cambridge University Press.

Caspi, A., Wright, B. R., Moffitt, T. E., & Silva, P. (in press). Early failure in the labor market: Childhood and adolescent predictors of unemployment in the transition to adulthood. *American Sociological Review.*

Caspi, A., Lynam, D., Moffitt, T. E., & Silva, P. A. (1993). Unravelling girls' delinquency: Biological, dispositional, and contextual contributions to adolescent misbehavior. *Developmental Psychology, 29,* 19–30.

Caspi, A., & Moffitt, T. E. (1993). When do individual differences matter? A paradoxical theory of personality coherence. *Psychological Inquiry, 4,* 247–271.

Caspi, A., & Moffitt, T. E. (1995). The continuity of maladaptive behaviour: From description to understanding in the study of antisocial behaviour. In D. Cicchetti & D. Cohen (Eds.), *Developmental psychopathology* (Volume 2, pp. 472–511). New York: Wiley.

Caspi, A., Moffitt, T. E., Newman, D. L., & Silva, P. A. (1996). Behavioral observations at age 3 predict adult psychiatric disorders: Longitudinal evidence from a birth cohort. *Archives of General Psychiatry, 53,* 1033–1039.

Chaiken, J. M., & Chaiken, M. R. (1990). Drugs and predatory crime. In M. Tonry & J. Q. Wilson (Eds.), *Drugs and crime* (pp. 203–240). Chicago: University of Chicago Press.

Champion, L. A., Goodall, G. M., & Rutter, M. (1995). Behaviour problems in childhood and stressors in early adult life: A twenty-year follow-up of London school children. *Psychological Medicine*, 25, 231–246.

Clark, L. A., Watson, D., & Reynolds, S. (1995). Diagnosis and classification of psychopathology: Challenges to the current system and future directions. *Annual Review of Psychology*, 46, 121–153.

Clausen, J. (1991). Adolescent competence and the shaping of the life course. *American Journal of Sociology*, 96, 805–842.

Cohen, P., Cohen, J., & Brook, J. (1993a). An epidemiological study of disorders in late childhood and adolescence: II. Persistence of disorders. *Journal of Child Psychology and Psychiatry*, 34, 869–877.

Cohen, P., Cohen, J., Kasen, S., Velez, C. N., Hartmark, C., Johnson, J., Rojas, M., Brook, J., & Struning, E. L. (1993b). An epidemiological study of disorders in late childhood and adolescence: I. Age- and gender-specific prevalence. *Journal of Child Psychology and Psychiatry*, 34, 851–867.

Crowe, R. R. (1974). An adoption study of antisocial personality. *Archives of General Psychiatry*, 31, 785–791.

Daly, K. (1993). *Gender crime and punishment*. New Haven: Yale University Press.

DiLalla, L. F., & Gottesman, I. I. (1989). Heterogeneity of causes for delinquency and criminality: Lifespan perspectives. *Development and Psychopathology*, 1, 339–349.

Dishion, T.J., French, D. C., & Patterson, G. R. (1995). The development and ecology of antisocial behavior. In D. Cicchetti & D. J. Cohen (Eds.), *Developmental psychopathology* (Vol. 2, pp. 421–471). New York: Wiley.

Dodge, K. A., Bates, J. E., & Pettit, G. S. (1990a). Mechanisms in the cycle of violence. *Science*, 250, 1678–1683.

Dodge, K. A., Pettit, G. S., Bates, J. E., & Valente, E. (1995). Social information-processing patterns partially mediate the effects of early physical abuse on later conduct problems. *Journal of Abnormal Psychology*, 104, 632–643.

Dodge, K. A., Price, J. N., Bachorowski, J. A., & Newman, J. P. (1990b). Hostile attributional biases in severely aggressive adolescents. *Journal of Abnormal Psychology*, 99, 385–392.

Dunn, G., Everitt, B., & Pickles, A. (1993). *Modelling covariances and latent variables using EQS*. London: Chapman & Hall.

Earls, F. (1994). Oppositional-defiant and conduct disorders. In M. Rutter, E. Taylor, & L. Hersov (Eds.), *Child and adolescent psychiatry: Modern approaches* (3rd ed., pp. 308–329). Oxford, UK: Blackwell Scientific Publications.

Elder, G. H. J. (1986). Military times and turning points in men's lives. *Developmental Psychology*, 22, 233–245.

Elder, G. H. J., & Caspi, A. (1990). Studying lives in a changing society: Sociological and personalogical explorations. In A. I. Rabin, R. A. Zucker, S. Frank, & R. A. Emmons (Eds.), *Studying persons and lives* (pp. 201–247). New York: Springer.

Elliott, D. S., Ageton, S. S., Huizinga, D., Knowles, B. A., & Canter, R. J. (1983). *The prevalence and incidence of delinquent behavior: 1976–1980*. (National Youth Survey Report No. 26). Boulder, CO: Behavioral Research Institute.

Esser, G., Schmidt, M. H., & Woerner, W. (1990). Epidemiology and course of psychiatric disorders in school-age children: Results of a longitudinal study. *Journal of Child Psychology and Psychiatry*, 31, 243–263.

Fagan, J. (1990). Intoxication and aggression. In M. Tonry & J. Q. Wilson (Eds.), *Drugs and crime* (pp. 241–320). Chicago: University of Chicago Press.

Farrington, D. P. (1986a). Age and crime. In M. Tonry & N. Morris (Eds.), *Crime and justice: An annual review of research* (Vol. 7, 189–250). Chicago: University of Chicago Press.

Farrington, D. P. (1986b). Stepping stones to adult criminal careers. In D. Olweus, J. Block, & M. R. Yarrow (Eds.), *Development of antisocial and prosocial behaviour* (pp. 359–384). New York: Academic Press.

Farrington, D. P. (1989). Early predictors of adolescent aggression and adult violence. *Violence and Victims, 4,* 79–100.

Farrington, D. P. (1990). Age, period, cohort and offending. In D. M. Gottfredson & R. V. Clarke (Eds.), *Policy and theory in criminal justice* (pp. 51–75). Aldershot, UK: Avebury.

Farrington, D. P. (1991). Antisocial personality from childhood to adulthood. *The Psychologist, 4,* 389–394.

Farrington, D. P. (1992). Criminal career research in the United Kingdom. *British Journal of Criminology, 32,* 521–536.

Farrington, D. P., Gallagher, B., Morley, L., St. Ledger, R. J., & West, D. J. (1986). Unemployment, school leaving and crime. *British Journal of Criminology, 26,* 335–356.

Farrington, D. P., Loeber, R., Elliott, D. S., Hawkins, J. D., Kandel, D. B., Klein, M. W., McCord, J., Rowe, D. C., & Tremblay, R. E. (1990b). Advancing knowledge about the onset of delinquency and crime. In B. B. Lahey & A. E. Kazdin (Eds.), *Advances in clinical child psychology* (pp. 283–342). New York: Plenum Press.

Farrington, D. P., Loeber, R., & Van Kammen, W. B. (1990a). Long-term criminal outcomes of hyperactivity–impulsivity–attention deficit and conduct problems in childhood. In L. N. Robins & M. Rutter (Eds.), *Straight and devious pathways from childhood to adulthood* (pp. 62–81). New York: Cambridge University Press.

Farrington, D. P., Sampson, R. J., & Wikström, P.-O. H. (Eds.). (1993). *Integrating individual and ecological aspects of crime.* Stockholm: National Council for Crime Prevention.

Farrington, D. P., & West, D. J. (1993). Criminal, penal and life histories of chronic offenders: Risk and protective factors and early identification. *Criminal Behaviour and Mental Health, 3,* 492–523.

Farrington, D. P., & West, D. J. (1995). Effects of marriage, separation, and children on offending by adult males. In Z. Smith Blau (Series Ed.) & J. Hagan (Vol. Ed.), *Current perspectives on aging and the life cycle: Delinquency and disrepute in the life course* (pp. 249–281). Greenwich: JAI Press.

Farrington, D. P., & Wikström, P.-O. H. (1994). Criminal careers in London and Stockholm: A cross-national comparative study. In E. G. M. Weitekamp & H.-J. Kerner (Eds.), *Cross-national longitudinal research on human development and criminal behavior* (pp. 65–89). Netherlands: Kluwer Academic Publishers.

Feehan, M., McGee, R., & Williams, S. M. (1993). Mental health disorders from age 15 to age 18. *Journal of the American Academy of Child and Adolescent Psychiatry, 32,* 1118–1126.

Ferdinand, R. F., & Verhulst, F. C. (1995). Psychopathology from adolescence into young adulthood: An 8-year follow-up study. *American Journal of Psychiatry, 152,* 1586–1594.

Ferdinand, R. F., Verhulst, F. C., & Wiznitzer, M. (1995). Continuity and change of self-reported problem behaviors from adolescence into young adulthood. *Journal of the American Academy of Child and Adolescent Psychiatry, 34,* 680–690.

Fergusson, D. M., & Horwood, L. J. (1995). Predictive validity of categorically and dimensionally scored measures of disruptive childhood behaviours. *Journal of the American Academy of Child and Adolescent Psychiatry, 34,* 477–485.

Fergusson, D. M., & Horwood, L. J. (1996). The role of adolescent peer affiliations in the continuity between childhood behavioral adjustment and juvenile offending. *Journal of Abnormal Child Psychology, 24,* 205–221.

Fergusson, D. M., Horwood, L. J., & Lynskey, M. T. (1995). The stability of disruptive childhood behaviors. *Journal of Abnormal Child Psychology, 23,* 379–396.

Fergusson, D. M., Lynskey, M. T., & Horwood, L. J. (1996). Origins of comorbidity between conduct and affective disorders. *Journal of the American Academy of Child and Adolescent Psychiatry, 35,* 451–460.

Fleming, J. P., Kellam, S. G., & Brown, C. H. (1982). Early predictors of age at first use of alcohol, marijuana, and cigarettes. *Drug and Alcohol Dependence, 9,* 295–303.

Frick, P. J., Lahey, B. B., Loeber, R., Tannenbaum, L., Van Horn, Y., Christ, M. A. G., Hart, E. A., & Hanson, K. (1993). Oppositional defiant disorder and conduct disorder: A meta-analytic review of factor analyses and cross-validation in a clinic sample. *Clinical Psychology Review, 13,* 319–340.

Furstenberg, F. F., Brooks-Gunn, J., & Chase-Lansdale, L. (1989). Teenage pregnancy and childbearing. *American Psychologist, 44,* 313–320.

Gottfredson, M. R., & Hirschi, T. (1990). *A general theory of crime.* Stanford: Stanford University Press.

Gould, M. S., Bird, H., & Jaramillo, B. S. (1993). Correspondence between statistically derived behavior problem syndromes and child psychiatric diagnoses in a community sample. *Journal of Abnormal Child Psychology, 21,* 287–313.

Graham, J., & Bowling, B. (1995). *Young people and crime.* London: Home Office.

Graham, P., & Rutter, M. (1973). Psychiatric disorder in the young adolescent: A follow-up study. *Proceedings of the Royal Society, 66,* 1226–1269.

Guiffra, L. A., & Risch, N. (1994). Diminished recall and the cohort effect of major depression: A simulation study. *Psychological Medicine, 24,* 375–383.

Hämäläinen, M., & Pulkkinen, L. (1996). Problem behavior as a precursor of male criminality. *Development and Psychopathology, 8,* 443–455.

Harada, Y. (1995). Adjustment to school, life course transitions and changes in delinquent behavior in Japan. In Z. Smith Blau (Series Ed.) & J. Hagan (Volume Ed.), *Current perspectives on aging and the life cycle: Delinquency and disrepute in the life course* (pp. 35–59). Greenwich: JAI Press.

Harrington, R. C., Fudge, H., Rutter, M., Pickles, A., & Hill, J. (1991). Adult outcomes of childhood and adolescent depression: II. Links with antisocial disorders. *Journal of the American Academy of Child and Adolescent Psychiatry, 30,* 434–439.

Hawkins, J. D., & Lishner, D. M. (1987). Schooling and delinquency. In E. H. Johnson (Ed.), *Handbook on crime and delinquency prevention* (pp. 179–221). New York: Greenwood Press.

Heidensohn, F. (1994). Gender and crime. In M. Maguire, R. Morgan, & R. Reiner. *The Oxford Handbook of Criminology.* Oxford, UK: Oxford University Press.

Helzer, J. E., Burnham, A., & McEvoy, L. T. (1991). Alcohol abuse and dependence. In L. N. Robins & D. A. Regier (Eds.), *Psychiatric disorders in America* (pp. 81–115). New York: Free Press.

Henry, B., Caspi, A., Moffitt, T. E., & Silva, P. A. (1996). Temperamental and familial predictors of violent and non-violent criminal convictions: From age 3 to 18. *Developmental Psychology, 32,* 614–623.

Hinshaw, S. P. (1992). Externalizing behaviour problems and academic underachievement in childhood and adolescence: Causal relationships and underlying mechanisms. *Psychological Bulletin, 111,* 127–155.

Hinshaw, S. P., Lahey, B. B., & Hart, E. L. (1993). Issues of taxonomy and comorbidity in the development of conduct disorder. *Development and Psychopathology, 5,* 31–49.

Hirschi, T., & Hindelang, M. J. (1977). Intelligence and delinquency: A revisionist review. *American Sociological Review, 42,* 571–587.

Hodgins, S. (Ed.). (1993). *Mental disorder and crime.* Newbury Park, CA: Sage.

Hogan, D. P., & Astone, N. M. (1986). The transition to adulthood. *Annual Review of Sociology,* *12,* 109–130.

Holmshaw, J., & Simonoff, E. (1996). The validity of a retrospective interview on childhood psychopathology. *International Journal of Methods in Psychiatric Research, 6,* 1–10.

Holtzworth-Munrow, A., & Anglin, K. (1993). Attributing negative intent to wife behavior: The attributions of maritally violent versus nonviolent men. *Journal of Abnormal Psychology, 102,* 206–211.

Home Office. (1995). *Criminal careers of those born between 1953 and 1973.* London: Her Majesty's Stationery Office.

Huesmann, L. R., Eron, L. D., Lefkowitz, M. M., & Walder, L. O. (1984). Stability of aggression over time and generations. *Developmental Psychology, 20,* 1120–1134.

Jeglum Bartusch, D. R., Lynam, D. R., Moffitt, T. E., & Silva, P. A. (1997). Is age important? Testing a general versus a developmental theory of antisocial behavior. *Criminology, 35,* 13–47.

Jensen, P. S., Watanabe, H. K., Richters, J. E., Roper, M., Hibbs, E. D., Salzberg, A. D., & Liu, S. (1996) Scales, diagnoses, and child psychopathology: II. Comparing the CBCL and the DISC against external validators. *Journal of Abnormal Child Psychology, 24,* 151–167.

Jessor, R., Donovan, J. E., & Costa, F. M. (1991). *Beyond adolescence: Problem behavior and young adult development.* Cambridge, UK: Cambridge University Press.

Jessor, R., & Jessor, S. L. (1977). *Problem behavior and psychosocial development: A longitudinal study of youth.* New York: Academic Press.

Kagan, J. (1969). The three faces of continuity in human development. In D. A. Goslin (Ed.), *Handbook of socialization theory and research* (pp. 983–1002). Chicago: Rand McNally.

Kagan, J. (1980). Perspectives on continuity. In O. Brim & J. Kagan (Eds.), *Constancy and change in human development* (pp. 26–74). Cambridge, MA: Harvard University Press.

Kandel, D. (1985). On processes of peer influences in adolescent drug use: A developmental perspective. *Alcohol and Substance Abuse in Adolescence, 4,* 139–163.

Kandel, D., Mednick, S. A., Kirkegaard-Sorensen, L., Hutchings, B., Knop, J., Rosenberg, R., & Schulsinger, F. (1988). IQ as a protective factor for subjects at high risk for antisocial behavior. *Journal of Consulting and Clinical Psychology, 56,* 224–226.

Kaplan, H. B. (Ed.). (1995). *Drugs, crime, and other deviant adaptations.* New York: Plenum Press.

Keenan, K., Loeber, R., Zhang, Q., Stouthamer-Loeber, M., & Van Kammen, W. (1995). The influence of deviant peers on the development of boys' disruptive and delinquent behavior: A temporal analysis. *Development and Psychopathology, 7,* 715–726.

Kendler, K. S. (1995). Genetic epidemiology in psychiatry: Taking both genes and environment seriously. *Archives of General Psychiatry, 52,* 895–899.

Kendler, K., & Eaves, L. (1986). Models for the joint effect of genotype and environment on liability to psychiatric illness. *American Journal of Psychiatry, 143,* 279–289.

Kerner, H.-J., Weitekamp, E. G. M., & Stelly, W. (1995). From child delinquency to adult criminality: First results of the follow-up of the Tuebingen Criminal Behavior Development Study. *Eurocriminology, 89,* 127–162.

Kerner, H.-J., Weitekamp, E. G. M., Stelly, W., & Thomas, J. (1996). *Patterns of criminality and alcohol abuse: Results of the Tuebingen Criminal Behavior Study.* Paper presented at a meeting of the Life History Research Society, London. October.

Kerr, M., Tremblay, R. E., Pagani, L., & Vitaro, F. (1997). Boys' behavioral inhibition and the risk of later delinquency. *Archives of General Psychiatry, 54,* 809–816.

Kessler, R. C., Foster, C. L., Saunders, W. B., & Stang, P. E. (1995). Social consequences of psychiatric disorder: I. Educational attainment. *American Journal of Psychiatry, 52,* 1026–1032.

Kessler, R. C., McGonagle, K. A., Zhao, S., Nelson, C. B., Hughes, M., Eshleman, S., Wittchen,

H.-U., & Kendler, K. S. (1994). Lifetime and 12 month prevalence of DSM-III-R psychiatric disorders in the United States. *Archives of General Psychiatry, 51,* 8–19.

Kovacs, M., Krol, R. S. M., & Voti, L. (1994). Early onset psychopathology and the risk for teenage pregnancy among clinically referred girls. *Journal of the American Academy of Child and Adolescent Psychiatry, 33,* 106–113.

Krazter, L., & Hodgins, S. (1996). *Childhood factors and adult criminality among women.* Paper presented at the 14th Biennial Meeting of the International Society for the Study of Behavioral Development (ISSBD), Quebec City, Canada.

Krueger, R. F., Caspi, A., Moffitt, T. E., & Silva, P. A. (in press). The structure and stability of common mental disorders (DSM-III-R): A longitudinal/epidemiological study. *Journal of Abnormal Psychology.*

Lahey, B. B., & Loeber, R. (1991). *A preliminary developmental-psychobiological model of conduct disorder.* Paper presented at the annual meeting of the Society for Research in Child and Adolescent Psychopathology, Amsterdam.

Lahey, B. B., McBurnett, K., Loeber, R., & Hart, E. L. (1995). Psychobiology. In G. P. Sholevar (Ed.), *Conduct disorders in children and adolescents: Assessments and interventions* (pp. 27–44). Washington, DC: American Psychiatric Press.

Lewinsohn, P. M., Rohde, P., & Seeley, J. R. (1995). Adolescent psychopathology: III. The clinical consequences of comorbidity. *Journal of the American Academy of Child and Adolescent Psychiatry, 34,* 510–519.

Loeber, R. (1982). The stability of antisocial and delinquent child behaviour: A review. *Child Development, 53,* 1431–1446.

Loeber, R., DeLamatre, M., Keenan, K., & Zhang, Q. (1997). Boys' experimentation and persistence in developmental pathways toward serious delinquency. *Journal of Child and Family Studies, 6,* 321–357.

Loeber, R., & Hay, D. (1994). Developmental approaches to aggression and conduct problems. In M. Rutter & D. Hay (Eds.), *Development through life: A handbook for clinicians* (pp. 488–517). Oxford, UK: Blackwell Scientific Publications.

Loeber, R., & Keenan, K. (1994). Interaction between conduct disorder and its comorbid conditions: Effects of age and gender. *Clinical Psychology Review, 14,* 497–523.

Loeber, R., & Schmaling, K. (1985). Empirical evidence for overt and covert patterns of antisocial conduct problems. *Journal of Abnormal Child Psychology, 13,* 337–352.

Loeber, R., Wung, P., Keenan, K., Giroux, B., Stouthamer-Loeber, M., Van Kammen, W., & Maughan, B. (1993). Developmental pathways in disruptive child behaviours. *Development and Psychopathology, 5,* 101–132.

Lyons, M. J., True, W. R., Eisen, S. A., Goldberg, J., Meyer, J. M., Faraone, S. V., Eaves, L. J., & Tsuang, M. T. (1995). Differential heritability of adult and juvenile antisocial traits. *Archives of General Psychiatry, 52,* 906–915.

Lytton, H. (1990). Child and parent effects in boys' conduct disorder: A reinterpretation. *Developmental Psychology, 26,* 683–697.

Magnusson, D. (1988). *Individual development from an interactional perspective: A longitudinal study.* Hillsdale, NJ: Erlbaum.

Magnusson, D., & Bergman, L. R. (1990). A pattern approach to the study of pathways from childhood to adulthood. In L. N. Robins & M. Rutter (Eds.), *Straight and devious pathways from childhood to adulthood* (pp. 101–115). Cambridge, UK: Cambridge University Press.

Magnusson, D., & Cairns, R. B. (1996). Developmental science: Toward a unified framework. In R. B. Cairns, G.H. Elder, & E. J. Costello (Eds.), *Developmental science* (pp. 7–30). Cambridge: Cambridge University Press.

Maguin, E., & Loeber, R. (1996). Academic performance and delinquency. *Crime and Justice, 20,* 145–264.

Markus, H., & Cross, S. (1990). The interpersonal self. In L. Pervin (Ed.), *Handbook of personality: Theory and research* (pp. 576–608). New York: Guilford.

Maughan, B., Gray, G., Smith, A., & Rutter, M. (1985). Reading retardation and antisocial behaviour: A follow-up into employment. *Journal of Child Psychology and Psychiatry, 26*, 741–758.

Maughan, B., & Hagell, A. (1996). Poor readers in adulthood: Psychosocial functioning. *Development and Psychopathology, 8*, 457–476.

Maughan, B., Hagell, A., Rutter, M., & Yule, M. (1994). Poor readers in secondary school. *Reading and Writing: An Interdisciplinary Journal, 6*, 125–150.

Maughan, B., & Lindelow, M. (1997). Secular change in psychosocial risks: The case of teenage motherhood. *Psychological Medicine, 27*, 1129–1144.

Maughan, B., Pickles, A., Hagell, A., Rutter, M., & Yule, W. (1996). Reading problems and antisocial behavior: Developmental trends in comorbidity. *Journal of Child Psychology and Psychiatry, 37*, 405–418.

Maughan, B., Pickles, A., & Quinton, D. (1995). Parental hostility, childhood behavior and adult social functioning. In J. McCord (Ed.), *Coercion and punishment in long-term perspectives* (pp. 34–58). New York: Cambridge University Press.

Maughan, B., & Rutter, M. (1997). Retrospective reporting of childhood adversity: Issues in assessing long-term recall. *Journal of Personality Disorders, 11*, 19–33.

McCord, W., & McCord, J. (1960). *Origins of alcoholism*. Stanford: Stanford University Press.

McCord, J. (1979). Some child-rearing antecedents of criminal behaviour in adult men. *Journal of Personality and Social Psychology, 37*, 1477–1486.

McCord, J. (1988). Identifying developmental paradigms leading to alcoholism. *Journal of Studies on Alcohol, 49*, 357–362.

McGee, R., Feehan, M., Williams, S., & Anderson, J. (1992). DSM-III disorders from 11 to 15 years. *Journal of the American Academy of Child and Adolescent Psychiatry, 31*, 50–59.

Menard, S., & Elliott, S. (1990). Longitudinal and cross-sectional data collection and analysis in the study of crime and delinquency. *Justice Quarterly, 7*, 11–55.

Moffitt, T. E. (1993a). Adolescence-limited and life-course-persistent antisocial behaviour: A developmental taxonomy. *Psychological Review, 100*, 674–701.

Moffitt, T. E. (1993b). The neuropsychology of conduct disorder. *Development and Psychopathology, 5*, 135–153.

Moffitt, T. E. (1994). Natural histories of delinquency. In E. G. M. Weitekamp & H.-J. Kerner (Eds.), *Cross-national longitudinal research on human development and criminal behavior* (pp. 3–61). Netherlands: Kluwer Academic Publishers.

Moffitt, T. E., Caspi, A., Dickson, N., Silva, P., & Stanton, W. (1996). Childhood-onset versus adolescent-onset antisocial conduct problems in males: Natural history from ages 3–18 years. *Development and Psychopathology, 8*, 399–424.

Moffitt, T., Caspi, A., Fawcett, P., Brammer, G. L., Raleigh, M., Yuwiler, A., & Silva, P. (in press). Whole blood serotonin and family background relate to male violence. In A. Raine, D. Farrington, P. Brennan, & S. A. Mednick (Eds.), *Unlocking crime: The biosocial key*. New York: Plenum Press.

Moffitt, T. E., Caspi, A., Harkness, A. R., & Silva, P. A. (1993). The natural history of change in intellectual performance: Who changes? How much? Is it meaningful? *Journal of Child Psychology and Psychiatry, 34*, 455–506.

Nagin, D. S., & Farrington, D. P. (1992). The stability of criminal potential from childhood to adulthood. *Criminology, 30*, 235–260.

Nagin, D. S., Farrington, D. P., & Moffitt, T. E. (1995). Life-course trajectories of different types of offenders. *Criminology, 33*, 111–139.

Nagin, D. S., & Paternoster, R. (1991). On the relationship of past and future participation in delinquency. *Criminology, 29*, 163–190.

Newman, D. L., Moffitt, T. E., Caspi, A., Magdol, L., & Silva, P. A. (1996). Psychiatric disorder in a birth cohort of young adults: Prevalence, comorbidity, clinical significance, and new case incidence from ages 11 to 21. *Journal of Consulting and Clinical Psychology, 64*, 552–562.

Nottelman, E. D., & Jensen, P. S. (1995). Comorbidity of disorders in children and adolescents: Developmental perspectives. In T. H. Ollendick & R. J. Prinz (Eds.), *Advances in clinical child psychology* (Vol. 17, pp. 109–155). New York: Plenum Press.

Offord, D. R., & Bennett, K. J. (1994). Conduct disorder: Long-term outcomes and intervention effectiveness. *Journal of the American Academy of Child and Adolescent Psychiatry, 33*, 1069–1078.

Offord, D. R., Boyle, M. H., Racine, Y. A., Fleming, J. E., Cadman, D. T., Blum, H. M., Byrne, C., Links, P. S., Lipman, E. L., & MacMillan, H. L. (1992). Outcome, prognosis and risk in a longitudinal follow-up study. *Journal of the American Academy of Child and Adolescent Psychiatry, 31*, 916–923.

Offord, D. R., Boyle, M. H., Szatmari, P., Rae-Grant, N. I., Links, P. S., Cadman, D. T., Byles, J. A., Crawford, J. W., Blum, M. H., & Byrne, C. (1987). Ontario Child Health Study II: Six-month prevalence of disorder and rates of service utilization. *Archives of General Psychiatry, 44*, 832–836.

Olweus, D. (1979). Stability of aggressive reaction patterns in males: A review. *Psychological Bulletin, 86*, 852–875.

Oyserman, D., & Markus, H. R. (1990). Possible selves and delinquency. *Journal of Personality and Social Psychology, 59*, 112–125.

Patterson, G. R. (1982). *Coercive family interactions.* Eugene, OR: Castalia Press.

Patterson, G. R., & Yoerger, K. (1993). Developmental models for delinquent behavior. In S. Hodgins (Ed.), *Mental disorder and crime* (pp. 140–172). Newbury Park, CA: Sage.

Patterson, G. R., & Yoerger, K. (in press). A developmental model for late-onset delinquency. In R. Dienstbier (Series Ed.) & D. W. Osgood (Vol. Ed.), *Nebraska symposium on motivation: Vol. 44. Motivation and delinquency.* Lincoln: University of Nebraska Press.

Pennington, B. F., & Ozonoff, S. (1996). Executive functions and developmental psychopathology. *Journal of Child Psychology and Psychiatry, 37*(1), 51–87.

Peters, P. L., Serbin, L. A., & Schwartzman, A. E. (1996). *Assortative mating among women with histories of aggressive childhood behavior.* Paper presented at the 14th Biennial Meeting of the International Society for the Study of Behavioral Development (ISSBD), Quebec City, Canada.

Pickles, A., & Rutter, M. (1991). Statistical and conceptual models of turning points in developmental processes. In D. Magnusson, L. R. Bergman, G. Rudinger, & B. Torestad (Eds.), *Problems and methods in longitudinal research: Stability and change* (pp. 131–165). Cambridge, UK: Cambridge University Press.

Pulkkinen, L. (1992). Life-styles in personality development {Special issue: Longitudinal research and personality}. *European Journal of Personality, 6*, 139–155.

Pulkkinen, L., & Pitkanen, T. (1993). Continuities in aggressive behavior from childhood to adulthood. *Aggressive Behavior, 19*, 249–263.

Quinton, D., Pickles, A., Maughan, B., & Rutter, M. (1993). Partners, peers and pathways: Assortative pairing and continuities in conduct disorder. *Development and Psychopathology, 5*, 763–783.

Quinton, D., & Rutter, M. (1988). *Parenting breakdown: The making and breaking of intergenerational links.* Avebury, UK: Gower.

Quinton, D., Rutter, M., & Gulliver, L. (1990). Continuities in psychiatric disorders from childhood to adulthood in the children of psychiatric patients. In L. Robins & M. Rutter (Eds.), *Straight and devious pathways from childhood to adulthood* (pp. 259–277).

Raine, A., Venables, P. H., & Williams, M. A. (1995). High autonomic arousal and electrodermal orienting at age 15 years as protective factors against criminal behavior at age 29 years. *American Journal of Psychiatry, 152,* 1595–1600.

Robins, L. N. (1966). *Deviant children grown up: A sociological and psychiatric study of sociopathic personality.* Baltimore: Williams & Wilkins.

Robins, L. N. (1978). Sturdy childhood predictors of antisocial behaviour: Replications from longitudinal studies. *Psychological Medicine, 8,* 611–622.

Robins, L. N. (1986). The consequences of conduct disorder in girls. In D. Olweus, J. Block, & M. Radke-Yarrow (Eds.), *Development of antisocial and prosocial behavior: Research, theories and issues* (pp. 385–414). New York: Academic Press.

Robins, L. N. (1991). Conduct disorder. *Annual Research Review, Journal of Child Psychology and Psychiatry, 32,* 193–213.

Robins, L. N. (1993). Childhood conduct problems, adult psychopathology and crime. In S. Hodgins (Ed.), *Mental disorder and crime* (pp. 173–193). Newbury Park, CA: Sage.

Robins, L. N., & McEvoy, L. (1990). Conduct problems as predictors of substance abuse. In L. Robins & M. Rutter (Eds.), *Straight and devious pathways from childhood to adulthood* (pp. 182–204). Cambridge, UK: Cambridge University Press.

Robins, L. N., & Price, R. K. (1991). Adult disorders predicted by childhood conduct problems: Results from the NIMH Epidemiologic Catchment Area Project. *Psychiatry, 542,* 116–132.

Robins, L. N., & Regier, D. (1991). *Psychiatric disorders in America.* New York: Free Press.

Robins, L. N., Tipp, J., & Przybeck, T. (1991). Antisocial personality. In L. N. Robins & D. A. Regier (Eds.), *Psychiatric disorders in America* (pp. 258–290). New York: Free Press.

Rodgers, B. (1986). Change in the reading attainment of adults: A longitudinal study. *British Journal of Developmental Psychology, 4,* 1–17.

Rodgers, B. (1990). Influences of early-life and recent factors on affective disorder in women: An exploration of vulnerability models. In L. Robins & M. Rutter (Eds.), *Straight and devious pathways from childhood to adulthood* (pp. 314–328). Cambridge, UK: Cambridge University Press.

Rowe, D. C., Woulbroun, E. J., & Gulley, B. L. (1994). Peers and friends as nonshared environmental influences. In E. M. Hetherington, D. Reiss, & R. Plomin (Eds.), *Separate social worlds of siblings: Impact of nonshared environment on development* (pp. 159–173). Hillsdale, NJ: Erlbaum.

Rutter, M. (1987). Continuities and discontinuities from infancy. In J. Osofsky (Ed.), *Handbook of infant development* (2nd ed., pp. 1256–1296). New York: Wiley.

Rutter, M. (1991). Childhood experiences and adult psychosocial functioning. In G. R. Bock & J. A. Whelan (Eds.), *The childhood environment and adult disease. CIBA Foundation Symposium No. 156* (pp. 189–200). Chichester, UK: Wiley.

Rutter, M. (1994). Continuities, transitions and turning points in development. In M. Rutter & D. F. Hay (Eds.), *Development through life: A handbook for clinicians* (pp. 1–26). Oxford, UK: Blackwell Scientific Publications.

Rutter, M. (1995). Causal concepts and their testing. In M. Rutter & D. J. Smith (Eds.), *Psychosocial disorders in young people: Time trends and their causes* (pp. 7–34). Chichester, UK: Wiley.

Rutter, M. (1996). Transitions and turning points in developmental psychopathology: As applied to the age span between childhood and mid-adulthood. *International Journal of Behavioral Development, 19*(3), 603–626.

Rutter, M. (1997a). Antisocial behavior: Developmental psychopathology perspectives. In D. Stoff, J. Breiling, & J. D. Maser (Eds.), *Handbook of antisocial behavior* (pp. 115–124). New York: Wiley.

Rutter, M. (1997b). Nature–nurture integration: The example of antisocial behavior. *American Psychologist, 52,* 390–398.

Rutter, M. (in press). Individual differences and levels of antisocial behavior. In A. Raine,

D. Farrington, P. Brennan, & S. A. Mednick (Eds.), *Unlocking crime: The biosocial key*. New York: Plenum Press.

Rutter, M., Champion, L., Quinton, D., Maughan, B., & Pickles, A. (1995). Understanding individual differences in environmental risk exposure. In P. Moen, G. H. J. Elder, & K. Luscher (Eds.), *Examining lives in context: Perspectives on the ecology of human development* (pp. 61–93). Washington, DC: American Psychological Association.

Rutter, M., Giller, H., & Hagell, A. (in press-a). *Antisocial behavior in young people*. New York: Cambridge University Press.

Rutter, M., Harrington, R., Quinton, D., & Pickles, A. (1994). Adult outcome of conduct disorder in childhood: Implications for concepts and definitions of patterns of psychopathology. In R. D. Ketterlinus & M. Lamb (Eds.), *Adolescent problem behaviors: Issues and Research* (pp. 57–80). Hillsdale, NJ: Erlbaum.

Rutter, M., Maughan, B., Meyer, J., Pickles, A., Silberg, J., Simonoff, S., & Taylor, E. (in press-b). Heterogeneity of antisocial behavior: Causes, continuities, and consequences. In R. Dienstbier (Series Ed.) & D. W. Osgood (Vol. Ed.), *Nebraska symposium on motivation: Vol. 44. Motivation and delinquency*. Lincoln, NE: University of Nebraska Press.

Rutter, M., & Pickles, A. R. (1991). Person–environment interactions: Concepts, mechanisms and implications for data analysis. In T. D. Wachs & R. Plomin (Eds.), *Conceptualization and measurement of organism-environment interaction* (pp. 105–141). Washington, DC: American Psychological Association.

Rutter, M., & Quinton, D. (1984). Parental psychiatric disorder: Effects on children. *Psychological Medicine, 14*, 853–880.

Rutter, M., Quinton, D., & Hill, J. (1990). Adult outcome of institution-reared children: Males and females compared. In L. N. Robins & M. Rutter (Eds.), *Straight and devious pathways to adulthood* (pp. 135–157). Cambridge, UK: Cambridge University Press.

Rutter, M., & Rutter, M. (1993). *Developing minds: Challenge and continuity across the lifespan*. Harmondsworth, UK & New York: Penguin & Basic Books.

Rutter, M., Tizard, J., Yule, W., Graham, P., & Whitmore, K. (1976). Research report: Isle of Wight Studies 1964–1974. *Psychological Medicine, 6*, 313–332.

Rutter, M., Yule, B., Quinton, D., Rowlands, O., Yule, W., & Berger, M. (1975). Attainment and adjustment in two geographical areas: III. Some factors accounting for area differences. *British Journal of Psychiatry, 126*, 520–533.

Rydelius, P. A. (1988). The development of antisocial behaviour and sudden violent death. *Acta Psychiatrica Scandinavica, 77*, 398–403.

Sampson, R. J. (1992). Family management and child development: Insights from social disorganization theory. In J. McCord (Ed.), *Facts, frameworks and forecasts: Advances in criminological theory* (Vol. 3, pp. 63–93). New Brunswick, NJ: Transaction Publishers.

Sampson, R., & Laub, J. (1993). *Crime in the making: Pathways and turning points through life*. Cambridge: Harvard University Press.

Sanford, M., Offord, D., McLeod, K., Boyle, M., Byrne, C., & Hall, B. (1994). Pathways into the work force: Antecedents of school and work force status. *Journal of the American Academy of Child and Adolescent Psychiatry, 33*, 1036–1046.

Scarr, S. (1992). Developmental theories for the 1990s; Development and individual differences. *Child Development, 63*, 1–19.

Scarr, S., & McCartney, K. (1983). How people make their own environments: A theory of genotype → environment effects. *Child Development, 54*, 424–435.

Schachar, R., Rutter, M., & Smith, A. (1981). The characteristics of situationally and pervasively hyperactive children: Implications for syndrome definition. *Journal of Child Psychology and Psychiatry, 22*, 375–392.

Shanahan, M. J., Elder, G. H., & Miech, R. A. (1996). History and agency in men's lives: Pathways to achievement in cohort perspective. *Sociology of Education, 70*, 54–67.

Serbin, L. A., Moskowitz, D. S., Schwartzman, A. E., & Ledingham, J. E. (1991). Aggressive, withdrawn and aggressive/withdrawn children in adolescence: Into the next generation. In D.J. Pepler & K. H. Rubin (Eds.), *The development and treatment of childhood aggression* (pp. 55–70). Hillsdale, NJ: Erlbaum.

Silberg, J., Meyer, J., Pickles, A., Simonoff, E., Eaves, L., Hewitt, J., Maes, H., & Rutter, M. (1996). Heterogeneity among juvenile antisocial behaviours: Findings from the Virginia Twin Study of Adolescent Behavioural Development. In G. R. Bock & J. A. Goode (Eds.), *Genetics of criminal and antisocial behaviour: CIBA Foundation Symposium, 194* (pp. 76–92). Chichester, UK: Wiley.

Slaby, R. G., & Guerra, N. G. (1988). Cognitive mediators of aggression in adolescent offenders: 1. Assessment. *Developmental Psychology, 24,* 580–588.

Smith, D. J. (1995). Youth crime and conduct disorders: Trends, patterns and causal explanations. In M. Rutter & D. J. Smith (Eds.), *Psychosocial disturbances in young people: Time trends and their causes* (pp. 389–489). Chichester, UK: Wiley.

Stattin, H., & Klackenberg-Larssen, I. (1993). Early language and intelligence development and their relationship to future criminal behavior. *Journal of Abnormal Psychology, 102,* 369–378.

Stattin, H., & Magnusson, D. (1989). The role of early aggressive behaviour in the frequency, seriousness, and types of later crime. *Journal of Consulting and Clinical Psychology, 576,* 210–218.

Stattin, H., & Magnusson, D. (1990). *Pubertal maturation in female development.* Hillsdale, NJ: Erlbaum.

Stattin, H., & Magnusson, D. (1995). Onset of official delinquency. *British Journal of Criminology, 35,* 417–449.

Steinhausen, H.-C., & Reitzle, M. (1996). The validity of mixed disorders of conduct and emotions in children and adolescents: A research note. *Journal of Child Psychology and Psychiatry, 37,* 339–343.

Stoff, D., Breiling, J., & Maser, J. D. (Eds.). (1997). *Handbook of antisocial behavior.* New York: Wiley.

Sudman, S., & Bradburn, N. M. (1973). Effects of time and memory factors on response in surveys. *Journal of the American Statistical Association, 63,* 805–815.

Taylor, E., Heptinstall, H., Chadwick, O., & Danckaerts, M. (1996). Hyperactivity and conduct problems as risk factors for adolescent development. *Journal of the American Academy of Child and Adolescent Psychiatry, 35,* 1213–1226.

Thornberry, T. P., & Krohn, M. D. (1997). Peers, drug use and delinquency. In D. Stoff, J. Breiling, & J. D. Maser (Eds.), *Handbook of antisocial behavior* (pp. 218–233). New York: Wiley.

Tolan, P. H., & Thomas, P. (1995). The implications of age of onset for delinquency risk: II. Longitudinal data. *Journal of Abnormal Child Psychology, 23,* 157–181.

Tonry, M., & Wilson, J. Q. (Eds.). (1990). *Drugs and crime.* Chicago: University of Chicago Press.

Tracey, P. E., Wolfgang, M. E., & Figlio, R. M. (1990). *Delinquency careers in two birth cohorts.* New York: Plenum Press.

Tremblay, R. E., Pihl, R. O., Vitaro, F., & Dobkin, P. L. (1994). Predicting early onset of male antisocial behavior from preschool behavior. *Archives of General Psychiatry, 51,* 732–739.

Vaillant, G. E. (1983). *The natural history of alcoholism: Causes, patterns and paths to recovery.* Cambridge, MA: Harvard University Press.

Waldman, I. D., Lilienfield, S. O., & Lahey, B. B. (1995). Toward construct validity in the childhood disruptive behavior disorders: Classification and diagnosis in DSM-IV and beyond. In T. H. Ollendick & R. J. Prinz (Eds.), *Advances in clinical child psychology* (Vol. 17, pp. 323–363). New York: Plenum Press.

Warr, M. (1993). Age, peers and delinquency. *Criminology, 31,* 17–40.

Weitekamp, E. G. M., Kerner, H.-J., Schubert, A., & Schindler, V. (1995). On the "dangerousness" of chronic/habitual offenders: A re-analysis of the 1945 Philadelphia Birth Cohort data. *Studies on Crime and Crime Prevention, 4,* 159–175.

West, D. J. (1982). *Delinquency: Its roots, careers, and prospects.* London: Heinemann.

West, D. J., & Farrington, D. P. (1977). *The delinquent way of life.* London: Heinemann.

White, J., Moffitt, T. E., Earls, F., Robins, L. N., & Silva, P. A. (1990). How early can we tell? Preschool predictors of boys' conduct disorder and delinquency. *Criminology, 28,* 507–533.

Wikström, P.-O. H. (1990). Age and crime in a Stockholm cohort. *Journal of Quantitative Criminology, 6,* 61– 84.

Wilson, J. Q., & Herrnstein, R. J. (1985). *Crime and human nature.* New York: Simon & Schuster.

Wolfgang, M. E., Figlio, R. M., & Sellin, T. (1972). *Delinquency in a birth cohort.* Chicago: University of Chicago Press.

Wolfgang, M. E., Thornberry, T. P., & Figlio, R. M. (1987). *From boy to man, from delinquency to crime.* Chicago: University of Chicago Press.

World Health Organization (1992). *The ICD-10 classification of mental and behavioral disorders. Clinical descriptions and diagnostic guidelines.* Geneva: Author.

Yoshikawa, H. (1994). Prevention as cumulative protection: Effects of early family support and education on chronic delinquency and its risks. *Psychological Bulletin, 115,* 28–54.

Zoccolillo, M. (1992). Co-occurrence of conduct disorder and its adult outcomes with depressive and anxiety disorders: A review. *Journal of the American Academy of Child and Adolescent Psychiatry, 31,* 547–556.

Zoccolillo, M. (1993). Gender and the development of conduct disorder. *Development and Psychopathology, 5,* 65–78.

Zoccolillo, M., Pickles, A., Quinton, D., & Rutter, M. (1992). The outcome of childhood conduct disorder: Implications for defining adult personality disorder and conduct disorder. *Psychological Medicine, 22,* 971–986.

2

Psychotherapy Outcome Research with Children and Adolescents

The State of the Art

JOHN R. WEISZ, STANLEY J. HUEY,
AND VANESSA ROBIN WEERSING

1. Introduction

After decades of sowing, weeding, harvesting, and winnowing, workers in the field of child and adolescent treatment research have produced a bumper crop. There are now scores of structured interventions for diverse forms of psychological dysfunction across a broad age spectrum. Research-based treatments exist for a substantial range of clinically significant problems and disorders. Although a majority of the more than 230 named therapies for youths have not been tested empirically (see Kazdin, 1988; Kazdin & Weisz, 1996), dozens of such therapies have been subjected to empirical scrutiny, with beneficial effects demonstrated in more than 300 studies. In this chapter, we describe the context of child and adolescent treatment and treatment research, summarize findings of that research, and offer a constructive critique. Finally, we suggest a number of issues that need to be addressed, and approaches that need to be taken, to advance the field. Throughout this chapter, we use the term *children* to encompass both children and adolescents, except where a distinction needs to be drawn between the two age groups.

JOHN R. WEISZ, STANLEY J. HUEY, AND VANESSA ROBIN WEERSING • Department of Psychology, University of California at Los Angeles, Los Angeles, California 90095.

Advances in Clinical Child Psychology, Volume 20, edited by Thomas H. Ollendick and Ronald J. Prinz. Plenum Press, New York, 1998.

2. Prevalence of Child Psychopathology and Use of Psychotherapy

Although disturbed children may differ markedly from one another in patterns of dysfunction, substantial numbers suffer from some kind of significant behavioral, emotional, or mental health problem. Several epidemiological studies in the late 1980s (summarized by Costello, 1989), taken together, suggested that more than 17% of children in the general population met criteria for at least one diagnosis in the *Diagnostic and Statistical Manual of Mental Disorders*, third edition (DSM-III; American Psychiatric Association, 1980), and many had multiple disorders; preliminary findings suggest that prevalence rates will be considerably higher for the most recent edition of the diagnostic manual (DSM-IV). Not evident in these rates of formal diagnosis are the many children who do not qualify for diagnosis but have very significant problems and may well need help. Of course, not all disturbed children receive psychotherapy. But the most recent estimates available in the United States indicate that about 2.5 million American children do receive treatment each year (Office of Technology Assessment, 1986). The annual cost is estimated at more than $1.5 billion (Institute of Medicine, 1989). The dates cited for these statistics reveal a need for more recent data, particularly given the marked changes seen in the U.S. mental health care delivery system (e.g., managed care) in the mid-1990s.

3. Distinctive Features of Child Treatment

Psychotherapy with children bears notable similarities to work with adults, but some important differences warrant attention here—differences that are relevant to our interpretation of the treatment research literature. First, unlike adults, children rarely perceive themselves as "disturbed" or as needing therapy. Thus, most treatment referrals, up until late adolescence, tend to be made by parents, teachers, or other adults, who contract for the therapy, pay the bill, and identify some or all of the goals the therapist is to pursue. The child may or may not participate in identifying target problems or setting treatment goals, or may participate but with less ultimate influence than the adults involved. In a sense, in child therapy, the child is often "the patient," whereas the parent or other adult is "the client." With therapy commissioned by adults, and its goals heavily influenced by adults, it is clear that children may sometimes enter the process with little motivation for treatment or personal change, or at least with different objectives than those shared by the adults involved.

Child therapy also differs from adult therapy in the sources of information used by the therapist to shape the goals and directions of treatment. Given developmental limitations in the self-awareness, psychological mindedness, and expressive ability of their clientele, child therapists must rely heavily on adults for information about the youngsters they treat, and this can present problems of several types. First, parents' and teachers' reports may be inaccurate, based on distorted samples of child behavior, influenced by their own adult agendas, calculated to conceal their own failings as parents (including neglect or abuse), or even biased by their own pathologies (see, e.g., Kazdin & Weisz, 1996); and levels of agreement among different adult informants reporting on the same child tend to be low (Achenbach, McConaughy, & Howell, 1987). Even where there is no blatant bias or intentional distortion, adult reports of child behavior and adult identification of reasons for referral are both apt to reflect the values, practices, and social ideals of their cultural reference group[1] (see Weisz, McCarty, Eastman, Chaiyasit, & Suwanlert, 1997; Weisz et al., 1988; Weisz & Weiss, 1991).

A third notable difference between adult and child treatment relates to environmental selection. To a much greater extent than adults, children are captives of their externally engineered environments. Thus, the "pathology" the child therapist treats may reside as much in a disturbed environment from which the child cannot escape as in the child's personality. This fact may limit the impact of interventions that focus on the child as solo or primary participant, and it may argue for involvement of others from the child's social context, but of course, such significant others are not always willing or cooperative. So, in a number of ways, the child therapist faces challenges that are rather different from those confronted by one who treats only adults. This being the case, it cannot simply be assumed that if therapy is effective with adults it is also effective with children; rather, a separate body of treatment outcome research is required. We turn now to that body of research, investigating whether psychological treatment of children is beneficial.

4. Evidence on the Effects of Child Treatment

Evidence on the effects of child treatment comes in several forms. The most widely recognized of these is the clinical trial, an outcome study

---

[1]The picture can grow complex when these values, practices, and social ideals are not shared by others who are involved in the process of therapy (e.g., a therapist and teacher whose culture differs from that of the child and family).

comparing posttreatment adjustment in a group of children who received a candidate intervention to that of one or more control groups who did not. It is these clinical trials studies that are most frequently pooled in reviews and meta-analyses (to follow) and thus constitute most of the evidence discussed in this chapter. However, other approaches to outcome assessment should be noted here. In circumstances where all the children with a particular condition must receive an active treatment, multiple baseline designs, ABAB (sometimes called "reversal") designs, and simultaneous/alternating treatment designs are useful. Such approaches are often used in treatment research with attention-deficit-hyperactivity disordered (ADHD) youth (see, e.g., Pelham et al., 1993), in studies where an entire classroom needs to receive an intervention (see, e.g., Wurtele & Drabman, 1984), and in cases (sometimes involving rare conditions) where only one or two children will be treated (e.g., McGrath, Dorsett, Calhoun, & Drabman, 1988; Tarnowski, Rosen, McGrath, & Drabman, 1987). These alternative outcome assessment designs have generated a rich body of outcome data that, unfortunately, still await an enterprising reviewer. For now, though, we will focus on the clinical trials research, which has been reviewed rather thoroughly in the form of several meta-analyses, as described here.

4.1. Meta-Analysis: Description, Interpretation, Cautionary Notes

Research findings on psychotherapy effects can be pooled via a technique called meta-analysis (see Mann, 1990; Smith, Glass, & Miller, 1980; but see also critiques, e.g., by Wilson, 1985). The technique uses effect size (ES) as the unit of analysis. ES is an index of the size and direction of treatment effects. For most clinical trials, it is the posttreatment mean on some outcome measure for the treated group minus the mean for the control group, with the difference divided by the standard deviation (SD) of the outcome measure. Figure 1 is a guide to interpreting ES values. As the figure indicates, ES values may be positive, indicating treatment benefit; zero, indicating no effect; or negative, indicating a detrimental effect.[2] Each ES value corresponds to a percentile standing of the average treated child on the outcome measure(s) if that child were placed in the control group after treatment. For example, an ES of 0.90 indicates that the average treated child scored better after treatment than 82% of the control group.

---

[2]For clarity, we are describing the situation in which positive scores on an outcome measure reflect good adjustment. In the cases where the opposite is true (e.g., where the outcome measure is a symptom count), calculations are typically done in such a way that a positive effect size continues to imply more improvement in the treatment than the control group.

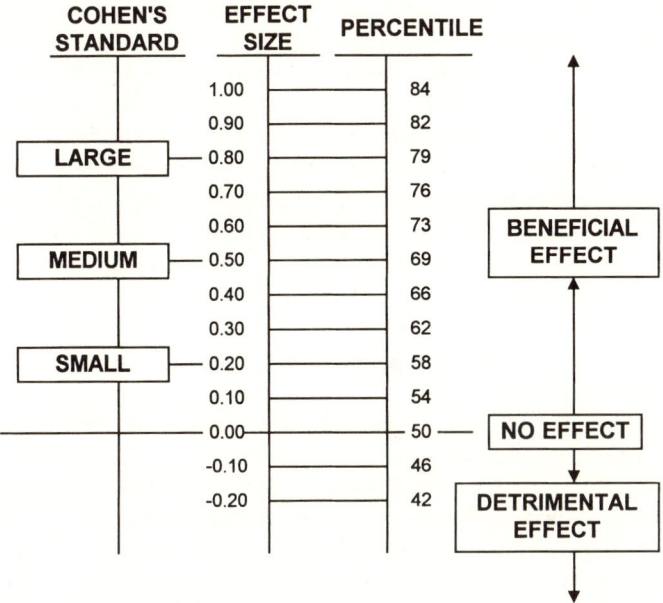

FIGURE 1. An aid to interpreting effect size (ES) statistics. Each ES value corresponds to a specific percentile standing of the average treated child, after treatment, across outcome measures, relative to the untreated group. Reprinted with permission from Weisz, Weiss, Donenberg, Han, and Weiss (1995).

As an aid to interpretation. Cohen's (1988) guidelines suggest that an ES of 0.20 may be considered a "small" effect, 0.50 a "medium" effect, and 0.80 a "large" effect.

By averaging across the various outcome measures used, a meta-analyst may compute a single mean ES for each study (or each treatment group) in the collection to be reviewed. This permits computation of an overall mean ES for the entire collection of studies; it also permits comparison of mean ES across studies differing in potentially important ways (e.g., in the type of therapy employed, the target problem being treated, or the age or gender of the children involved). The results of such comparisons can suggest promising hypotheses—for example, about direct causes, moderators, and mediators of treatment outcome. Thus, meta-analyses can be useful both descriptively, in summarizing the knowledge base and trends therein, and heuristically, in generating questions and predictions for further study.

Like any technique, however, meta-analysis has limitations, some warranting attention here. First, the output of meta-analyses must necessarily reflect limitations of the input. As an example, ES means in the child treatment area reflect a limited range of methods, because there are many more studies of behavioral (including cognitive-behavioral) than non-behavioral treatments. Another limitation is the inevitable confounding among independent variables (e.g., certain target problems tend to be treated with certain methods); such confounding can be addressed partly via eliminating and interaction tests (see, e.g., Weisz, Weiss, Han, Granger, & Morton, 1995c), but the problem can never be completely solved, and this complicates interpretation of findings. More broadly, every meta-analysis requires scores of decisions (e.g., how inclusive to be across studies varying in methodological rigor, which outcome measures to accept, whether to use raw ES or adjust for sample size), any of which may influence the obtained ES values and group means (see relevant findings in a methodological meta-analysis by Weiss & Weisz, 1990). Because no two investigative teams could possibly make all these decisions exactly alike, conclusions of different meta-analyses may differ in part because of differences in meta-analytic method, not just because of substantive differences in study findings. For this reason, convergent findings across separate meta-analyses are particularly useful. With these cautionary notes in place, we now consider findings of meta-analyses in the child area.

4.2.   Findings from Meta-Analyses of Child Psychotherapy Research

We know of four published, broad-based child psychotherapy meta-analyses, that is, meta-analyses involving diverse collections of studies, with few limits imposed on the kinds of treated problems or types of intervention that are included. Together, these four meta-analyses encompass more than 300 separate treatment outcome studies. In the first of the four, Casey and Berman (1985) included outcome studies published between 1952 and 1982, involving treatment of children aged 12 and younger. The mean ES was 0.71 for those studies that included treatment–control comparisons; in percentile terms (see our discussion of Figure 1), the average treated child scored better after treatment than 76% of control group children, averaging across outcome measures. In a second meta-analysis, Weisz, Weiss, Alicke, and Klotz (1987) reviewed outcome studies published between 1952 and 1983, involving children aged 4–18. The mean ES was 0.79, indicating that, after treatment, the average treated child was at the 79th percentile of control group peers, across outcome measures.

The third broad-based meta-analysis was carried out by Kazdin, Bass, Ayers, and Rodgers (1990a). It included studies published between 1970 and 1988, with children aged 4–18. For the subset of studies that compared treatment and no-treatment control groups, the mean ES was 0.88; this indicated that the average treated child scored higher on outcome measures, after treatment, than 81% of the no-treatment comparison group. For studies in the Kazdin et al. collection that involved comparison of treatment groups to active control groups, mean ES was 0.77; the average treated child was functioning better, posttreatment, than 78% of the control group. The fourth broad-based meta-analysis was conducted by Weisz et al. (1995c); it included studies published between 1967 and 1993, involving children aged 2–18. The mean ES was 0.71; this indicated that, after treatment, the average treated child was functioning better than 76% of comparison children in the control groups. (For more detailed descriptions of the procedures and findings of both broad-based and more narrowly focused meta-analyses, see Weisz & Weiss, 1993.)

These four broad-based meta-analyses present a uniformly positive picture. Their mean ES values ranged from 0.71 to 0.84 (0.84 is the estimated overall mean for Kazdin et al., 1990), hovering near Cohen's (1988) threshold of 0.80 for a "large" effect. (Note, however, that recent analyses [in Weisz et al., 1995c] suggests that true population ES means, adjusting for heterogeneity of variance, may be closer to the "medium" level.) Figure 2 shows findings from the four child meta-analyses presented together with the findings of two frequently cited meta-analyses with older groups— that is, Smith and Glass's (1977) meta-analysis of primarily adult psychotherapy outcome studies, and Shapiro and Shapiro's (1982) meta-analysis of exclusively adult outcome studies. As the figure suggests, mean effects found in child meta-analyses fall within the range of effects found in these two adult meta-analyses. Thus, the evidence suggests that empirically tested child and adolescent treatments may approximate the effects of empirically tested adult treatments.

4.3. Findings of Focused Meta-Analyses

Complementing the broad-based analyses just described, some meta-analysts have addressed rather specific questions by focusing on select subsets of treatment outcome studies. Meta-analyses focused specifically on cognitive-behavioral therapy have found substantial positive effects across a range of target problems (Durlak, Fuhrman, & Lampman, 1991) and on impulsivity considered alone (Baer & Nietzel, 1991). And Dush, Hirt, and Schroeder (1989) found significant positive effects associated with the specific cognitive-behavioral technique of self-statement modification. Two teams (Hazelrigg, Cooper, & Borduin, 1987; Shadish et al., 1993) have found respectable mean effects of family therapy, somewhat higher for measures of individual family members' behavior than for

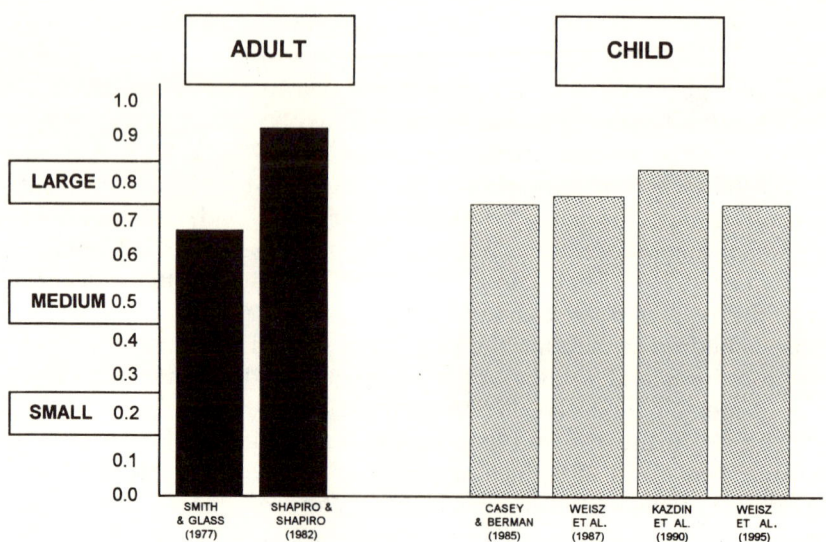

FIGURE 2.   Mean effect sizes found in the predominantly adult meta-analysis by Smith and Glass (1977), in the exclusively adult meta-analysis by Shapiro and Shapiro (1982), and in four broad-based meta-analyses of psychotherapy outcome studies with children and adolescents. Reprinted with permission from Weisz, Donenberg, Han, and Weiss (1995).

family interaction measures. Moderate positive effects have been found for interventions used to prepare children for medical and dental procedures (Saile, Burgmeier, & Schmidt, 1988), and for psychotherapeutic interventions administered in school settings (Prout & DeMartino, 1986). Finally, illustrating the range of questions to which meta-analysis may be relevant, Russell, Greenwald, and Shirk (1991) used a sample of treatment studies to test whether child language proficiency improved with psychotherapy; it did, particularly with therapies that emphasized spontaneous verbal interaction.

4.4.   A Sampler of Additional Meta-Analytic Findings: Outcome as a Function of Therapy, Therapist, and Child Factors

A potpourri of other meta-analytic findings illustrates both the descriptive summarizing, debate-provoking, and hypothesis-generating/research-provoking potential of the technique. In the two meta-analyses from our lab (Weisz et al., 1987; Weisz et al., 1995c), we found that studies involving behavioral treatments (e.g., behavioral contracting, modeling, cognitive-behavioral therapy) generated larger effects than studies using nonbehavioral treatments (e.g., insight-oriented therapy, client-centered counseling). (The Casey–Berman [1985] meta-analyses showed the same effect at $p = .06$; Kazdin et al. [1990a] did not address the question.) By contrast, meta-analyses have generally not found that treatment outcomes differ reliably for different types of treated problems (e.g., internalizing vs. externalizing; for one exception, see Casey & Berman, 1985, pp. 392–393).

The relation between treatment outcome and age has varied across meta-analyses. However, the meta-analysis involving the most recent collection of studies (Weisz et al., 1995c) found that mean ES was larger for adolescents than for children. Notably, this main effect was qualified by an age x gender interaction (shown in Figure 3): Mean ES for samples of predominantly or exclusively adolescent girls was twice as large as mean ES for adolescent boys and for children of both genders. One possible interpretation might be that adolescent girls are more likely to be treated for internalizing problems than are younger children or adolescent boys; however, we found no reliable difference in mean ES for internalizing versus externalizing problems, and in any event, the age x gender interaction shown in Figure 3 was not qualified by type of treated problem (internalizing vs. externalizing), type of treatment (behavioral vs. nonbehavioral), or level of therapist training (professional vs. clinical trainee

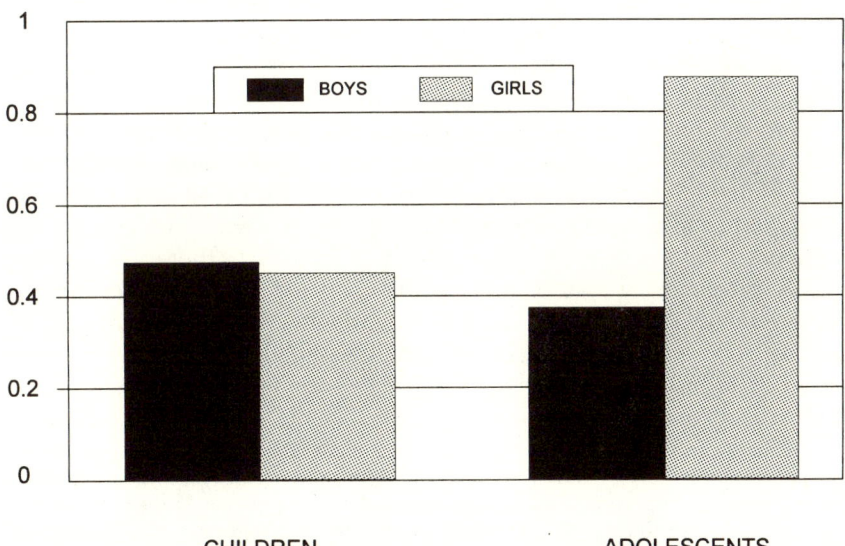

FIGURE 3. Mean effect size for samples of predominantly male and female children (11 years of age and younger) and adolescents (12 years of age and older). Reprinted with permission from Weisz, Weiss, Han, Granger, and Morton (1995).

vs. paraprofessional). Perhaps there is something about the treatments encompassed in these studies in the 1995 meta-analysis that fits the characteristics and needs of adolescent girls particularly well. If so, we are left to speculate about what that elusive quality may be.

Two additional findings illustrate two additional ways meta-analytic data can be used. First, meta-analysis can be used to assess the holding power of intervention effects. We have found in both our meta-analyses (Weisz et al., 1987; Weisz et al., 1995c) that treatment effects measured immediately after treatment are quite similar to effects measured at follow-up assessments, which average about 6 months after treatment termination. This suggests that treatment benefits tend to be durable, at least within typical follow-up time frames.

A second finding (from Weisz et al., 1995c) concerns the specificity of treatment effects. Obviously, children differ markedly from one another in problem profile, and the various therapies differ from one another in the problems they are designed to address, but do these individual differences actually influence treatment outcome? Some (e.g., Frank, 1973) have argued that psychotherapy has general, "nonspecific" effects (e.g., helping people through such unfocused means as promoting a feeling of being understood, or inducing an expectancy of relief). In an alternative view, therapies help in specific ways, and thus have their most pronounced influence on the specific problems they are designed to address.

In Weisz et al. (1995c), we addressed this controversy by testing whether effect sizes were larger for the specific problem domains targeted by a treatment than for other, more incidental domains. As an example, we asked whether a treatment designed to reduce anxiety produced bigger changes in anxiety levels than in related but more peripheral problems such as depression. Across multiple comparisons like these, our analyses showed that ES means were about twice as large for the specific problems addressed in treatment as for related problems that were not specifically targeted. This suggests that the tested child psychotherapies are not merely producing global or nonspecific good feelings that influence diverse outcomes equally; instead, the treatments appear to have rather precise, focused effects consistent with the specific changes they were designed to bring about.[3]

---

[3]An alternative perspective on these findings warrants consideration as well. If one focuses on the "nonspecific factor" of *client expectancy*, it might be argued that the findings cut in the other direction; that is, because the domains targeted in treatment may be the most reactive for the client, those outcome domains would be expected to change more than nontargeted domains, given the impact of client expectancy. In summary, the findings support the notion that outcomes are target-problem-specific, but the precise mechanism driving this specificity may continue to be a matter of debate in the field.

To summarize the evidence, meta-analyses of child psychotherapy outcome studies point to positive, durable, and problem-specific effects of mental health interventions for a variety of child problems. Clearly, child psychotherapy research is generating a number of encouraging findings. On the other hand, significant limitations in conceptualization, sampling, study design, and outcome assessment methodology make research in this area less useful and less edifying than it might otherwise be. We turn our attention now to some of the limitations of child treatment outcome research, and we offer suggestions for future research that we believe could help advance the field.

5. Representativeness of Outcome Research vis-à-vis Clinical Practice

One significant limitation of child psychotherapy outcome research to date is that much of it has been conducted with nonreferred children and under conditions that may have rather limited external validity for clinical practice. Most of the 300-plus studies in the meta-analyses reviewed earlier (especially the recent and behavioral studies) involved samples, treatments, and/or treatment conditions that are not very representative of what typically happens in most clinical practice with referred children. In many of the studies, for example, (1) children were recruited for treatment and were not actual clinic cases; (2) homogeneous samples were selected, with therapy addressing only one focal problem (e.g., a specific phobia) or a narrow range; (3) therapists received extensive pretherapy training and between-session supervision in the specific intervention techniques they would use; and/or (4) the therapy involved more or less exclusive adherence to those specific techniques. In addition, (5) therapy was frequently highly structured, guided by a manual, and/or monitored for adherence to a treatment plan.

These features of the experimental studies tend to coalesce around an abstract category that we (Weisz, Weiss, & Donenberg, 1992) have called *research therapy*, as distinguished from conventional *clinic therapy*. Table 1 summarizes some illustrative differences between the two therapy genres. The two are best construed as two poles of a multidimensional continuum; certainly no single feature listed in the table under Research Therapy is present in all laboratory outcome studies, nor is any single feature listed under Clinic Therapy present in all clinic-based treatment. Moreover, we do not intend to imply that either pole is somehow "better" than the other; rather, the two poles reflect characteristics that are driven in part by the rather different objectives and requirements of outcome research and

TABLE 1
*Some Characteristics Frequently Associated with Child Psychotherapy
in Outcome Research (Research Therapy) and in Clinics (Clinic Therapy)*

Research therapy	Clinic therapy
Recruited cases (less severe, study volunteers)	Clinic-referred cases (more severe, some coerced into treatment)
Homogeneous groups	Heterogeneous groups
Narrow or single-problem focus	Broad, multiproblem focus
Treatment in lab, school settings	Treatment in clinic, hospital settings
Researcher as therapists	Professional career therapists
Very small caseloads	Very large caseloads
Heavy pretherapy preparation	Little/light pretherapy preparation
Preplanned, highly structured treatment (manualized)	Flexible, adjustable treatment (no treatment manual)
Monitoring of therapist behavior	Little monitoring of therapist behavior
Behavioral methods	Nonbehavioral methods

clinic treatment, respectively. However, differences between child therapy in outcome studies and child therapy in clinics are common enough and substantial enough that it is fair to ask whether the positive outcomes generated in the research therapy studies, and summarized in the previous meta-analyses, are representative of the outcomes achieved in actual clinical practice with children.

5.1. Evidence on the Effects of Child Treatment in Clinical Practice

We sought to find out what outcomes are achieved in clinical practice with children, but we found it difficult to locate much relevant evidence. We conducted a search (described in Weisz, Donenberg, Han, & Weiss, 1995b) for published outcome studies that focused on what might fairly be called "clinic therapy." The search aimed for studies that involved (1) treatment of clinic-referred (i.e., not "analog" or recruited) youngsters; (2) treatment in service-oriented clinics or clinical agencies, not in research settings (e.g., not public schools or university labs); (3) therapy carried out by practicing clinicians (as opposed to trained research assistants); and (4) therapy that was part of the regular service provided by the clinic, not a treatment program designed specifically for research. For inclusion, we required that the studies involve direct comparison between youngsters who received treatment and a control group who received no treatment or a placebo condition.

Clinic studies that met the criteria outlined here proved to be very rare. We had done one study that met the criteria (Weisz & Weiss, 1989), but we found only eight others (spanning a period of 50 years) that seemed to fit; most of these had been published many years earlier. The studies all compared treatment and control groups, but via several different method-ologies (for details, see Weisz, Donenberg, Han, & Kauneckis, 1995a). To facilitate comparison of findings from these nine studies with the meta-analytic findings, we computed an ES or ES estimate for each of the nine studies (for studies that did not report the statistics needed for standard ES calculation, we used estimation procedures described by Smith et al., 1980, and Glass, McGaw, & Smith, 1981). As shown in Figure 4, ES values ranged from −0.40 to +0.29, with mean ES for the nine clinic studies (0.01) falling well below the mean ES of the four broad-based meta-analyses discussed earlier (0.77). This certainly points to outcomes of clinic therapy that were less positive than the outcomes of research therapy, at least for the pool of studies we have identified.

These findings are complemented by recent evidence on "system of care" or "continuum of care" programs for children, that is, efforts to provide an array of conventional mental health services to children, often with the services organized and coordinated by a case manager (see, e.g.,

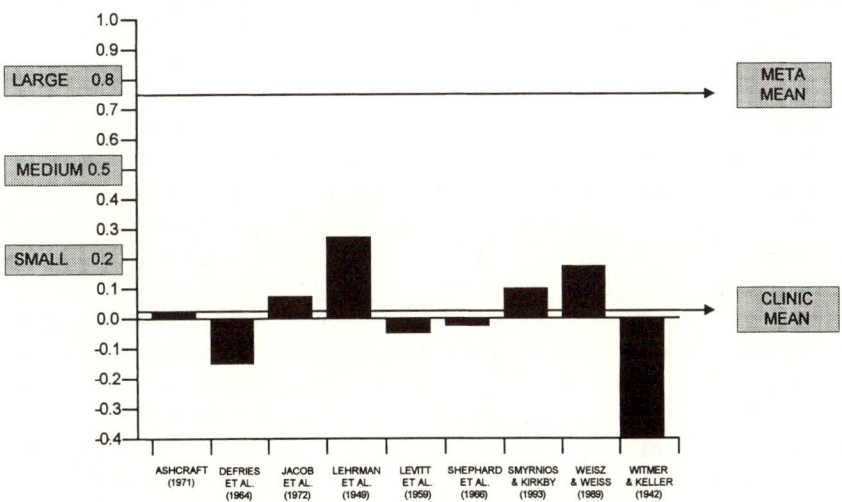

FIGURE 4.   Estimated effect sizes for nine studies of clinic-based psychotherapy with chil-dren and adolescents. Horizontal arrows show mean effect size for four broad-based meta-analyses of laboratory outcome studies (top), and averaging across the nine clinic-based studies (bottom). Reprinted with permission from Weisz, Weiss, Donenberg, Han, and Weiss (1995).

Stroul & Friedman, 1986). In one of the most recent and ambitious of these efforts, the Fort Bragg Project (see Bickman, 1996; Bickman et al., 1995), the U.S. Army spent $80 million to provide an organized continuum of mental health care for children in the Ft. Bragg (North Carolina) catchment area, and to test its cost effectiveness relative to the more typical fragmented services in a matched comparison site. The Fort Bragg program apparently did produce well-integrated services. It was judged by the American Psychological Association's section on Child Clinical Psychology and the Division of Child, Youth, and Family Services Joint Task Force to be

> the most comprehensive program to date, integrating many of the approaches demonstrated by other service programs ... integrated and flexibly con- structed, yet comprehensive, [with] services available to be adapted to meet the needs of children and their families, rather than a simplistic application of a single approach. (Roberts, 1994, p. 215)

There is good evidence (see Bickman et al., 1995) that the program pro- duced better access to treatment and higher levels of client satisfaction; the program also cost a good deal more than services in the comparison site. Unfortunately, clinical and functional outcomes were no better among Fort Bragg children than among children in the comparison site. Fort Bragg children received more mental health intervention at greater cost, but their outcomes were not improved by the increased intensity and cost.

Rather similar findings have emerged from other studies designed to modify, link, or otherwise improve delivery of conventional clinical ser- vices (see, e.g., Evans et al., 1994; Lehman, Postrado, Toth, McNary, & Goldman, 1994). Certainly, a number of alternative interpretations of these null findings may be plausible, but one interpretation that must be consid- ered is this: The various treatments that are linked and coordinated within these continua of care may simply not be very effective, individually or in combination (see Weisz, Han, & Valeri, 1997). Because there is no indica- tion that the individual interventions employed in these various continua of care have been tested empirically and shown to be effective, it is possible that the various interventions are simply not very helpful to children. By extension, it is also possible that a broad array of relatively ineffective services will not produce much true benefit, regardless of the extent to which they are multiplied and organized into continua or systems of care, and regardless of whether they are coordinated by case managers.

To summarize findings on representative clinical interventions with children, (1) the limited evidence on conventional clinical treatments pro- vides little support for their effectiveness, and (2) the modest number of available studies on effects of integrating conventional interventions into systems or continua of care also shows little evidence of treatment benefit. These conclusions may certainly be reversed or otherwise modified by future research findings. But the findings to date offer little support for the effectiveness of conventional clinical intervention for young people.

5.2. Directions for Future Research

The research findings on community- and clinic-based interventions suggest a number of useful directions for future research. First, we certainly need a richer base of information than is currently available on outcomes of treatment under representative clinical conditions. Research on this question is difficult but certainly not impossible to carry out, as the nine studies shown in Figure 4 demonstrate (for a discussion of the pros and cons of various methods, see Weisz & Weiss, 1993). Our base of information on psychotherapy effects in public clinics is obviously quite thin, but the situation is even worse for other treatment contexts. For example, as best we can determine, there is currently no methodologically sound investigation of treatment effects in such now-common treatment configurations as group and individual private practice and health maintenance organizations (HMOs). We need evidence on the child outcomes generated by these forms of practice if we are to know how outcomes across the range of today's clinic therapies compare to the outcomes of laboratory interventions. Moreover, without such information, we will lack the kind of baseline data needed to assess the impact of significant changes in clinical practice conditions—for example, such changes as the implementation of empirically validated treatments (to follow) or even the introduction of managed care.

If further research on conventional clinical treatment continues to show rather poor effects, we will also need research to identify factors that account for the difference between the strong positive effects of therapy in lab studies and the weak effects in clinical settings. We have made two attempts to address this issue (Weisz et al., 1995a; Weisz et al., 1995b). In both, we used our meta-analytic data sets to assess which, if any, of the factors that distinguish research therapy from clinic therapy (e.g., of those shown in Table 1) might account for substantial variance in treatment outcome. In our most recent effort, using our most compete sample (Weisz et al., 1995b), we examined eight potentially relevant factors and we found two that were significantly related to treatment outcome: (1) Behavioral treatments generated better outcomes than nonbehavioral treatments, and (2) analog cases had better outcomes than clinic-referred children. The first finding suggests the possibility that effects of clinic treatment might be enhanced if more behavioral treatments were used in those settings; recent evidence does indicate that behavioral treatments are not the first choice of most practitioners (see Kazdin, Siegel, & Bass, 1990b), and this suggests that such therapies may not be used as frequently as nonbehavioral approaches. The second finding suggests that even the lab-tested treatment methods may be less successful in treating truly clinic-referred children than in treating the less disturbed children who are so often the subjects in lab studies. This, in turn, suggests that one reason clinical practice outcomes may be less positive than research therapy outcomes is simply that the clients referred to clinics are more difficult to treat.

A third useful direction for future research is relevant to the current emphasis on moving empirically supported treatments into clinical practice and clinical training programs (Chambless et al., 1996; Task Force, 1995). At first blush, it would seem that the array of findings presented earlier points to a clear need to emphasize empirically supported treatments in clinical practice. The logic is simple: (1) Evidence from clinical trials research with children, as summarized in meta-analyses, shows that the treatments represented in this literature generally produce positive effects; (2) research on conventional treatments in clinical settings has shown little evidence of positive effects; thus, (3) to generate beneficial effects in clinical settings, we should identify those treatments that have been supported in clinical trials and export them to clinics. This logic may prove to be sound in the long term; however, it may be a mistake to assume that the empirically supported treatments are ready for immediate export.

The problem is that the subjects and treatment conditions involved in tests of the empirically supported treatments tend to differ so much from everyday clinic cases and conditions that it is not entirely clear how workable or effective the supported treatments will be in practicing clinics. Some of the relevant differences are those noted earlier, in our discussion of Table 1. For example, consider the samples frequently employed in clinical trials research. We cannot be certain that treatments supported in clinical trials studies with subclinical samples recruited from schools will be equally effective with seriously disturbed children referred to clinics. Indeed, in a recent analysis (Weisz et al., 1995b, p.695), we found that mean ES in even the clinical trials research was significantly lower for studies using clinic-referred children than for those using analog samples. As a second example, clinical trials studies frequently focus on homogeneous groups, selected for the presence of one or two target problems, and with exclusionary criteria applied to exclude children who have additional unwanted problems. We cannot be sure that treatments supported with such samples will be equally effective with the heterogeneous groups of multiproblem children frequently seen in everyday clinical practice.

What these concerns suggest is that before manualized treatments from the empirical literature are implemented in our clinics and clinical training programs, we may need a new genre of treatment outcome research. This research would involve taking empirically supported treatments out of the laboratories where they were developed and experimenting with them in the crucible of clinical practice. The idea would be to find out what modifications are needed to make the treatments effective with the clientele, and under the real-life constraints, of clinical practice. Several investigators have taken steps in this direction, for example, by treating truly disturbed children in university-based lab clinics (see, e.g., Kendall, 1994; Lovaas, 1987). However, more extensive attempts may be needed to incorporate lab-tested treatments into clinical practice, and test their effects, before we can know (1) what changes will be needed to make these treatments work with seriously disturbed children, and (2) what steps must be taken for the treatments to operate within the policy and personnel parameters of most clinics.

6. Assessment of Therapy Process in Clinical Practice

To the extent that we begin to focus outcome research on treatment by practitioners in clinical settings with referred children, we are apt to need a much richer armamentarium than is now available to assess the processes that may account for outcome. When treatment works well, we need to know what therapy processes were involved, so we can repeat them and build on them; and when treatment fails, we need to know what to *stop* doing. This is especially important—but especially difficult methodologically—in research on nonmanualized treatments in conventional clinical practice. By contrast, structured interventions frequently involve detailed accounts of the treatment techniques used by therapists, but even those treatment studies that involve structured, manual-driven interventions rarely include efforts to determine what particular aspects of therapy were the "active ingredients" of treatment.

The typical clinical trial in the child area provides a rather global comparison of a control group to a treatment program involving multiple techniques. Significant global group differences at posttreatment and follow-up are indeed important elements of treatment validation, and for cost-effectiveness probably the most useful first step in treatment development. However, the lack of specificity regarding which elements of the treatment are producing which aspects of client change has led to calls for a more fine-grained analysis of the processes of child psychotherapy that influence treatment outcome (Kazdin & Weisz, in press; Kendall & Morris,

1991). Kazdin et al. (1990a) reported that one-fourth of their sample of 223 outcome studies varied some technique components across groups, and only 2% evaluated outcome in relation to treatment processes, such as the therapeutic relationship; this suggests that there is room for growth in research on what therapist, client, and relationship factors over the course of the therapy process actually influence change. There are at least four ways of construing such research.

6.1. Treatment Components

Wherever well-replicated effects indicate that a treatment program is effective, a logical next step is to test the effects of various program components, in combinations that make sense logically and theoretically. At least two variations on this theme are well recognized in the field. A *dismantling* approach involves breaking a program down into technique components and varying these across groups; an *additive* approach involves progressive addition of new components, or combining two or more treatments into one. In the Kazdin et al. (1990a) analysis of 223 child treatment outcome studies, 26% involved the first approach, to some extent, and 19% involved the second approach. If these numbers seem surprisingly large, it should be borne in mind that 60% of the Kazdin et al. sample of studies involved comparison of two or more treatments, not necessarily with a no-treatment or active control group. So, the data suggest that research involving "unpacking" specific treatment components is underway in the child area, but that much work remains to be done.

6.2. Therapist Behavior during Treatment

A second dimension of therapy process that deserves scrutiny is the behavior and style of the therapist, independent of the specific components of an outline or manual. For example, a good deal of research has focused on therapist directness in communication with clients. In a series of studies, Patterson and his colleagues have noted that therapists' direct instructions to parents of antisocial children to change their parenting style are frequently met with noncompliance in session and resistance to change outside sessions (e.g., Patterson & Chamberlain, 1994; Patterson & Forgatch, 1985). On the other hand, with a similar sample of delinquent children, Truax and Wittmer (1973) found evidence that directness by the therapist may have positive effects in confronting defense mechanisms in psychodynamic child therapy. As the findings of these two investigative teams suggest, any one aspect of therapist style or behavior may have differential effects depending on the content and objectives of the treatment, and, of course, therapist style may well interact with client style and personality to shape the ultimate effects. Despite the complexity of the task, and the infinite array of therapist style and behavior dimensions that might be addressed, research on this theme may be well worth the investment of time and intellectual resources it will require. Of all the research discussed in this chapter, this is perhaps the most relevant to the task of therapist training. Many directors of training programs for clinical psychologists and child psychiatry fellows would, no doubt, agree that we have a great deal to learn about this task.

6.3. Child and Family Behavior during Treatment

A third aspect of the treatment process that requires attention is the behavior of treated children and their families over the course of therapy. Research on this theme is illustrated by the work of Gorin (1993) and Braswell, Kendall, Braith, Carey, and Vye (1985) indicating that positive treatment outcomes are associated with clients' active on-task participation in therapy. Braswell et al. sampled therapist and child behavior from several sessions of cognitive-behavioral, behavioral, and attention-control treatment of impulsivity and attentional problems. Across groups, measures of child involvement, as indexed by child requests for information, clarification, or elaboration of the task at hand, were significantly related to positive outcome. Therapists' attempts to foster child involvement through eliciting feedback, encouraging children's performance, and correcting mistakes, were also related to outcome. Self-disclosure and non-task-related verbalization (i.e., off-task involvement) were not related to outcome.

Causality is difficult to nail down in such research, and it is certainly possible that such client behavior as active participation may be either a cause of the ultimate treatment benefit, a signal that the treatment is resonating with the client and producing change, or both. But, causality aside, the identification of child and family behavior during therapy that can predict ultimate outcome can, in principle, provide a much-needed tool for therapists: a means of determining—before the entire intervention program has ended—whether the treatment is working or not, and thus whether adjustments are needed.

6.4. The Therapeutic Relationship

The fourth dimension is perhaps the most elusive but possibly also the most important. The therapeutic relationship, or working alliance, has been construed as involving two interrelated parts: (1) the client's positive emotional connection to the therapist and (2) a shared conceptualization between the client and therapist of the tasks and goals of therapy (Bordin, 1979). In the adult literature, development of a therapeutic relationship has emerged as a particularly significant process correlate of positive outcome in several studies (Horowitz, Marmar, Weiss, DeWitt, & Rosenbaum, 1984; Luborsky, Crits-Christoph, Mintz, & Aurerbach, 1988). Shirk and Saiz (1992) have argued that this process variable may be an even more significant contributor to outcome for children due to the "involuntary client" status of many children at the beginning of therapy, the nonverbal nature of many forms of client-centered and play therapy for children, and the social deficits that are hypothesized to be central in the development and maintenance of many serious child problems (e.g., aggression). But only a few studies have examined the therapeutic relationship in the context of child treatment.

Researchers in the child area have studied the therapeutic relationship in play therapy (Howe & Silvern,1981; Truax, Altmann, Wright, & Mitchell, 1973), family therapy (Friedlander, Wildman, Heatherington, & Skowron, 1994; Pinsoff & Catherall, 1986), individual psychodynamic therapy (Shirk & Saiz, 1992), cognitive-behavioral treatment (Kendall, 1994), child behavior therapy (Motta & Lynch, 1990; Motta & Tobin, 1992), and parent training (Webster-Stratton & Herbert, 1993). However, unlike the consistently positive findings in the adult process literature relating the working alliance to therapeutic success, evidence from child psychotherapy has been mixed, with Truax et al. (1973) reporting positive associations between their measures of the therapeutic relationship and outcome in child psychodynamic psychotherapy, and both Kendall (1994) and Motta and Lynch (1990) finding no significant association between relationship quality and outcome with cognitive-behavioral treatment for anxiety and behavioral therapy for learning and disruptive behavior problems, respectively. The lack of agreement across studies is difficult to interpret, given the study-to-study differences in the way therapeutic relationship has been operationalized and assessed, and in the types of therapy to which these varied assessments have been applied. Table 2 summarizes some of the variations across studies.

Early assessment of the therapeutic relationship focused on evaluating therapist-generated conditions of empathy, warmth, and genuineness by coding therapist behavior *in vivo*, as observed live or on therapy tapes. Little attention was given to the child client's perception of these or other therapist behaviors, or to direct assessment of the reciprocal therapeutic relationship. The majority of these studies also focused on a single type of treatment (nondirective play therapy), involved small numbers of therapists and children, and did not evaluate the association between the

TABLE 2
Assessment of Therapeutic Relationship/Therapist Style in Various Studies of Child Psychotherapy Process

Study	Category	Method	Respondents/ coding targets	Type of treatment
Kendall (1994)	Relationship	Questionnaire	Child	Cognitive-behavioral
Motta & Lynch (1990)	Relationship	Questionnaire	Parent	Behavioral
Pinsoff & Catherall (1986)	Relationship	Questionnaire	Family members over age 10	Family
Shirk & Saiz (1992)	Relationship	Questionnaire	Therapist, child	Psychodynamic-eclectic
Smith-Acuna et al. (1991)	Affect, warmth, and acceptance	Questionnaire	Therapist, child	Psychodynamic
Mook (1982)	Empathy and respect	Coding system	Therapist	Rogerian-psychodynamic
Moustakas & Schalock (1955)	"Being there" empathy	Coding system	Therapist	Nondirective play
Moustakas et al. (1956)	"Being there" empathy	Coding system	Therapist	Nondirective play
Siegel (1972)	Warmth, genuineness	Coding system	Therapist	Nondirective play
Truax et al. (1973)	Warmth, genuineness	Coding system	Therapist	Psychodynamic-eclectic
Wright et al. (1972)	Warmth, genuineness	Coding system	Therapist	Psychodynamic-eclectic

therapeutic relationship and treatment outcome (Truax et al., 1973, is an exception to this generalization). More recent research has taken a different approach emphasizing the development and application of questionnaires designed to assess the perception of the therapeutic relationship by key players in the treatment process. However, various investigators have differed in their choices of the key players on which to focus (i.e., child vs. parent vs. therapist), the length and comprehensiveness of their scales (e.g., 7 items for Shirk & Saiz [1992] vs. 32 items for one subscale of the Smith-Acuna, Durlak, & Kaspar [1991] scale), and typical item content (e.g., "How important were the therapist's personal qualities such as warmth, sincerity, genuineness, or ability to relate, in the treatment?" [Motta & Lynch, 1990] vs. "I wish my therapist would leave me alone" [Shirk & Saiz, 1992]).

To untangle the different effects of the therapeutic relationship reported across studies, our field needs a well-validated set of measures for assessing the relationship. Developing such measures for child therapy will be a challenging task. Among the difficulties confronted, two are particularly notable: (1) the complexity of the relationship concepts involved relative to the limited verbal and conceptual facility of many of the children who will be the targets of the assessment; and (2) the need to encompass not only the child–therapist dyad, but also various family members whose relationship to therapist and child may be critical to the success of treatment. It is clear that studying this elusive entity known as the therapeutic relationship will be a challenging task, but the rewards of success may be very significant.

7. Ethnicity and Culture of Treated Children and Their Families

Another issue that has remained relatively unaddressed in research on child treatments is that of ethnicity and culture. In most child outcome studies, the samples are probably predominantly Caucasian, but authors have frequently failed to specify sample composition. In the Kazdin et al. (1990a) survey of 223 child outcome studies, 80% failed to identify the ethnic composition of their sample. While mere reporting of the relevant numbers is rare, actual tests of ethnicity as a moderator of outcome are even rarer. Some have suggested that treatments tested primarily with mainstream samples may not necessarily be optimal for members of ethnic minority groups (Gibbs & Huang, 1989; Rogler, Malgady, Costantino, & Blumenthal, 1987; Spurlock, 1985; Sue, 1977; Tharp, 1991). The treatments may not, for example, take into account the language, values, customs, child-rearing traditions, expectancies for child and parent behavior, and distinctive stressors and resources associated with different cultural groups. In the treatment setting, such cultural factors may lead to miscommunication and misunderstanding between the therapist and the client and family, thus increasing the likelihood of premature termination and poor treatment outcome (Ho, 1992; Sue & Zane, 1987). Tharp (1991) has also suggested that even therapy modality requires attention, and that family and group interventions may be more appropriate than individual treatment for many minority youth. Such interventions, Tharp suggests, may also generate information on cultural issues relevant to the child, family, and community—information the therapist can use in adjusting and focusing the treatment.

The published literature on culture and psychotherapy is rich in recommendations for how to treat specific ethnic groups but relatively poor in controlled empirical assessment. Most of the recommendations appear to be based on anecdotal and experiential reports (see Gibbs & Huang, 1989; Ho, 1992). The array of hypotheses now available should provide fertile ground for experimentation in the future. For the present, though, a modest base of evidence suggests trends that bear further study. We identified this evidence through the following search procedures: (1) We reviewed the Method section of all the articles included in our two broad-based meta-analyses of child treatment outcome studies (Weisz et al., 1987; Weisz et al., 1995c); (2) we carried out a Psychinfo search using the keywords *therapy, treatment, child(ren), adolescent(s), minority, ethnic, black(s), African American(s), Hispanic(s), Latino(s),* and *Asian(s)*: and (3) we searched reference trails from the studies identified, and from several review papers on the subject of ethnicity and child treatment. Through this process, we identified 19 treatment outcome studies in which the majority of the sample were ethnic minority children or families. The studies are briefly characterized in Table 3. Here we consider a few of the findings of these studies, and we note four key questions about treatment outcome and culture that need attention in future studies.

7.1. Effectiveness of Treatments with Ethnic Minority Children

As shown in Table 3, treated children in the 19 studies with large minority samples tended to improve more than children in control conditions, although the extent of improvement appears to vary somewhat with problem type. As summarized in Table 4, treatment showed a significant beneficial effect in 79% of the group comparisons with externalizing problems, 75% with internalizing problems, and only 43% with other problems (e.g., social skills, family functioning). The magnitude of improvement is

TABLE 3

Outcomes of Controlled Treatment Studies with Predominantly Minority Samples of Children and Adolescents

Study	Modality	Percentage ethnic minority	Control group	Culturally adjusted component?	Improvement on externalizing problems?	Improvement on internalizing problems?	Improvement on other problems?
Block (1978)	Rational-emotive education	100% black and Hispanic	No treatment	No	Yes	—	—
Costantino, Malgady, & Rogler (1986)	Cuento therapy. A modeling therapy utilizing folktales with moral lessons.	100% Puerto Rican	No treatment and art/play therapy	Hispanic, bilingual therapists. Cuento (folktales) rooted in Puerto Rican culture	No (vs. no treatment) Yes (vs. art/play therapy)	Yes	No (self-concept of competence)
Dubow, Huesmann, & Eron (1987)	Cognitive-behavior therapy	70% black and Hispanic	Attention/play condition	No	Yes	—	No (prosocial behavior)
Fling & Black (1984/1985)	Relaxation training with covert rehearsal	55% with "Spanish surnames"	Waiting list	No	No	—	No (self-esteem, tension, academic performance)
Forman (1980)	Cognitive restructuring/ Response cost treatment	89% black	Attention only	No	Yes/yes	—	—
Guerra & Slaby (1990)	Cognitive mediation training	60% ethnic minorities (mostly black and Hispanic)	Attention only and no treatment	No	Yes	—	Yes (social problem-solving skills) No (recidivism)
Hayes, Cunningham, & Robinson (1977)	Child behavior management/ Role playing with modeling treatment	100% black	No treatment	50% of counselors black	—	Yes/no	Yes/No (motivation toward school, self-esteem)

Study	Intervention	Sample	Control condition	Cultural adaptation		Outcome
Henggeler, Melton & Smith (1992)	Multisystemic therapy	66% black	"Usual" treatment through youth services	33% of therapists black	Yes	No	Yes (rearrests, recidivism, incarceration rate, family cohesion)
Henggeler et al. (1986)	Multisystemic therapy	65% black	"Usual" treatment through youth services	No	Yes	Yes	Yes (warmth, affection and aggressive verbalizations in family interactions)
Hudley & Graham (1993)	Attributional intervention	100% black	Attention only and no treatment	Both interventionists black	Yes	—	Yes (hostile judgements) No (prosocial behavior and academic performance)
Huey & Rank (1984)	Assertive training	100% black	Discussion groups	All therapists black. Made unspecified adaptations for cultural differences	Yes	—	—
Lewis (1974)	Modeling with participation treatment	100% black	Attention only	Modeling film depicted black males performing tasks	—	Yes	—
Lockman, Burch, Curry, & Lampron (1984)	Cognitive behavior treatment	53% black	No treatment	No	Yes	—	—

(continued)

TABLE 3 (Continued)

Study	Modality	Percentage ethnic minority	Control group	Culturally adjusted component?	Improvement on externalizing problems?	Improvement on internalizing problems?	Improvement on other problems?
Malgady, Rogler, & Costantino (1990)	Hero/Heroine therapy. A modeling therapy using folktales with moral lessons.	100% Puerto Rican	Attention only	All therapists Puerto Rican. Folktales rooted in Puerto Rican culture	—	Yes	Yes (Puerto Rican identity)
Niles (1986)	Problem solving of moral dilemmas treatment	"Primarily" black and Hispanic	No treatment and noninteractive values clarification condition	No	No	—	Yes (moral maturity)
Porter & Hoedt (1985)	Adlerian counseling	64% black	Attention only	No	—	—	No (total problems) Yes (insight ratings)
Scherer, Brondino, Henggeler, Melton, & Hanley (1994)	Multisystemic therapy	78% black	"Usual" services through youth services	50% of therapists black. Active efforts to ensure racially mixed treatment teams	Yes	Yes	Yes (parental monitoring)
Strayhorn & Weidman (1989)	Child behavior management	64% Black, 6% other nonwhite	Minimal attention only	All interventionists black women from community	Yes	Yes	Yes (parenting behavior)
Szcapocznik et al. (1989)	Structural family therapy / psychodynamic play therapy	100% Hispanic (80% Cuban, 20% other Hispanic)	Recreational activities only	All therapists bilingual, Hispanic women	—	—	No/no (total behavior); yes/no (family functioning)

TABLE 4
Percentage of Studies Showing Improvement in Externalizing,
Internalizing, and Other Problems, by Presence or Absence
of a Culturally Adjusted Treatment Component

	Culturally adjusted component	No culturally adjusted component	Total
Number of studies	10	9	19
Proportion reporting improvement in externalizing problems	5/6 = 83% (1 mixed outcome)	6/8 = 75%	11/14 = 79%
Proportion reporting improvement in internalizing problems	5/7 = 71% (1 mixed outcome)	1/1 = 100%	6/8 = 75%
Proportion reporting improvement in other problems	4/8 = 50% (3 mixed outcomes)	2/6 = 33% (2 mixed outcomes)	6/14 = 43%

difficult to compare to that seen in meta-analyses cited earlier because of numerous study-to-study differences in specific treated problems, types of treatment, and so on. Direct within-study comparison is far superior, but only one such comparison was identified in the 19 studies: Henggeler, Melton, and Smith (1992) found that African-American and Caucasian delinquents responded equally well to multisystemic treatment. In general, our initial look at the question does *not* suggest that structured treatments are *in*effective with samples that include large proportions of minority youth.

7.2. Differential Effectiveness of Various Treatments with Different Ethnic Groups

Another potentially important question is whether outcome is influenced by treatment type *x* ethnic group interactions. However, we find little research bearing on the question. In our sample of 19 outcome studies, only one involved an initial step toward such a test. Szapocznik and colleagues (Szapocznik et al., 1989; Szapocznik, Kurtines, Santisteban, & Rio, 1990) tested the efficacy of structural family therapy (SFT) and individual psychodynamic child therapy (IPCT) with Hispanic families of boys with behavioral and emotional problems. Following treatment, SFT-treated children had fewer behavior problems than IPCT children, but neither group differed significantly from children in a recreational control condition. At follow-up, family functioning had improved substantially following SFT and had actually worsened following IPCT. The findings seem consistent with Tharp's (1991) contention that family-based therapies are more appropriate than individual treatment for minority children. However, Szapocznik et al. (1989) did not include comparison groups of non-Hispanic youth treated with SFT and IPCT. So, as best we can determine, our field still awaits a fully developed test of interactions between ethnicity and treatment type.

7.3. Impact of Matching Therapist and Client on Ethnicity

Are outcomes enhanced when therapist and treated child are matched for ethnicity? No definite answer emerges from the studies we have found. Although nine of the 19 studies in the collection involved some attempt at ethnicity and/or language match, none provided a direct test of the impact of the match (e.g., by comparing matched and unmatched therapist–child pairs). Hayes, Cunningham, and Robinson (1977) did report that counselor race (African American vs. Caucasian) did not appear to influence target outcomes of test anxiety and poor school motivation among African-American children, but they did not report substantiating analyses. In general, the nine studies in which some form of matching was reported appear to show only slightly better success rates than the remaining 10 studies. Rates of significant improvement in the matching versus non-matching studies were 83% versus 75% for externalizing problems and 50% versus 33% for other problems (only one "unadjusted" study included any internalizing problem outcome measure, so we do not report the comparison here, but see Table 4 for data). Again, we must note that such global comparison across studies lacks the precision of the direct, within-study tests that are most needed to address the "matching" question. Moreover, in most of the studies, ethnicity matching is confounded with other efforts to adjust treatments to fit minority youth, and this brings us to a related issue.

7.4. Impact of Adapting Therapies to Fit Ethnic Minority Children

Perhaps the most overarching issue related to ethnicity and child treatment is that of whether standard therapies may be administered in standard ways to minority youth, or whether outcomes are improved by adapting the therapies to relevant group characteristics. Relevant to this question, we found that 10 of the 19 studies involved some sort of treatment adaptation designed to fit cultural characteristics of the minority sample. The adaptations ranged from narrowly focused changes, such as depicting minority figures in modeling tasks, to such pervasive change as redesigning entire programs for a particular minority group. The fact that only one of the "unadapted" studies focused on internalizing problems ruled out comparisons on that dimension; however, the percentage of comparisons showing significant positive treatment effects was slightly higher for externalizing problems (83% vs. 75%) and for problems in the "other" category (50% vs. 33%). For reasons noted here, such comparisons are suggestive at best. Much to be preferred are direct comparisons of adapted and unadapted methods within the same study, but such comparisons are difficult to find. One study, by Costantino, Malgady, and Rogler (1986) did find that maladjusted Puerto Rican children in a culturally adapted modeling program involving *Cuento* or Folklore Therapy were less aggressive following treatment than those in an art/play therapy control condition (APT). However, since APT subjects were even more aggressive than those in the no-therapy (NT) condition, the findings may reflect the ineffectiveness of APT as much as superiority of *Cuento* Therapy. A more robust test of any culture-specific treatment approach would entail comparison with another empirically supported approach (e.g., social skills training for aggression). In future research, wherever culture-linked changes have been made to a standard treatment program, it will be important to carry out direct comparison of outcomes for minority children receiving the altered program versus outcomes for minority children receiving the standard program. Without such comparisons, clear conclusions may continue to elude us.

To summarize, the state of affairs regarding culture and child psychotherapy is this: We have intriguing hypotheses and important questions that need attention, but thus far we lack the numerous direct comparisons needed to test the hypotheses and answer the questions. With concern about culture and mental health in our society growing steadily, the situation is likely to improve in the years ahead. As the volume of relevant research increases, we hope the agenda will include the four themes we have identified here.

8. Sensitivity of Child Treatments to Social and Family Contexts

Most treatment research with children can be faulted not only for relative inattention to ethnicity and culture but also for a failure to link treatments closely to the contexts in which children live their lives. Most of us would agree that children do not develop as solitary beings in a sterile environment, but rather as active participants in complex physical and social systems. Yet most treatment research with children involves interactions with a single therapist, or sometimes with a small group of unfamiliar children, in the sterile environment of the therapist's office or therapy room. Pretherapy assessment and treatment planning typically involve very limited sampling of the child's life circumstances and behavior at home, at school, or with familiar peers, and limited application of treatment-related gains to life in those settings. This may limit the capacity of the therapist to fit interventions precisely to the conditions and context of the individual child's problems. In some cases, the problem may tilt treatment development in the direction of "one-size-fits-all" or "cookie-cutter" therapies. In other cases, therapists may try to adjust aspects of their work to fit the child's situation but lack the information needed to do so precisely and effectively.

Some of our most valued theorists and researchers (e.g., Bronfenbrenner, 1979, 1986; Masten, Best, & Garmezy, 1991) have emphasized the context-boundedness of development and discussed implications for child adaptation and dysfunction. Others (e.g., Cicchetti & Toth, 1997; Mash & Dozois, 1996) have noted the diverse ways in which the child's contexts and ecological systems can influence the development and expression of dysfunctional behavior and emotional states. Still others (e.g., Forehand, Lautenschlager, Faust, & Graziano, 1986; Kazdin, 1989) have noted that even what parents report (e.g., to assessors and therapists) regarding deviance and dysfunction in their children can be influenced by such diverse factors as parental psychopathology, marital discord, stress in the home, and even an intent to conceal harmful parental practices (e.g., abuse or neglect). Finally, it seems self-evident that the impact of psychotherapy with children may vary depending on the extent to which significant others in the child's contexts (e.g., parents, teachers) are involved and supportive of the process. The power of all the influences noted in this paragraph may be felt disproportionately in childhood, because, as we noted earlier, children have so little freedom to select their own contexts.

The pervasive power of environmental forces in the lives of children suggests an important message for treatment planners and treatment outcome researchers: Contextual factors and key individuals in the child's social environment (e.g., parents, teachers, siblings, peers) may need to figure significantly in pretreatment assessment, in treatment planning, in treatment delivery, and even in outcome assessment. In general, these steps have only been taken in very limited and tentative ways in child psychotherapy research to date. There are some exceptions to this generalization, however. Noting a few of these may help illustrate what is possible in future child psychotherapy research, and why such steps may have value.

As one example, Lewinsohn and colleagues (see Lewinsohn, Clarke, Hops, & Andrews, 1990; Lewinsohn, Rohde, Clarke, Hops, & Seeley, 1994; Rohde, Lewinsohn, & Seeley, 1994) have created a parent counterpart to their Adolescent Coping with Depression group intervention. The objective is to promote parental understanding and acceptance of the intervention, and to reduce family conflict by teaching parents the kinds of communication and problem-solving skills their adolescents are learning. In a related approach, Barrett, Dadds, and Rapee (1996) have added a Family Management program to a standard child anxiety treatment (from Kendall, 1994), with the intent of helping parents and children to work as a team in managing anxiety and rewarding successful coping. In another program, addressing a variety of child problems, Szapocznik and colleagues (e.g., Szapocznik et al., 1989) treat Hispanic boys by means of structural family therapy. Webster-Stratton and colleagues (e.g., Webster-Stratton, Kolpacoff, & Hollinsworth, 1988) have developed a self-administered videotape therapy for families with conduct-problem children. And Henggeler and colleagues (e.g., Henggeler & Borduin, 1990; Henggeler et al., 1992; Borduin et al., 1995), in perhaps the most context-sensitive approach yet developed, send therapists into the settings where juvenile offenders live their lives, working with them to develop treatments tailored to the strengths and limitations of their family, school, peer groups, and neighborhood. Each of the intervention approaches cited here has shown positive effects relative to control groups. Although Lewinsohn and colleagues did not find that adding parent training alone to their adolescent intervention led to greater reductions in depression than their basic program, Barrett et al. (1996) found that adding a family component led to several significant improvements over and above the basic individual child treatment program for anxiety. As these examples suggest, there are numerous ways environment can be included in treatment, and without the loss of basic structure and even manualization.

Treatment researchers who move in the directions illustrated by these research teams will certainly find that their work has grown more complex. This may well be true at every level of the process, from treatment planning to outcome assessment. On the other hand, such efforts may be essential if we are ever to gauge the impact of making treatments fit the contexts in which children are developing. In our view, there is a real need to learn what can be gained if we push beyond a narrow focus on child characteristics and toward a broader focus on potentiating and inhibiting forces in the child's social systems.

9. Enriching Research Design in Treatment-Outcome Research

Beyond the substantive issues discussed earlier, there are many ways that child treatment outcome research can be strengthened at the level of research design. Some of the elements are implicit within suggestions

TABLE 5
Steps toward Enriched Child Treatment Outcome Research

1. Explication and tests of conceptual basis for treatment
   • Hypothesized causal, maintaining, and exacerbating factors
   • Hypothesized mechanisms by which treatment addresses these factors
   • Tests of the hypothesized mechanisms vis-à-vis outcome
2. Tests of other potential mediators of treatment–outcome relation
   • Comprehension of the "lessons" of treatment
   • Therapy "process" factors (e.g., therapeutic bond, alliance, etc.)
   • Out-of-therapy processes (e.g., parent and/or peer support)
3. Tests of potential outcome moderators
   • Child demographic factors (e.g., age, gender, ethnictiy)
   • Context factors (e.g., family composition, school support)
   • Clinical/personality factors (e.g., comorbid conditions, motivation)
4. Expanded outcome assessment
   • Broader range of measures (e.g., child symptoms, functioning, satisfaction
     with treatment, environmental change, use of systems)
   • Extended duration of assessment
   • Tests for bonus and incidental effects (e.g, on comorbid conditions)
5. Tests of varied models of treatment delivery
   • Blunderbuss MaxTreat vs. Rifle models with disaggregated components
   • Booster sessions, checkups (sessions added as assessment shows a need)
   • Deputizing therapists to extend treatment (e.g., parents, sibs, teachers)

noted earlier, but here we offer a more comprehensive list, summarized briefly in Table 5.

9.1. Explication and Tests of the Conceptual Basis for the Treatment

First, treatment outcome research could be enriched by a systematic effort by investigators to explain the conceptualization that guides their treatment and then provide corresponding tests. In many cases, this would include explication of the investigator's view as to causal processes that contribute to the target problem, with attention to risk factors, primary causes, maintaining factors, and exacerbating conditions. Clarification is needed as to which of these elements is addressed via the treatment program and in what way the elements of the treatment connect to the hypothesized causal processes. In cases where the treatment is not construed as addressing causes—and we do not assume here that all effective treatments must necessarily address original causes—it is important, nonetheless, to specify the hypothesized mechanism by which the treatment is seen as operating and having its effects.

Of course, all this specification of the conceptual basis for treatments is needed so that tests of the treatment models can be carried out. Such tests may affirm the hypothesized connection between processes linked to dysfunction and specified elements of the treatment, and such affirmation may fuel the further development and refinement of treatment. Or such tests may disconfirm hypothesized connections and thus suggest the need for restructured models, and perhaps restructured treatments. An example of the kind of surprise that may await researchers can be seen in the Durlak et al. (1991) meta-analysis of cognitive-behavioral treatments (CBT) for children. In contrast to the CBT model, which explicitly links behavior change to cognitive change, Durlak et al. reported that averaging across multiple studies, behavior change was not significantly related to changes in cognition.

9.2. Tests of Other Potential Mediators of the Treatment–Outcome Relation

The kinds of analyses just described are essentially tests of potential mediators of the relation between treatment and outcome. There are other mediational tests that certainly warrant consideration by researchers. We have already stressed the need for therapy process research testing such potential mediators of change as therapeutic bond. In addition, there is much about the child's comprehension of and participation in treatment activities that may play a role in shaping outcome, but this dimension is rarely addressed in outcome research. For example, one rarely sees tests designed to determine which of the key lessons or skills taught in therapy were actually assimilated by the children, and to what degree such assimilation relates to treatment outcome. Beyond such intrachild processes, critical mediators may be found in events within the child's social surround. For example, for some children, the degree to which parents or teachers are a part of the treatment program *and* respond by actively engaging the child in treatment-related activities may be a critical factor mediating child outcomes. We know little about these and numerous other mediational possibilities at present, because mediators of any kind are rarely tested in the extant literature.

9.3. Tests of Potential Outcome Moderators

Earlier, we noted the importance of testing such potential demographic moderators of treatment outcome as child age, gender, and ethnicity. Even when such factors are noted in sample descriptions, their significance for outcome is very rarely assessed. Children's clinical characteristics, such as their level or subtype of the target diagnosis, or their pattern of comorbidities, may also moderate outcome of some treatments. Beyond these individual child "person" factors, moderators may well be found in characteristics of the child's physical and social environment. Factors such as family income, degree of crowding, and family composition (e.g., single-parent vs. two-parent), for instance, may all relate to the family's ability to support the treatment process. The general objective of all this moderator research is to identify those youth who are most and least likely to profit from a particular form of treatment. Findings on this question can facilitate diversification of treatment forms and increasingly precise matching of treatment forms to types of children.

9.4. Expanded Range of Outcome Assessment

Child outcome research could profit from several kinds of expansion within the domain of outcome assessment. First, the range of outcomes measured has tended to be rather restricted, with emphasis placed on symptom or problem assessment. Recently, Hoagwood, Jensen, Petti, and Burns (1996) have called for assessment of not only symptoms (e.g., impulsivity, anxiety) but also the child's role functioning in usual life contexts (e.g., grades in school, participation in peer activities), consumer responses to treatment (e.g., child's and parents' satisfaction, perceived improvement), changes in the child's environment that were targeted in treatment (e.g., parental discipline practices, classroom disruptions), and system-related outcomes (e.g., the child's use of mental health services after the treatment program ends). Appropriate broadening, even at the "symptom" level, could also include the use of structured diagnostic interviews, thus to generate the information needed to assess the clinical significance of treatment-related change.

We also encourage expansion in the duration of outcome assessment. In our meta-analyses (Weisz et al., 1987; Weisz et al., 1995c), only about one-third of the studies we found included any assessment other than immediate posttreatment. And for that one-third, the average follow-up lag time was only 6 months. Consequently, we know relatively little to date about the long-term holding power of the effects generated by most treatments, and thus little about whether and/or when there may be a need for treatment enhancement, booster sessions, and the like, to maintain gains.

One other kind of expansion should be noted here. For those studies that include children with comorbid diagnoses over and above the condition targeted in treatment, outcome assessment might well be profitably directed to those comorbid conditions. It is useful to know, for example, that treatments targeting anxiety may also have beneficial effects on depression (see, e.g., Barrett et al., 1996; Kendall, 1994). Such knowledge can improve our efficiency in allocating treatments to conditions, in addition to helping us expand our models of treatment and outcome.

9.5. Tests of Varied Models of Treatment Delivery

Finally, we suspect that there could be considerable payoff from experimentation with various models of treatment delivery. Along one dimension, treatment approaches may range from the Blunderbuss model—in which all promising techniques are packed into one treatment program, in the hope of generating maximum bang for the buck—to the Rifle model—precise fitting of a few well-chosen techniques to very specific problems. Along another dimension, data from an expanded duration of outcome assessment (see above) could go hand-in-hand with efforts to extend treatment benefit over time. Such efforts might include regularly scheduled booster sessions, brief refresher courses on the basics of a previously learned treatment package. An alternative might be the "yearly checkup" model, patterned after the "yearly physical," in which assessment is conducted and areas of slippage are addressed by retraining in the relevant components of a treatment program. Finally, there is room for tinkering with our venerable models holding that treatment must be provided by qualified experts. Our meta-analytic findings (in both Weisz et al., 1987, and Weisz et al., 1995c) point to effects (particularly for externalizing problems) that are as positive for parents and teachers trained in specific therapy techniques as for fully trained professionals in mental health careers (see also Christensen & Jacobson, 1993). This suggests that much-needed person power and outreach may be gained by deputizing and training those who live their daily lives in close proximity to our child clients, thus to ensure that our treatment programs can be extended into the settings where the children live their lives.

10. Conclusion

There is much to admire about child psychotherapy outcome research to date, including a rich and extensive body of evidence supporting the efficacy of a substantial number of treatment programs. However, there are also significant limitations in the extant research. These give rise to numerous suggestions for reconceptualization, refinement, study of treatment components and processes, tests of client factors that may moderate treatment impact, experimentation with treatment delivery models, and approaches to outcome assessment. The suggestions are offered with appreciation for all that has been accomplished thus far, and with optimism about all that can be done in the future to enhance the lives of children and their families.

ACKNOWLEDGMENTS

Preparation of this chapter was facilitated by a research grant (R01 MH49522) and a Research Scientist Award (KO5 MH01161) to John Weisz from the National Institute of Mental Health. We are grateful to the many researchers, clinic administrators, therapists, parents, and children whose participation in treatment outcome research has given form and substance to this review and analysis.

11. References

Achenbach, T. M., McConaughy, S. H., & Howell, C. T. (1987). Child/adolescent behavioral and emotional problems: Implications of cross-informant correlations for situational specificity. *Psychological Bulletin, 101*, 213–232.

American Psychiatric Association. (1980). *Diagnostic and statistical manual of mental disorders* (3rd ed.). Washington, DC: Author.

Ashcraft, C. W. (1971). The later school adjustment of treated and untreated emotionally handicapped children. *Journal of School Psychology, 9*, 338–342.

Baer, R. A., & Nietzel, M. T. (1991). Cognitive and behavioral treatment of impulsivity in children: A meta-analytic review of the outcome literature. *Journal of Clinical Child Psychology, 2*, 400–412.

Barrett, P. M., Dadds, M. R., & Rapee, R. M. (1996). Family treatment of childhood anxiety: A controlled trial. *Journal of Consulting and Clinical Psychology, 64*, 333–342.

Bickman, L. (1996). A continuum of care: More is not always better. *American Psychologist, 51*, 689–701.

Bickman, L., Guthrie, P. R., Foster, E. M., Lambert, E. W., Summerfelt, W. T., Breda, C. S., & Heflinger, C. A. (1995). *Evaluating managed mental health services: The Fort Bragg experiment.* New York: Plenum Press.

Block, J. (1978). Effects of a rational-emotive mental health program on poorly achieving, disruptive high school students. *Journal of Counseling Psychology, 25*(1), 61–65.

Bordin, E. S. (1979). The generalizability of the psychoanalytic concept of the working alliance. *Psychotherapy: Theory, Research, and Practice, 16*, 252–260.

Borduin, C. M., Mann, B. J., Cone, L. T., Henggeler, S. W., Fucci, B. R., Blaske, D., & Williams, R. A. (1995). Multisystemic treatment of serious juvenile offenders: Long-term prevention of criminality and violence. *Journal of Consulting and Clinical Psychology, 63*, 569–578.

Braswell, L., Kendall, P. C., Braith, J., Carey, M. P., & Vye, C. S. (1985). "Involvement" in cognitive-behavioral therapy with children: Process and its relationship to outcome. *Cognitive Therapy and Research, 9*, 611–630.

Bronfenbrenner, U. (1979). *The ecology of human development.* Cambridge, MA: Harvard University Press.

Bronfenbrenner, U. (1986). Ecology of the family as a context for human development. *Developmental Psychology, 22*, 723–742.

Casey, R. J., & Berman, J. S. (1985). The outcome of psychotherapy with children. *Psychological Bulletin, 98*, 388–400.

Chambless, D. L., Sanderson, W. C., Shoham, V., Bennett-Johnson, S., Pope, K. S., Crits-Cristoph, P., Baker, M., Johnson, B., Woody, S. R., Sue, S., Beutler, L., Williams, D. A., & McCurry, S. (1996). An update on empirically validated treatments. *Clinical Psychologist, 49*, 5–18.

Christensen, A., & Jacobson, N. S. (1993). Who or what can do psychotherapy: The status and challenge of nonprofessional therapies. *Psychological Science, 5*, 8–14.

Cicchetti, D., & Toth, S. L. (1997). Transactional ecological systems in developmental psychopathology. In S. S. Luthar, J. A. Burack, D. Cicchetti, & J. R. Weisz (Eds.), *Developmental psychopathology: Perspectives on adjustment, risk, and disorder* (pp. 273–313). New York: Cambridge University press.

Cohen, J. (1988). *Statistical power analysis for the behavioral sciences* (2nd ed.). Hillsdale, NJ: Erlbaum.

Costantino, G., Malgady, R., & Rogler, L. (1986). Cuento therapy: A culturally sensitive modality for Puerto Rican children. *Journal of Consulting and Clinical Psychology, 54*, 639–645.

Costello, E. J. (1989). Developments in child psychiatric epidemiology, *Journal of the American Academy of Child and Adolescent Psychiatry, 28*, 836–841.

DeFries, Z., Jenkins, S., & Williams, E. C. (1964). Treatment of disturbed children in foster care. *American Journal of Orthopsychiatry, 34*, 615–624.

Dubow, E. F., Huesmann, L. R., & Eron, L. D. (1987). Mitigating aggression and promoting prosocial behavior in aggressive elementary schoolboys. *Behavioral Research and Therapy, 25*(6), 527–531.

Durlak, J. A., Fuhrman, T., & Lampman, C. (1991). Effectiveness of cognitive-behavior therapy for maladapting children: A meta-analysis. *Psychological Bulletin, 110*, 204–214.

Dush, D. M., Hirt, M. L., & Schroeder, H. E. (1989). Self-statement modification in the treatment of child behavior disorders: A meta-analysis. *Psychological Bulletin, 106*, 97–106.

Evans, M. E., Armstrong, M. I., Dollard, N., Kuppinger, A. D., Huz, S., & Wood, V. M. (1994). Development and evaluation of treatment foster care and family-centered intensive case management in New York. *Journal of Emotional and Behavioral Disorders, 2*, 228–239.

Fling, S., & Black, P. (1984/1985). Relaxation convert rehearsal for adaptive functioning in fourth-grade children. *Psychology and Human Development, 1*(2), 113–123.

Forehand, R., Lautenschlager, G. J., Faust, J., & Graziano, W. G. (1986). Parent perceptions and parent–child interactions in clinic-referred children: A preliminary investigation of the effects of maternal depressive moods. *Behavior Research and Therapy, 24*, 73–75.

Forman, S. G. (1980). A comparison of cognitive training and response cost procedures in modifying aggressive behavior of elementary school children. *Behavior Therapy, 11*, 594–600.

Frank, J. D. (1973). *Persuasion and healing: A comparative study of psychotherapy*. Baltimore: Johns Hopkins University Press.

Friedlander, M. L., Wildman, J., Heatherington, L., & Skowron, E. A. (1994). What we do and don't know about the process of family therapy. *Journal of Family Psychology, 8*, 390–416.

Gibbs, J. T., & Huang, L. N. (1989). *Children of color: Psychological interventions with minority children*. San Francisco: Jossey-Bass.

Glass, G.V., McGaw, B., & Smith, M. L. (1981). *Meta-analysis in social research*. Beverly Hills, CA: Sage.

Gorin, S. S. (1993). The prediction of child psychotherapy outcome: Factors specific to treatment. *Psychotherapy, 30*, 152–158.

Guerra, N. G., & Slaby, R. G. (1990). Cognitive mediators of aggression in adolescent offenders: 2. Intervention. *Developmental Psychology, 26*(2), 269–277.

Hayes, E. J., Cunningham, G. K., & Robinson, J. B. (1977). Counseling focus: Are parents necessary? *Elementary School Guidance and Counseling, 12,* 8–14.

Hazelrigg, M. D., Cooper, H. M., & Borduin, C. M. (1987). Evaluating the effectiveness of family therapies: An integrative review and analysis. *Psychological Bulletin, 101,* 428–442.

Henggeler, S. W., & Borduin, C. M. (1990). *Family therapy and beyond: A multisystemic approach to treating the behavior problems of children and adolescents.* Pacific Grove, CA: Brooks/Cole Publishing.

Henggeler, S. W., Melton, G. B., & Smith, L. A. (1992). Family preservation using multisystemic therapy: An effective alternative to incarcerating serious juvenile offenders. *Journal of Consulting and Clinical Psychology, 60*(6), 953–961.

Henggeler, S. W., Rodick, J. D., Borduin, C. M., Hanson, C. L., Watson, S. M., & Urey, J. R. (1986). Multisystemic treatment of juvenile offenders: Effects on adolescent behavior and family interaction. *Developmental Psychology, 22*(1), 132–141.

Ho, M. K. (1992). *Minority children and adolescents in therapy.* Newbury Park, CA: Sage.

Hoagwood, K., Jensen, P. S., Petti, T., & Burns, B. J. (1996). Outcomes of mental health care for children and adolescents: I. A comprehensive conceptual model. *Journal of the American Academy of Child and Adolescent Psychiatry, 35,* 1055–1063.

Horowitz, M. J., Marmar, C. R., Weiss, D. S., DeWitt, K. N., & Rosenbaum, R. L. (1984). Brief psychotherapy of bereavement reactions: The relationship of process to outcome. *Archives of General Psychiatry, 41,* 438–448.

Howe, P. A., & Silvern, L. E. (1981). Behavioral observation of children during play therapy: Preliminary development of a research instrument. *Journal of Personality Assessment, 45,* 168–182.

Hudley, C., & Graham, S. (1993). An attributional intervention to reduce peer-directed aggression among African-American boys. *Child Development, 64*(1), 124–138.

Huey, W. C., & Rank, R. C. (1984). Effects of counselor and peer-led group assertive training on Black adolescent aggression. *Journal of Counseling Psychology, 31,*(1), 95–98.

Institute of Medicine. (1989). *Research on children and adolescents with mental, behavioral, and developmental disorders.* Washington, DC: National Academy Press.

Jacob, T., Magnussen, M. G., & Kemler, W. M. (1972). A follow-up of treatment terminators and remainers with short-term and long-term symptom duration. *Psychotherapy: Theory, Research, and Practice, 9,* 139–142.

Kazdin, A. E. (1988). *Child psychotherapy: Developing and identifying effective treatments.* Elmsford, NY: Pergamon.

Kazdin, A. E. (1989). Developmental psychopathology: Current research, issues, and directions. *American Psychologist. 44,* 180–187.

Kazdin, A. E., Bass, D., Ayers, W. A., & Rodgers, A. (1990a). Empirical and clinical focus of child and adolescent psychotherapy research. *Journal of Consulting and Clinical Psychology, 58,* 729–740.

Kazdin, A. E., Siegel, T. C., & Bass, D. (1990b). Drawing on clinical practice to inform research on child and adolescent psychotherapy: Survey of practitioners. *Professional Psychology: Research and Practice, 21,* 189–198.

Kazdin, A. E., & Weisz, J. R. (in press). Identifying and developing empirically supported child and adolescent treatments. *Journal of Consulting and Clinical Psychology.*

Kendall, P. C. (1994). Treating anxiety disorders in children: Results of a randomized clinical trial. *Journal of Consulting and Clinical Psychology, 62,* 100–110.

Kendall, P. C., & Morris, R. J. (1991). Child therapy: Issues and recommendations. *Journal of Consulting and Clinical Psychology, 59,* 777–784.

LaFromboise, T. D., & Rowe, W. (1983). Skills training for bicultural competence: Rationale and application. *Journal of Counseling Psychology, 30*, 589–595.

Lehman, A. E., Postrado, L. T., Roth, D., McNary, S. W., & Goldman, H. H. (1994). Continuity of care and client outcomes in the Robert Wood Johnson Foundation program on chronic mental illness. *Milbank Quarterly, 72*, 105–122.

Lehrman, L. J., Sirluck, H., Black, B. J., & Glick, S. J. (1949). *Success and failure of treatment of children in the child guidance clinics of the Jewish Board of Guardians, New York City.* Jewish Board of Guardians Research Monographs, No. 1.

Levitt, E. E., Beiser, H. R., & Robertson, R. E. (1959). A follow-up evaluation of cases treated at a community child guidance clinic. *American Journal of Orthopsychiatry, 29*, 337–347.

Lewinsohn, P. M., Clarke, G. N., Hops, H., & Andrews, J. A. (1990). Cognitive-behavioral treatment for depressed adolescents. *Behavior Therapy, 21*, 385–401.

Lewinsohn, P. M., Rohde, P., Clarke, G. N., Hops, H., & Seeley, J. R. (1994). *Cognitive-behavioral treatment for depressed adolescents: Treatment outcome and the role of parental involvement.* Unpublished manuscript, Oregon Research Institute, Eugene.

Lewis, S. (1974). A comparison of behavior therapy techniques in the reduction of fearful avoidance behavior. *Behavior Therapy, 5*, 648–655.

Lochman, J. E., Burch, P. R., Curry, J. F., & Lampron, L. B. (1984). Treatment and generalization effects of cognitive-behavioral and goal-setting interventions with aggressive boys. *Journal of Consulting and Clinical Psychology, 52*(5), 915–916.

Lovaas, O. I. (1987). Behavioral treatment and normal educational and intellectual functioning in young autistic children. *Journal of Consulting and Clinical Psychology, 55*, 3–9.

Luborsky, L., Crits-Christoph, P., Mintz, J., & Auerbach, A. (1988). *Who will benefit from psychotherapy?* New York: Basic Books.

Malgady, R. G., Rogler, L. H., & Costantino, G. (1990). Hero/heroine modeling for Puerto Rican adolescents: A preventive mental health intervention. *Journal of Consulting and Clinical psychology, 58*, 469–474.

Mann, C. (1990). Meta-analysis in the breech. *Science, 249*, 476–480.

Mash, E. J., & Dozois, D. J. A. (1996). Child psychopathology: A developmental-systems perspective. In E. J. Mash & R. A. Barkley (Eds.), *Child psychopathology* (pp. 3–60). New York: Guilford.

Masten, A., Best, K., & Garmezy, N. (1991). Resilience and development: Contributions from the study of children who overcome adversity. *Development and Psychopathology, 2*, 425–444.

McGrath, M. L., Dorsett, P. G., Calhoun, M. E., & Drabman, R. S. (1988). "Beat-the-buzzer": A method for decreasing parent–child morning conflicts. *Child and Family Behavior Therapy, 9*, 35–48.

Meichenbaum, D., & Goodman, S. (1979). Clinical use of private speech and critical questions about its study in natural settings. In G. Zivin (Ed.), *The development of self-regulation through private speech* (pp. 325–360). New York: Wiley.

Minuchin, P. P. (1985). Families and individual development: Provocations from the field of family therapy. *Child Development, 56*, 289–302.

Mook, B. (1982). Analyses of therapist variables in a series of psychotherapy sessions with two child clients. *Journal of Clinical Psychology, 38*, 63–76.

Motta, R. W., & Lynch, C. (1990). Therapeutic techniques vs. therapeutic relationships in child behavior therapy. *Psychological Reports, 67*, 315–322.

Motta, R. W., & Tobin, M. I. (1992). The relative importance of specific and nonspecific factors in child behavior therapy. *Psychotherapy in Private Practice, 11*, 51–61.

Moustakas, C. E., & Schalock, H. D. (1955). An analysis of therapist–child interaction in play therapy. *Child Development, 26*, 143–157.

Moustakas, C. E., Sigel, I. E., & Schalock, H. D. (1956). An objective method for the measurement and analysis of child–adult interaction. *Child Development, 27,* 109–134.

Nicholson, R. A., & Berman, J. S. (1983). Is follow-up necessary in evaluating psychotherapy? *Psychological Bulletin, 93,* 261–278.

Niles, W. J. (1986). Effects of a moral development discussion group on delinquent and predelinquent boys. *Journal of Counseling Psychology, 33,* 45–51.

Office of Technology Assessment. (1986). *Children's mental health: Problems and services—A background paper* (Publication No. OTA-BP-H-33). Washington, DC: U.S. Government Printing Office.

Orlinsky, D. E., Grawe, K., & Parks, B. K. (1994). Process and outcome in psychotherapy: Noch einmal. In A. E. Bergin & S. L. Garfield (Eds.). *Handbook of psychotherapy and behavior change* (4th ed., pp. 270–376). New York: Wiley.

O'Sullivan, M. J., Peterson, P. D., Cox, G. B., & Kirkeby, J. (1989). Ethnic populations: Community mental health services ten years later. *American Journal of Community Psychology, 17,* 17–30.

Patterson, G. R., & Chamberlain, P. (1994). A functional analysis of resistance during parent training therapy. *Clinical Psychology: Science and Practice, 1,* 53–70.

Patterson, G. R., & Forgatch, M. S. (1985). Therapist behavior as a determinant for client noncompliance: A paradox for the behavior modifier. *Journal of Consulting and Clinical Psychology, 53,* 846–851.

Pelham, W. E., Carlson, C., Sams, S., Vallano, G., Dixon, J., & Hoza, B. (1993). Separate and combined effects of methylphenidate and behavior modification on boys with attention-deficit hyperactivity disorder in the classroom. *Journal of Consulting and Clinical Psychology, 55,* 76–85.

Piaget, J. (1929). *The child's conception of the world.* Totowa, NJ: Littlefield, Adams.

Piaget, J. (1955). *The language and thought of the child.* New York: Meridian. (Originally published, 1923.)

Piaget, J. (1962). *Play, dreams, and imitation.* New York: Norton.

Piaget, J. (1970). *Piaget's theory.* In P. H. Mussen (Ed.). *Carmichael's manual of child psychology* (Vol. 1, pp. 703–732). New York: Wiley.

Pinsoff, W. M., & Catherall, D. R. (1986). The integrative psychotherapy alliance: Family, couple, and individual therapy scales. *Journal of Marital and Family Therapy, 12,* 137–151.

Porter, B. A., & Hoedt, K. C. (1985). Differential effects of an Adlerian counseling approach with preadolescent children. *Individual Psychology, 41,* 372–385.

Prout, H. T., & DeMartino, R. A. (1986). A meta-analysis of school-based studies of psychotherapy. *Journal of School Psychology, 24,* 285–292.

Roberts, M. C. (1994). Models for service delivery in children's mental health: Common characteristics. *Journal of Clinical Child Psychology, 23,* 212–219.

Rogler, L. H., Malgady, R. G., Costantino, G., & Blumenthal, R. (1987). What do culturally sensitive mental health services mean? The case of Hispanics. *American Psychologist, 42*(6), 565–575.

Rohde, P., Lewinsohn, P. M., & Seeley, J. R. (1994). Responses of depressed adolescents to cognitive-behavioral treatment: Do differences in initial severity clarify the comparison of treatments? *Journal of Consulting and Clinical Psychology, 62,* 851–854.

Russell, R. L., Greenwald, S., & Shirk, S. R. (1991). Language change in child psychotherapy: A meta-analytic review. *Journal of Consulting and Clinical Psychology, 59,* 916–919.

Saile, H., Burgmeier, R., & Schmidt, L. R. (1988). A meta-analysis of studies on psychological preparation of children facing medical procedures. *Psychology and Health, 2,* 107–132.

Scherer, D. G., Brondino, M. J., Henggeler, S. W., Melton, G. B., & Hanley, J. H. (1994). Multisystemic family preservation therapy: Preliminary findings from a study of rural and minority serious adolescent offenders. *Journal of Emotional and Behavioral Disorders*, 2(4), 198–206.

Schinke, S. P., Orlandi, M. A., Botvin, G. J., Gilchrist, L. D., Trimble, J. E., & Locklear, V. S. (1988). Preventing substance abuse among American Indian adolescents: A bicultural competence skills approach. *Journal of Counseling Psychology, 35,* 87–90.

Schoenwald, S. K., Henggeler, S. W., Pickrel, S. G., & Cunningham, P. B. (1996). Treating seriously troubled youths and families in their contexts: Multisystemic Therapy. In M. C. Roberts (Ed.), *Model programs in service delivery in child and family mental health* (pp. 317–332), Hillsdale, NJ: Erlbaum.

Shadish, W. R., Montgomery, L. M., Wilson, P., Wilson, M. R., Bright, I., & Okwumabua, T. (1993). Effects of family and marital psychotherapies: A meta-analysis. *Journal of Consulting and Clinical Psychology, 61,* 992–1002.

Shapiro, D. A., & Shapiro, D. (1982). Meta-analysis of comparative therapy outcome studies: A replication and refinement. *Psychological Bulletin, 92,* 581–604.

Shepherd, M., Oppenheim, A. N., & Mitchell, S. (1966). Childhood behavior disorders and the child-guidance clinic: An epidemiological study. *Journal of Child Psychology and Psychiatry, 7,* 39–52.

Shirk, S. R., & Saiz, C. S. (1992). Clinical, empirical, and developmental perspectives on the therapeutic relationship in child psychotherapy. *Development and Psychopathology, 4,* 713–728.

Shirk, S., Saiz, C., Green, B., & Hanze, D. (1990, June). *Measuring patient participation in child psychotherapy.* Poster presented at meetings of the Society for Psychotherapy Research, Wintergreen, VA.

Siegel, C. L. F. (1972). Changes in play therapy behaviors over time as a function of differing levels of therapist-offered conditions. *Journal of Clinical Psychology, 28,* 235–236.

Smith, M. L., & Glass, G. V. (1977). Meta-analysis of psychotherapy outcome studies. *American Psychologist, 32,* 752–760.

Smith, M. L., Glass, G. V., & Miller, T. L. (1980). *Benefits of psychotherapy.* Baltimore: Johns Hopkins University Press.

Smith-Acuna, S., Durlak, J. A., & Kaspar, C. J. (1991). Development of child psychotherapy process measures. *Journal of Clinical Child Psychology, 20,* 126–131.

Smyrnios, K. X., & Kirkby, R. J. (1993). Long-term comparison of brief versus unlimited treatments with children and their parents. *Journal of Consulting and Clinical Psychology, 61,* 1020–1027.

Spurlock, J. (1985). Assessment and therapeutic intervention of black children. *Journal of the American Academy of Child Psychiatry, 24(2),* 168–174.

Stiles, W. B., & Shapiro, D. A. (1989). Abuse of the drug metaphor in psychotherapy process-outcome research. *Clinical Psychology Review, 9,* 521–543.

Stoolmiller, M., Duncan, T., Bank, L., & Patterson, G. R.(1993). Some problems and solutions in the study of change: Significant patterns in client resistance. *Journal of Consulting and Clinical Psychology, 61,* 920–928.

Strayhorn, J. M., & Weidman, C. S. (1989). Reduction of attention deficit and internalizing symptoms in preschoolers through parent–child interaction training. *Journal of the American Academy of Child and Adolescent Psychiatry, 28(6),* 888–896.

Strayhorn, J. M., & Weidman, C. S. (1991). Follow-up one year after parent–child interaction training: Effects on behavior of preschool children. *Journal of the American Academy of Child and Adolescent Psychiatry, 30(1),* 138–143.

Stroul, B. A., & Friedman, R. (1986). *A system of care for children and youth with severe emotional disturbances* (rev. ed.). Washington, DC: Georgetown University Child Development Center, CASSP Technical Assistance Center.

Sue, S. (1977). Community mental health services to minority groups: Some optimism, some pessimism. *American Psychologist, 32,* 616–624.

Sue, S., & Zane, N. (1987). The role of culture and cultural techniques in psychotherapy: A critique and reformulation. *American Psychologist, 42*(1), 37–45.

Szapocznik, J., Kurtines, W., Santisteban, D. A., & Rio, A. T. (1990). Interplay of advances between theory, research, and application in treatment interventions aimed at behavior problem children and adolescents. *Journal of Consulting and Clinical Psychology, 58,* 696–703.

Szapocznik, J., Rio, A., Murray, E., Cohen, R., Scopetta, M., Rivas-Vasquez, A., Hervis, O., Posada, V., & Kurtines, W. (1989). Structural family versus psychodynamic child therapy for problematic Hispanic boys. *Journal of Consulting and Clinical Psychology, 57,* 571–578.

Tarnowski, K. J., Rosen, L. A., McGrath, M. L., & Drabman, R. S. (1987). A modified habit reversal procedure in a recalcitrant case of trichotillomania. *Journal of Behavior Therapy and Experimental Psychiatry, 18,* 157–163.

Task Force on Promotion and Dissemination of Psychological Procedures, Division of Clinical Psychology, American Psychological Association. (1995, Winter). Training in and dissemination of empirically validated psychological treatments: Report and Recommendations. *Clinical Psychologist, 48,* 3–24.

Tharp, R. G. (1991). Cultural diversity and treatment of children. *Journal of Consulting and Clinical Psychology, 59*(6), 799–812.

Truax, C. B., Altmann, H., Wright, L., & Mitchell, K. M. (1973). Effects of therapeutic conditions in child therapy. *Journal of Community Psychology, 1,* 313–318.

Truax, C. B., & Wittmer, J. (1973). The degree of therapist focus on defense mechanisms and the effect on therapeutic outcome with institutionalized juvenile delinquents. *Journal of Community Psychology, 1,* 201–203.

Webster-Stratton, C., & Herbert, M. (1993). What really happens in parent training? *Behavior Modification, 17,* 407–456.

Webster-Stratton, C., Kolpacoff, M., & Hollinsworth, T. (1988). Self-administered videotape therapy for families with conduct-problem children: Comparison with two cost-effective treatments and a control group. *Journal of Consulting and Clinical Psychology, 56,* 558–566.

Weiss, B., & Weisz, J. R. (1990). The impact of methodological factors on child psychotherapy outcome research: A meta-analysis for researchers. *Journal of Abnormal Child Psychology, 18,* 639–670.

Weisz, J. R., Donenberg, G. R., Han, S. S., & Kauneckis, D. (1995a). Child and adolescent psychotherapy outcomes in experiments versus clinics: Why the disparity? *Journal of Abnormal Child Psychology, 23,* 83–106.

Weisz, J. R., Donenberg, G. R., Han, S. S., & Weiss, B. (1995b). Bridging the gap between lab and clinic in child and adolescent psychotherapy. *Journal of Consulting and Clinical Psychology, 63*(5), 688–701.

Weisz, J. R., Han, S. S., & Valeri, S. M. (1997). More of what? Issues raised by the Fort Bragg Study. *American Psychologist, 52,* 541–545.

Weisz, J. R., McCarty, C. A., Eastman, K. L., Chaiyasit, W., & Suwanlert, S. (1997). Developmental psychopathology and culture: Ten lessons from Thailand. In S. S. Luthar, J. A. Burack, D. Cicchetti, & J. R. Weisz (Eds.), *Developmental psychopathology: Perspectives on adjustment, risk, and disorder* (pp. 568–592). New York: Cambridge University Press.

Weisz, J. R., Suwanlert, S., Chaiyasit, W., Weiss, B., Walter, B. R., & Anderson, W. (1988). Thai and American perspectives on over- and undercontrolled child behavior problems: Exploring the threshold model among parents, teachers, and psychologists. *Journal of Consulting and Clinical Psychology, 56,* 601–609.

Weisz, J. R., & Weiss, B. (1989). Assessing the effects of clinic-based psychotherapy with children and adolescents. *Journal of Consulting and Clinic Psychology, 57,* 741–746.

Weisz, J. R., & Weiss, B. (1991). Studying the "referability" of child clinical problems. *Journal of Consulting and Clinical Psychology, 59,* 266–273.

Weisz, J. R., & Weiss, B. (1993). *Effects of psychotherapy with children and adolescents.* Newbury Park, CA: Sage.

Weisz, J. R., Weiss, B., Alicke, M. D., & Klotz, M. L. (1987). Effectiveness of psychotherapy with children and adolescents: A meta-analysis for clinicians. *Journal of Consulting and Clinical Psychology, 55,* 542–549.

Weisz, J. R., Weiss, B., & Donenberg, G. R. (1992). The lab versus the clinic: Effects of child and adolescent psychotherapy. *American Psychologist, 47,* 1578–1585.

Weisz, J. R., Weiss, B., Han, S. S., Granger, D. A., & Morton, T. (1995c). Effects of psychotherapy with children and adolescents revisited: A meta-analysis of treatment outcome studies. *Psychological Bulletin, 117*(3), 450–468.

Wilson, G. T. (1985). Limitations of meta-analysis in the evaluation of the effects of psychological therapy. *Clinical Psychology Review, 5,* 35–47.

Witmer, H. L., & Keller, J. (1942). Outgrowing childhood problems: A study in the value of child guidance treatment. *Smith College Studies in Social Work, 13,* 74–90.

Wright, L., Truax, C. B., & Mitchell, K. M. (1972). Reliability of process ratings of psychotherapy with children. *Journal of Clinical Psychology, 28,* 232–234.

Wurtele, S. K., & Drabman, R. S. (1984). "Beat-the-buzzer" for classroom dawdling: A one-year trial. *Behavior Therapy, 15,* 403–409.

3

Child Psychotherapy Process Research

ROBERT L. RUSSELL AND STEPHEN R. SHIRK

1. Introduction

Relative to studies of treatment outcome, psychotherapy process research has been the ignored stepchild of child psychotherapy investigators. In their review of the child therapy literature, Kazdin, Bass, Ayers, and Rodgers (1990) found that less than 3% of all child therapy studies examined treatment processes. Although research on therapy process with adults has waxed and waned over time in both the behavioral and non-behavioral traditions (Orlinsky & Russell, 1994; Russell & Orlinsky, 1996), the study of therapy process is "perhaps the area of work that is most discrepant between child and adult therapy" (Kazdin, 1995, p. 268). In recent years, however, there have been increasing calls for studies of child therapy processes (cf. Kazdin, 1995; Kendall & Morris, 1991; Russ, 1995), due, in part, to growing evidence from the adult therapy literature that variation in patterns of transactions within sessions contributes to the prediction of treatment outcome (cf. Orlinsky, Grawe, & Parks, 1994).

Does the paucity of research on child therapy process mean that we must follow the lead of adult process researchers—a form of delayed imitation—or essentially start from scratch? In fact, the adult literature is rich in studies of therapy process; however, our review of the child therapy literature has uncovered a body of research that can provide guideposts for the systematic evaluation of processes in child treatment (Shirk & Russell, 1996). Although a finished map of child therapy processes does not emerge from the historical record, there is something important to be

ROBERT L. RUSSELL • Department of Psychology, Loyola University Chicago, Chicago, Illinois 60626. STEPHEN R. SHIRK • Department of Psychology, University of Denver, Denver, Colorado 80208.

Advances in Clinical Child Psychology, Volume 20, edited by Thomas H. Ollendick and Ronald J. Prinz. Plenum Press, New York, 1998.

gained by marking the productive paths and blind alleys that have been encountered by child therapy investigators over the last 50 years.

2. Scope and Organization of the Review

The literature that we review mainly concerns empirical research on what actually transpires between therapist and child during their face-to-face meetings.[1] Often these transactions are studied in their own right with the aim of discovering what actually comprises "therapy" of one type or another. Less frequently, aspects of transactions are measured and related to outcomes at the session or treatment level. We restrict our review to what we have defined elsewhere as psychotherapy, not behavior therapy, research (Shirk & Russell, 1996). Although the distinction is not faultless, it is our aim to review empirical investigations of those therapies that give prominence to internal, psychological processes in their theories of pathogenesis and in their attempts to define targets of intervention. If we must revert to brand-name labels, such therapies would be considered psychodynamic, client-centered, cognitive, and cognitive-behavioral.

Our main interest, however, is in compiling and summarizing the research record over the past 50 years as it pertains to key emotional, interpersonal, and language/cognitive processes as they have been studied across types of therapy. As we have argued elsewhere (Russell & Orlinsky, 1996; Shirk & Russell, 1996), clients do not respond to brand-name therapies any more than therapists respond to diagnostic labels in the here-and-now of face-to-face therapeutic interaction. However, in all therapies, therapist–client interactions are always comprised of and often focused on emotional, interpersonal, and language/cognitive processes. In ongoing, face-to-face meetings, all three of these dimensions seamlessly coalesce. For analytic and expository purposes, we attempt to disassociate them and track progress (or lack thereof) in the investigation of each of these aspects of therapy process. Studies have been organized within each substantive area by decade, and divided for summary purposes into early and recent investigations. Detailed critiques of the methodological quality of these and other related studies have been offered elsewhere (Greenwald & Russell, 1991; Shirk & Russell, 1992; Shirk & Russell, 1996). We conclude our review of the substantive findings with summaries of the major meth-

---

[1]The studies reviewed include both children and adolescents. The use of the term *child* or *children* does not imply that developmental differences are inconsequential but is used rather than the more cumbersome phrase *children and adolescents* throughout the text. Where noted in the original studies, the ages of the participants are presented in this review.

odological flaws found in this literature and present a set of recommendations for future research on child psychotherapy process.

3. Emotion Processes in Child Psychotherapy

3.1. Early Studies of Emotion Processes

As one might expect, the very first empirical study of child psychotherapy process was focused on "feelings" in client-centered therapy. Landisberg and Snyder (1946) conducted a pure process study in which they sought to describe what took place in nondirective therapy using a client and therapist coding system comprised of eight major and numerous minor categories. The four clients were 5- or 6-year-olds with a mix of behavioral and emotional problems. Surprisingly, the authors studied contingencies between therapist and client verbal behaviors, possibly the first "sequential" process study in the history of child or adult psychotherapy research.

Landisberg and Snyder (1946) reported that the therapists' reflection of feelings were most often followed by client information-giving and positive action. The authors noted several phase phenomena as well. Positive client feelings occurred more frequently in the first two-fifths of therapy than negative feelings, and the expression of negative feelings increased over the last three-fifths of therapy. Overall, clients' expression of feelings, positive or negative, increased over the course of therapy, as did their physical action. The authors interpreted these findings as evidence of increased emotional catharsis over the course of therapy.

The findings of Landisberg and Snyder (1946) suggest that in the context of relatively high and stable levels of therapist reflections of feelings, children increase their levels of emotional expression, permitting themselves to vent pent-up negative feelings. Of special note is the fact that these authors were able to demonstrate effects of therapist technique at the level of the *exchange* and to begin to map changes in therapist and client interaction through various phases of therapy, even for clients of such a young age.

Lebo (1952, 1955) published two studies concerned with the classification of children's behavior in therapy. Dissatisfied with the coding system used by Landisberg and Snyder (1946) because it was adopted from the adult literature with few changes, Lebo attempted to craft a developmentally appropriate category system. Of note, in his 1955 measure development study, Lebo pointed out that emotion expression took form in and through both verbalizations and vocalizations, the latter category being especially important for younger clients. Consequently, he included categories that were meant to capture vocalizations children emit, especially during dramatic play (e.g., sound effects, mumblings, cries, etc.). These two studies are noteworthy in that they point to the need for developmentally sensitive coding systems for child psychotherapy.

In 1955, Moustakas presented the first hypothesis-testing study in which he compared the expressions and intensities of negative attitudes of normal and disturbed 4-year-old children in a four-session course of therapy. His findings were consistent with his hypothesis that disturbed children would express more negative attitudes than normal children, and that their expressions would also be more intense. Interestingly, the disturbed children's expressions of negative emotions were more diffuse and less focused than those of nondisturbed children. Moustakas speculated that therapeutic improvement might be signaled as disturbed children's expression of negative attitudes approached those of the normal children's in terms of frequency, intensity, and focus. In this sense, Moustakas may have conducted the first process study of child psychotherapy that incorporated social comparisons with a nondisturbed control group in its design.

Moustakas and Schalock (1955) conducted a second process study that examined verbal exchanges between child and therapist. In it, 5 normal and 5 disturbed 4-year-olds were assigned to client-centered therapies, and each of the therapists' and each of the children's turns at talk were coded using an extensive coding scheme (82 categories for the therapists and 72 for the children). Moreover, anxiety and hostility ratings were made at 5-second intervals. As in the previous study, Moustakas and Schalock reported that the disturbed children verbally expressed hostility far more frequently than did their nondisturbed counterparts. In fact, the disparity was enormous: The disturbed group evinced hostility in 418 exchanges, whereas the normal children expressed hostility in only 23. Neither disturbed nor normal children sought positive therapist responses in the form of displays of affection or rewards. The authors concluded that "such approaches as reward, praise, affection, giving reassurance, and so on have been overemphasized in such interaction" (p. 150).

Lebo and Lebo (1957) conducted a study of the expression of aggression in relation to age, hypothesizing that younger children (4 and 6 years old) would be more aggressive in their speech than 9- and 12-year-olds. They also expected that younger children would be less polite and abide by playroom rules less than older children. Note that these hypotheses are clearly developmental in character and, in fact, among normal children, seem subsequently to have been well established (Brown & Levinson, 1987). To test these hypotheses, the authors formed groups of aggressive children, roughly about 28 children in each of three levels of aggression, on the basis of teacher ratings. Children participated in three sessions of nondirective therapy conducted by the same therapist; roughly 3% of the utterances were randomly selected for coding using Lebo's 24-category system.

Lebo and Lebo reported that there were significant effects of age and level of aggression on nearly half of the categories. As expected, younger and more aggressive children both expressed more aggression and tested the limits of the counseling session. Unfortunately, interaction effects were not reported, but the authors concluded that the process of therapy, and in particular, the expression of affect, differed depending both on age level and pretherapy measures of aggressiveness. Such findings appear to be consistent with the client-centered assumption that a permissive therapeutic relationship will facilitate expression of negative emotion, especially among aggressive children. Unfortunately, no attempt was made to examine the relationship between in-session expressions of anger and extrasession changes in aggressiveness.

In the 1940s and 1950s, then, we see some remarkable initiatives in the study of affect in child therapy. Sequential, social comparison, and phase analyses were all begun, even if conducted in a rudimentary fashion by today's standards. We learn that the expression of affect differs in frequency, intensity, and degree of focus between normal and disturbed children in therapy as indicated across several studies, and that age effects need to be taken into account as well. Therapist reflection of feelings also seems to have proximal effects on affect expression. In their search for the active ingredients in child psychotherapy, Shirk and Russell (1996) concluded from these sets of studies that "there may be something corrective in therapists' behaviors that formulate, emphasize, and highlight the clients' moods or feelings or affects, as these create the subjective contexts through which objective events are understood" (p. 194).

Guerney, Burton, Silverberg, and Shapiro (1965) applied a four-category system to roughly two hundred 15-second samples of six different child therapy play sessions. Two of their categories directly concerned affect and were labeled positive feeling and negative feeling. The authors reported that the therapists' and children's category usage across segments evidenced a very high ("nearly perfect") rank-order correlation. Although findings were interpreted to reflect correspondence between therapist and child behavior, or emotional "tracking," there was little evidence in the study to support such a phenomenon. There could be a near-perfect rank-order correlation between adult and child category usage without there being any contingency between them.

In several studies in the 1970s (Boll, 1971; Siegel, 1972; Truax, Altmann,

Wright, & Mitchell, 1973), changes in affect expression in and outside of therapy were studied as consequences of different levels of therapist-offered relationship conditions (genuineness, accurate empathy, and non-possessive warmth). Boll's study compared sessions of therapies conducted by an active, directive therapist with those of a nondirective therapist. Each saw four or five children for 15 to 20 sessions. Although only a descriptive study, Boll concluded that children seen by the nondirective therapist were both more hostile and aggressive over time than children being seen by the directive therapist.

More sophisticated in method was Siegel's (1972) study, in which the emotional expressions of 16 children in grades two through four were examined across treatments of 16 sessions. Siegel sampled 4-minute excerpts from sessions 3, 8, 12, and 16, coding the verbal behavior according to Lebo's (1955) categories and rating therapist-offered conditions. He compared children receiving the highest and lowest therapist-offered relationship conditions of warmth, genuineness, and accurate empathy. In terms of affect, he reported that children in the high condition expressed more negative affect in later sessions than did the children in the low condition. Interestingly, the same children also produced more verbalizations labeled as insight. Siegel's research represents one of the first attempts to relate children's in-session behavior to the quality of therapists' interpersonal behavior. Although it is tempting to conclude that children's emotional expression varied as a function of therapist-offered relationship conditions, it is equally plausible that therapists varied their behavior in response to variations in children's emotional presentations.

Truax et al. (1973) also studied the differential effects of levels of therapist-offered conditions on emotional expression, only here the effects were assessed, not from analyses of later sessions, but as posttherapy outcomes. Sixteen therapists, of various schools, treated 16 children averaging 9 years old, who were described as having neurotic or character disorders. On teacher and parent rating forms, children with the highest therapist-offered conditions changed more than did the children with the lower offered conditions on such items as "Less emotionally disturbed," "Fears have decreased," "Laughs more," and "More able to express feelings." These results suggest that variation in process may account for changes in emotion expression posttreatment.

In summary, then, in the 1960s and 1970s, studies began to document that emotions could be tracked within and across sessions, and assessed at outcome from various perspectives. Linkages between emotion processes and outcomes, and other aspects of therapy process, specifically, relationship conditions, were demonstrated. Although limited in number, studies in this period introduced comparative process and process–outcome studies to child psychotherapy research.

3.2. Recent Studies of Emotion Processes

Howe and Silvern (1981) presented a complex measure development study that attempted to describe basic underlying factors in child therapy. Two raters rated 31 variables across 76 twelve-minute segments that were drawn from a variety of therapies. Factor analyses of reliable ratings revealed three stable factors: Emotional Discomfort, Fantasy Play, and Social Inadequacy. Items on the emotion scale concerned aggression, worries, conflict in play, quality and intensity of affect, and play disruption. Whereas previous studies used only single items to assess affect or emotion expression, notably categories pertaining to aggression or expression of feeling, Howe and Silvern attempted to identify the underlying organization of children's affect expression in therapy.

The research of Howe and Silvern (1981) suggests that children's affect expression in therapy is associated with their play activity. In a comparative outcome study with young children who evinced high levels of separation anxiety, Milos and Reiss (1982) coded the quality of children's play in three treatment conditions—free play, directed play, and modeling—for level of emotional involvement and mastery efforts. They found that high-quality play was associated with lower posttest anxiety scores as assessed by level of speech disturbance (e.g., word repetitions, slips, in response to separation-relevant questions). This study is particularly noteworthy in that it was one of the first to examine within-session process in the context of a comparative outcome study.

Smith-Acuna, Durlak, and Kaspar (1991) developed a set of child therapy process scales that assessed therapist and child perceptions of therapy. Child clients, ($N = 20$, mean age = 8.9 years) and their therapists rated their perceptions of six sessions of long-term, dynamically oriented therapy. Two of the four therapist scales and two of the three child scales focused on affect. Therapists rated their own positive and negative affect, and their perceptions of their clients' positive and negative affect. Children made comparable ratings. The authors reported that, after dropping several items from the therapist and client scales, moderate levels of internal consistency were obtained. Interestingly, there were no significant correlations between any of the child and therapist scales. However, they noted that the lack of association between therapist and client scales, even when assessing the same dimension or phenomenon, is not uncommon in the adult literature. The authors indicated that comparisons of participant ratings with observer ratings were needed in the future.

Russell, Bryant, and Estrada (1996) examined emotion processes in a methodologically oriented paper that integrated empirically derived observational ratings of molar aspects of child therapy process with both exploratory and confirmatory P-technique analyses of ratings of microanalytic processes in the form of therapist utterances. P-technique factor analysis was devised to assess underlying patterns of covariation between variables rated repeatedly over time for a single subject or across the normalized, chained data of several subjects. The authors' goals were to discover and compare the underlying structure of therapist participation in high- and low-quality sessions of dynamically oriented child therapy and to validate it by use of confirmatory factor analyses.

In order to evaluate the overall quality of therapy sessions, ratings of multiple dimensions of process were made first with the Child Psychotherapy Process Scales (Estrada & Russell, 1996). Patterned after the Vanderbilt Psychotherapy Process Scales for adults (Suh, O'Malley, & Strupp, 1986), these scales involve ratings of videotaped therapy sessions by trained observers. Principal components analysis of three segments of 39 therapy sessions with children between the ages of 6 and 16 revealed three factors for child and therapist items, respectively. The three child factors were identified as therapeutic relationship, therapeutic work, and therapeutic readiness. The three therapist factors referred to technical work, therapeutic relationship, and technical lapses.

After rating sessions with the Child Psychotherapy Process Scales, overall session quality scores for the child and therapist scales were rank ordered. The discourse of children and therapists in the three highest quality sessions and the three lowest quality sessions was then independently coded. A total of 907 therapist utterances were rated on 15 language interaction scales. In the principal components analysis, the third extracted factor for both high- and low-quality sessions concerned affect. Accounting for about 10% of the total variance, factor 3, named Positive Regard, had two affect-laden items that loaded most heavily: positive evaluation and positive affect. The results suggested that therapist participation in child therapy sessions of high or low quality was partially organized around provision of positive feedback and engagement. However, when Russell et al. (1996) attempted to confirm the exploratory analyses by use of confirmatory analysis, which posits and then tests a stipulated model, the third factor could not be confirmed.

The authors suggested that the lack of confirmation of the affect factor could have been due to the fact that it only had two variables that loaded highly on it, and that it accounted for the least amount of total variance. This could mean that the therapists' participation in child therapy was not organized strongly enough around affect expression to be confirmed. Alternatively, this third factor could have been comprised of more error variance than common variance, both of which are included in exploratory principal components analysis. However, factors in confirmatory factor analysis contain only common variance. The authors suggest that more reliable and numerous affect scales need to be developed so as to enable improved model-building attempts to understand the underlying organizational structure of therapist affect expression over the course of child psychotherapy.

An alternative approach to evaluating emotion in child therapy has been advanced by Russ (1995), who developed the Affect in Play Scale. Ratings for amount, type, and intensity of affect are derived from a standardized, videotaped puppet-play task. One major advantage of this scale involves the breadth of affective categories assessed, 11 in all. This represents a significant departure from earlier studies that tended to focus on single emotions (e.g., hostility) or lumped emotions according to positive or negative valence. Although the scale has shown promise as a predictor of effective coping with invasive dental procedures (Christiano & Russ, 1996), and has been presented as a potential indicator of treatment responsiveness (Russ, 1995), it has not been applied to actual therapeutic transactions. Given the range of emotions assessed by the scale, if modified for therapeutic play, it could help clarify the organization of emotion processes in child treatment.

In the 1980s and 1990s, then, we can see a flurry of measure development studies that at least partially focus on affect. Interestingly, we see developments in the use of different perspectives to assess affect: participant and nonparticipant perspectives. Moreover, we see a growing interest in the identification of the structure of affect expression in child therapy, signaled by increasing use of multiple-item scales and factor analyses. Finally, the first study intent on confirmation as well as description is presented.

3.3. Summary of Research on Emotion Processes

Substantively, these studies suggest that emotion expression is a key ingredient in many forms of child therapy, from both the child and therapist perspective. Because "emotion" factors do not emerge as the single or first factor in these studies, we might infer that child therapy is more centrally organized around other interactional phenomena than affect expression. Such a conclusion, however, might be premature, simply because researchers have yet to generate a sufficiently complex method to assess emotion processes with the same thoroughness as other phenomena (e.g., therapist technique or the alliance). Moreover, because affect expression seems inherently tied to positivity and negativity, and these cut across other domains, it may be difficult to isolate affective phenomena, even though few correlations were reported between affect and other factors.

It is important to note that this literature is plagued both by general design and method problems, and specific shortcomings as pertains to the study of emotion in child therapy. On the general level, many of the studies provide little information about the specific problems of the child clients that are treated; heterogeneity in patient samples is rampant. On the therapist side, many studies either use one therapist, often an author of the research report, or use multiple therapists, without attending or controlling for therapist effects. Assignment of children to treatments is rarely randomized, measures are often neither standardized nor appropriately normed, and reporting and levels of reliability are often less than optimal. Statistical conclusion validity is further jeopardized by low-power, inappropriate use of statistical tests, and frequent mixing of sources of variation in the data submitted to factor analyses (as is the case in every factor-analytic study of child therapy process done in the 1980s and 1990s).

The most prevalent problems specific to the study of emotion concern the degree of underdevelopment of complex coding and rating schemes. Most scales have little content validity, if the universe of emotional expression is the targeted area of study. Furthermore, as was pointed out early in the research history, emotion expression cuts across many channels of communication, and its study should not be restricted to verbalizations or verbalizations plus vocalizations (see Wiener, Budney, Wood, & Russell, 1989, for review of studies of nonverbal behavior in therapy). Last, there is still little focus on the interactional complexities of emotion expression in child psychotherapy and its relation to phase of treatment phenomena or to outcome.

To conclude, the history of research on child psychotherapy has always concerned itself with emotion processes. The focus has been either broad-banded or extremely narrow (e.g., focus on hostility) and has cut across types of study (i.e., pure process, comparative process, process–outcome) and types of methodology (i.e., use of self-report or objective observer scales; sequential or frequency studies). In addition, there is indication that emotion expression in therapy and at outcome are both affected by the therapists' reflective and empathic engagement. Clearly, far more detailed, developmentally informed investigations of emotion expression in child therapy are called for. Nevertheless, the history of research on this topic provides initiatives that can be fruitfully and programmatically developed.

4. Interpersonal Processes in Child Psychotherapy

Although the importance of the therapeutic relationship was stressed from the beginning in the client-centered and psychodynamic traditions, coding systems often did not include categories that directly addressed interpersonal phenomena. In the review of interpersonal processes in child psychotherapy, we included only those studies that directly assessed interpersonal phenomena, and not studies that merely emphasized the importance of interpersonal factors in child treatment.

4.1. Early Studies of Interpersonal Processes

A number of early studies examined interpersonal processes as well as emotional and language processes in child psychotherapy. For example, Lebo (1952, 1955), who evaluated children's emotion expression within sessions, also coded verbalizations as markers of interpersonal process. In what may have been the first "analogue" study of child therapy, Lebo (1955) categorized the verbal behavior of 20 normal children across three sessions of client-centered therapy. He reported that there was a significant trend across age levels in the children's attempts to form a relationship with the therapist, as indexed by their verbal behavior. Lebo interpreted this finding to indicate that children become more independent in therapy, and in relation to the therapist, with increasing age.

In a series of studies, Moustakas and his colleagues examined interpersonal behavior between child and therapist. In their previously mentioned 1955 study, contingencies between therapist and child behavior were examined, albeit in a rudimentary way. Here, we find the first investigation of therapeutic interaction, that is, an analysis of interrelationships between therapist and child behaviors. Although the study included both disturbed and nondisturbed children, surprisingly few differences emerged in their responses to therapist behaviors. For example, to therapist verbal suggestions, the predominant response of both groups was cooperation, despite the fact that the disturbed group evinced higher levels of hostility within sessions than their nondisturbed counterparts. Similarly, in response to children's directive behavior, the therapists' predominant response was straightforward cooperation. In fact, one of the most frequently coded therapist behaviors was Attentive Observation, which led Moustakas and Schalock to conclude that the essential character of the therapist's interpersonal orientation was "being there" for the child.

In a follow-up study, Moustakas, Sigel, and Schalock (1956) examined the interactions of a therapist who treated 2 anxious and 2 withdrawn children. Innovatively, the authors also assessed the children's interactions with their mothers in the laboratory playroom and at home. Consistent with their earlier findings, Moustakas et al. found that approximately 93% of the therapist's behavior consisted of attentively observing the child, with his most frequent responses involving watching or listening to the child. The children's behavior was also limited in range, with nearly 95% of their time spent in solitary play. This pattern of findings suggests that this form of therapy, at least with this therapist, could hardly be characterized as interpersonally interactive; instead, the results indicate that the participants were engaged in parallel activities! In contrast, observations of the children with their mothers across both situations revealed higher levels of interaction than with the therapist. One interesting contribution of this study involves its "normative" comparative process design, which revealed that "therapeutic" play interactions differed significantly from typical play interactions between mother and child. It is not clear, empirically or conceptually, how the parallel process found in therapy interactions would facilitate change in the presenting problems of these children.

Although these early studies focused primarily on client-centered play therapy, they introduced empirical methods for the microanalysis of interpersonal processes in child therapy. Substantive results are sparse, although there is some evidence to suggest age differences in children's interpersonal behavior in therapy, and for differences in the character of therapeutic versus typical play between an adult and a child. The latter finding suggests what might be expected: a natural suppression of a child's basic response rate with a stranger in a strange situation, at least in the early stages of relationship formation. However, one must wonder if this pattern would typify other initial therapy interactions with different therapists, with diagnostically different types of children, and of course, with different therapeutic parameters.

Over 15 years passed before there was another study of interpersonal processes in child psychotherapy. Across this gap, there was a substantial shift in the way that these processes were conceptualized and operationalized. Three studies conducted in the 1970s examined the therapeutic relationship in terms of therapist-offered conditions and assessed these conditions with scales measuring accurate empathy, nonpossessive warmth, and genuineness. Molar ratings of relational dimensions replaced microanalytic coding of verbal utterances. Wright, Truax, and Mitchell (1972) conducted a measure development study to determine whether client-centered scales of empathy, warmth, and genuineness could be reliably applied to child treatment. To assess reliabilities of the scales, the authors sampled three 5-minute segments drawn from 16 different therapists. Only the empathy scale showed adequate reliability, and the authors recommended that further scale development was needed. In the same year, Siegel (1972) applied the same scales to an analysis of 4-minute therapy segments drawn from the treatment of 16 school-aged children. His results indicated adequate reliability for all three scales, ranging from .70 to .84. After classifying cases in terms of high versus low therapist-offered conditions, Siegel found that children in the two groups showed different patterns of verbalization over the course of treatment. Most striking was the tendency for children in the high-condition group to show more positive statements about the self somewhat early in treatment, then an increase in levels of aggressive statements at midtreatment, and then a return to relatively high levels of positive self-statements in the final phase of treatment. This was the first study to explicitly document that changes occurred over the course of therapy on key process variables in association with the quality of the therapist-offered relationship. The absence of sequential data, however, precludes unambiguous inferences about the direction of effect. Furthermore, despite the identification of different patterns of process, no attempt was made to relate these patterns to treatment outcome.

This gap in the literature was partially filled by a study by Truax et al. (1973), who examined the association between the quality of therapist-offered relationship and interpersonal treatment outcomes. Again, children were divided into high and low therapist-offered relationship condition groups. Among the most important findings of this study were significant relationships between parental report of improved relationship functioning and group membership. Children in the high therapist-offered condition showed the greatest gains. Moreover, deterioration effects were noted: "Children seen by the therapists in the lower half on therapeutic conditions showed deterioration on five times as many measures as children in the upper half on conditions" (p. 317). As the authors noted, "Depending on the therapist's level of interpersonal skill, (therapy) can be for better or for worse" (p. 317). Although the study was not without serious limitations (e.g., lack of random assignment), it introduced the process variation design into the child psychotherapy literature.

4.2. Recent Studies of Interpersonal Processes

During the 1980s, two studies advanced the investigation of interpersonal processes in child treatment. Mook (1982a, 1982b) presented the first P-technique study of child therapy, describing the structure of two therapists' and two clients' participation in treatment. P-technique is a form of factor analysis that is applied to a matrix comprised of repeated measurements of the same subject on a range of variables. It reveals underlying patterns of covariation between the variables over time within a single subject. Using this technique, Mook factor-analyzed scores on 28 variables assessed at 221 points in time for one therapist–child dyad and 163 points in time for another. Variables focused on what Mook called empathy, verbal response categories, and grammatical categories.

Several factors for both therapists involved the empathic quality of the therapist-offered relationship and included such behaviors as encouragement, approval, and affirmation. These findings suggested that across clients there may be a stable pattern to therapists' behavior, and that it is organized around the provision of an empathic relationship. There were, however, important differences in other therapist factors, thus indicating individual differences across therapists as well. The fact that the therapists were utilizing, and supervised in, the "same" therapeutic approach (dynamic/humanistic) raises some interesting points. Most obviously, the structure of therapist behavior might be quite different across therapeutic orientations. On the other hand, even within the same orientation there were differences in the structure of therapists' behavior across sessions. As we have argued elsewhere, therapist process variation within treatment "brands" is likely to account for significant variation in treatment outcome, and should be addressed by child therapy researchers (Shirk & Russell, 1996).

In an effort to assess level of "involvement" in cognitive-behavioral therapy, Braswell, Kendall, Braith, Carey, and Vye (1985) coded child and therapist verbal responses assumed to be indicative of level of participation in therapy. For the child, verbal categories included self-disclosure, suggesting positive change in the task, self-evaluations of performance, and task-irrelevant statements. For therapists, self-disclosure, emphasizing feelings, correcting self-statements, asking for feedback, and verbal reinforcement were coded. Verbalizations were assessed at three points in time within sessions across the course of treatment. Although there were numerous correlations between verbal responses and multiple outcome measures taken at posttreatment and follow-up, the overall pattern of results suggested that indices of active involvement were predictive of therapeutic gains. Specifically, children's tendency to make spontaneous verbal elaborations about tasks and therapists' encouragement and corrective feedback appeared to be among the best predictors of change in teacher ratings of self-control. Again, this study provides some evidence that *within* a well-defined treatment approach, differences in child and therapist process account for variation in treatment outcome.

The early 1990s was marked by a notable increase in the number of studies that addressed interpersonal processes. As previously discussed, the therapist and child rating scales devised by Smith-Acuna et al. (1991) included dimensions that assessed both the therapist's and the child's perceptions of the therapist-offered relationship. This study represented a shift in the *source* of interpersonal process evaluations with ratings obtained from both child and therapist perspectives. The study demonstrated that school-aged children could make reliable judgments of aspects of interpersonal process; however, their perceptions of therapist-offered conditions were largely uncorrelated with their therapists' perceptions.

In an effort to bring focus to the study of interpersonal processes in child therapy, Shirk and Saiz (1992) advanced a model of the therapeutic alliance in child treatment. Drawing on the work of Bordin (1979) and Luborsky (1976), two components of the alliance were investigated, the emotional quality of the treatment relationship and the child's collaboration with therapeutic tasks. Shirk and Saiz (1992) hypothesized that a positive relationship between child and therapist would promote collaboration with therapy tasks. In a study with a diagnostically heterogeneous sample of 7- to 12-year-old children who were hospitalized and seen in intensive, short-term, dynamically oriented child therapy, children and their therapists rated the quality of the working alliance. Reliabilities for both therapist and child ratings ranged from acceptable to excellent. Moreover, there were moderate levels of shared variance between therapist and child reports of the affective quality of the alliance. For both therapist and child reports, the affective quality of the relationship was associated with task collaboration in the predicted direction. The alliance scales appeared to be promising, especially the dimensions assessing the affective quality of the treatment relationship. Regarding task collaboration, Shirk and Saiz (1992) suggested that observational ratings might be better for assessing this aspect of the alliance than child self-report, given the constraints of the child's level of cognitive development and limited therapeutic experience.

As previously discussed, Estrada and Russell (1996) developed observational scales to assess aspects of child therapy process, including participation in what they called "therapeutic work." Factor analyses of observational ratings of 117 session segments revealed three therapist and three child factors. One of the child factors and one of the therapist factors concerned the quality of the therapeutic relationship. As in previous studies, items such as Empathy, Warmth, and Positive Relationship loaded heavily on the therapist relationship factor; items such as Trust and Openness loaded highly on the child relationship factor. There was evidence of a significant degree of covariation between the two relationship factors. In addition, factors emerged that concerned participation in the tasks of therapy for both children and therapists. Observational ratings of therapeutic work for child and therapist were highly correlated. Furthermore, there was evidence that technical lapses by the therapist (e.g., low responsiveness or inattentiveness) were negatively associated with ratings of the child's relationship with the therapist. When viewed in relation to the findings of Shirk and Saiz (1992), these results suggest that it is possible to reliable assess multiple aspects of the therapeutic relationship from multiple perspectives, and that aspects of the alliance, specifically, quality of relationship and task collaboration, are associated in predictable ways.

Unfortunately, there have been very few attempts to relate indices of the alliance or therapy relationship to treatment outcome. As part of the evaluation of a cognitive-behavioral treatment for anxiety disordered children, Kendall (1994) assessed the child's perception of the therapeutic relationship with a seven-item child self-report scale. Similar to the alliance measure of Shirk and Saiz (1992), the scale tapped the child's feelings for the therapist and comfort with talking with the therapist. In this controlled outcome study, there was some, albeit limited, evidence for associations between alliance scores and measures of treatment outcome. From pretreatment to posttreatment and follow-up, 7 of 24 correlations were significant in the predicted direction; however, five of these involved shared source variance (child self-reports). The strongest pattern of results was between alliance scores and child reports of symptoms of anxiety and depression, with significantly less improvement for those cases that reported a poorer therapeutic relationship. The tendency for most children to report positive relationships may have limited variability and attenuated other potential relationships with outcome. Multiple perspectives on the alliance could potentially address this problem.

Eltz, Shirk, and Sarlin (1995) examined relationships among maltreatment experience, therapeutic alliance formation, and treatment outcome in a sample of psychiatrically hospitalized adolescents. The alliance was measured from both the adolescents' and therapists' perspectives at two points in time with the Penn Helping Alliance Scales (Alexander & Luborsky, 1987). Results indicated that maltreatment status, multiplicity of maltreatment, and type of perpetrator were all associated with initial alliance problems. None of these variables was associated with change in the alliance over time, which was best predicted by severity of pretreatment interpersonal problems. Adolescents who showed more positive change in alliance quality, regardless of maltreatment status, evinced greater treatment gains across sources of outcome ratings. These results suggest that changes in the pattern of alliance may be a better predictor of outcome than "one-shot" assessments of relationship quality.

In the 1980s and 1990s, then, scale development continued, but at a quickened pace and with more theoretical and methodological sophistication. Noteworthy is the turn to use of multiple-item scales constructed on the basis of factor analyses or reliability studies. In these two decades, then, there seems to be a concerted effort to discover and describe the underlying organization of the therapeutic relationship in child treatment. Finally, we find initial efforts to relate interpersonal processes, specifically, the alliance, to treatment outcome.

4.3.   Summary of Research on Interpersonal Processes

Methodological and statistical problems are evident throughout the history of research on interpersonal processes in child psychotherapy. One common problem boils down to the use of just too few therapists and too few clients, even in measure development studies, where independence of observations is assumed in standard factor analyses, or where there is a need for a very large number of repeated measurements in P-technique studies that use numerous rating scales. Furthermore, there is a virtual dearth of validity studies—concurrent, predictive, or discriminant—that might serve as a basis for an assessment of the construct validity of the interpersonal dimensions that are purportedly assessed.

One does note some development in the specificity of the constructs that figure in the interpersonal process literature. The field appears to have moved from global characterizations of the therapist "being there," through an examination of therapist-offered relationship conditions, and finally to a components analysis of the therapeutic alliance. However, much more is needed to adequately assess the role of various aspects of the child–therapist relationship in treatment process and outcome. Clearly, more attention must be directed to developmental constraints on the complexity of interpersonal information processing in order to guide construction of scales that are appropriate for use with children of varying capacities.

5.   Language/Cognitive Process in Child Psychotherapy

To be included in this section, studies had to employ category systems that targeted speech acts or therapeutic techniques focused on processive contents that were neither explicitly emotional nor interpersonal in character. In addition, studies that report findings about discourse processes or amounts of verbalization were included.

5.1.   Early Studies on Cognitive/Language Processes

As we have noted in previous sections, many of the earliest studies of therapy process assessed language interaction or speech acts as a means of evaluating emotional and interpersonal processes. These studies also shed light on the linguistic content of specific forms of child psychotherapy, especially client-centered therapy. For example, in the study by Landisberg and Snyder (1946), therapists' and children's verbal behavior were coded into a set of speech act categories. Three types of verbal behavior accounted for almost 80% of all child–therapist exchanges; these included 30% therapist nondirective statements, 25% clients giving information, and 24% client positive play action. As noted earlier, this was the first study to examine dependencies between client and therapist speech. One noteworthy finding was that client information-giving and positive play action followed therapist reflection of feeling more frequently than any other child speech actions.

Other descriptive findings emerged from early studies of language interaction in child therapy. For example, Lebo (1952) found that children's most frequently used speech category was descriptions or stories about family, school, pets, teachers, the playroom, or the self. These utterances accounted for almost one-third of all speech acts. It should be noted that this was the first study to focus on narratives in child or adult therapy, thus defining a new unit for language analysis. In two later studies, Lebo (1956; Lebo & Lebo, 1957) found that the number of verbalizations decreased with increasing age (between 4 and 12), and that younger children's speech contained more stories, as well as more sound effects and unclassifiable statements, than did the speech of older children. These findings suggest that therapeutic talk may not increase, at least during the school-aged years, as a function of increasing verbal capacity. This conclusion, though consistent with clinical observation, is offered tentatively, in that Lebo did not assess verbal capacity, nor did he report diagnostic information that could represent a potential confound for the reported age trends.

Other descriptive findings emerged from the studies of Moustakas and his colleagues, who classified over 1,000 therapist and 1,000 child utterances in nondirective therapy. For example, in their comparison of disturbed and nondisturbed children's verbalizations, Moustakas and Schalock (1955) found that 67% of the nondisturbed group's behavior could be classified as verbal behavior, whereas only 53% of the disturbed children's behavior met the same criterion. As the authors noted, the disturbed children appeared to be more likely to "act out" rather than symbolize their experience compared to the nondisturbed children. In the same study, contingencies were also examined. To therapist interpretations, children most frequently responded with statement of condition or action, recognition, or rejection. Conversely, to children's information seeking, the therapist most frequently responded with information giving. These results point to some basic patterning in child therapy, at least in nondirective therapy; however, no attempt was made to examine such patterns in relation to outcomes at the level of the session or overall treatment.

In the earliest studies of language processes, then, investigators turned to language analysis to assess not only frequency of use of specific speech acts, but also overall verbal output and dependencies between therapist and child utterances. With these strategies, they were able to provide empirical characterizations of what went on in nondirective therapy, to document age trends during the school-age years, and to begin to characterize differences in the quality and quantity of participation in therapy of children with or without behavioral disorders. Amount of verbalization, information seeking and giving, aggressiveness in speech, and reflective and attentive responding seem to be the predominant categories of use in the earliest studies.

Two studies appeared in the 1960s that addressed language process. Guerney et al. (1965) found that raters could reliably code verbal utterances, and that these utterances appeared to provide an index of the child's in-session behavior. Dana and Dana (1969) applied a six category coding system, only two of which were focused on vocal and verbal behavior, in a comparison of nondirective versus dynamic group therapy with children ages 3 to 8. Despite the absence of formal statistical analyses, the authors concluded that nondirective treatments tended to inhibit play, vocalization, and speech more than dynamic treatments. These results were not replicated by Boll (1971), who reported, on the basis of a qualitative analysis of the data, results that were the opposite of the previous study. It is unfortunate that the systematic efforts to code samples of therapy process in these studies were not complemented by systematic analyses of the resulting data.

Many of the limitations of early language process research are addressed in the Truax and Wittmer (1973) investigation of therapists' use of confrontation in treatment. In this study, the relationship between a specified therapist discourse tactic, confrontation, and a specified pathogenic process, maladaptive defense mechanisms, was investigated with a sample of delinquents. Seventy-three adolescents between the ages of 14 and 18 were treated in dynamically oriented group therapy during residential treatment. The study focused on the relationship between degree of confrontation of the adolescents' defense mechanisms and treatment outcome. High- and low-confrontation groups were contrasted by comparing change scores on over 20 measures, while controlling for pretherapy levels of the target variables. The authors found substantial evidence across most outcome measures for a relationship between confrontation of defenses and treatment progress.

This study represents a dramatic shift in the strategy used to investigate process–outcome relations. It attempts to link concrete therapist interventions and underlying pathogenic mechanisms in the client, and to relate the interplay between these units to treatment outcome. This approach not only represents a major advance in the history of child process research, but it also stands in sharp contrast to most studies of treatment outcome that focus on the impact of treatment *packages* on children who share similar behavioral phenotypes. In this sense, this study, undertaken in the early 1970s, predates the current focus on change events and plan-focused interventions that were initiated in the adult literature in the early 1980s (cf. Orlinsky & Russell, 1994).

The few studies conducted during the 1960s and 1970s provide limited substantive findings. As in other areas of process research, there is evidence for reliable coding of child and therapist verbalizations. Initial evidence on the impact of types of treatment on language process is equivocal, largely because of unsystematic treatment of the coded data. The one bright spot to emerge during this period is found in the work on specific therapist discourse strategies. This new strategy redirects attention to specific therapist interventions in relation to specific pathogenic processes. Such an approach seems to have the potential to realign studies of treatment outcome by addressing the interventions that constitute brand-name treatments and the mechanisms that underlie specific disorders.

5.2. Recent Studies on Cognitive/Language Processes

The 1980s witnessed both continuities and new directions in the study of language and cognitive processes in child psychotherapy. Mook's (1982a, 1982b) studies represent a continuation of the focus on speech acts in dynamically oriented child therapy. Several new developments are also evident in this work. First, Mook included a new language coding system that focused on grammatical variation (present, past, and future tenses) in child and therapist language use. Second, a new method for organizing language use in therapy, the P-technique, was introduced in order to identify the underlying organization of the therapist's or client's participation over time. Utilizing this approach with two therapists who each treated one child, Mook found that the therapists' discourse was organized around several strategies, including questioning the client about neutral and painful topics, information giving, affirmation, and self-disclosure. For the children, factors emerged that also reflected discourse strategies. Talking about uneventful topics, engaging in self-exploration of problems and feelings, and information seeking organized the children's discourse. Interestingly, there was some evidence for a developmental difference in the structures that characterized the children's cognitive and language activities; a play factor emerged for the younger child, whereas an insight and understanding factor emerged for the older child.

A series of process–outcome studies in cognitive-behavioral child therapy established several new directions in the study of cognitive and language processes. First, these studies marked the expansion of process research beyond the relatively narrow confines of nondirective or dynamic child therapies. Second, these studies represented the first systematic manipulation of cognitive or language processes in therapy, and the first analyses of how *controlled* variations in process related to treatment outcome.

Common to these studies is the focus on self-instructional training to enhance self-control and an interest in the potential moderating influence of the child's age or cognitive developmental level on the efficacy of such interventions. Given the emphasis on teaching thinking strategies in self-control training, a number of investigators hypothesized that such interventions could interact with children's cognitive capacities to produce differential outcomes (cf. Cohen & Myers, 1984; Kendall, Lerner, & Craighead, 1984). In order to investigate this possibility, Cohen, Myers, and their colleagues conducted a series of studies that systematically varied the programmed dialogue between child and therapist in self-instructional training. In the first study, Schleser, Meyers, and Cohen (1981) taught preoperational and concrete operational children of similar age a set of self-guiding statements in one of two conditions. In the traditional condition, the therapist provided the child with direct examples of self-instructions (e.g., "What is it that I need to do?"); in the *directed-discovery* condition, children were induced to discover basic self-instructions through dialogue with the therapist. For example, the therapist might ask, "What is the first thing you need to ask yourself when you start a task?" One of the main findings to emerge from this study was that the discovery procedure had a differential effect on children at different cognitive levels. Specifically, in the discovery condition, concrete operational children showed greater generalization to new tasks than preoperational children. Thus, the type of programmed dialogue appeared to have an impact on treatment outcome for children at different developmental levels. Nichol, Cohen, Meyers, and Schleser (1982) conducted a follow-up study in which children were presented with a linguistic variation of the *directed-discovery* approach to self-instructional training. In this study, children were presented with general content (e.g., "I'm going to ask myself a question, I have to stop and think about what the question is asking") rather than specific self-instructions. A comparison group received no treatment. Children at both levels of cognitive development showed greater gains in self-control relative to the no-treatment group, but again generalization was limited to concrete operational children in the treatment group. The authors concluded that in contrast to preoperational children, concrete operational children learn not only a specific set of self-instructions but also a procedure for generating such statements. From the perspective of language process in child therapy, these studies are important in that they draw attention to differences in patterns of language interaction within a well-defined treatment protocol that influence the generalization of treatment effects, at least for more cognitively advanced children.

In a related study, Kendall and Wilcox (1980) manipulated the manner in which self-instructional training was administered to children between the ages of 8 and 12. Children in the *concrete* condition received training that involved procedures that were specific to the training task; in the *conceptual* condition, children were presented with procedures that were general and relevant to a range of problem situations. The conceptual approach produced larger gains than the concrete approach in teacher ratings of self-control, and conceptual training was superior in producing generalization of behavior change. These results suggest that variations in the conceptual level of training instructions influence treatment outcome, even for treatments that target the same cognitive skill. Although language interaction was not systematically examined in this study, it is possible that the two groups might show differences in the character of language processes corresponding to the nature of the training tasks.

Russell, Greenwald, and Shirk (1991) attempted to relate types of in-session conversational interaction to changes in child clients' language achievement and other outcome variables. Eighteen studies were coded for one of three types of verbal interaction—spontaneous conversation, task-framed conversation, or behavioral or non-language-oriented treatment—that had been purportedly used in the children's treatment. Using meta-analytic techniques, the authors reported that treatments using spontaneous conversation obtained outcome effect sizes over 10 times as large as those using task-framed conversation, and over four times as large as those treatments that deemphasized verbal interaction. Interestingly, changes in language outcomes and other behavioral outcomes were not correlated. This study is noteworthy in that it stressed the relationship between types of discourse organization and achievement on language tasks, an important but often overlooked domain of child functioning.

Russell, van den Broek, Adams, Rosenberger, and Essig (1993) presented a study of Richard Gardner's (1971) mutual storytelling technique. The authors were interested in identifying if and how the therapist's story differed from the child's story, which served as its basis. Three narrative dimensions were assessed, including the causal and temporal connectedness of the story, the degree of elaboration of subjectivity in the stories, and the grammatical complexity of the stories. Sixteen child and therapist counterpart stories were coded. Findings indicated that the therapist provided stories that were more connected causally and temporally, representing subjectivity more frequently, but were equally or less complex than the children's stories. For the therapist's stories, those segments that were most connected causally and temporally also contained the most representations of subjectivity. The authors concluded that the therapist may have been trying to repair, augment, or foster the development of the children's theories of mind, specifically, by modeling sensitivity to causal connections between internal cognitive processes such as intentions, plans, wishes, and overt behavior. This was the first study in the child area to relate therapist and child narrative activity and to suggest, on the basis of empirical findings, how narrative processes might function in child therapy.

In addition to analyzing emotional and relational processes in their P-technique study (see earlier sections), Russell, Bryant, and Estrada (1996) examined discourse strategies in high- versus low-quality child therapy sessions. Exploratory P-technique factor analyses revealed three descriptively comparable therapist factors for both types of sessions—responsive informing, initiatory questioning, and positive regard; however, confirmatory analyses confirmed only the first two factors. Important differences in discourse distinguished high- from low-quality sessions. Specifically, relative to sessions of low quality, high-quality sessions were organized more systematically around two developmentally significant discourse strategies: (1) efforts by the therapist to continue the child's topic of discussion in a manner that produced richer information, and (2) attempts to acquire new information about the recent past that was focused in relation to the child. The authors related these two discourse strategies to findings from the developmental literature, which suggest that each is critical for structuring children's basic language and cognitive abilities (Feldman, 1988; Shirk & Russell, 1996).

In summary, recent studies of language and cognitive processes in child psychotherapy are marked by a significant shift in strategy and target of study. In earlier research, frequencies of nominally scaled language categories were tallied, described, and compared. Underlying patterns of organization or molar descriptions of discourse styles were not systematically investigated. Recent studies begin to overcome these limitations. Moreover, one finds initial attempts to evaluate cognitive and language processes that have been systematically manipulated in comparative outcome designs.

Substantively, there is indication that therapist discourse styles influence outcomes and can be differentiated across high- and low-quality sessions. A number of aspects of therapist–child language interaction appear to be potential candidates for promoting or enhancing therapeutic change, including discovery-oriented dialogue, topic continuation, and narratives that focus on causal connections and child subjectivity. It is not clear if all effective treatments are characterized by high levels of these processes, or if such processes are differentially relevant to specific types of interventions.

Clear methodological developments emerge in this period as well. Meta-analysis of processes, fine-grained linguistic analyses of narratives, and confirmatory P-technique studies surface for the first time. Limitations, however, also abound. Small sample sizes, use of few or training therapists, and heterogeneous client samples continue to be a problem. Furthermore, there appears to be a growing need to devise methods whereby findings from P-technique studies can be aggregated systematically. Idiographic strategies will need to be augmented in such a way as to build an idiothetic science, one built on the confirmation and compilation of $N = 1$ studies (Czogalik & Russell, 1994).

5.3. Summary of Research on Cognitive/Language Processes

The study of cognitive and language processes in child psychotherapy has progressed substantially over its six-decade history. This progressive trend remedies the oversimplification inherent in the construction of mutually exclusive classification systems comprised of a limited number of categories and in use of the frequency approach (Russell & Trull, 1986). Contemporary researchers have placed more emphasis on the multiplicity of meanings and functions characteristic of human discourse and have thus begun to assess each discourse unit on sets of ordinal scales. In addition, recent investigators have focused on ways to assess process—relationships between language units that emerge over time—thereby reestablishing a link with the very first child process study. Recent work has also considered different language units for analysis, thereby moving beyond a singular focus on the utterance. These include narratives, broad discourse patterns, and patterns of exchange that typify whole treatments. Finally, language processes have begun to be modeled. Here investigators are searching to identify and confirm underlying patterns characteristic of therapist–child discourse. In these current developments, the structures of effective processes are beginning to be discovered.

Substantially, several language/cognitive processes repeatedly surface as significant constituents of child therapy. These processes might be described as information-exchange, cognitive-emotional work, instructional guidance, and disclosure paired with acknowledgment. These processes, although similar to those identified in the adult literature, were found to vary developmentally, and in sessions of varying quality. Future programs of research will need to address how such processes shape outcomes at the level of the session and the full treatment. Initial investigations suggest that it may be the *form* and not the quantity of these processes that are predictive of successful outcomes.

6. Conclusions and Future Directions

In reviewing the 50-year history of research on child psychotherapy process, it is evident that there are both promising beginnings and recurrent problems. Although this body of research is often disparaged, present authors included, a close look at it reveals some striking facts. First, process researchers in the child area have been repeatedly innovative, introducing, often before their appearance in the "more developed" adult literature, such strategies as sequential analysis, social comparison techniques, analogue process studies, rudimentary phase of treatment analyses, assessment of therapist interventions in relation to pathogenic mechanisms, fine-grained narrative analyses, confirmatory P-technique, and meta-analysis of language process in relation to outcomes. Second, although there has been little continuity in programs of research across generations, there is notable confluence with regard to the key therapist and client variables that are included in process studies, some of which have been shown to be related to changes in process and outcomes. Not surprisingly, aspects of emotion identification, expression, and regulation; aspects of the process and structure of the therapeutic relationship; and aspects of therapist and client language use have repeatedly been used to assess therapist and client participation in therapy and to index treatment mechanisms. Third, although there are many methodological shortcomings in this research, there has been a consistent focus on measurement construction that has included a recurrent concern with developmental parameters, even in the earliest studies.

The internal, external, statistical conclusion, and construct validity of this body of research would have to be considered less than optimal. The methodological problems found in many of these studies cast serious doubts about the validity or generalizability of their findings (see Shirk and Russell, 1996, for a study by study methodological critique). It is important to note that many of the methodological limitations found in this research stem from the fact that studies were often conducted with samples and therapists of "convenience," a problem that follows from the lack of funding for process research. Some of these problems are likely to persist as long as funding sources are more inclined to invest in studies assessing which of several treatments works best, rather than in studies assessing how and which therapeutic processes are responsible for change.

There have been, needless to say, a number of productive pathways and blind alleys etched across this field of research. Several "method-specific" and "paradigm-level" blind alleys should be noted. At the method-specific level, most process research in the child tradition has been conducted by use of nominal coding categories for in-session behavior or participant/observer rating scales administered after sessions. Most of the category systems have been constructed with a limited number of mutually exclusive language categories, and most analyses have consisted of simply tallying category frequencies. Several inherent limitations to this approach can be noted (cf. Russell & Trull,1986; Russell & Czogalik, 1989). First of all, it should be noted that language and discourse are the most complicated human behaviors; it would be odd if their complexity could be adequately gauged by the use of 5 or 10 broad-band categories. Second, utterances are typically polysemantic and polyfunctional; they mean more than one thing, and they attempt to accomplish more than one act or function. Consequently, the multiple meanings and functions of utterances can be captured more adequately with a set of ordinal scales on which each utterance is rated. Third, the use of the frequency approach, that is, simply tallying instances over a segment or course of therapy, reveals little about the temporal or causal organization of discourse, or the relationships between utterances. The same applies to the analysis of interpersonal interactions. Sequential, time series, growth curve, and P-technique methods of analysis each offer more sophisticated alternatives to the frequency approach. Fourth, use of the frequency approach has often been applied to randomly selected segments of therapy sessions. It is possible that the change events responsible for patient improvement are not evenly distributed throughout the course of treatment. Discriminative sampling procedures aimed at first locating significant change events in therapy may provide a better corpus of data on which to apply sophisticated analytic strategies to discover mechanisms of change (Russell, 1987).

Use of participant/observer scales for assessment of therapy process has also been limited at the method-specific level. Most obvious has been the lack of the necessary series of studies, including sufficient numbers of patients and therapists, to assess an instrument's reliability and validity. Scale development in this area has been consistently neglectful in securing content validity, particularly with regard to emotion and interpersonal processes. Few studies have examined the concurrent or predictive validity of process rating scales.

Studies that have used coding systems or participant ratings have often assessed process at one point in time. Such an approach provides little insight into the course of therapy and the pattern of therapeutic processes. In some areas, such as the therapeutic alliance, differential *patterns* in the quality of the therapeutic relationship may be more predictive of outcome than "one-shot" assessments. Research by Patterson and his colleagues on resistance in parent training (Patterson & Chamberlain, 1994; Stoolmiller, Duncan, Bank, & Patterson, 1993) has shown that *patterns* of change in this interpersonal process are better predictors of outcome than single assessments or averaged process scores from multiple points in time. At present, we know preciously little about the pattern of development of most process variables and whether differing linear or nonlinear patterns of process are predictive of treatment outcomes. In fact, too few studies have examined the relation between process variables, however measured, and treatment outcome. This task represents the major challenge for the next generation of child therapy process researchers.

At the paradigm level, we saw that many of the studies were aimed at describing and comparing treatment "brands" when applied to clients whose problems were either poorly described or categorized by diagnostic criteria alone. Research on adult psychotherapy has shown that there is substantial variation among therapists who deliver the "same" treatment, the so-called therapist effect (cf. Crits-Christoph & Mintz, 1991; Lambert, 1989), and developmental research has indicated that children with the "same" disorder may not share underlying pathogenic processes (cf. Kazdin & Kagan, 1994; Shirk & Russell, 1996). Furthermore, it is unlikely that therapists respond to the child's diagnostic label any more than children respond to the therapist's espoused brand of therapy. In the heart of the therapy hour, therapists respond to the verbal and nonverbal activities of the child, just as the child responds to the varied actions of the therapist. By neglecting these transactions, the time-honored research paradigm that organizes outcome and process–outcome studies in terms of treatment packages and descriptive diagnostic groupings may miss the real phenomena of therapeutic treatment. Thus, process research should be recalibrated to examine patterns of transactions in and across sessions and their relation to changes in children's underlying pathogenic processes.

Although these blind alleys may seem prohibitive, several productive pathways are evident in the history of child psychotherapy process research and worth following. For example, early in this tradition, an interest was evident in social comparison methodology as applied to process. Exposed to similar treatment conditions, is there a difference in the form and function of therapist–client interaction when comparing healthy and disturbed children, and do the interactions of the therapists with the disturbed children begin to approximate patterns found with healthy or healthier children over time? Of equal importance, do disturbed children's patterns of interaction with the therapist begin to approximate healthy children's interactions with non-mental-health providers? Although these questions are rarely asked, such analyses could provide in-session markers of progress (processive outcomes). Recently, investigators have begun to devise sophisticated methods for applying social comparison methodology to process (Russell, 1995; Stinson, Milbrath, & Horowitz, 1995).

In the 1980s and 1990s, investigators began to turn to multivariate methods for assessing process. This trend was evident in research using either microanalytic ratings of in-session behaviors or molar ratings of process taken after sessions. Future research should build on this trend, with appropriate efforts to establish the reliability and validity of the measurement systems, and with concern to replicate and confirm findings with additional samples. Consequently, we recommend use of confirmatory factor analyses to validate and confirm measurement models suggested by exploratory factor analyses of process. In this regard, replicated P-technique factor analyses, based on $N = 1$ or chained samples, can contribute to the nomothetic goals of the more traditional R-technique factor analyses evident in this literature.

Attentive observation or "being there," therapist-offered conditions, and the alliance have served as overarching characterizations of the therapeutic relationship. There is, however, a trend toward conceptualizing the therapeutic relationship as multidimensional and to assess such dimensions with multiple-item scales. These developments in construct and scale development should be continued, especially insofar as such variables have proven to be consistent predictors of treatment progress in the adult literature (cf. Horvath & Luborsky, 1993). Furthermore, the structure of such scales needs to be assessed at multiple time points during therapy, as there may be qualitative as well as quantitative variations across phases of treatment in interpersonal constructs.

Child process research has highlighted the importance of stories and narratives in psychotherapy, and continued research in this area could prove to be especially productive. Narratives are common in everyday discourse, as well as in therapy, and function to organize social experience. It is possible that the core schema of self and other working models that primes maladaptive emotional and behavioral reactions is represented in narrative form (Buchsbaum, Toth, Clyman, Cicchetti, & Emde, 1992; Shirk & Russell, 1996). Thus, narratives represent an important target for assessment and intervention. Research on the process of narrative transformation and its relation to changes in social functioning appears to be a particularly promising path for future research.

In conclusion, our review has uncovered a tradition of child psychotherapy process research that extends across six decades. Although the methodological shortcomings of this literature are evident, there are numerous examples of innovative approaches to the study of child therapy transactions. Child therapy investigators who take up the study of process and process–outcome relations are advised to examine the productive paths and blind alleys that have been encountered by their predecessors in order to advance this field.

Finally, the study of therapy process may represent one of the best ways to bridge the gap between clinical research and clinical practice. Studies on the utilization of psychotherapy research by practitioners indicate that clinicians are unlikely to implement a treatment, even a treatment with known efficacy, "if they do not know what the treatment consists of or how it should be delivered" (Cohen, Sargent, & Sechrest, 1986, p. 204). Not surprisingly, then, Kazdin et al. (1990) found that child practitioners viewed studies of therapeutic processes and their relation to outcome to be a top priority for future research. It appears that for treatment research to be relevant to clinical practice, the processes that constitute treatments must be detailed and directly investigated in relation to outcome. The studies reviewed here mark potential points for bridging the gap between research and practice.

7. References

Alexander, L., & Luborsky, L. (1987). The Penn Helping Alliance Scales. In L. Greenberg & W. Pinsof (Eds.), *The psychotherapeutic process: A research handbook* (pp. 325–366). New York: Guilford.

Boll, T. J. (1971). Systematic observation of behavior change with older children in group therapy. *Psychological Reports, 28,* 26.

Bordin, E. S. (1979). The generalizability of the psychoanalytic concept of working alliance. *Psychotherapy: Theory, Research, and Practice, 16,* 252–260.

Braswell, L., Kendall, P., Braith, J., Carey, M., & Vye, C. (1985). "Involvement" in cognitive-behavioral therapy with children: Process and its relationship to outcome. *Cognitive Therapy and Research, 9,* 611–630.

Brown, R., & Levinson, S. (1987). *Politeness: Some universals in language use.* Cambridge, UK: Cambridge University Press.

Buchsbaum, H., Toth, S., Clyman, R., Cicchetti, D., & Emde, R. (1992). The use of narrative story stem technique with maltreated children: Implications for theory and practice. *Development and Psychopathology, 4,* 603–625.

Christiano, B., & Russ, S. (1996). Play as a predictor of coping and distress in children during invasive dental procedure. *Journal of Clinical Child Psychology, 25,* 130–138.

Cohen, L., Sargent, M., & Sechrest, L. (1986). Use of psychotherapy research by professional psychologists. *American Psychologist, 41,* 188–197.

Cohen, R., & Meyers, A. (1984). The generalization of self-instructions. In B. Gholson & T. Rosenthal (Eds.), *Applications of cognitive-developmental theory* (pp. 95–114). New York: Academic Press.

Crits-Christoph, P., & Mintz, J. (1991). Implications of therapist effects for the design and analysis of comparative studies of psychotherapies. *Journal of Consulting and Clinical Psychology, 59,* 20–26.

Czogalik, D., & Russell, R. L. (1994). Structures of therapist participation in psychotherapy. *Psychotherapy Research, 4,* 75–94.

Dana, R. H., & Dana, J. M. (1969). Systematic observation of children's behavior in group therapy. *Psychological Reports, 24,* 134.

Eltz, M., Shirk, S., & Sarlin, N. (1995). Alliance formation and treatment outcome among maltreated adolescents. *Child Abuse and Neglect, 19,* 419–431.

Estrada, A. U., & Russell, R. L. (1996). *The development of the Child Psychotherapy Process Scales.* Manuscript submitted for publication.

Feldman, C. F. (1988). Early forms of thought about thoughts: Some simple linguistic expressions of mental state. In J. Astington, P. Harris, & D. Olson (Eds.), *Developing theories of mind* (pp. 126–137). Cambridge, UK: Cambridge University Press.

Gardner, R. (1971). *Therapeutic communication with children: The mutual storytelling technique.* New York: Aronson.

Greenwald, S., & Russell, R. L. (1991). Assessment rationales for inclusiveness in meta-analytic samples. *Psychotherapy Research, 1,* 17–24.

Guerney, B., Jr., Burton, J., Silverberg, D., & Shapiro, E. (1965). Use of adult responses to codify children's behavior in a play situation. *Perceptual and Motor Skills, 20,* 614–616.

Horvath, A., & Luborsky, L. (1993). The role of the therapeutic alliance in psychotherapy. *Journal of Consulting and Clinical Psychology, 61,* 561–573.

Howe, P. A., & Silvern, L. E. (1981). Behavioral observation of children during play therapy: Preliminary development of a research instrument. *Journal of Personality Assessment, 45*(2), 168–182.

Kazdin, A. (1995). Bridging child, adolescent, and adult psychotherapy: Directions for research. *Psychotherapy Research, 5,* 258–277.

Kazdin, A. E., Bass, D., Ayers, W. A., & Rodgers, A. (1990). Empirical and clinical focus of child and adolescent psychotherapy research. *Journal of Consulting and Clinical Psychology, 58*(6), 729–740.

Kazdin, A., & Kagan, J. (1994). Models of dysfunction in developmental psychopathology. *Clinical Psychology: Science and Practice, 1,* 35–52.

Kendall, P. (1994). Treating anxiety disorders in children: Results of a randomized clinical trial. *Journal of Consulting and Clinical Psychology, 62,* 100–110.

Kendall, P., Lerner, R., & Craighead, W. (1984). Human development and intervention in child psychopathology. *Child Development, 55,* 71–82, 777–784.

Kendall, P., & Morris, R. (1991). Child therapy: Issues and recommendations. *Journal of Consulting and Clinical Psychology, 59,* 777–784.

Kendall, P., & Wilcox, L. (1980). A cognitive-behavioral treatment for impulsivity: Concrete versus conceptual training. *Journal of Consulting and Clinical Psychology, 48,* 80–91.

Lambert, M. (1989). The individual therapist's contribution to psychotherapy process and outcome. *Clinical Psychology Review, 9,* 217–224.

Landisberg, S., & Snyder, W. U. (1946). Nondirective play therapy. *Journal of Clinical Psychology, 2*(3), 203–214.

Lebo, D. (1952). The relationship of response categories in play therapy to chronological age. *Journal of Child Psychiatry, 2,* 330–336.

Lebo, D. (1953). The present status of research on nondirective play therapy. *Journal of Consulting Psychology, 17*(3), 177–183.

Lebo, D. (1955). Quantification of the nondirective play therapy process. *Journal of Genetic Psychology, 86,* 375–378.

Lebo, D. (1956). Age and suitability for nondirective play therapy. *Journal of Genetic Psychology, 89,* 231–238.

Lebo, D., & Lebo, E. (1957). Aggression and age in relation to verbal expression in nondirective play therapy. *Psychological Monographs: General and Applied*, 71(20), 1–12.

Luborsky, L. (1976). Helping alliances in psychotherapy. In J. Cleghorn (Ed.), *Successful psychotherapy* (pp. 92–116). New York: Brunner/Mazel.

Milos, M., & Reiss, S. (1982). Effects of three play conditions on separation anxiety in children. *Journal of Consulting and Clinical Psychology, 50*, 389–395.

Mook, B. (1982a). Analyses of therapist variables in a series of psychotherapy sessions with two child clients. *Journal of Clinical Psychology, 38*, 63–76.

Mook, B. (1982b). Analyses of client variables in a series of psychotherapy sessions with two child clients. *Journal of Clinical Psychology, 38*, 263–274.

Moustakas, C. E. (1955). The frequency and intensity of negative attitudes expressed in play therapy: A comparison of well-adjusted and disturbed young children. *Journal of Genetic Psychology, 86*, 309–325.

Moustakas, C. E., & Schalock, H. D. (1955). An analysis of therapist–child interaction in play therapy. *Child Development, 26*(2), 143–157.

Moustakas, C. E., Sigel, I. E., & Schalock, H. D. (1956). An objective method for the measurement and analysis of child–adult interaction. *Child Development, 27*, 109–134.

Nichol, G., Cohen, R., Meyers, A., & Schleser, R. (1982). Generalization of self-instructional training. *Journal of Applied Developmental Psychology, 3*, 205–215.

Orlinsky, D., Grawe, K., & Parks, B. (1994). Process and outcome in psychotherapy—Noch einmal. In A. E. Bergin & S. L. Garfield (Ed.), *Handbook of psychotherapy and behavior change* (4th ed., pp. 477–502). New York: Guilford.

Orlinsky, D., & Russell, R. L. (1994). Tradition and change in psychotherapy research: Notes on the fourth generation. In R. L. Russell (Ed.), *Psychotherapy research: Assessing and redirecting aspects of the tradition* (pp. 185–214). New York: Guilford.

Patterson, G., & Chamberlain, P. (1994). A functional analysis of resistance during parent training therapy. *Clinical Psychology: Science and Practice, 1*, 53–70.

Russ, S. W. (1995). Play psychotherapy research: State of the science. In T. Ollendick & R. Prinzer (Eds.), *Advances in clinical child psychology* (Vol. 17, pp. 365–391). New York: Plenum Press.

Russell, R. L. (Ed.). (1987). *Language in psychotherapy: Strategies of discovery.* New York: Plenum Press.

Russell, R. L. (Ed.). (1994). *Reassessing psychotherapy research.* New York: Guilford.

Russell, R. L. (1995). Introduction to the special section on multivariate psychotherapy process research: Structure and change in the talking cure. *Journal of Consulting and Clinical Psychology, 63*, 3–5.

Russell, R. L., Bryant, F., & Estrada, A. U. (1996). Confirmatory P-technique analyses of therapist discourse: High versus low quality child therapy sessions. *Journal of Consulting and Clinical Psychology, 64*, 1366–1376.

Russell, R. L., & Czogalik, D. (1989). Strategies for analyzing conversations: Frequencies, sequences, or rules. *Journal of Social Behavior and Personality, 4*, 221–236.

Russell, R. L., Greenwald, S., & Shirk, S. R. (1991). Language in child psychotherapy: A meta-analytic review. *Journal of Consulting and Clinical Psychology, 6*, 916–919.

Russell, R. L., & Orlinsky, D. (1996). Psychotherapy research in historical perspective: Some implications for mental health care policy. *Archives of General Psychiatry, 53*, 708–713.

Russell, R. L., & Trull, T. J. (1986). Sequential analysis of language variables in psychotherapy process research. *Journal of Consulting and Clinical Psychology, 54*, 16–21.

Russell, R. L., van den Broek, P., Adams, S., Rosenberger, K., & Essig, C. (1993). Analyzing narratives in psychotherapy: A formal framework and empirical analysis. *Journal of Narrative and Life History, 3,* 337–360.

Schleser, R., Meyers, H., & Cohen, R. (1981). Generalization of self-instructions: Effects of general versus specific content, active rehearsal, and cognitive level. *Child Development, 52,* 335–340.

Shirk, S., & Russell, R. (1992). A reevaluation of estimates of child therapy effectiveness. *Journal of the American Academy of Child and Adolescent Psychiatry, 31,* 703–709.

Shirk, S., & Russell, R. (1996). *Change processes in child psychotherapy: Revitalizing treatment and research.* New York: Guilford.

Shirk, S. R., & Saiz, C. C. (1992). Clinical, empirical, and developmental perspectives on the therapeutic relationship in child psychotherapy. *Development and Psychopathology, 4,* 713–728.

Siegel, C. L. F. (1972). Changes in play therapy behaviors over time as a function of differing levels of therapist-offered conditions. *Journal of Clinical Psychology, 28,* 235–236.

Smith-Acuna, S., Durlak, J. A., & Kaspar, C. J. (1991). Development of child psychotherapy process measures. *Journal of Clinical Child Psychology, 20,* 126–131.

Stinson, C., Milbrath, C., & Horowitz, M. (1995). Dysfluency and topic orientation in bereaved individuals: Bridging individual and group studies. *Journal of Consulting and Clinical Psychology, 63,* 37–45.

Stoolmiller, M., Duncan, T., Bank, L., & Patterson, G. (1993). Some problems and solutions to the study of change: Significant patterns in client resistance. *Journal of Consulting and Clinical Psychology, 61,* 920–928.

Suh, C. S., O'Malley, S., & Strupp, H. H. (1986). The Vanderbilt process measures: The Vanderbilt Psychotherapy Process Scale and the Vanderbilt Negative Indicator Scale. In L. S. Greenberg & W. M. Pinsof (Eds.), *The psychotherapy process: A research handbook* (pp. 285–324). New York: Guilford.

Truax, C. B., Altman, H., Wright, L., & Mitchell, K. M. (1973). Effects of therapeutic conditions in child therapy. *Journal of Community Psychology, 1*(3), 313–318.

Truax, C., Wargo, D., & Silber, L. (1966). Effects of group psychotherapy with accurate empathy and nonpossessive warmth upon female institutionalized delinquents. *Journal of Abnormal Psychology, 71,* 267–274.

Truax, C., & Wittmer, J. (1973). The degree of therapist's focus on defense mechanisms and the effect on therapeutic outcome with institutionalized juvenile delinquents. *Journal of Community Psychology, 1,* 201–203.

Wiener, M., Budney, S. E., Wood, L., & Russell, R. L. (1989). Research in psychotherapy and nonverbal behavior. *Clinical Psychology Review, 9,* 487–504.

Wright, L., Truax, C. B., & Mitchell, K. M. (1972). Reliability of process ratings of psychotherapy with children. *Journal of Clinical Psychology, 28,* 232–234.

4

Parent–Child Interaction Approaches to the Treatment of Child Behavior Problems

REBECCA FOOTE, SHEILA EYBERG,
AND ELENA SCHUHMANN

1. Introduction

Behavioral parent training, or parent management training (PMT), refers to procedures in which parents are trained to alter their child's behavior at home (Kazdin, 1996). The recognition that parents can become effective agents of therapeutic change in their children has resulted in the development and empirical evaluation of numerous parent training programs. Today, PMT is considered the treatment of choice for child conduct problems (Azar & Wolfe, 1989; Kazdin, 1987) and is gaining popularity as a component in the treatment of child internalizing problems as well (Albano & Barlow, 1996; Brent et al., 1996; Kendall & Treadwell, 1996; Lewinsohn, Clark, Rohde, Hops, & Seeley, 1996; Stark, Swearer, Kurowski, Sommer, & Bowen, 1996).

With the growing body of scientific evidence highlighting the role of parents in shaping and maintaining child behavior problems (Denham, Renwick, & Holt, 1991; Dix, Ruble, & Zambrano, 1989; Parpal & Maccoby, 1985), parents are moving from cotherapist to coclient, or even primary client for problems in dysfunctional parenting (Kendziora & O'Leary, 1993). Parent–child interactional approaches to the treatment of child behavior problems view parents as coclients. Although the child, not the parent, typically receives the diagnosis (e.g., Oppositional Defiant Dis-

REBECCA FOOTE, SHEILA EYBERG, AND ELENA SCHUHMANN • Department of Clinical and Health Psychology, University of Florida, Gainesville, Florida 32610.

Advances in Clinical Child Psychology, Volume 20, edited by Thomas H. Ollendick and Ronald J. Prinz. Plenum Press, New York, 1998.

order), his or her behavior problems are considered in the broader context of the parent–child interaction and overall relationship. From this perspective, treatment involves changing both the child's and parent's behaviors, thoughts, and feelings that affect the well-being of the other.

In addition, the recognition of the multifaceted nature of clinical dysfunctions and adjustment (Kazdin, 1995) underscores the need to expand the goals of parent training beyond the child's symptoms. Clinical child psychologists are increasingly turning to the developmental literature in an effort to understand how childhood problems evolve and how to foster positive child outcomes. Baumrind's (1967) developmental research associating parenting practices with child outcomes in normal populations has important implications for intervention. She formulated the authoritative–authoritarian–permissive parenting theory (Baumrind, 1991) after finding that middle-class parents of preschoolers who were less nurturant, less involved, and more controlling and punitive had more discontented, withdrawn, and mistrustful children (Baumrind, 1967). More recently, Baumrind (1991) has demonstrated that parents who do not adequately meet young children's dual needs for nurturance and for limits are less likely to have successful and healthy adolescents. The strong and consistent relation between certain parenting styles and problematic child outcomes has been shown in numerous other studies (e.g., Azar & Wolfe, 1989; Franz, McClelland, & Weinberger, 1991; Olson, Bates, & Bayles, 1990; Power & Chapieski, 1986). This research clearly suggests that clinicians' efforts should be directed toward fostering optimal parenting styles if they are interested in promoting optimal child outcomes.

1.1. Scope of Review

This review focuses on interactional approaches to parent training, which we refer to as parent–child treatments (PCTs). Although they are indeed part of the same family, PCT can be distinguished from PMT in several important ways. PMT programs typically target specific problem behaviors of children, utilize available incentives, and emphasize contingent application of consequences (Eyberg, 1992; Kazdin, 1996). Although PMT can result in positive changes in the interaction between parent and child, the progress of therapy is guided by changes in the child's behaviors rather than by changes in the interaction. Therapists work with parents to teach them fundamental principles of child behavior change (e.g., the function of positive reinforcement), as well as how to implement changes at home. The major task of the therapy session is to review how the treatment program was implemented at home, identify how it can be modified, and give feedback, model, and rehearse specific skills with the parent. The child is typically not included in the sessions but may be brought in to ensure that he or she understands the program, that the program is implemented as reported by the parent, and to negotiate behavioral contracts between parent and child (Eyberg, 1992; Kazdin, 1996).

In contrast, PCT targets the interaction patterns between parent and child for change, rather than specific child behavior problems, and emphasizes training in nurturance as well as discipline. This approach attempts to reduce children's maladaptive and inappropriate behaviors by strengthening the parent–child bond via positive communications, effective discipline, and problem-solving skills. Because the target of change is the interaction and overall relationship, both parent and child attend the treatment sessions. Therapists engage in direct coaching of parents as they interact with their child. This strategy enables therapists to provide parents with immediate feedback on the implementation of the interaction skills taught (Eyberg, 1992).

Most PCTs target young children and their parents when the patterns of parent–child interaction are taking shape, and when children are most vulnerable to poor quality parenting (Loeber, 1990). In addition, PCTs have thus far focused on children with disruptive behavior problems. There are three DSM-IV categories that address these behavior problems: Oppositional Defiant Disorder (ODD), Conduct Disorder (CD), and Attention-Deficit/Hyperactivity Disorder (ADHD). Even among preschoolers, disruptive behavior problems represent the majority of referrals seen at mental health centers (Offord, Boyle, & Racine, 1991; Schuhmann, Durning, Eyberg, & Boggs, 1996). These early problems also show considerable stability in childhood (Campbell & Ewing, 1990). Furthermore, epidemiological research suggests that preschool conduct problems may be part of a common pathway for a wide range of adolescent and adult disorders of both an externalizing and internalizing nature (Fisher, Rolf, Hasazi, & Cummings, 1984; Lerner, Inui, Trupin, & Douglas, 1985).

2. Theoretical Foundations

PCT, with its special emphasis on changing parent–child interaction patterns and improving the quality of the parent–child relationship, is informed by the developmental psychology literature and draws on both attachment and social learning theories. Even when the child's problem behaviors are strongly influenced by biological characteristics such as a difficult temperament or the neurological deficits suspected in hyperactive, developmentally delayed, or autistic children, many of the behavior problems seem to be intensified by the parent–child interactional patterns (Eyberg & Boggs, in press). Quality of parenting as well as the nature of the home environment (e.g., marital discord, poverty) are strongly implicated in most cases of child behavior problems (Bearss & Eyberg, 1996; Farrington, 1988; Hawkings, Catalano, & Miller, 1992; Loeber & Dishion, 1983; Patterson, 1986).

2.1. Attachment Theory

Recent theory and observational research on the antecedents and correlates of the child's attachment to primary caregivers has provided a new perspective and methodology for understanding how the quality of the parent–child relationship might influence the child's risk for antisocial behavior in later years (Sroufe, Egeland, & Kreutzer, 1990). It has been found that preschool children referred to clinics for disruptive behavior are more likely to be distressed during separations and to display behaviors thought to indicate insecure attachments with their mothers (Greenberg, Speltz, DeKlyen, & Endriga, 1991; Speltz, Greenberg, & DeKlyen, 1990).

2.1.1. Early Child–Parent Attachment Relationships

The nature of the parent–child relationship during infancy and toddlerhood, as assessed through the attachment paradigm, is believed to be a central causal factor in the child's personality development and behavioral adjustment (Bowlby, 1982; Bronfenbrenner, 1979). Numerous empirical findings indicate that secure attachment with a caregiver in the first 2 years of life is related to sociability with other adults and children, compliance with parents, and more effective emotional regulation (Ainsworth, Blehar, Waters, & Wall, 1978; Richters & Waters, 1991). Insecure attachment prior to age 2, in contrast, has been related to lower sociability, anger, poorer peer relations, and lower behavioral self-control during the preschool years (Greenberg & Speltz, 1988).

Attachment theory asserts that sensitive and responsive parenting during infancy leads the child to develop a cognitive-affective working model that he or she will be responded to when necessary. Thus, infants whose parents show greater warmth, responsiveness, and sensitivity to the child's signals during the first year are more likely to develop a secure working model of their relationships (Ainsworth et al., 1978; Bates, Maslin, & Frankel, 1985; Egeland & Sroufe, 1981) and more effective emotional regulation (Stern, 1985). Isabella & Belsky (1991) demonstrated that it is contingent responsiveness, not sheer frequency of involvement, that is most important.

2.1.2. Early Attachment and Later Behavior Problems

One of the most informative series of studies has come from the Minnesota Mother–Child Project, which followed a high-risk sample of children of young, single mothers from birth through adolescence (Egeland & Sroufe, 1981; Erikson, Sroufe, & Egeland, 1985; Sroufe, 1983). Findings from this project have consistently shown that children in high social risk environments showing early insecure relations are significantly more likely to have poor peer relations, depression, and aggression than those children who showed early security. Despite a strong relationship between the quality of the early attachment relationship and preschool measures of behavior problems, this association is mediated by subsequent variations in the parent–child relationship and family circumstances such as home environment, parenting practices, and maternal psychopathology (Erikson et al., 1985; Sroufe et al., 1990). These findings suggest that information about attachment security as well as later parent–child and family relationships are necessary to predict later behavior problems accurately.

2.1.3. Attachment during the Preschool Years

In discussing the nature of attachment during the preschool years, Greenberg et al. (1991) reported that the development of joint verbal planning in the parent–child relationship serves to support the child's rudimentary coping repertoire, reduce the child's anxiety regarding separation, and increase the child's autonomy. However, Greenberg et al. (1991) maintain that, as in infancy, the security of the attachment relationship depends on a parent's ability to be responsive to the preschooler's emotional needs during separations and reunions. Malatesta-Magai (1991) suggested that a parent who responds to a child's emotional expression with empathy and labeling is essentially teaching the young child that emotional expressions are tolerable experiences. In relationships characterized by behavior and emotional problems, children often express negative affect (Campbell, 1988); however, these expressions, which are often stimuli that elicit coercive cycles, are frequently viewed by the parent as intolerable (Patterson, 1982). A pattern is then established in which the parent indicates to the child that these negative affects are "bad" and does not assist the child in developing more mature forms of emotional expression (Greenberg & Speltz, 1988). Although parents of children with behavior problems may show deficiencies in strategies for child control/discipline (Patterson, 1986), a more fundamental problem may be their inability to be sensitive and responsive to their child's needs for security and attention (Greenberg & Speltz, 1988). Furthermore, it has been hypothesized that many of the behaviors labeled as problems are themselves necessary strategies to engage the attachment/caregiving behaviors of some parents, although clearly maladaptive in the social world at large (Speltz et al., 1990).

Classification systems have been developed for assessing the quality of attachment in children between the ages of 3 and 6 years (Cassidy & Marvin, 1989; Main & Cassidy, 1985). Two recent studies examined the concurrent relations between attachment and peer relations. Cohn (1990) found that 6-year-old boys, but not girls, with insecure attachments were perceived as more aggressive by peers and were reported by their teacher to show significant behavior problems. Using a low-risk sample of English 4-year-olds, Turner (1991) found that boys with concurrent insecurity showed more aggression, disruption, and attention seeking in preschool than secure boys. Insecure girls showed more dependent, less assertive, and less controlling behavior than did secure girls, but no differences were found in aggression or disruption.

Two studies have examined attachment security in clinic-referred samples of children who met criteria for ODD and comparison children matched for age, social class, and family composition (Greenberg et al., 1991; Speltz et al., 1990). In both studies, approximately 80% of the clinic children demonstrated insecure attachments in comparison to 30% of the comparison children, with the insecure–controlling pattern being especially prominent.

2.2. Social Learning Theory

Consistent with social learning theory, PCT assumes that child conduct problems are inadvertently established and/or maintained by the young child's interaction with the parent (Eyberg, 1992). The dysfunctional parent–child interaction is characterized by habitual aversive behaviors on the part of both parent and child. Each member in this relationship attempts to control the behaviors of the other through behaviors (e.g., arguing, criticizing, whining, aggression) that are maintained by intermittent positive reinforcement (e.g., compliance, attention). Parents of conduct-problem children have commonly been found to be both power-assertive and lax in their discipline (Baumrind, 1967; Dumas, LaFreniere, Beaudin, & Verlaan, 1992; Dumas & Wahler, 1985). These parents often issue vague instructions that cannot be obeyed and respond to their children's disruptive behavior in an inconsistent manner, giving it both positive and negative attention (Dumas & Lechowicz, 1989; Patterson, 1982). Exposure to parental coercion and inconsistency fails to control child disruptive behavior, but rather serves to maintain and strengthen it (Dumas & Wahler, 1985; Patterson, 1982; Snyder, 1977).

Specific interaction patterns have been identified in families of children with disruptive behavior problems. Mothers of ADHD children, for example, have been found to be more commanding and negative, and less responsive to positive or neutral communications from their children than mothers of normal children. ADHD children, in turn, have been found to be less compliant, more negative, more off-task, and less able to sustain compliance to maternal directives than normal children (Cunningham & Barkley, 1979).

Differences in parent–child interaction styles have also been reported in the literature on children with developmental delays and/or language difficulties (Cross, 1981, 1984; Hopman, 1989). Just as parents of children with behavior problems are less positive and accepting of their child's conduct, parents of language-delayed children tend to be less positive and accepting of their children's utterances than parents of normally developing children (Cross, 1984). Other studies showed that parent of children with developmental delay speak at a significantly faster rate (Hopman, 1989) and with less fluency and intelligibility during parent–child interactions (Cross, 1981) than parents of nondelayed children.

Interactional variables appear to suggest whether a family will seek help. In a recent study, Dumas (1996) concluded that low levels of positiveness and compliance, coupled with high levels of aggression, especially in the mother–child relationship, may play an important role in determining whether a family will seek professional services for disruptive child behavior problems.

3. Intervention Models

3.1. A Relationship Approach to Parent Training

A pioneer in relationship-enhancement therapy for parents and children, Guerney and colleagues (1964) developed filial therapy for treating emotionally disturbed children. The core feature of this approach is training parents to conduct client-centered play-therapy sessions at home. The goals are to foster increased intimacy between parent and child, greater independence and self-acceptance on the part of the child, and an increased acceptance of the child by the parent. In addition, parents are expected to improve their own self-concepts through the learning and application of general parenting and relationship skills. Although not well controlled, several studies have provided preliminary empirical support for the efficacy of this intervention (Oxman, 1971; Sensue, 1981; Stover & Guerney, 1967; Sywulak, 1977).

3.2. Early Behavioral Approaches to Parent Training

Early behavioral approaches to parent training such as those developed by Wahler, Winkel, Peterson, and Morrison (1965) and Patterson (1974, 1982) focused not on the parent–child relationship but on modifying specific child behaviors by application of principles of learning. Outcome studies have repeatedly demonstrated the success of these approaches (Kazdin, 1987). It is important to note that although this application can result in positive changes in the interaction between parent and child, the progress of therapy is guided by changes in the child's behaviors rather than by changes in the interaction. The importance of changing interactional patterns in addition to teaching behavior modification strategies in parent training is suggested by research showing that mothers who are not successful in behavioral parent training are more aversive than successful mothers in their interactions during pretreatment, treatment, and at follow-up phases (Dumas, 1984).

3.3. A Two-Stage Model

Hanf (1969) developed a two-stage operant conditioning model for treating dysfunctional interactional patterns of multiply handicapped young children and their mothers within a play context. In the first stage, mothers were taught to allow their children to lead a play activity while providing positive attention for appropriate child behavior and ignoring all inappropriate behavior. The second stage focused on teaching parents to lead the play by giving clear commands, praising obedience, and punishing disobedience using time-out. As opposed to working with parents alone, Hanf's format involved coaching parents *in vivo* with their child.

Forehand applied Hanf's model to the treatment of noncompliant children. Forehand's program has been evaluated extensively and shown to produce positive changes in both parent and child behavior (Forehand, Cheney, & Yoder, 1974; Forehand, Griest, & Wells, 1979; Forehand & King, 1977; Humphreys, Forehand, McMahon, & Roberts, 1978; Peed, Roberts, & Forehand, 1977; Wells, Forehand, & Griest, 1980). Studies also indicate that treatment effects generalize over time and to nontargeted behaviors (Forehand & Atkeson, 1977). More recently, Pisterman et al. (1989, 1992) have demonstrated that the program is effective in treating the behavior problems of preschoolers with Attention-Deficit/Hyperactivity Disorder (ADHD). In treated parents, there was a significant decrease in the percentage of directive and negative behavior, and a significant increase in the percentage of positive behavior. All of these changes in parent behavior were maintained at a 3-month follow-up (Pisterman et al., 1992).

4. Parent–Child Interaction Therapy: An Integration

Parent–child interaction therapy (PCIT; Eyberg & Boggs, 1989) was developed as an integration of the traditional and behavioral approaches to the treatment of behavior problems in young children. The PCIT program borrows from Hanf the two-stage model focusing on modifying dysfunctional parent–child interactions through direct coaching of treatment skills. The PCIT program, however, may be distinguished from other Hanf-model programs in its emphasis on teaching the relationship-enhancement skills espoused by Axline (1969) with the primary goal of improving the quality of the parent–child relationship. Thus, with its dual emphasis on strengthening the parent–child bond and establishing firm parental control over disruptive child behavior, PCIT helps parents adopt the authoritative parenting style described by Baumrind (1967).

PCIT is conducted within the context of natural play situations between each parent and child and has two basic stages labeled child-directed interaction (CDI) and parent-directed interaction (PDI). The CDI focuses most directly on strengthening the emotional bond between the parent and child. In this stage, parents are taught nondirective interaction skills similar to the techniques used by traditional play therapists to provide a safe and therapeutic dyadic situation that allows the child to experiment with change. Interpersonal factors such as parental warmth, attention, and praise serve as nontangible incentives that assist the child toward developing internal attributions of self-control (Robinson, 1985). Differential reinforcement of child behavior through praise directed toward the child's appropriate play and consistent ignoring of any undesirable activity provides a positive form of behavior management throughout this stage.

PDI focuses on helping parents gain firm control over their child's disruptive behavior. Methods of incorporating clearly communicated and age-appropriate instructions to the child are taught. Using techniques based directly on operant principles of behavior change, parents are trained to provide consistent positive and negative consequences following the child's obedience and disobedience. In addition, the therapist assists the parents in learning how the principles and methods taught in

PCIT can be applied to new problems as they arise. These functional problem-solving skills serve to increase the generalization of clinic-based parent training efforts (Boggs, Stokes, & Danforth, 1986).

PCIT can be administered in an individual or group format. Therapy sessions are conducted once a week and are 1 hour in length. The average length of treatment is 10–12 sessions, although there is no fixed number of sessions. Termination is dependent on parents' mastery of the skills presented, improvements in the child's behavior, and increased feelings of parental competence. The skills of both phases of treatment are taught via didactic presentation, modeling, role play, and direct coaching of the parent and child during structured play sessions. In addition, parents are required to practice the skills at home during daily play sessions (5 minutes per day during CDI, 10–15 minutes per day during PDI) with their child.

PCIT outcome research has demonstrated statistically and clinically significant improvements in child conduct-problem behavior (Eisenstadt, Eyberg, McNeil, Newcomb, & Funderburk, 1993; Eyberg, Boggs, & Algina, 1995; Eyberg & Robinson, 1982; Zangwill, 1984). These studies have documented change in the interactional style of the fathers and mothers in play situations with the child, as evidenced by increases in reflective listening, physical proximity, and the percentage of praise; and decreases in percentage of criticism and sarcasm. Changes in child compliance and disruptive behaviors generalize to the home (Boggs, 1990) and to the child's behavior at school (McNeil, Eyberg, Eisenstadt, Newcomb, & Funderburk, 1991). In addition, parent behaviors generalize to interactions with other children in the family and are reflected in improved behavior of siblings (Brestan, Eyberg, Boggs, & Algina, 1997; Eyberg & Robinson, 1982). Newcomb (1995) demonstrated maintenance of treatment gains at 1-year follow-up for both children and parents, although by 2 years following treatment, approximately half of the treated children again met diagnostic criteria for a disruptive behavior diagnosis.

4.1. Other Applications of the Hanf Model

4.1.1. Videotape Modeling

Webster-Stratton (1981b) has developed a low-cost videotape modeling program for parents with conduct-problem children based on the Hanf model. Concepts such as nurturance, sensitivity, authoritative style, individual differences in children, and behavioral management skills are presented to parents in 10 videotape programs. A more complete description of the 10-videotape training programs is available (Webster-Stratton, 1981b, 1987). Webster-Stratton has demonstrated the short- and long-term effectiveness of videotape modeling combined with either clinic or nonclinic parent discussion groups for changing a broad range of parent–child interactions (Webster-Stratton, 1981a, 1981b, 1982a, 1982b, 1984). In addition, the program has been found to be equally effective when administered individually or in groups (Webster-Stratton, 1984). More recently, she found that an individually self-administered videotape modeling treatment with or without therapist consultation was effective in reducing child behavior problems and parent stress levels (Webster-Stratton, 1990).

4.1.2. Adaptation for Children with Attention-Deficit/Hyperactive Disorder

Barkley has applied the Hanf model to a treatment program designed specifically for parents of 3- to 11-year-old children with ADHD (Barkley, 1981, 1987, 1990). This program shares with other PCTs an emphasis on changing dysfunctional parent–child interactions and using playtime as a means of enhancing the parent–child relationship. However, Barkley's multimodal program is unique in several ways. First, a psychoeducational component is included in order to increase parental knowledge and understanding of ADHD. A second distinctive feature is its explicit incorporation of cognitive therapy strategies, such as identifying and correcting faulty perceptions and Socratic questioning. Finally, a token reinforcement system is used. Parenting skills are taught primarily through didactic training rather than direct coaching of parent–child interactions, although treatment skills are practiced in playtime sessions and other homework assignments.

Significant improvements have been found in child behavior following parental participation in the treatment program (Pisterman, McGrath, Firestone, Goodman, Webster, & Malory, 1989; Pollard, Ward, & Barkley, 1983). Anastopolous and colleagues (1993) demonstrated significant improvements in school-age children's ADHD symptomatology. In addition, they found reduced parent stress immediately following treatment and at 2-month follow-up (Anastopolous, Shelton, DuPaul, & Guevremont, 1993).

4.1.3. Adaptation for Children with Language Delays

Cunningham (1989) has developed an intervention program based on the Hanf model for language-delayed children who experience significant behavior problems. Like other PCTs, the program coaches parents as they interact with their child and uses play as a medium to enhance parent–

child interactions. Parents develop strategies for improving relationships via play, for avoiding escalating conflicts, for encouraging children to use problem-solving techniques, for encouraging cooperative prosocial behavior, for establishing limits, and for enforcing these limits with effective consequences. The latter part of the program is designed to foster generalization of the parents' skills. Cunningham's program formally includes siblings of the target children. The sibling group, run conjointly with the parent sessions, primarily involves play activities designed to foster the development of language and social skills. For siblings with normal language skills, the program is designed to assist in developing their own solutions to situational problems involving the target child. The effectiveness of parent training derived from the Hanf model has been demonstrated with specifically language-delayed children and generally delayed children (Cunningham, Siegel, van der Spuy, Clark, Elbard, Nielson, & Richards, 1983).

4.2. Summary of Parent–Child Treatments

The primary goal of PCTs is to improve parent–child interactions and enhance the parent–child relationship by helping parents develop an authoritative parenting style. The assumption is that teaching parents to apply an appropriate balance between nurturance and firm control will result in improvements in the overall adaptive functioning of the child and family. In PCTs, the therapist usually works directly with parent–child dyads, a format that enables the therapist to coach parents to modify their behavior as they interact with their children. In this way, the therapist can closely monitor the changes in the parent–child relationship through the course of treatment. Although PCTs may draw on different theoretical explanations to account for change, they recognize the importance of increasing the sense of warmth and intimacy in the parent–child relationship before addressing conflict areas.

Research has demonstrated that PCTs are effective in reducing child behavior problems such as noncompliance and aggressiveness and improving parenting skills and parent functioning more generally. PCTs have been demonstrated to result in improvements in the child's behavior at home (Boggs, 1990; Eyberg, Boggs, & Algina, 1995) and at school (McNeil et al 1991), and to result in improved behavior in untreated siblings (Brestan et al., 1997). In discussing the outcome of PCTs, it is important to note that treatment evaluation is not restricted to posttreatment assessment. PCTs also depend on close and continuous monitoring of parent–child interactions to guide the course of treatment.

5. The Important Role of Measurement in Parent–Child Treatments

To measure most accurately parent–child interactions, it is necessary to use instruments that capture their reciprocal nature. Direct observational measures of parent–child interactions serve this purpose and are central to PCTs. Not only do they provide baseline data of behaviors that will be the direct targets of treatment, but they also guide the rate and progress of treatment. In PCIT, we use the Dyadic Parent–Child Interaction Coding System II (DPICS-II; Eyberg, Bessmer, Newcomb, Edwards, & Robinson, 1994) to assess the quality of the parent–child interaction in three 5-minute standardized situations that vary in the degree to which parental control is required. The DPICS-II Clinic Version provides a quick and easy, paper-and-pencil method of recording basic parenting skills in addition to child compliance and disruptive behavior. This version allows us to give parents immediate feedback about the kinds of skills we emphasize in PCIT.

Important process variables associated with healthy parent–child interaction patterns that we are only beginning to identify and operationalize for clinical assessment include warmth, genuineness, and other affective variables. Rather than focusing solely on quantitative approaches, assessment researchers may want to incorporate qualitative approaches to measurement in order to identify process variables relevant to dyads with different demographic and developmental characteristics (Eyberg, 1995).

Attachment variables can contribute an added dimension to assessing the interactive process in dysfunctional parent–child relationships. Advances in clinic observations of parent–child separations/reunions have allowed for the reliable assessment of attachment in the preschool years, and preliminary studies have supported the validity of these assessments to show distinctly different reunion patterns among clinic dyads with highly similar symptom topographies (e.g., Greenberg et al., 1991; Speltz et al., 1990). The assessment of reunion and separation patterns may be particularly germane to outcome assessment, in that the tasks are developmentally pertinent yet not directly taught during treatment.

One essential quality of parent–child interactions that has emerged in factor-analytic studies is warmth (MacDonald, 1992). Observational attempts to measure warmth in the parent–child relationship have met with limited success (Eisenstadt et al., 1993). In Maccoby and Martin's (1983) empirically derived model, parent–child interactions range from warm (parental acceptance, responsiveness, and child centeredness) to hostile (parental rejection, nonresponsiveness, and parent centeredness). This classification scheme might provide a useful framework for the assessment of warmth in parent–child relations.

Developmentally appropriate measures of the relationship quality can not only aid in treatment outcome research, but can also guide the type and intensity of recommended treatments. Some families in treatment, for example, may show poor behavior management skills but warm and nurturing parent–child relationships despite frequent conflict, whereas other families may show strong behavior management skills but distant and/or hostile affective relationships (Greenberg et al., 1993). Although the child's behavior might meet criteria for ODD in both cases, different intervention formats (e.g., stage sequence, stage emphasis) may be indicated. For example, the former parent–child dyad may benefit from earlier or more intensive focus on PDI skills, whereas the latter may need more focus on CDI skills (Eisenstadt et al., 1993).

In addition to measuring parent–child interactions, PCTs use multiple measures to assess other child, parent, and family domains relevant to child behavior problems. Such measures include clinical and structured diagnostic interviews with parents, cognitive screenings of both parent and child, self-report measures of child behavior at home and at school, parent psychopathology, parenting stress, parent locus of control, marital satisfaction, and parenting alliance.

6.   Methodological Issues and Future Directions

6.1.   Client-to-Treatment Matching

One compelling area of interest is the issue of treatment specificity or prescriptive treatments (Beutler & Clarkin, 1990). It is important to investigate whether PCTs are more effective for families at certain developmental stages and with certain types of child and parent problems.

6.1.1.   Child Age

Although we have focused on the treatment of young children in this chapter, there is evidence from the family therapy literature that treatments combining behavioral and relationship-enhancement components are effective in treating adolescents with conduct-problem behavior. In numerous studies, youth antisocial behavior has been predicted either directly or indirectly by central aspects of family relations such as low parental monitoring and weak parental attachment (for review, see Henggeler, 1991). Multisystemic therapy (MST; Henggeler & Borduin, 1990) intervenes directly in systemic processes known to be related to antisocial behavior in adolescents, including both parenting discipline and family affective relations, as well as peer associations and school performance. Several controlled outcome studies have shown that MST is a promising approach to the treatment of adolescents and multiproblem families (Borduin, Henggeler, Blaske, & Stein, 1990; Henggeler et al., 1986; Mann, Borduin, Henggeler, & Blaske, 1990). Thus, it appears that integrated approaches can be adapted to children at different ages and developmental levels. More empirical work that compares alternative and combined approaches in families with children at different developmental levels is needed.

6.1.2. Child and Parent Dysfunctions

Within the clinical intervention literature, outcome studies of PCTs have focused on externalizing problems in young children and have yet to examine rigorously the impact of parent–child relationship enhancement on any of the internalizing disorders. Given that improvements in the parent–child relationship have been found to result in improvements in self-esteem in children diagnosed with externalizing problems (Eisenstadt et al., 1993), the relationship-enhancement component alone might be sufficient for young children whose primary diagnosis is related to a mood disorder. In regard to parent dysfunctions, a relationship-approach seems particularly well-suited for the problem of child abuse, in which repairing and strengthening the parent–child bond is essential. PMT has been found to be effective with this population (Denicola & Sandler, 1980; Sandler, Van Dercar, & Milhoan, 1978; Wolfe & Sandler, 1981; Wolfe, Sandler, & Kaufman, 1981), although PCTs have yet to be evaluated.

6.1.3. Comorbidity of Child and Parent Disorders

A related issue is that of comorbidity as it affects the outcome of PCTs. Indeed, comorbidity has been described as the premiere challenge facing mental health professionals in the 1990s (Kendall & Clarkin, 1992). Comorbidity, which generally refers to the co-occurrence of two disorders, is typical among childhood disorders. For example, the co-occurrence of Oppositional Defiant Disorder (ODD) or Conduct Disorder (CD) among children with Attention-Deficit/Hyperactivity Disorder (ADHD) has been estimated to range between 20% (Barkley, 1990) and 60% (Biederman, Munir, & Knee, 1987).

Comorbidity can also be considered as a dyadic phenomenon, between child behavior problems and parent problems (e.g., parent psychopathology, social isolation, marital distress). Some researchers have suggested that these parent or family problems need to be treated adjunctly (Webster-Stratton, 1994), whereas others have suggested that PCTs may lead to generalized family improvements that might not require additional modules (Eyberg & Boggs, in press). These hypotheses are important to pursue further, particularly in light of research findings associating parent, family, and environmental variables with treatment efficacy (Dumas & Wahler, 1983; McMahon, Forehand, Griest, & Wells, 1981; Patterson, 1974, 1976; Reisinger, Frangia, & Hoffman, 1976; Strain, Young, & Horowitz, 1981). Webster-Stratton (1994) has taken steps to address these problems by adding a treatment component (ADVANCE) on coping with distress to a basic videotape PCT program (GDVM). In her study, parents who received ADVANCE treatment versus GDVM alone showed additional significant improvements in problem solving, communication, and consumer satisfaction.

Miller and Prinz (1990) have reviewed the use of adjunctive treatments to improve outcomes of social learning interventions with conduct-disordered children. They conclude that although much progress has been made, the task is far from complete. Specifically, they emphasize the need for long-term evaluation of treatment outcome, and for assessment of potential side effects in nontargeted areas. In addition, they discuss the need for studies to specify the timing of adjunctive components as well as the influence of individual difference variables on the success of adjunctive social learning components.

6.1.4. Attrition

PCTs, like other family treatments, make numerous demands on the parents. Parents are required to attend weekly treatment sessions consistently, master educational material, practice techniques at home, and actively respond to therapist feedback. Furthermore, PCTs require parents to recognize their influence on their child's behavior. PCTs require parents not only to have the financial resources (e.g., fees, transportation, child care for siblings) to engage in therapy, but also to be motivated and cognitively able to change their own behaviors. Premature dropout, unfortunately, is more the rule than the exception in treating childhood conduct-disorder populations (Firestone & Witt, 1982; McMahon et al., 1981; Patterson, 1982; Reid & Patterson, 1976). In a recent study evaluating the effectiveness of PCIT, 38% of 100 families dropped out of treatment prematurely (Eyberg, 1996). Clearly, attrition is an important problem that warrants further attention.

Prinz and Miller (1994) systematically studied dropout of family-based treatment for childhood antisocial behavior. They found that families whose treatment focused exclusively on parent training and child behavior dropped out more often than families who had many opportunities during treatment to discuss life concerns beyond child management. This finding was particularly true for families facing greater adversity. Prinz and Miller suggest that addressing broader contextual issues in treatment may be necessary to keep some families in treatment and promote greater consumer satisfaction. Engaging families in treatment, particularly those experiencing multiple stressors, may require more flexible treatment models (Miller & Prinz, 1990), including home-based implementation, provision of transportation, flexible hours, and greater sensitivity to cultural variation (Prinz & Miller, 1991).

To reduce attrition in research studies, Mash and Terdal (1980) have stressed the importance of presenting a clear and concise rationale at the outset that makes the expectations for participation clear. Capaldi and Patterson (1987) demonstrated empirically the importance of ongoing personal relationships with participating families, as well as the influential role of monetary incentives for improving retention rates with families. Such monetary incentives may act by allowing economically disadvantaged families to afford the costs of treatment (e.g., transportation, child care) (Eyberg, Edwards, Boggs, & Foote, in press). Black and Holden (1995) reviewed several strategies that reduced attrition in previous longitudinal studies, including tracking the family's whereabouts by recording the names and addresses of other family contacts who would always know the location of the family. In addition, strategies that maintain rapport, such as sending birthday and holiday cards to the families, sending reminder notices, and providing baby-sitting, are effective in reducing attrition (Black & Holden, 1995).

6.1.5. Maintenance of Treatment Gains

To know whether the effects of PCT are generalizable and durable, there is a critical need for follow-up studies. The results of studies that have assessed maintenance of effects of PMT beyond 1 year have been mixed (Bank, Marlowe, Reid, Patterson, & Weinrott, 1991; Baum & Forehand, 1981; Dumas & Wahler, 1983; Forehand & Long, 1988; Long, Forehand, Wierson, & Morgan, 1994; Patterson & Fleischman, 1979; Wahler, 1980). Forehand and colleagues have conducted the longest-term studies following treatment of young noncompliant children, and these studies suggest normal conduct in the youngsters several years later. Most studies, however, suggest that a substantial proportion of families fail to demonstrate continued benefit.

Webster-Stratton (1985, 1990) has examined long-term maintenance in PCTs. She obtained 3-year follow-up data on approximately 82% of fami-

(

lies who participated in videotape-based parent training (Webster-Stratton, 1990). At a 3-year follow-up assessment, only about half of the children maintained treatment gains at home. Similarly, only half of those whose school behavior was initially problematic were able to maintain treatment gains. Those children who did maintain treatment gains tended to come from intact, higher SES families without psychopathology.

Newcomb (1995) examined long-term outcomes in a small sample of 13 preschoolers and their mothers following PCIT. She found that the families in the study moved from outside of normal limits at pretreatment to within normal limits at posttreatment and 1-year follow-up on measures of compliance, conduct problems, activity level, and parenting stress. In addition, 12 of the children no longer met diagnostic criteria for a disruptive behavior disorder immediately posttreatment. However, after 2 years, only 50% of the children still demonstrated clinically significant improvements in behavior. Data from individual families showed that in this sample, more parents than children obtained and maintained clinically significant levels of improvement in behavior (i.e., parenting skills) over the course of follow-up. These findings raise questions about why some children fail to maintain treatment gains. For example, is the maintenance of certain parenting skills (e.g., praise, direct commands) more important than others in maintaining gains in child behavior? Are certain children more vulnerable to peer or other influences? What role do child and/or parent comorbid conditions play in long-term maintenance of treatment gains? Controlled studies that investigate these and other specific hypotheses are needed to determine why PCTs fail to produce durable results in some families.

In summary, the immediate and short-term outcome for families of young children with conduct-problem behavior who participate in PCT is successful. However, the continued impact of such training on the development of conduct problems in childhood and adolescence is less clear. Long-term follow-up studies suggest PCTs may achieve long-term positive outcomes in only about half those who complete treatment. Additional studies on long-term maintenance, comparing families who receive treatment to those who do not, are necessary before we can be confident in the durability of current treatments and our understanding of variables associated with long-term outcomes.

7. Conclusion

We have attempted to identify the theoretical, clinical, and empirical merits of a parent–child interaction approach to the treatment of child dysfunctions. In reviewing PCTs, we have discussed their common emphasis on treating the parent–child dyad by improving interaction patterns and enhancing the overall relationship. We are excited by the broad implications of an approach to child treatment that teaches parents to adopt an appropriate balance between nurturance and effective discipline. We readily acknowledge that we have asked more empirical questions than we have answered, and hope that our discussion will stimulate needed research on PCTs.

8. References

Abikoff, H., Klein, R., Klass, E., & Ganeles, D. (1987, October). Methylphenidate in the treatment of conduct disordered children. In H. Abikoff (Chair), *Diagnosis and treatment issues in children with disruptive behavior disorders*. Symposium presented at the annual meeting of the American Academy of Child and Adolescent Psychiatry, Washington, DC.

Ainsworth, M. D., Blehar, M. C., Waters, E., & Wall, S. (1978). *Patterns of attachment*. Hillsdale, NJ: Erlbaum.

Albano, A. M., & Barlow, D. H. (1996). Breaking the vicious cycle: Cognitive-behavioral group treatment for socially anxious youth. In E. D. Hibbs, & P. S. Jensen (Eds.), *Psychosocial treatments for child and adolescent disorders: Empirically based strategies for clinical practice* (pp. 43–62). Washington, DC: American Psychological Association.

American Psychiatric Association. (1994). *Diagnostic and statistical manual of mental disorders* (4th ed.). Washington, DC: Author.

Anastopoulos, A. D., Shelton, T. L., Du Paul, G. J., & Guevremont, D. C. (1993). Parent training for attention-deficit hyperactivity disorder: Its impact on parent functioning. *Journal of Abnormal Child Psychology, 21*, 581–596.

Axline, U. (1969). *Play therapy*. New York: Ballantine.

Azar, S. T., & Wolfe, D. A. (1989). Child abuse and neglect. In E. J. Mash & R. A. Barkley (Eds.), *Treatment of childhood disorders* (pp. 451–489). New York: Guilford.

Bank, L., Marlow, J. H., Reid, J. B., Patterson, G. R., & Weinrott, M. R. (1991). A comparative evaluation of parent-training interventions for families of chronic delinquents. *Journal of Abnormal Child Psychology, 19*, 15–33.

Barkley, R. A. (1981). *Hyperactive children: A handbook for diagnosis and treatment*. New York: Guilford.

Barkley, R. A. (1987). *Defiant children: A clinician's manual for parent training*. New York: Guilford.

Barkley, R. A. (1990). *Attention-deficit-hyperactivity disorder: A handbook for diagnosis and treatment*. New York: Guilford.

Bates, J. E., Maslin, C. A., & Frankel, K. A. (1985). Attachment security, mother–child interaction, and temperament as predictors of behavior problem ratings at age three years. In I. Bretherton & E. Waters (Eds.), Growing points in attachment theory and research (pp. 167–193). *Monographs of the Society for Research in Child Development, 50*(1-2), Serial No. 209.

Baum, C. G., & Forehand, R. (1981). Long-term follow-up of parent training by use of multiple outcome measures. *Behavior Therapy, 12*, 643–652.

Baumrind, D. (1967). Child care practices anteceding three patterns of preschool behavior. *Genetic Psychology Monographs, 75*, 43–88.

Baumrind, D. (1991). The influence of parenting style on adolescent competence and substance use. *Journal of Early Adolescence, 11,* 56–95.

Bearrs, K., & Eyberg, S. (1996). Construct validity of the Parenting Alliance Inventory. *Early Education and Development.*

Beutler, L. E., & Clarkin, J. E. (1990). *Systematic treatment selection: Toward targeted therapeutic interventions.* New York: Brunner/Mazel.

Biederman, J., Munir, K., & Knee, D. (1987). Conduct and oppositional disorder in clinically referred children with attention-deficit-hyperactivity disorder: A controlled family study. *Journal of the American Academy of Child and Adolescent Psychiatry, 26,* 724–727.

Black, M. M., & Holden, W. E. (1995). Longitudinal intervention research in children's health and development. *Journal of Clinical Child Psychology, 24,* 163–172.

Boggs, S. R. (1990). *Generalization of treatment to the home setting: Direct observation analysis.* In S. Eyberg (Chair), Parent–Child Interaction Therapy (PCIT) outcome studies: Multiple method assessment. Symposium presented at the American Psychological Association, Boston.

Boggs, S. R., Stokes, T. F., & Danforth, J. (1986, August). *Functional problem-solving skills: Increasing the generality of parent training.* Paper presented at the annual meeting of the American Psychological Association, Washington, DC.

Borduin, C. M., Mann, B. J., Cone, L., Henggeler, S. W., Fucci, B. R., Blaske, D. M., & Williams, R. A. (1992). Multisystemic treatment of adolescents referred for serious and repeated antisocial behavior.

Borduin, C. M., Henggeler, S. W.,Blaske, D. M., & Stein, R. (1990). Multisystemic treatment of adolescent sexual offenders. *International Journal of Offender Therapy and Comparative Criminology, 34,* 105–113.

Bowlby, J. (1982). *Attachment and loss: Vol. 2. Separation.* New York: Basic Books.

Brent, D. A., Roth, C. M., Holder, D. P., Kolko, D. J., Birmaher, B., Johnson, B. A., & Schweers, J. A. (1996). Psychosocial interventions for treating adolescent suicidal depression: A comparison of three psychosocial interventions. In E. D. Hibbs & P. S. Jensen (Eds.), *Psychosocial treatments for child and adolescent disorders: Empirically based strategies for clinical practice* (pp. 187–206). Washington, DC: American Psychological Association.

Brestan, E. V., Eyberg, S. M., Boggs, S. R., & Algina, J. (1997). Parent–child interaction therapy: Parent's perceptions of untreated siblings. *Child and Family Behavior Therapy, 19,* 13–28.

Bronfenbrenner, U. (1979). *The ecology of human development.* Cambridge, MA: Harvard University Press.

Campbell, S. B. (1988). The socialization and social development of hyperactive children. In M. Lewis & S. Miller (Eds.), *The handbook of developmental psychopathology.* New York: Plenum Press.

Campbell, S. B. (1990). *Behavior problems in preschool children: Clinical and developmental issues.* New York: Guilford.

Campbell, S. B., & Ewing, L. J. (1990). Follow-up of hard to manage preschoolers: Adjustment at age 9 and predictors of continuing symptoms. *Journal of Child Psychology and Psychiatry, 31,* 871–889.

Capaldo, D., & Patterson, R. (1987). An approach to the problem of recruitment and retention rates for longitudinal research. *Behavioral Assessment, 9,* 169–177.

Cassidy, J., Marvin, R. S., & MacArthur Working Group on Attachment. (1989). *Attachment organization in three- and four-year-olds: Coding Manual.* Unpublished scoring manual.

Cohn, D. A. (1990). Child–mother attachment of six-year-olds and social competence at school. *Child Development, 61,* 152–162.

Cross, T. G. (1981). The linguistic experience of slow language learners. In A. R. Nesdale, C.

Pratt, R. Grieve, J. Field, D. Illingworth, & J. Hogben (Eds.), *Advances in child development*. Proceedings of the First National Conference on Child Development, University of Western Australia.

Cross, T.G. (1984). Habilitating the language impaired child: Ideas from studies of parent–child interaction. *Topics in Language Disorders, 4*, 1–14.

Cunningham, C. E. (1989). A family-systems-oriented training program for parents of language-delayed children with behavior problems. In C. E. Schaefer & J. M. Briesmeister (Eds.), *Handbook of parent training: Parent as cotherapists for children's behavior problems*. New York: Wiley.

Cunningham, C. E., & Barkley, R. A. (1979). The interactions of hyperactive and normal children with their mothers during free play and structured tasks. *Child Development, 50*, 217–224.

Cunningham, C. E., Siegel, L. S., van der Spuy, H. I. J., Clark, M. L., Elbard, H., Nielson, B., & Richards, J. (1983, November). *The effects of parent training, classroom, and community programs on the parent–child interactions, language and cognitive development of language-delayed preschoolers*. Poster presented at the Conference of the Association for the Advancement of Behavior Therapy, Washington, DC.

Denham, S. A., Renwick, S. M., & Holt, R. W. (1991). Working and playing together: Prediction of preschool social-emotional competence from mother–child interaction. *Child Development, 62*, 242–249.

Denicola, J., & Sandler, J. (1980). Training abusive parents in cognitive behavioral techniques. *Behavior Therapy, 11*, 263–270.

Dix, T., Ruble, D. N., & Zambarano, R. J. (1989). Mothers' implicit theories of discipline: Child effects, parent effects, and the attribution process. *Child Development, 60*, 1373–1391.

Dumas, J. E. (1984). Indiscriminant mothering: Empirical findings and theoretical speculation. *Advances in Behavior Research and Therapy, 6*, 13–27.

Dumas, J. E. (1996). Why was this child referred? Interactional correlates of referral status in families of children with disruptive behavior problems. *Journal of Clinical Child Psychology, 25*, 106–115.

Dumas, J. E., LaFreniere, P. J., Beaudin, L., & Verlaan, P. (1992). Mother–child interactions in competent and aggressive dyads: Implications of relationship stress for behavior therapy with families. *New Zealand Journal of Psychology, 21*, 3–13.

Dumas, J. E., & Lechowicz, J. G. (1989). When do noncompliant children comply? Implications for family behavior therapy. *Child and Family Behavior Therapy, 11*, 21–38.

Dumas, J. E., & Wahler, R. G. (1983). Predictors of treatment outcome in parent training: Mother insularity and socioeconomic disadvantage. *Behavioral Assessment, 5*, 301–313.

Dumas, J. E., & Wahler, R. G. (1985). Indiscriminant mothering as a contextual factor in aggressive–oppositional child behavior: "Damned if you do and damned if you don't!" *Journal of Abnormal Child Psychology, 13*, 1–17.

Egeland, B., & Sroufe, L. A. (1981). Developmental sequelae of maltreatment in infancy. *New Directions for Child Development, 11*, 77–92.

Eisenstadt, T. E., Eyberg, S., McNeil, C. B., Newcomb, K., & Funderburk, B. (1993). Parent–child interaction therapy with behavior problem children: Relative effectiveness of two stages and overall treatment outcome. *Journal of Clinical Child Psychology, 22*, 42–51.

Emery, R. E. (1982). Interparental conflict and the children of discord and divorce. *Psychological Bulletin, 92*, 310–330.

Erikson, M. F., Sroufe, L. A., & Egeland, B. (1985). The relationship between quality of attachment and behavior problems in preschool in a high risk sample. In I. Bretherton & E. Waters (Eds.), Growing points in attachment theory and research (pp. 147–186). *Monographs of the Society for Research in Child Development, 50*(1-2), Serial No. 209.

Eyberg, S. M. (1992). Assessing therapy outcome with preschool children: Progress and problems. *Journal of Clinical Child Psychology, 221,* 306–311.

Eyberg, S. M. (1995). Jigsaws: Introduction to the special issue on methodological issues in clinical child psychology research. *Journal of Clinical Child Psychology, 24,* 122–124.

Eyberg, S. M. (August, 1996). Parent–child interaction therapy. In T. Ollendick, *Developmentally based integrated psychotherapy with children: Emerging models.* Symposium presented at the annual meeting of the American Psychological Association, Toronto.

Eyberg, S., Bessmer, J., Newcomb, K., Edwards, D., & Robinson, E. (1994). Dyadic Parent–Child Interaction Coding System II: A manual. *Social and Behavioral Sciences Documents* (Ms. No. 2897). San Raphael, CA: Select Press.

Eyberg, S., & Boggs, S. R. (1989). Parent training for oppositional-defiant preschoolers. In C. E. Schaefer & J. M. Breismeister (Eds.), *Handbook of parent training: Parents as cotherapists for children's behavior problems* (pp. 105–132). New York: Wiley.

Eyberg, S., & Robinson, E. (1982). Parent–child interaction training: Effects on family functioning. *Journal of Clinical Child Psychology, 11,* 130–137.

Eyberg, S., Edwards, D., Boggs, S., & Foote, R. (in press). Maintaining the treatment effects of parent training: The role of "booster sessions" and other maintenance strategies. *Clinical Psychology: Science and Practice.*

Eyberg, S. M., & Boggs, S. R. (in press). Parent–child interaction therapy for oppositional preschoolers. In C. E. Schaefer & J. M. Briesmeister (Eds.), *Handbook of parent training: Parents as co-therapists for children's behavior problems* (2nd ed.). New York: Wiley.

Eyberg, S. M., Boggs, S. R., & Algina, J. (1995). Parent–child interaction therapy: A psychosocial model for the treatment of young children with conduct problem behavior and their families. *Psychopharmacology Bulletin, 31,* 83–91.

Farrington, D. P. (1988). Studying changes within individuals: The causes of offending. In M. Rutter (Ed.), *Studies of psychosocial risk* (pp. 158–183). New York: Cambridge University Press.

Firestone, P., & Witt, J. E. (1982). Characteristics of families completing and prematurely discontinuing behavioral parent training. *Journal of Pediatric Psychology, 7,* 209–222.

Fischer, M., Rolf, J. E., Hasazi, J. E., & Cummings, L. (1984). Follow-up of a preschool epidemiological sample: Cross-age continuities and predictions of later adjustment with internalizing and externalizing dimensions of behavior. *Child Development, 55,* 137–150.

Forehand, R., & Atkeson, B. M. (1977). Generality of treatment effects with parents as therapists: A review of assessment and implementation procedures. *Behavior Therapy, 8,* 575–593.

Forehand, R. L., Cheney, T., & Yoder, P. (1974). Parent behavior training: Effects on the non-compliance of a deaf child. *Journal of Behavior Therapy and Experimental Psychiatry, 5,* 575–593.

Forehand, R. L., Griest, D., & Wells, K. C. (1979). Parent behavioral training: An analysis of the relationship among multiple outcome measures. *Journal of Abnormal Child Psychology, 7,* 228–242.

Forehand, R. L., & King, H. E. (1977). Noncompliant children: Effects of parent training on behavior and attitude change. *Behavior Modification, 1,* 93–108.

Forehand, R. L., & Long, N. (1988). Outpatient treatment of the acting out child: Procedures, long-term follow-up data, and clinical problems. *Advances in Behavior Research and Therapy, 10,* 129–177.

Forehand, R. L., & McMahon, R. J. (1981). *Helping the noncompliant child.* New York: Guilford.

Franz, C. E., McClelland, D. C., & Weinberger, J. (1991). Childhood antecedents of conventional social accomplishment in midlife adults: A 36-year prospective study. *Journal of Personality and Social Psychology, 60,* 586–595.

Greenberg, M. T., & Speltz, M. L. (1988). Contributions of attachment theory to the understanding of conduct problems during the preschool years. In J. Belsky and T. Nezworski (Eds.), *Clinical implications of attachment* (pp. 177–218). Hillsdale, NJ: Erlbaum.

Greenberg, M. T., Speltz, M. L., & DeKlyen, M. (1993). The role of attachment in the early development of disruptive behavior problems. *Development and Psychopathology, 5*, 191–213.

Greenberg, M. T., Speltz, M. L., DeKlyen, M. C., & Endriga, M. C. (1991). Attachment security in preschoolers with and without externalizing problems: A replication. *Development and Psychopathology, 3*, 413–4310.

Guerney, B. G., Jr. (1964). Filial therapy: Description and rationale. *Journal of Consulting Psychology, 28*, 303–310.

Hanf, C. (1969, April). *A two stage program for modifying maternal controlling during mother–child (M-C) interaction.* Paper presented at the meeting of the Western Psychological Association, Vancouver, BC.

Hawkings, J. D., Catalano, R. F., & Miller, J. Y. (1992). Risk and protective factors for alcohol and other drug problems in adolescence and early adulthood: Implications for substance abuse prevention. *Psychological Bulletin, 112*, 64–105.

Henggeler, S. W. (1991). Multidimensional causal models of delinquent behavior and their implications for treatment. In R. Cohen & A. W. Siegel (Eds.), *Context and development* (pp. 211–231). Hillsdale, NJ: Erlbaum.

Henggeler, S. W., & Borduin, C. M. (1990). *Family therapy and beyond: A multisystemic approach to treating the behavior problems of children and adolescents.* Pacific Grove, CA: Brooks/Cole.

Henggeler, S. W., Rodick, J. D., Borduin, C. M., Hanson, C. L., Watson, S. M., & Urey, J. R. (1986). Multisystemic treatment of juvenile offenders: Effects on adolescent behavior and family interaction. *Developmental Psychology, 22*, 132–141.

Hetherington, E. M., & Martin, B. (1986). Family factors and psychopathology in children. In H. C. Quay & J. S. Werry (Eds.), *Psychopathological disorders of childhood* (3rd ed.). New York: Wiley.

Hopman, W. M. (1989). Interactional approaches to parent training. *Childhood Education, 65*, 167–171.

Humphreys, L., Forehand, R., McMahon, R. J., & Roberts, M. W. (1978). Parent behavioral training to modify child noncompliance: Effects on untreated siblings. *Journal of Behavior Therapy, 9*, 235–238.

Isabella, R. A., & Belsky, J. (1991). Interactional synchrony and the origins of infant–mother attachment: A replication study. *Child Development, 62*, 373–384.

Kazdin, A. E. (1987). Treatment of antisocial behavior in children: Current status and future directions. *Psychological Bulletin, 102*, 187–203.

Kazdin, A. E. (1995). Scope of child and adolescent psychotherapy research: Limited sampling of dysfunctions, treatments, and client characteristics. *Journal of Child Clinical Psychology, 24*, 125–140.

Kazdin, A. E. (1996). Problem solving and parent management in treating aggressive and antisocial behavior. In E. D. Hibbs & P. S. Jensen (Eds.), *Psychosocial treatments for child and adolescent disorders: Empirically based strategies for clinical practice* (pp. 386–387). Washington, DC: American Psychological Association.

Kazdin, A. E., Bass, D., Ayers, W. A., & Rodgers, A. (1990). The empirical and clinical focus of child and adolescent psychotherapy research. *Journal of Consulting and Clinical Psychology, 58*, 729–740.

Kendall, P. C., & Clarkin, J. F. (1992). Introduction to special section: Comorbidity and treatment implications. *Journal of Consulting and Clinical Psychology, 60*, 833–834.

Kendall, P. C., & Treadwell, K. R. (1996). Cognitive-behavioral treatment for childhood anxiety disorders. In E. D. Hibbs & P. S. Jensen (Eds.), *Psychosocial treatments for child and adolescent disorders: Empirically based strategies for clinical practice* (pp. 23–41). Washington, DC: American Psychological Association.

Kendziora, K. T., & O'Leary, S. G. (1993). Dysfunctional parenting as a focus for prevention and treatment of child behavior problems. *Advances in Child Psychology, 15,* 175–206.

Lerner, J. A., Inui, T. S., Trupin, E. W., & Douglas, E. (1985). Preschool behavior can predict future psychiatric disorders. *Journal of the American Academy of Child Psychiatry, 24,* 42–48.

Lewinsowhn, P. M., Clarke, G. N., Rohde, P., Hops, H., & Seeley, J. R. (1996). A course in coping: A cognitive-behavioral approach to the treatment of adolescent depression. In E. D. Hibbs & P. S. Jensen (Eds.), *Psychosocial treatments for child and adolescent disorders: Empirically based strategies for clinical practice* (pp. 109–135). Washington, DC: American Psychological Association.

Loeber, R. (1990). Development and risk factors of juvenile antisocial behavior and delinquency. *Clinical Psychology Review, 10,* 1–41.

Loeber, R., & Dishion, T. J. (1983). Early predictors of male delinquency: A review. *Psychological Bulletin, 94,* 68–99.

Long, P., Forehand, R., Wierson, M., & Morgan, A. (1994). Does parent training with young noncompliant children have long-term effects? *Behavior Research and Therapy, 32,* 101–107.

Maccoby, E. E., & Martin, J. (1983). Socialization in the context of the family: Parent–child interaction. In P. Mussen (Ed.), *Handbook of child psychology* (Vol. 2, pp. 1–101). New York: Wiley.

MacDonald, K. (1992). Warmth as a developmental construct: An evolutionary analysis. *Child Development, 63,* 753–773.

Main, M., & Cassidy, J. (1985). *Assessments of child–parent attachment at six years of age.* Unpublished scoring manual.

Main, M., & Cassidy, J. (1988). Categories of response to reunion with the parent at age six: Predictable from infant attachment classifications and stable over a one-month period. *Developmental Psychology, 24,* 415–426.

Main, M., Cassidy, J., & Kaplan, N. (1985). Security in infancy, childhood, and adulthood: A move to the level of representation. In I. Bretherton & E. Waters (Eds.), Growing points in attachment theory and research (pp. 64–104). *Monographs of the Society for Research in Child Development, 50*(1-2), Serial No. 209.

Main, M., & Hesse, E. (1990). Adult lack of resolution of attachment-related trauma related to infant disorganized/disoriented behavior in the Ainsworth strange situation: Linking parental states of mind to infant behavior in a stressful situation. In M. T. Greenberg, D. Cicchetti, & M. Cummings (Eds.), *Attachment in the preschool years: Theory, research and intervention* (pp. 339–426). Chicago: University of Chicago Press.

Malatesta-Magai, C. (1991). Emotional socialization: Its role in personality and developmental psychopathology: *Rochester Symposium on Developmental Psychopathology: Vol. 2. Internalizing and externalizing expressions of dysfunction* (pp. 203–224). Hillsdale, NJ: Erlbaum.

Mann, B. J., Borduin, C. M., Henggeler, S. W., & Blaske, D. M. (1990). An investigation of systemic conceptualizations of parent–child coalitions and symptom change. *Journal of Consulting and Clinical Psychology, 58,* 336–344.

Mash, E. J., & Terdal, L. G. (1980). Follow-up assessment in behavior therapy. In P. Karoly & J. Steffan (Eds.). *The long-range effects of psychotherapy: Models of durable outcome* (pp. 99–147). New York: Gardner.

McMahon, R. J., Forehand, R., Griest, D. L., & Wells, K. C. (1981). Who drops out of treatment during parent behavioral training? *Behavioral Counseling Quarterly, 1,* 79–85.

McNeil, C., Eyberg, S., Eisenstadt, T., Newcomb, K., & Funderburk, B. (1991). Parent–child interaction therapy with behavior problem children: Generalization of treatment effects to the school setting. *Journal of Clinical Child Psychology, 20,* 140–151.

Miller, G. E., & Prinz, R. J. (1990). Enhancement of social learning family interventions for childhood conduct disorder. *Psychological Bulletin, 108,* 291–307.

Newcomb, K. E. (1995). *The long-term effectiveness of parent–child interaction therapy with behavior problem children and their families: A two-year follow-up.* Unpublished doctoral dissertation, University of Florida, Gainesville.

Offord, D. R., Boyle, M. C., & Racine, Y. A. (1991). The epidemiology of antisocial behavior in childhood and adolescence. In D. J. Pepler & K. H. Rubin (Eds.), *The development and treatment of childhood aggression* (pp. 31–54). Hillsdale, NJ: Erlbaum.

Olson, S. L., Bates, J. E., & Bayles, K. (1990). Early antecedents of childhood hyperactivity: The role of parent–child interaction, cognitive competence, and temperament. *Journal of Abnormal Child Psychology, 18,* 317–334.

Oxman, L. (1971). *The effectiveness of filial therapy: A controlled study.* Unpublished doctoral dissertation, Rutgers University, New Brunswick, NJ.

Parpal, M., & Maccoby, E. (1985). Maternal responsiveness and subsequent child compliance. *Child Development, 56,* 1326–1334.

Patterson, G. R. (1974). Interventions for boys with conduct problems: Multiple settings, treatments, and criteria. *Journal of Consulting and Clinical Psychology, 42,* 471–481.

Patterson, G. R. (1976). The aggressive child: Victim and architect of a coercive system. In E. Mash, L. Hamerlynck, & L. Handy (Eds.), *Behavior modification and families* (pp. 267–316). New York: Brunner/Mazel.

Patterson, G. R. (1982). *A social learning approach to family intervention: III. Coercive family process.* Eugene, OR: Castalia.

Patterson, G. R. (1986). Performance models for antisocial boys. *American Psychologist, 41,* 432–444.

Patterson, G. R., & Fleischman, M. J. (1979). Maintenance of treatment effects: Some considerations concerning family systems and follow-up data. *Behavior Therapy, 10,* 168–185.

Peed, S., Roberts, M., & Forehand, R. (1977). Evaluation of the effectiveness of a standardized parent training program in altering the interaction of mothers and their noncompliant children. *Behavior Modification, 1,* 323–350.

Pisterman, S., McGrath, P., Firestone, P., Goodman, J., Webster, I., & Mallory, R. (1989). Outcome of parent-mediated treatment of preschoolers with attention deficit disorder with hyperactivity. *Journal of Consulting and Clinical Psychology, 57,* 628–635.

Pisterman, S., McGrath, P., Firestone, P., Goodman, J., Webster, I., Mallory, R., & Goffin, B. (1992). The effects of parent training on parenting stress and sense of competence. *Canadian Journal of Behavioral Science, 24,* 41–58.

Pollard, S., Ward, E. M., & Barkley, R. A. (1983). The effects of parent training and Ritalin on the parent–child interactions of hyperactive boys. *Child and Family Therapy, 5,* 51–69.

Power, T. G., & Chapieski, M. L. (1986). Child rearing and impulse control in toddlers: A naturalistic investigation. *Developmental Psychology, 22,* 271–275.

Prinz, R. J., & Miller, G. E. (1991) Issues in understanding and treating childhood conduct problems in disadvantaged populations. *Journal of Clinical Child Psychology, 20,* 379–385.

Prinz, R. J., & Miller, G. E. (1994). Family-based treatment for childhood antisocial behavior: Experimental influences on dropout and engagement. *Journal of Consulting and Clinical Psychology, 62,* 645–650.

Reid, J. B., & Patterson, G. R. (1976). The modification of aggression and stealing behavior of boys in a home setting. In E. Ribes-Inesta & A. Bandura (Eds.), *Analysis of delinquency and aggression* (pp. 123–145). Hillsdale, NJ: Erlbaum.

Reisinger, J. J., Frangia, G. W., & Hoffman, E. H. (1976). Toddler management training: Generalization and marital status. *Journal of Behavior Therapy and Experimental Psychiatry, 7*, 335–340.

Richters, J. E., & Waters, E. (1991). Attachment and socialization: The positive side of social influence. In M. Lewis & S. Feinman (Eds.), *Social influences and socialization in infancy* (pp. 185–213). New York: Plenum Press.

Robinson, E. A. (1985). Coercion theory revisited: Toward a new theoretical perspective on the etiology of conduct disorders. *Clinical Psychology Review, 5*, 597–625.

Sandler, J., Van Dercar, C., & Milhoan, M. (1978). Training child abusers in the use of positive reinforcement practices. *Behavior Research and Therapy, 16*, 169–175.

Sensue, M. E. (1981). *Filial therapy follow-up study: Effects on parental acceptance and child adjustment.* Unpublished doctoral dissertation, Pennsylvania State University, University Park, PA.

Schuhmann, E. M., Durning, P. E., Eyberg, S. M., & Boggs, S. R. (1996). Screening for conduct problem behavior in pediatric settings using the Eyberg Child Behavior Inventory. *Ambulatory Child Health, 2*, 35–41.

Snyder, J. J. (1977). Reinforcement analysis of interaction in problem and non-problem families. *Journal of Abnormal Psychology, 86*, 528–535.

Speltz, M. L., Greenberg, M. T., & DeKlyen, M. (1990). Attachment in preschoolers with disruptive behavior: A comparison of clinic-referred and non-problem children. *Development and Psychopathology, 2*, 31–46.

Sroufe, L. A. (1983). Infant caregiver attachment and patterns of adaptation in preschool: The roots of maladaptation and competence. In M. Perlmutter (Ed.), *Minnesota Symposium on Child Psychology* (Vol. 16, pp. 41–81). Hillsdale, NJ: Erlbaum.

Sroufe, L. A., Egeland, B., & Kreutzer, T. (1990). The fate of early experience following developmental change: Longitudinal approaches to individual adaptation in childhood. *Child Development, 61*, 1363–1373.

Stark, K. D., Swearer, S., Kurowski, C., Sommer, D., & Bowen, B. (1996). Targeting the child and the family: A holistic approach to treating child and adolescent depressive disorders. In E. D. Hibbs & P. S. Jensen (Eds.), *Psychosocial treatments for child and adolescent disorders: Empirically based strategies for clinical practice* (pp. 207–238). Washington, DC: American Psychological Association.

Stern, D. N. (1985). *The interpersonal world of the infant.* New York: Basic Books.

Stover, L., & Guerney, B. G., Jr. (1967). The efficacy of training procedures for mothers in filial therapy. *Psychotherapy: Theory, Research and Practice, 4*, 110–115.

Strain, P. S., Young, C. C., & Horowitz, J. (1981). Generalized behavior change: During oppositional child training. *Behavior Modification, 5*, 15–26.

Sywulak, A. E. (1977). *The effect of filial therapy on parental acceptance and child adjustment.* Unpublished doctoral dissertation, Pennsylvania State University, University Park, PA.

Turner, P. (1991). Relations between attachment, gender, and behavior with peers in the preschool. *Child Development, 62*, 1475–1488.

Wahler, R. G. (1980). The insular mother: Her problems in parent–child treatment. *Journal of Applied Behavior Analysis, 13*, 207–219.

Wahler, R. G., Winkel, G. H., Peterson, R.F., & Morrison, D.C. (1965). Mothers as behavior therapists for their own children. *Behavior Research and Therapy, 3*, 113–124.

Webster-Stratton, C. (1981a). Modification of mother's behavior and attitudes through a videotape modeling group discussion program. *Behavior Therapy, 12*, 634–642.

Webster-Stratton, C. (1981b). Videotape modeling: A method of parent education. *Journal of Clinical Child Psychology, 10*, 93–97.

Webster-Stratton, C. (1982a). Long-term effects of a videotape modeling parent education program: Comparison of immediate and 1-year follow-up results. *Behavior Therapy, 13,* 702–714.

Webster-Stratton, C. (1982b). Teaching mothers through videotape modeling to change their children's behaviors. *Journal of Pediatric Psychology, 7,* 279–294.

Webster-Stratton, C. (1984). Randomized trial of two parent training programs for families with conduct disordered children. *Journal of Consulting and Clinical Psychology, 52,* 666–678.

Webster-Stratton, C. (1985). Predictors of treatment outcome in parent training for conduct disordered children. *Behavior Therapy, 16,* 223–243.

Webster-Stratton, C. (1987). *Parents and children: A 10-program videotape parent training series with manuals.* Eugene, OR: Castalia Press.

Webster-Stratton, C. (1990). Enhancing the effectiveness of self-administered videotape parent training for families with conduct-problem children. *Journal of Abnormal Child Psychology, 18,* 479–492.

Webster-Stratton, C. (1994). Advancing videotape parent training: A comparison study. *Journal of Consulting and Clinical Psychology, 62,* 583–593.

Wells, K. C., Forehand, R., & Griest, D. L. (1980). Generality of treatment effects from treated to untreated behaviors resulting from a parent training program. *Behavior Research and Therapy, 18,* 347–358.

Wolfe, D., & Sandler, J. (1981). Training abusive parents in effective child management. *Behavior Modification, 5,* 320–335.

Wolfe, D. A., Sandler, J., & Kaufman, K. (1981). A competency-based parent training program for child abusers. *Journal of Consulting and Clinical Psychology, 49,* 633–640.

Zangwill, W. M. (1984). An evaluation of a parent training program. *Child and Family Behavior Therapy, 5,* 1–16.

5

Children's Perception of Physical Symptoms

The Example of Asthma

SIMON RIETVELD AND PIER J. M. PRINS

1. Introduction to Symptom Perception

Distinction between physiological changes and the conscious awareness of associated sensations and symptoms is a common phenomenon in health and disease. Throughout the chapter, the term *sensation* will be used to denote what subjects feel, whereas the term *symptom* will be used in association with a pathological condition.

Generally, human beings are incapable of *accurately* perceiving vegetative functions as well as pathophysiological reactions, such as heartbeat, blood-glucose level, and cancer or asthmatic airway obstruction (Gannon, 1984; Skelton & Croyle, 1991). These phenomena are the topic of symptom perception research, a relatively new field of medical psychology. Specific knowledge on children's symptom perception is just beginning to be established (Pennebaker, 1982). This chapter introduces symptom perception as a concept to explain and understand the often remarkable discordance between objective and subjective symptoms of disease. Contemporary models describing symptom perception and factors that influence these symptom perceptual processes are evaluated in light of recent empirical advantages.

The accuracy of symptom perception is defined in terms of the relationship between objective (physiological) and subjective variables. However, *accurate symptom perception* is a relative term, because for human beings a continuous flow of specific afferent stimulation would be impos-

SIMON RIETVELD AND PIER J. M. PRINS • Department of Clinical Psychology, University of Amsterdam, 1018 WB Amsterdam, The Netherlands.

Advances in Clinical Child Psychology, Volume 20, edited by Thomas H. Ollendick and Ronald J. Prinz. Plenum Press, New York, 1998.

sible to cope with. In the course of development, children learn to interpret specific peripheral stimuli as high-order sensations, such as hunger, fatigue, or breathlessness. Nevertheless, with respect to disease, it is surprising that physiological deviations with harmful consequences remain largely unrecognized or cannot be perceived with more specificity.

Accurate symptom perception in disease encompasses (1) early awareness of pathophysiology, and (2) a close relationship between pathophysiology and magnitude of subjective complaints. The exception of a linear relationship between objective and subjective symptoms is based on psychophysics, where subjective sensation is a logarithmic function of physiological change. Two basic assumptions in this model are that the physiological changes are variable and that all other factors are held constant. In reality, subjective sensations are not coded in the same way as the underlying physiological changes are measured, whereas other factors are very rarely constant (Pennebaker, 1982). The difference between objective and subjective symptoms is highlighted by an abundance of clinical cases of patients who do not recognize a serious condition in time for proper medical treatment, which shows that the adequate perception of serious symptoms is often illusionary.

The perceptual systems are an inheritance of the early human environment. Unfortunately, this "kindergarten" of human development did not provide the broad range of medical remedies for rapidly and properly perceived symptoms. Hence, accurate symptom perception was not selected during human phylogenetic development.

In this chapter, symptom perception is viewed as a process that is subject to a variety of influences, both within and outside the individual. The output of the symptom perceptual process can be formalized by borrowing response options from signal detection theory (Green & Swets, 1966): (1) correct awareness of a symptom; (2) correct awareness of a normal sensation; (3) false awareness of a symptom (during a normal condition); and (4) false awareness of a normal sensation (during a pathological condition). Although a false-negative response (option 3) may be as inaccurate as a false-positive one (option 4), the latter would imply neglect of actual pathology and thereby pose a threat to health and survival. On the other hand, erroneously "perceiving" the symptoms of a pathological condition can lead to unnecessary consumption of possibly dangerous medication, as well as negative affect and unwarranted illness behavior.

The concept of symptom perception is often overlooked when discussing issues in medical psychology. For instance, the four response options may also be applied to understand aspects of unexplained pain, lack of compliance with a medical regimen, placebo responses, somatoform disorders, and fatal pathophysiology that is not recognized in time for treatment.

A striking feature of symptom perception is the impressive variability in perceptual accuracy, both between and within subjects (Gannon & Haynes, 1986; Pennebaker, 1982). For instance, several investigators in respiratory diseases have claimed that differences in the accuracy of symptom perception cannot be understood within medical parameters (Jones, 1992; Pratter & Barter, 1991). Because biofeedback research shows that neural pathways are often available and that subjects can learn to master the use of at least some of them, psychological or situational factors may explain differences in symptom perception.

The study of symptom perception is interesting from both a theoretical and clinical point of view; it can be studied, for example, in diabetes mellitus, childhood cancer, or asthma. There are three arguments why asthma provides an excellent opportunity to study children's symptom perception in chronic disease. First, asthma may turn into a life-threatening condition, provoking cognitions and emotions that are believed to play an important role in symptom perception. Second, asthma is characterized by remarkable fluctuations in symptom severity, ranging from the absence of symptoms to high severity, allowing investigation of a complete asthma attack. Third, objective, pathophysiological variables as well as subjective symptoms of asthma can quickly, validly, and reliably be measured.

In the next section, childhood asthma is introduced, and specific features of asthma as well as general features of chronic diseases are addressed. Then, seven biomedical and psychological factors that explain aspects of symptom perception are evaluated. Finally, developmental and gender issues are examined. The chapter attempts to integrate this corpus of knowledge and to formulate a new perspective on children's perception of physical symptoms in chronic disease.

2. Childhood Asthma

Obstructive pulmonary diseases range from episodic exacerbations of airway obstruction (asthma) to more chronic obstructive diseases, as are usually diagnosed in adults, such as chronic obstructive pulmonary disease and emphysema. Asthma is the most common chronic disorder in childhood, affecting up to 10% of school-aged children in the Western world (Creer & Gustafson, 1989). Asthma is characterized by airway hypersensitivity to a number of stimuli (e.g., animal products, smoke, and physical exercise). There are acute reactions of airway smooth muscle constriction, as well as long-term or chronic inflammation and edema of lung tissue (Sterk & Bell, 1989). Clinical manifestations are episodic attacks of airway obstruction association with difficult breathing, asthmatic wheezing sounds, coughing, breathlessness (dyspnea), and eventually hypoxia and cardiorespiratory arrest (Rietveld & Dooijes, 1996). Considering that a life-threatening attack of airway obstruction can develop within 1 hour, accurate symptom perception is essential for the early medication of symptoms (Carswell, 1985). Other benefits of accurate symptom perception would be that children learn to leave asthma-provoking situations in time, favoring perceived control over symptoms and elevated self-efficacy, which in turn are likely to decrease illness-related distress (Bandura, 1990; Pennebaker, Burnam, Schaeffer, & Harper, 1977; Yellowlees & Kalucy, 1990). Alternatively, poor symptom perception poses a major threat to children's well-being. A young boy who loves swimming but is forced to stop with his sport after repeated accidents in the swimming pool may eventually develop depression. The adolescent girl who experiences unexpected attacks of faintness in the discotheque may be desperate with embarrassment and may suffer from a loss of self-esteem. Statistics confirm the high incidence of emotional problems in asthmatic children and of psychopathology in asthmatic adults (Boyce et al., 1995; Yellowlees & Ruffin, 1989).

2.1. Symptom Perception in Asthma

In symptom perception research in asthma at least two variables need to be measured and compared: lung function and breathlessness. A practical definition of the accuracy of symptom perception would be a high correlation between subjective degrees of breathlessness and objective lung function parameters, which, in turn, reflect airway obstruction. The assessment of lung function is usually conducted with a spirometer by a lung function technician. The subject is breathing through a mouthpiece, quietly as well as with maximum effort, while wearing a nose clip. Common lung function parameters are the *vital capacity, peak expiratory flow,* and the *forced expiratory volume in one second,* the latter being the golden standard of lung physicians. In order to measure fluctuations in peak expiratory flow, peak flow meters are increasingly used by family doctors and asthmatic patients in the home situation. After initial testing, asthmatics become familiar with their regular values and may use deviations as a basis for medication. Generally, the assessment of lung function in children under 7 years of age may be very difficult, restricting symptom perception research to the older age groups.

Breathlessness is the sensation associated with difficult, labored breathing, and common descriptions include shortness of breath, tightness of the chest, and wheeziness. Breathlessness is usually measured with self-report scales, such as a Likert-type or a visual analogue scale. The etiology of the breathlessness response is still a subject of dispute. This illustrates that the origin of the subjective symptoms associated with a disease is often diffuse, puzzling clinicians and experimenters alike.

Over the years, the occurrence of breathlessness has been related to arterial gas mixtures, particularly to increased levels of carbon dioxide. In a series of classic psychophysic experiments, Campbell and colleagues refuted the importance of gas mixtures in the etiology of the breathlessness response and tested the alternative hypothesis that breathlessness is caused by afferent information from the respiratory muscles (Campbell, Godfrey, Clark, Freedman, & Norman, 1969; Campbell, Robson, & Norman, 1967). They tested this by blocking the afferent pathways with curare. Indeed, the paralysis significantly lengthened the time that the subjects could hold their breath without breathlessness. Their model predicts that the intensity of breathlessness not only arises as the tension in the inspiratory muscles increases, but also as their length becomes smaller and the inspiratory airflow increases, hence the term *length–tension inappropriateness*. This model properly explains that breathlessness during prolonged exercise results from an increase in both motor command and respiratory effort due to inspiratory muscle fatigue.

Nevertheless, some investigators have maintained that afferent information from respiratory muscles is not a necessary condition to evoke breathlessness and instead presented findings that supported the assumed influence of gas mixtures (Banzett, Lansing, Reid, Adams, & Brown, 1989). For example, with a sample of quadriplegic adults paralyzed below the neck and fully dependent upon mechanical ventilation of gases, Banzett et al. (1990) showed that increased carbon dioxide in the administered gas mixture indeed caused substantial "air hunger." Unfortunately, research has yielded mixed results, supporting and refuting predictions by the two models. For instance, contrary to expectations, normal adults reported no breathlessness either during respectively high levels of arterial carbon dioxide, or during voluntarily breathing as during an asthma attack (Adams, Lane, Shea, Cockcroft, & Guz, 1985).

Results of a recent study by Rietveld (1997) also provided no support for the assumption that breathlessness follows difficult, labored breathing. Normal adolescents reported mild levels of breathlessness during respectively one 30-minute, or two 30-minute trials of labored breathing through a face mask, which interrupted airflow to a degree analogous to a severe asthma attack. Some of these subjects were quite at ease while reading a magazine during breathing against an interruption of 64% reduction in lung function. Continuous monitoring of respiration sounds in another study by Rietveld (1996a) showed that children often did not wake up during severe asthma attacks at night. It is evident from these findings that the afferent sensory information associated with respiratory changes often lacks clarity and specificity.

Whereas the above studies demonstrate that breathlessness is not a sensitive marker of airway obstruction or inadequate ventilation of gases, breathlessness is also not specific for these conditions. In fact, breathlessness is common in normal controls (e.g., after physical exercise, as well as during anxiety attacks in patients with agoraphobia or panic disorder; Carr, Lehrer, & Hochron, 1992). As a consequence, the current view on the etiology of breathlessness centers around the notion of a multisystem control of respiratory adequacy, in accordance with metabolic demands, most of which takes place beyond awareness.

Because it is difficult to induce a complete asthma-like attack of airway obstruction, an analogous method of externally applied resistive loads on breathing has been used to investigate symptom perception in obstructive respiratory disease. In line with signal detection theory, responses to a series of sensory stimuli are assessed, usually airflow interruptions of varying intensity (Green & Swets, 1966). The distinction between the perception of actual symptoms and the analogous signal-detection method addresses the difference between the conscious perception of a pathological stimulus and the associated aversive sensations of breathlessness. This distinction has been neglected in (medical) studies using the term *breathlessness perception*, but should be advocated (Barness, 1992, 1994; Burdon, Juniper, Killian, Hargreave, & Campbell, 1982; Burdon, Pain, Rubinfeld, & Nana, 1994; Teramoto, 1995).

Theoretically, each stimulus relevant to human survival is believed to be emotionally connotated and to trigger extensive cognitive and emotional elaboration. This elaboration can be directed to particular aspects of a stimulus. Instead of focusing on the actual stimulus features, subjects may unconsciously mobilize interpretative cognitive strategies to attend to either the objective, sensory component of the stimulus, or to the subjective, cognitive, and evaluative components (Pennebaker, 1982). Consequently, airflow detection or perception of asthma symptoms may be a perceptual event without negative emotions being involved. On the other hand, patients with obstructive diseases may report aversive sensations without actually knowing that something is wrong with their airways (Dirks & Schraa, 1983; Rietveld, 1996a). A child may feel miserable and complain of the flu, when in fact a severe degree of airway obstruction could explain the condition. A 10-year-old boy in a study by Rietveld (1996a) reported chronic fatigue, which his mother attributed to family problems (divorce); however, lung function testing revealed a reduction of up to 70% of the capacity predicted for a healthy boy.

Although the perception of airway obstruction and the sensation of breathlessness are usually mutually influential, they should be regarded as distinct response systems. In this respect, the classic psychological definition of breathlessness is still valid (although subjects may feel breathless without recognizing its origin): "Breathlessness encompasses (a) the real or fantasized perception of airway obstruction, as well as, (b) the reaction to this perception" (Heim, Blaser, & Waidelich, 1972). The difference between perception and breathlessness is evident from the modest correlation (r = .31) between the accuracy of detection of airflow obstruction and the accuracy of perception of actual airway obstruction (Mas, Dahme, & Richter, 1992). In clinical reality, asthmatics may consider themselves symptom-free in the midst of an asthma attack, whereas they may also report severe breathlessness without airway obstruction (Boulet, Deschesnes, Turcotte, & Gignac, 1991).

Clinicians may commonly observe patients with very poor lung function who produce obvious asthmatic wheezing sounds, but who maintain that they feel quite well. By testing the physical condition of school-aged children, school physicians or epidemiologists often diagnose asthma in children who are unaware of having the disease. In the often-cited study by Rubinfeld and Pain (1977), approximately 15% of adult asthmatics were incapable of perceiving a reduction as large as 50% in lung function. Other experimental data confirmed that some asthmatics are completely incompetent perceivers of airway obstruction, and that probably all asthmatics may occasionally fail to perceive the symptoms of asthma properly (McFadden, Kiser, & de Groot, 1973; Perrin, MacLean, & Perrin, 1989; Silverman et al., 1987; Wolkove et al., 1992; Yamamoto, Inaba, Nishimura, Kishi, & Kawakami, 1978). Detection experiments—with all variables being held constant except for resistive load intensity—also showed that a majority of subjects poorly perceive differences in airflow obstruction (Burki, Mitchel, Chaudhary, Zechman, & Campbell, 1978).

Children seem also be to inaccurate in the perception of airway obstruction, although experimental results are just beginning to provide insight into their perceptual capacity (Ergood, Epstein, Ackerman, & Fireman, 1985; Sly, Landau, & Weymouth, 1985). For example, in a study by Rietveld, Prins, and Kolk (1996d) only 7 of 36 children with asthma had a "just noticeable difference" (analogous to a reduction in lung function of 64%), compared with 16 of 36 normal controls. Note that in signal detection theory, a just noticeable difference (jnd) is defined as the stimulus intensity that is properly detected in >50% of stimulus presentations. Ten of the normal controls in this study had also a jnd at the stimulus intensity analogous to 39%. Whereas some children responded remarkably accurately within seconds to airflow interruptions, other youngsters did not respond at all, or responded falsely.

To summarize, the accuracy of symptom perception in asthma is assessed by measuring and comparing lung function and breathlessnes, or by means of the analogous method of detecting external airflow interruptions. Clinical and experimental studies showed that adults and children are predominantly inaccurate perceivers of airway obstruction, although some asthmatics can quite properly perceive an upcoming attack of asthma and may accurately estimate the state of their airways.

Thus, inaccurate symptom perception is not a general characteristic of asthma. Breathlessness is a highly subjective sensation. Moreover, its origin is subject to debate, and its magnitude is not well understood.

3. Factors Influencing Symptom Perception

There are at least seven factors that influence symptom perception in asthma, and most of these factors would be applicable to symptom perception in other chronic diseases as well. The factors refer to biomedical and psychological influences.

3.1. Biomedical Factors

Biomedical factors consist of biological circadian influences, differences in pathophysiology, and organic or neurological pathology.

3.1.1. Biological Circadian Influences

The correlations between breathlessness and lung function are generally significantly smaller in the afternoon than in the early morning. This suggests a biological/circadian influence on the accuracy of symptom perception (Bagg & Hughes, 1980; Peiffer, Marsac, & Lockhart, 1989). Obviously, circadian influences are often difficult to assess and may be intertwined with other influences, such as the competition of stimulus cues as described below.

3.1.2. Differences in Pathophysiology

In asthma and other obstructive respiratory diseases, three general and overlapping physiological explanations for variance in accuracy of symptom perception are present. The mediators between pathophysiology and perceptual accuracy include the different clusters of receptors and afferent pathways involved.

Acute versus gradual or chronic airway obstruction. There is modest support that acute obstructive reactions are more accurately perceived and evaluated than a gradual deterioration of airway quality (Rietveld, 1997; Turcotte, Corbeil, & Boulet, 1990). In other words, the perception of acute smooth muscle contraction is perceived more accurately than chronic obstruction due to airway inflammation and edema. The contraction of smooth muscles, for instance, to protect against inhalation of noxious gases, would be an adaptive response, likely to reach awareness. An explanation for the phenomenon of absence of breathlessness during airway obstruction would be that asthmatics habituate to the modest signals associated with a prolonged or chronic obstruction (Bonnel, Mathiot, Jungas, & Grimaud, 1987). Breathlessness is associated with physical exercise and fatigue, and, eventually, asthmatics with prolonged or chronic obstruction may learn to protect themselves against breathlessness by restricting high-energy activities.

Acute obstructive reactions, however, could overwhelm asthmatics in the midst of an activity and would be reflected in relatively high breathlessness. Consequently, acute versus chronic obstructive reactions would be associated with robust differences in accuracy of symptom perception, although this has not been studied systematically. Rietveld (1997) found no support for habituation in a sample of normal adolescents in a signal detection experiment. While subjects were breathing through a face mask and a tube device that interrupted airflow, breathlessness did not diminish after an hour of labored breathing. Other studies have revealed that repeated exposure to external airflow obstruction leads to diminished breathlessness reporting upon subsequent occasions (Wilson & Jones, 1990). A similar effect with actual airway obstruction in asthma patients should be doubted, however, as we will argue in a later section (see 3.2).

Different agents provoking obstructive reaction. Asthma can be provoked by a variety of stimuli, and various patterns of subjective responses are likely (Rietveld, 1996a). High levels of breathlessness in asthmatic children during histamine provocation (which is an aversive test to assess hyperresponsiveness of airways) as compared to physical exercise has been attributed to excessive saliva and mucus secretion, and test-related distress (Rietveld, 1996a). However, Turcotte et al. (1990) found no significant difference in breathlessness reporting by adult asthmatics during three different forms of induction of airway obstruction. Although children may respond differently to a particular medical setting than adults, a problem is that secondary symptoms or levels of negative affect are generally not assessed in symptom perception research.

Central versus peripheral airway obstruction. Sensory information from obstruction in the central airways may be different from sensory information from central as well as peripheral obstruction, although this difference may not be evident from lung function parameters (McFadden, 1975). For instance, asthmatics could experience breathlessness associated with peripheral airway obstruction, which could be underestimated by a peak flow meter. Naturally, this would affect the correlation between breathlessness and lung function.

To summarize, differences in pathophysiology may often influence the relationship between objective and subjective variables, affecting the accuracy of symptom perception. The three factors described would often be overlapping and may be difficult to test and control in symptom perception research.

3.1.3. Organic or Neurological Pathology

An influential assumption in symptom perception research has been that the accuracy of symptom perception can be affected by a deterioration of receptor sensitivity and neurological pathways, resulting from chronic pulmonary pathology (Cherniack, 1987). Detection experiments provided some support for this assumption, because normal controls generally performed somewhat better than asthmatics, whereas the latter performed better than patients with chronic obstructive pulmonary disease (Burki et al., 1978; Cote, Leblanc, & Boulet, 1987; Gottfried, Altose, Kelsen, & Cherniack, 1981). This suggests that some variance in accuracy of symptom perception can be explained by variables denoting airway quality. However, Montserrat et al. (1988) found no effect of severe asthma and near-fatal asthma attacks on the ability to detect external resistive loads on breathing. Other empirical studies showed that the accuracy of symptom perception generally does not relate to objective variables of asthma, such as duration of the disease, symptom severity, prescribed medication, airway hyperresponsiveness, or current lung function (Burdon et al., 1982; Janson-Bjerklie, Ruma, Stulbarg, & Kohlman-Carrieri, 1987; Rietveld, 1996a; Rubinfeld & Pain, 1977). This suggests that pathophysiology may affect the accuracy of symptom perception in asthma only occasionally.

An evaluation of the three biomedical factors indicates support for the general notion that these factors are of some importance, but convincing empirical data on group effects have not been presented in the literature. To the contrary, results have shown that subjective symptoms are generally independent of objective, medical variables. In addition, these biomedical influences would usually remain beyond testable parameters for a psychologist.

3.2. Psychological Factors

The psychological factors consist of competition of sensory information, selective perception, cognitive compensation, and emotional influences.

3.2.1. Competition of Sensory Information

A basic model in symptom perception research relates to the competition between internal and external stimuli (Blitz & Dinnerstein, 1977; Pennebaker & Lightner, 1980). The main idea is that the human capacity to process sensory information is limited and that the probability of noticing internal cues can be expressed as a function of the ratio of available internal and external information. For instance, with an abundance of external stimulation, hardly any capacity for processing internal cues is left. Cioffi (1991) illustrated this by pointing toward a sudden worsening of an ache or pain in the dead of night, as the house grows still, and the previously ignored internal state comes to attention. This is also illustrated by the fact that children's complaints of breathlessness are more severe at night than during daytime, irrespective of degree of airway obstruction (Weiss, 1966). In an experiment with adult subjects who performed an exercise task of treadmill running, it was found that those who listened to magnified street noise reported significantly less bodily symptoms than those who were not distracted by sounds (Pennebaker & Lightner, 1980). The subjects in a third condition listened to magnified breath sounds and reported the most symptoms, which was interpreted in line with the concept. However, the manipulation in this condition could best be interpreted in terms of selective attention (see next paragraph).

In a second experiment, subjects ran significantly faster across country than on a monotonous training track, although the physiological parameters in the two settings were similar. The result supported the hypothesis that running pace depends on the perception of fatigue, and that subjects processed more internal cues on the training track—facilitating perception of fatigue—than running across country (Pennebaker, 1982). Pennebaker extrapolated these experimental results to lifestyle and medical consumption. People with demanding jobs and a rich social life would be less likely to report symptoms than those unemployed and lonely, presumably because their highly taxed processing capacities only allow for "real emergencies."

The concept of a "competition of cues" seems attractive for the explanation of variance in the accuracy of symptom perception, particularly the within-subject variability. However, several studies provided mixed empirical support for the concept. Fillingim and Fine (1986) studied joggers in an exercise setting and observed that distraction only influenced task-related symptoms. In another experiment, adult subjects rated their heartbeat while watching a variety of slides. The degree of interest for the slides correlated significantly with heartbeat estimates ($r = -.51$), showing that very interesting slides coincided with a poor estimation of heartbeat.

However, the accuracy was similar for pleasant or aversive, interesting or boring, slides (Pennebaker, 1982).

A limitation of the concept of "a competition of cues" was elucidated in one of our signal detection experiments with samples of asthmatic and nonasthmatic children who were to detect externally applied airflow interruptions. Children generally responded less frequently to perceived airflow interruptions when they were distracted by the external stimulation of film clips (Rietveld, Kolk, Prins, & Van Beest, 1996a). Because there were much fewer false-positive responses during distraction, the overall accuracy of detection remained similar in nonasthmatic children and improved significantly in asthmatics. This may indicate that the quality (correct responses) and quantity of responses (correct + false responses) should be differentiated in the "competition of cues" model (Fillingim, Roth, & Haley, 1988; Williams & Lees-Haley, 1993).

3.2.2. Selective Perception

Symptom perception comprises the integration of afferent stimuli with knowledge structures from memory. Instead of passive information processors, human beings can be activated to attend selectively to particular sensations that influence the outcome of their symptom perception. In other words, whereas afferent sensory information may eventually reach conscious awareness (bottom-up information processing), selective attention may facilitate conscious awareness of symptoms (top-down information processing).

When healthy individuals are requested to report illness-related symptoms, they may selectively attend to their sensations and report one or two symptoms. Medical students are often inclined to "interpret" their own harmless general sensations in terms of the serious diseases they have studied (Fitzpatrick, O'Donnell, Getson, & Sahler, 1993). Selective attention for particular symptoms in line with knowledge-based expectations has also been experimentally demonstrated. Normal subjects who were presented with an ambiguous physical stimulus reported pleasant or unpleasant sensations, depending on the information they had received prior to testing (Anderson & Pennebaker, 1980; Burnam & Pennebaker, 1977).

As will be argued herein, patients with a chronic disease are more likely to perceive symptoms following top-down perceptual strategies. The lay assumption would be that the symptom perception of a particular disease becomes more accurate with an increasing knowledge of, and experience with, its symptoms. Consequently, experienced patients with chronic diseases and a long history of symptoms would be more accurate than novices (Bishop, 1987; Pennebaker, 1982). However, in reality, symptom perception in chronic disease often becomes less accurate over time. Pennebaker (1982) emphasized that selective perception comprises the following mechanisms: (1) selective monitoring of particular sensory sources; (2) priority for processing of illness-related information; and (3) illness-congruent interpretation of ambiguous sensory information.

As has been emphasized by Pennebaker (1982), selective perception of illness-related information will usually enhance the magnitude of self-reported symptoms. During experiments in a physical exercise setting, children with asthma reported consistently more breathlessness than normal controls, which could not be explained by differences in physical condition or lung function. This result could, however, be explained by selective perception of a wide array of potentially relevant information, facilitating the integration of relatively irrelevant, exercise-related sensations in the symptom perceptual process, which increases breathlessness. Whereas some children may either unconsciously or consciously attend to possible illness-related information, others would either neglect such information or apply strategies to keep this sensory information beyond conscious awareness. Yellowlees and Ruffin (1989) confirmed the existence of such distinct symptom perceptual strategies in adult asthmatics, who were either anxious perceivers of real or fantasized symptoms, or neglected their symptoms completely. These strategies had a decisive influence on asthma management and medical consumption.

The process of selective symptom perception would be triggered by asthma-related external cues and by emotions associated with asthma. Another factor may be worrying, which is viewed as a special state of the cognitive system, and which prepares the individual to anticipate a future danger. Worry involves rehearsing possible aversive events and outcomes, coincident with a search for ways of avoiding them (Matthews, 1990). Different levels of worry seem to differentiate children with mild versus high levels of anxiety, and likewise, illness-related worry could differentiate high versus low levels of perceptual accuracy via the mediating impact of schema-driven symptom perception (Silverman, LaGreca, & Wasserstein, 1995). Rietveld and Brosschot (1996) suggested that the highest impact of selective perception could be expected in a situation in which asthmatics were uncertain about the condition of their airways, particularly with availability of ambiguous sensory information.

To summarize, the tendency to selectively attend to aspects of physical symptoms gradually increases in chronic diseases as a result of the influence of illness schemas that contain illness-related information and associated emotional experiences. This process of selective perception and illness-schema-guided information processing may become a self-enhancing system toward distorted symptom perception, fitting psychopathological disorders.

3.2.3. Cognitive Compensation

Perception and cognition are complementary processes. Cognition may dominate the symptom perceptual process. The term *cognitive compensation* refers to the relative dominance of top-down over bottom-up information processing. A maximum effect of cognition can be expected when sensory information is highly emotionally connotated and ambiguous, particularly in subjects with a tendency to dwell extensively on the consequences of the disease (Rietveld & Brosschot, 1996).

A first information-processing strategy would be that subjects attend to secondary symptoms or to external, situational information and integrate this information in the process of symptom perception, either fully aware or not (Rietveld, 1996a). This implies that sensory information that is merely associated with, and not causally linked to the disease may influence symptom perception. Children who were familiar with using peak-flow meters in the self-management of asthma appeared easily influenced by false peakflow information when reporting breathlessness (Rietveld, Kolk, & Prins, 1996c; Higgs, Richardson, Lea, Lewis, & Laszlo, 1986). After a running task, these children unknowingly were presented peakflow meters with a scale value of either 30% below or 30% above the actual value. The "optimistic" lung function indicated by the second meter had no impact on self-reported breathlessness. However, asthmatic children who saw that their lung function after exercise went down by at least 30% reported high breathlessness. This difference suggested that false peak-flow information was potent only when it confirmed children's expectations with respect to their airways. A reduction in peakflow after exercise would be understandable, whereas an increased value would not. Children without asthma were not at all influenced by false peakflow information (Rietveld, Kolk, & Prins, 1996c). In another study, asthmatic children who listened to false feedback of wheeze after physical exercise reported significantly more breathlessness than children who did not listen to recorded sounds (Rietveld, Kolk, Colland, & Prins, 1996b). Asthmatic respiration sounds or wheezes are associated with airway obstruction. In this study, all children were invited to listen through a headphone to their actual respiration sounds and after physical exercise were again invited to listen, but this time recorded sounds were presented, varying from asthmatic wheezes to quiet respiration sounds. Immediately following this, the children were requested to report breathlessness. False feedback of respiration sounds did not enhance breathlessness in nonasthmatics, and false feedback of quiet respiration sounds had no effect in either group. It was assumed that children who listened to false feedback of respiration sounds would likely interpret the false wheezes as a confirmation of their expectation of exercise-induced airway obstruction. It may be worthwhile to speculate how such external information affects the child's symptom reporting. First, a child with asthma knows that a running task may induce symptoms of airway obstruction. Second, sensory information associated with airway obstruction generally lacks specificity. Third, the child is to evaluate his/her condition after running. In this ambiguous situation, with diffuse, general, exercise-related sensations available, and the need to introspect, the child is likely to interpret sensations in line with expectations, irrespective of objective symptoms of asthma.

A second information-processing strategy would be a false interpretation of sensory information, with two reciprocal mechanisms affecting the accuracy of symptom perception: false interpretation of general bodily sensations as the symptoms of asthma, and false interpretation of actual symptoms as general, harmless sensations (Dirks & Schraa, 1983). Clinical studies have confirmed that adult asthmatics may erroneously interpret worry, general sensations, and emotional arousal as the symptoms of asthma (e.g., irritability, anxiety, fatigue, hyperventilation/hypocapnia, or heart pounding; Dirks, Schraa, & Robinson, 1982; Silverglade, Tosi, Wise, & D'Costa, 1993). Dirks and Schraa (1983) suggested that all asthmatics make these interpretative errors occasionally, and some of them quite often.

Whereas the information-processing strategies so far described would generally favor the overperception or overprediction of symptoms, other strategies may favor underperception. The absence of breathlessness during severe pathophysiology is one of the remarkable features of asthma and has never been explained sufficiently, although some investigators have suggested the mechanism of repression. Because sensory information associated with potential harm is extensively elaborated beyond cortical control, following phylogenetically old pathways, keeping such information from awareness could possibly be reached only via biased symptom perception, that is, false interpretation of actual symptoms as general, innocent sensations (Rietveld & Brosschot, 1996). This mechanism, however, would be distinguishable from higher order cognitions only with great difficulty. Because the assessment of subjective symptoms demands some evaluation and reasoning, high-order cognition may dominate the outcome of symptom perceptual processes. Although biased symptom perception would seem to be associated with very severe asthma, empirical results suggest that all asthmatics are vulnerable to biased symptom perception (Costa & McCrae, 1985; Watson & Pennebaker, 1989). In fact, mild symptoms with ambiguous clarity and specificity would be most likely subjected to biased symptom perception.

To summarize, the cognitive compensation for the often ambiguous sensory information associated with pathophysiology is characterized by integration of external, situational information in the symptom perceptual process and by interpretation of information in congruence with illness-schemas. There are two reciprocal mechanisms responsible for a false interpretation of sensations and symptoms, resulting in either overperception or underperception of pathophysiology. The eventual verbal expression of symptoms is subjected to high-order cognitions. Hence, the process of biased symptom perception may operate from the stimulus-level to high-order reasoning, and the latter may either facilitate or interfere with the results of unconscious perceptual processes. As shall be argued in the following paragraph, emotional factors may constitute alternative or complementary explanations for inaccuracies in symptom perception.

3.2.4. Emotional Influences

The strong relationship between stress, negative emotions, and asthma has been demonstrated by a longitudinal study between 1939 and 1949. By far the highest incidence of fatal asthma occurred during the Second World War, particularly during the Battle of Britain (Friedman, 1984). Part of this mortality may have been associated with asthmatics living under continuous stress, interfering with adequate symptom perception. Asthmatics are aware of the risks of severe airway obstruction, and exacerbations of asthma are associated with worry, irritability, anxiety, fear, and eventually depression (Badoux & Levy, 1994; Colland, 1993). In fact, approximately two-thirds of children experience panic when they notice the onset of airway obstruction (Janson, Bjornsson, Hetta, & Boman, 1994). Major topics that children worry about are school, health, and personal harm—all of which are involved in childhood asthma and likely to enhance illness-related distress and anxiety (Band & Weisz, 1988; Bennett, 1989).

Symptom perception, negative affect, and subjective symptoms are to some degree mutually influential (Davis & Offenkrantz, 1976). There is some evidence that negative affect may induce airway obstruction, but irrespective of this relationship, substantial evidence supports the effect of negative affect on both accuracy of symptom perception and magnitude of reported subjective symptoms.

3.2.4.1. Effect of Emotions on Accuracy of Symptom Perception. The relationship between negative affect and symptom perception comprises at least three different mechanisms. First, the accuracy of symptom perception generally relates negatively to anxiety and distress (Dahme, Konig, Nussbaum, & Richter, 1991; Hollandsworth, Kirkland, Jones, Van Norman, & Glazesky, 1979; Hudgel, Cooperson, & Kinsman, 1982). High levels of emotional arousal may either completely block pain perception or make conscious awareness of symptoms a function of survival-related behavior (Flor & Turk, 1989; McGrath, 1990; Peterson, Kimmel, Sacks, & Mesquita, 1991). Second, the occurrence of negative emotions may trigger the interpretation of general bodily sensations as the symptoms of disease. As discussed earlier, the false interpretation of sensations is one of the features of distorted symptom perception in chronic disease. The presence of negative affect, coinciding with previous asthma attacks and, as such, stored in memory, may trigger selective symptom perception and asthma-congruent interpretation of ambiguous symptoms. This suggestion was supported by the results of the study by Rietveld and Prins (1996) with asthmatic children who participated in one of four experimental conditions with (1) induction of negative affect, and (2) induction of sensations by means of physical exercise, presented in different order. The highest breathlessness was observed in the condition with negative affect preceding exercise. Exercise-induced sensations seemed to be interpreted in congruence with asthma when asthmatics were in a negative mood. Indirect support for this assumption came from a study in which asthmatics who frequently falsely interpreted symptoms had the highest incidence of emotional lability, anxiety, and depression (Dirks et al., 1982). Third, negative emotions may be interpreted as actual symptoms of a chronic disease (Rainville, Feine, Bushnell, & Duncan, 1992; Watson & Clark, 1984; Watson & Pennebaker, 1989). Dirks and Schraa (1983) suggested that asthmatic adults may falsely interpret negative emotions as the symptoms of asthma. Cardiac patients may interpret the emotional arousal associated with sexual excitement as cardiac symptoms and may be overwhelmed with distress (Cioffi, 1991; Easterling & Leventhal, 1989; Ehlers, Margrat, Roth, Taylor, & Birbaumer, 1988). In chronic-pain patients, a negative relation between pain and anxiety supported the hypothesis of a somatic instead of a cognitive interpretation of anxious arousal (DeGood, Buckeelew, & Tait, 1985). As Johnson (1973) emphasized, subjects who can attribute their psychological arousal to a neutral source will be less apt to label their state "emotional" than when the arousal is to be attributed to a threatening source. Considering the close association between severe chronic disease and emotions, asthmatics may have more problems finding such neutral causes than normal controls.

To summarize, asthma and negative affect are intertwined, and independent causal relationships are hard to distinguish. The main theme would be the mutual enhancement of negative affect and symptoms. This illustrates the importance in assessing negative affect when conducting symptom perception research. The main conclusion from the current paragraph would be that negative affect worsens perceptual accuracy, may trigger extensive elaboration of possibly relevant sensory information, and may be interpreted as actual symptoms of asthma.

3.2.4.2. Effect of Emotions on Breathlessness. Factor analysis of symptoms during asthmatic exacerbations showed that breathlessness may consist of five distinct factors: panic–fear, awareness of airway obstruction, hyperventilation, fatigue, and irritability (Brooks et al., 1989). Only panic–fear appeared to be a stable factor. It has been hypothesized that the weight of these constituents would determine the magnitude of breathlessness, whereas different configurations of factors could correlate with particular conditions (Rietveld, 1996a). Simon et al. (1990) went so far as to suggest that different configurations of factors could be associated with different respiratory diseases. Wilson and Jones (1991) confirmed that breathlessness and distress during induced airway obstruction overlap broadly. However, a methodological problem may be that emotional arousal influences the respiratory pattern and may eventually provoke airway obstruction—and breathlessness (Bass & Gardner, 1985). This illustrates the close relationship between asthma and negative affect but also suggests that the occurrence of either negative affect or the awareness of asthma may initiate a vicious circle of negative emotions and illness-related distress.

Another influence in excessive-breathlessness reporting would be neuroticism, perhaps less influential in children, but nevertheless a potent determinant of subjective symptom reporting in adults (Affleck, Tennen, Urrows, & Higgins, 1992; Costa & McCrae, 1987). The negation of negative affect that enhances subjective symptoms is that absence of negative affect diminishes the magnitude of breathlessness, irrespective of the level of airway obstruction (Lehrer, Isenberg, & Hochron, 1993; Osward, Waller, & Drinkwater, 1970). This would be an explanation for the classic experimental observations by Rubinfeld and Pain (1977) on adult asthmatics who reported no symptoms at the end of a provocation test, while their lung function was still severely reduced (see also the cognitive explanation in 3.2.3.) Support for this explanation (i.e., lack of negative affect) could only be a matter of reasoning, because the levels of distress and negative affect were not assessed in this study. Rietveld (1996a) argued that subjects regained control and felt relief by the end of the test, which was reflected in low levels of negative affect and breathlessness.

In a signal detection experiment by Rietveld (1996b), children with and without asthma breathed through a face mask with airflow interruptions of different magnitude, ranging from 5% to 64% reduction in forced expiratory volume in 1 second. The children continuously reported breathlessness by moving a lever. Remarkably, the magnitude of breathlessness was completely independent of the intensity of airflow interruption. Overall breathlessness remained mild, and there was no difference between asthmatics and normal controls. These results showed that when negative emotions are held constant by random presentation of different intensities of airflow interruption, breathlessness is not linearly related to intensity of airflow interruption, remains quite mild, even during severe airflow interruption, and is fairly similar in children with and without asthma. In other words, breathlessness without emotional influences becomes a reflection of increased respiratory effort. Labored breathing to an external obstruction may be exhausting or unpleasant but seems quite distinct from the suffering during an actual asthma attack. Consequently, the lack of subjective symptoms during severe pathophysiology, previously attributed to impaired perception, repression, ignorance, or neglect of symptoms, could be explained by the absence of negative affect (Steiner, Higgs, Fritz, Lazlo, & Harvey, 1987). The distinction between unconscious repression of symptoms and conscious neglect of symptoms has not been addressed in asthma research. However, as Cioffi (1991) pointed out, aversive sensations cannot be ignored for long, and attempts to distract from them will fail (Avia & Kanfer, 1980). Consequently, a lack of subjective symptoms during obvious pathophysiology could well be explained by the false interpretation of symptoms or by the absence of negative affect.

In summary, negative affect and breathlessness are overlapping categories, and presence and magnitude of emotions may favor either overperception or underperception of physical symptoms.

4. Developmental and Gender Influences

In ontogenetic development, children's cognitive and perceptual capacities gradually become more sophisticated. They may recognize specific sensory information, and, at the same time, learn to interpret specific sensory information as general sensations. Symptom appraisal in toddlers is in accordance with the mother's attitudes and eventually will be internalized, influencing subsequent symptom perception (Gauthier et al., 1977; Jordan & O'Grady, 1982; Steinberg & Laird, 1989).

Campbell (1975) suggested that mothers modify their children's experiences of symptoms in a casual learning process. Occasionally, parental influence may exceed the normal pattern, with the child's symptom per-

ception and symptom evaluation completely overruled by parental dominance, such as is the case in Munchausen by proxy syndrome (Harbeck-
Weber & Peterson, 1996). As was addressed in 3.2.2., external information
with respect to illness, including parental verbal interpretations of symptoms, is stored in cognitive schemas that guide and influence subsequent
sensory information processing. Consequently, developmental level plays
a crucial role in symptom perception but has not been studied systematically. The relationship between children's growth from concrete conceptions of reality to more complex ones and changes in the content of illness-
related fears has been emphasized (Burbach & Peterson, 1986). Future
studies should address these factors within the framework of child–parent
interactions.

The interaction between developmental level and fear may play an
important role in the perception of symptoms associated with diseases
with a life-threatening connotation. Parental expressions of fear may dominate children's rudimentary awareness of symptoms. Although these
parental characteristics are eventually internalized, children's own, real
experiences are gradually modifying their attitudes toward negative
events. They become increasingly able to anticipate future events and to
reason about their implications. They develop the capacity to worry about
an ever-increasing variety of threats (Vasey, 1993; Weinberger & Bushnell,
1994). This capacity may closely be related to the cognitive distortions
addressed in 3.2.3.

Another important developmental issue would be the capability to
select topics to which to attend. Attending to a particular feature of sensory information requires (1) that irrelevant stimuli can be analyzed automatically at semantic levels (where they may cause intrusion/interference
effects), and (2) that selection can be achieved by habituation to and
inhibition of the irrelevant stimuli (Tipper, Bourque, Anderson, & Brehat,
1989). The inhibitory mechanism may only be developed after second
grade (i.e., 7 to 8 years of age), suggesting that from that age on, cognitive
sophistication on the one hand may favor adequate symptom perception,
and on the other hand may make biased symptom perception possible. In
addition, the lesser capability of younger children to master inhibitory
strategies in attentional tasks would make them vulnerable to greater
distractibility. This suggests that younger children are less inclined to false
symptom perception. Empirical results confirm that young subjects are
generally more accurate symptom perceivers than the elderly (Tack, Altose, & Cherniack, 1982). On the other hand, toddlers with severe illness
may not be able to (1) perceive and evaluate symptoms beyond parental
dominance, (2) integrate available sensory information into adequate
symptom perception, and (3) have lower levels of illness-related worry.

Experimental studies showed that at least some 7- and 8-year-old children were influenced by false feedback of illness-related information (lung function information and respiration sounds) when reporting breathlessness, demonstrating that "sophisticated" symptom perception can be developed in school-aged children (Rietveld et al., 1996b). Studies with children under 7 years of age have not been conducted, but empirical results suggest that there is generally no age effect on the accuracy of symptom perception in school-aged children and adolescents, neither in airflow detection nor actual airway obstruction (Fritz, Klein, & Overholser, 1990; Rietveld, 1996a). Some modest age effects have been reported on the magnitude of breathlessness. Janson-Bjerklie et al. (1987) observed a negative correlation between age and breathlessness, suggesting that young children reported more breathlessness at a given degree of airway obstruction (see Quirk & Jones, 1990).

Generally, females score more subjective symptoms than males, which was confirmed for breathlessness in the study by Janson-Bjerklie et al. (1987). However, Quirk and Jones (1990) found no gender influence in the level of breathlessness-related distress. In children, young girls worry more than boys, which could be reflected in levels of breathlessness, but several studies have found no such effect (Fritz et al., 1990; Rietveld, 1996a). It may be concluded that knowledge on developmental and gender influences on symptom perception is severely limited.

5. Conclusions

There is abundant support that the sensory information underlying the symptom perceptual process in a chronic disease, such as asthma, is often neither clear nor specific. The *accuracy of symptom perception* is defined as the correlation between objective measures of pathophysiology and subjective symptoms. Additional information can be provided by experiments involving signal detection. The commonly observed discordance between objective, pathophysiological, and subjective symptoms often poses a threat to illness management, with both medical, psychological and psychosocial consequences.

There are seven factors influencing symptom perception, gathered under the headings "biomedical" and "psychological" factors. The biomedical factors include biological circadian influences, differences in pathophysiology, and organic or neurological pathology. The circadian influence may affect many research findings. The correlation between objective and subjective symptoms may vary as a function of this circadian influence. The concept has hardly been investigated in symptom perception and may be of marginal explanatory power, however. The modest empirical findings do not address symptom severity, confounding data-based conclusions. For instance, a lack of a correlation between objective and subjective variables during particular hours of the day may simply be explained by limited variance in symptom severity, whereas high correlations in the early morning may coincide with relative high symptom severity. Generally, subjective symptoms are relatively higher during the night than during the day, affecting such correlations too. It may be that circadian influence merely affects physiological changes as reflected in lung function parameters.

The accuracy of symptom perception may differ as a result of the influence of (1) acute versus prolonged or chronic airway obstruction, (2) central versus peripheral obstruction, and (3) different agents provoking obstruction. These differences are probably associated with different receptors and neurological pathways, determining the afferent information in the symptom perceptual process. Different agents provoking airway obstruction may be associated with different subjective symptoms (e.g., excessive mucus or saliva). These physiological differences may not be reflected in lung function measures and thereby enhance a discordance between objective and subjective symptoms. Although chronic asthma may eventually affect receptor sensitivity, results so far have demonstrated that the accuracy of symptom perception is independent of objective variables denoting asthma severity, suggesting that organic pathology may only modestly explain variance in perceptual accuracy.

Four different psychological factors influencing symptom perception have been described: competition of sensory information, selective perception, cognitive compensation, and emotional influences. The human capacity to process information is limited, and the probability of detecting internal cues can be expressed as a function of the ratio of available internal and external information. Although this concept may to some degree be useful in explaining intraindividual differences in the accuracy of symptom perception, several issues are yet to be investigated, such as the difference between quality and quantity of subjects' responses. Information and experiences with respect to a disease are integrated in cognitive illness-schemas, guiding and influencing subsequent information processing. The result may be selective perception of possible illness-related information, favoring the likelihood that symptoms are really perceived. Some perceptual processes are unconscious, but subjects may also actively and selectively monitor for possible relevant information. Selective perception for particular information will generally enhance the reporting of subjective symptoms.

Considering that asthma is a potential life-threatening condition, asthma-related information undergoes extensive cognitive and emotional elaboration. With sensory information often being vague or ambiguous, cognition may have a dominant effect. First, as a consequence of illness-schema-guided symptom perceptual strategies, sensory information with possible relevance to the disease may be subjected to illness-congruent interpretation. Second, external, situational information with possible relevance to the disease may be integrated in the symptom perceptual process. Information-processing biases or distortions are likely to result in either overperception or underperception of symptoms. High-order cognitions may modify the outcome of the symptom perceptual process when reporting subjective symptoms. Emotional factors may constitute alternative or complementary explanations for inaccuracy in symptom perception. Negative emotions are particularly dominant in magnitude of subjective symptoms. First, negative affect and the accuracy of symptom perception correlate negatively. Second, negative emotions may trigger the illness-congruent interpretation of ambiguous sensory information in terms of the disease. Third, negative emotions may be interpreted as symptoms of the disease (e.g., anxious arousal may be subjected to a somatic interpretation). Fourth, high levels of negative emotions enhance subjective symptoms, whereas a lack of negative emotions may explain the absence of subjective symptoms during pathophysiology. A child may perceive symptoms of asthma in full awareness, knowing that symptoms are generally mild and can be cured easily. Hence, negative affect remains minimal and so does breathlessness. On the other hand, a child who panics when perceiving asthma onset is likely to report high levels of anxiety, illness-related distress, and breathlessness.

The capacity of children to integrate illness-related sensory information may be developed by the age of 7 years. However, the influence of age and gender influences has not been studied systematically. Initial findings suggest that they may be of marginal influence in school-aged children and adolescents. The concept of symptom perception deals adequately with a number of problems associated with the discordance between objective and subjective symptoms in health and disease across both gender and age. Finally, symptom perception could also be used to investigate aspects of a wide array of problems facing physicians and psychologists, such as unexplained pain, lack of compliance with a medical regimen, placebo responses, somatoform disorders, and fatal pathology not recognized in time for treatment.

6. References

Adams, L., Lane, R., Shea, S. A., Cockcroft, A., & Guz, A. (1985). Breathlessness during different forms of ventilatory stimulation: A study of mechanisms in normal subjects and respiratory patients. *Clinical Science, 69,* 663–672.

Affleck, G., Tennen, H., Urrows, S., & Higgins, P. (1992). Neuroticism and the pain–mood relation in rheumatoidarthritis: Insights from a prospective daily study. *Journal of Consulting and Clinical Psychology, 60,* 119–126.

Anderson, D., & Pennebaker, J. W. (1980). Pain and pleasure: Alternative interpretations of identical stimulation. *European Journal of Social Psychology, 10,* 207–212.

Avia, M., & Kanfer, F. (1980). Coping with aversive stimulation. *Cognitive Therapy and Research, 4,* 73–81.

Badoux, A., & Levy, D. A. (1994). Psychologic symptoms in asthma and chronic urticaria. *Annals of Allergy, 72,* 229–234.

Bagg, L. R., & Hughes, D. T. D. (1980). Diurnal variation in peak expiratory flow rate in asthmatics. *European Journal of Respiratory Disease, 61,* 298–302.

Band, E. B., & Weisz, J. R. (1988). How to feel better when it feels bad: Children's perspectives on coping with everyday stress. *Developmental Psychology, 24,* 247–253.

Bandura, A. (1990). Perceived self-efficacy in the exercise of control over AIDS infection. In K. L. Kaemingle & L. Sechrist (Eds.), *The primary prevention of AIDS: Psychological approaches* (pp. 128–141). Newbury Park, CA: Sage.

Banzett, R. B., Lansing, R. W., Brown, R., Topulos, G. P., Yager, D., Stelle, S. M., Londoo, B., Loring, S. H., Reid, M. B., Adams, L., & Nations, C. S. (1990). "Air hunger" from increased PCO_2 persists after complete neuromuscular block in humans. *Respiratory Physiology, 81,* 1–18.

Banzett, R. B., Lansing, R. W., Reid, M. B., Adams, L., & Brown, R. (1989). "Air hunger" arising from increased PCO_2 in mechanically ventilated quadriplegics. *Respiratory Physiology, 76,* 53–68.

Barness, P. J. (1992). Poorly perceived asthma (Editorial). *Thorax, 47,* 408.

Barness, P. J. (1994). Blunted perception and death from asthma (editorial comment). *New England Journal of Medicine, 12,* 1383–1384.

Bass, C., & Gardner, W. (1985). Emotional influences on breathing and breathlessness. *Journal of Psychosomatic Research, 29,* 599–609.

Bennett, M. (1989). Children's self-attribution of embarrassment. *British Journal of Developmental Psychology, 7,* 207–217.

Bishop, G. (1987). Lay conceptions of physical symptoms. *Journal of Applied Social Psychology, 17,* 127–146.

Blitz, B., & Dinnerstein, A. (1977). Role of attentional focus in pain perception: Manipulation of response to noxious stimulation by instructions. *Journal of Abnormal Psychology, 77,* 42–45.

Bonnel, A. M., Mathiot, M. J., Jungas, B., & Grimaud, M. C. (1987). Breathing discomfort in asthma: Role of adaptation level. *Bulletin Européän de Physiopathology Respiratoire, 23,* 23–29.

Boulet, L. P., Deschesnes, F., Turcotte, H., & Gignac, F. (1991). Near fatal asthma, clinical and physiologic features, perception of broncho constriction and psychological profile. *Journal of Allergy and Clinical Immunology, 88,* 838.

Boyce, W., Chesney, M., Alkon, A., Tschamm, J., Adams, S., Chesterman, B., Cohen, F., Kaiser, P., Folkman, S., & Wara, D. (1995). Psychobiologic reactivity to stress and childhood respiratory illnesses: Results of two prospective studies. *Psychosomatic Medicine, 57,* 411–422.

Brooks, C. M., Richards, E. J., Bailey, W. C., Martin, B., Windsor, R. A., & Soong, S. J. (1989). Subjective symptomatology of asthma in an outpatient population. *Psychosomatic Medicine, 51,* 102–108.

Burbach, D., & Peterson, L. (1986). Children's concepts of physical illness: A review and critique of the cognitive developmental literature. *Health Psychology, 15,* 307–325.

Burdon, J. G. W., Juniper, E. F., Killian, K. J., Hargreave, F. E., & Campbell, E. J. M. (1982).

The perception of breathlessness in asthma. *American Review of Respiratory Disease*, *126*, 825–828.

Burdon, J. G. W., Pain, M. C. F., Rubinfeld, A. R., & Nana, A. (1994). Chronic lung disease and the perception of breathlessness: Clinical perspective. *European Respiratory Journal*, *7*, 1342–1349.

Burki, N. K., Mitchel, K., Chaudhary, B. A., Zechman, F. W., & Campbell, E. J. M. (1978). The ability of asthmatics to detect added resistive loads. *American Review of Respiratory Disease*, *117*, 71.

Burnam, M. A., & Pennebaker, J. W. (1977). *Cognitive labelling of physical symptoms*. Boston: Eastern Psychological Association.

Campbell, E. J. M., Godfrey, T. J. H., Clark, T. J. H., Freedman, S., & Norman, J. (1969). The effect of muscular paralysis induced by tubocurarine on the duration and sensation of breath-holding during hypercapnia. *Clinical Science*, *36*, 323–328.

Campbell, E. J. M., Robson, J. G., & Norman, J. (1967). The effect of muscular paralysis induced by tubocurarine on the duration and sensation of breath-holding. *Clinical Science*, *32*, 425–432.

Campbell, J. D. (1975). Illness is a point of view: The development of children's concepts of illness. *Child Development*, *46*, 92–100.

Carr, R. E., Lehrer, P. M., & Hochron, S. M. (1992). Panic symptoms in asthma and panic disorder: A preliminary test of the dyspnea-fear theory. *Behaviour Research and Therapy*, *30*, 251–261.

Carswell, F. (1985). Thirty deaths from asthma. *Archives of Disease in Childhood*, *60*, 25–28.

Cherniack, N. S. (1987). The perception of changes in airflow resistance in normal subjects and patients with chronic airway obstruction. *Chest*, *2*, 286–288.

Cioffi, D. (1991). Beyond attentional strategies: A cognitive perceptual model of somatic interpretation. *Psychological Bulletin*, *109*, 25–41.

Colland, V. T. (1993). Learning to cope with asthma, a behavioral self-management program. *Patient Education and Counseling*, *22*, 141–152.

Costa, P. T., Jr., & McCrae, R. R. (1987). Neuroticism, somatic complaints and disease: Is the bark worse than the bite? *Journal of Personality*, *55*, 299–316.

Cote, J., LeBlanc, P., & Boulet, L. P. (1987). Perception of bronchospasm in normal and asthmatic subjects. *American Review of Respiratory Disease*, *135*, 231.

Creer, T. L., & Gustafson, K. E. (1989). Psychological problems associated with drug therapy in childhood asthma. *Pediatrics*, *115*, 850–855.

Custrini, R. J., & Feldman, R. S. (1989). Children's social competence and nonverbal encoding and decoding of emotions. *Journal of Clinical Child Psychology*, *18*, 336–342.

Dahme, B., Konig, R., Nussbaum, B., & Richter, R. (1991). Haben Asthmatiker defizite in der Symptomwahrnehmung? *Psychotherapie: Psychosomatik Medizinische Psychologie*, *12*, 465–500.

Davis, D. I., & Offenkrantz, W. (1976). Is there a reciprocal relationship between symptoms and affect in asthma? *Journal of Nervous and Mental Disease*, *163*, 369–389.

DeGood, D. E., Buckeelew, S. P., & Tait, R. C. (1985). Cognitive-somatic anxiety response patterning in chronic pain patients and non-patients. *Journal of Consulting and Clinical Psychology*, *53*, 137–138.

Dirks, J. F., & Schraa, J. C. (1983). Patient mislabelling of symptoms and rehospitalization in asthma. *Journal of Asthma*, *20*, 43–44.

Dirks, J. F., Schraa, J. C., & Robinson, S. K. (1982). Patients mislabelling lof symptoms: Implications for patient–physician communication and medical outcome. *International Journal of Psychiatry in Medicine*, *12*, 15–27.

Easterling, D. V., & Leventhal, H. (1989). Contribution of concrete cognition to emotion:

Neutral symptoms as elicitors of worry about cancer. *Journal of Applied Psychology, 74,* 787–796.

Ehlers, A., Margrat, J., Roth, W., Taylor, C., & Birbaumer, M. (1988). Anxiety induced by false heartrate feedback in patients with panic disorder. *Behaviour Research and Therapy, 26,* 1–11.

Ergood, J., Epstein, L. H., Ackerman, M., & Fireman, P. (1985). Perception of expiratory flow by asthmatics and non-asthmatics during rest and exercise. *Health Psychology, 4,* 545–554.

Fillingim, R. B., & Fine, M. A. (1986). The effects of internal versus external information processing on symptom perception in an exercise setting. *Health Psychology, 5,* 115–123.

Fillingim, R. B., Roth, D. L., & Haley, W. E. (1988). The effects of distraction on the perception of exercise-induced symptoms. *Journal of Psychosomatic Research, 33,* 241–248.

Fiske, S., & Linville, P. (1980). What does the schema concept buy us? *Personality and Social Psychology Bulletin, 6,* 543–557.

Fitzpatrick, S. B., O'Donnell, R., Getson, P., Sahler, O. J. (1993). Medical students' experiences with and perceptions of chronic illness prior to medical school. *Medical Education, 27,* 355–359.

Flor, H., & Turk, D. C. (1989). Psychophysiology of chronic pain: Do chronic pain patients exhibit symptom-specific psychophysiological responses? *Psychological Bulletin, 105,* 215–259.

Friedman, M. S. (1984). Psychological factors associated with pediatric asthma death: A review. *Journal of Asthma, 21,* 97–117.

Fritz, G. K., Klein, R. B., & Overholser, J. C. (1990). Accuracy of symptom perception in childhood asthma. *Developmental Behavior Pediatrics, 11,* 69–72.

Gannon, L. R. (1984). Awareness of internal cues and concordance among verbal, behavioral, and physiological systems in dysfunction. *Psychological Reports, 54,* 631–650.

Gannon, L. R., & Haynes, S. N. (1986). Cognitive-physiological discordance as an etiological factor in psychophysiologic disorders. *Advances in Behavioural Research and Therapy, 8,* 223–226.

Garden, G. M., & Ayres, J. G. (1993). Psychiatric and social aspects of brittle asthma. *Thorax, 48,* 501.

Gauthier, Y., Fortin, C., Drapeau, P., Breton, J., Gosselin, J., Quintal, L., Weisnagel, J., Tetreault, L., & Pinard, G. (1977). The mother–child relationship and the development of autonomy and self-assertion in young (14 to 30 months) asthmatic children. *Journal of the American Academy of Child Psychiatry, 16,* 109–131.

Gottfried, S. B., Altose, M. D., Kelsen, S. G., & Cherniack, N. S. (1981). Perception of changes in airflow resistance in obstructive pulmonary disorders. *American Review of Respiratory Disease, 124,* 566.

Green, D. M., & Swets, J. A. (1966). *Signal detection theory and psychophysics.* New York: Wiley.

Harbeck-Weber, C., & Peterson, L. (1996). Health-related disorders. In E. Mash & R. Barkley (Eds.), *Child Psychopathology.* New York: Guilford.

Heim, E., Blaser, A., & Waidelich, E. (1972). Dyspnea: Psychophysiologic relationships. *Psychosomatic Medicine, 34,* 405–423.

Higgs, C. M. B., Richardson, R. B., Lea, D. A., Lewis, G. T. R., & Laszlo, G. (1986). Influence of the knowledge of peakflow on self assessment of asthma. Studies with a coded peak flow meter. *Thorax, 41,* 671–675.

Hollaender, J., & Florin, I. (1983). Expressed emotion and airway conductance in children with bronchial asthma. *Journal of Psychosomatic Research, 27,* 307–311.

Hollandsworth, J., Kirkland, R., Jones, G., Van Norman, L. R., & Glazesky, R. C. (1979). An analysis of the nature and effects of test anxiety: Cognitive, behavioral, and physiological components. *Cognitive Therapy and Research, 3,* 165–180.

Hudgel, H. D., Cooperson, D. M., & Kinsman, R. A. (1982). Recognition of added resistive loads in asthma: The importance of behavioral styles. *American Review of Respiratory Disease, 126*, 121–125.

Isenberg, S. A., Lehrer, P. M., & Hochron, S. (1992). The effects of suggestion and emotional arousal on pulmonary function in asthma: A review and a hypothesis regarding vagal mediation. *Psychosomatic Medicine, 54*, 192–216.

Jahnson, J. E. (1973). Effects of accurate expectations about sensations on the sensory and distress components of pain. *Journal of Personality and Social Psychology, 27*, 261–275.

Janson, C., Bjornsson, E., Hetta, J., & Boman, G. (1994). Anxiety and depression in relation to respiratory symptoms and asthma. *American Journal of Respiratory and Critical Care Medicine, 149*, 930–934.

Janson-Bjerklie, S., & Clarke, E. (1982). The effects of biofeedback training on bronchial diameter in asthma. *Clinical Techniques in Critical Care, 11*, 200–207.

Janson-Bjerklie, S., Kohlman-Carrieri, V. K., & Hudes, M. (1986). The sensations of pulmonary dyspnea. *Nursing Research, 35*, 154–159.

Janson-Bjerklie, S., Ruma, S. S., Stulbarg, M., & Kohlman-Carrieri, V. K. (1987). Predictors of dyspnea intensity in asthma. *Nursing Research, 36*, 179–183.

Johnson, J. H. (1973). Effects of accurate expectations about sensations on the sensory and distress components of pain. *Journal of Personality and Social Psychology, 27*, 261–275.

Jones, P. W. (1992). Breathlessness perception in airways obstruction. *European Respiratory Journal, 5*, 1035–1036.

Jordan, M. K., & O'Grady, D. J. (1982). Children's health beliefs and concepts: Implications for child health care. In P. Karoly, J. J. Steffen, & D. J. O'Grady (Eds.), *Child health psychology, concepts and issues.* New York: Pergamon.

Lehrer, P. M., Isenberg, S., & Hochron, S. M. (1993). Asthma and emotion. *Journal of Asthma, 30*(1), 5–21.

Mas, R., Dahme, B., & Richter, R. (1992). Vergleich zweier unterschiedlicher Messmethoden zur Interozeption von Obstruktionen bei Asthmapatienten. *Pneumologie, 5*, 183–189.

Matthews, A. (1990). Why worry? The cognitive function of anxiety. *Behaviour Research and Therapy, 28*, 455–468.

McFadden, E. R. (1975). Exertional dyspnoea and cough as preludes to acute attacks of bronchial asthma. *New England Journal of Medicine, 292*, 555–559.

McFadden, E. R., Kiser, R., & de Groot, W. J. (1973). Acute bronchial asthma: Relations between clinical and physiological manifestations. *New England Journal of Medicine, 288*, 221–225.

McGrath, P. A. (1990). Pain assessment in children—a practical approach. *Advances in Pain Research Therapy, 15*, 4–27.

Meyer, R., Kroner-Herwig, B., & Sporkel, H. (1990). The effect of exercise and induced expectations on visceral perception in asthmatic patients. *Journal of Psychosomatic Research, 34*, 445–460.

Montserrat, J. M., Picado, C., Lloberas, P., Serra, J., Luengo, M., & Agusti-Vidal, A. (1988). Ability of asthmatics with and without respiratory arrest to detect added resistive loads. *Journal of Asthma, 25*, 131.

Oswald, N. C., Waller, R. E. & Drinkwater, J. (1970). Relationship between breathlessness and anxiety in asthma and bronchitis: A comparative study. *British Medical Journal, 2*, 14–17.

Peiffer, C., Marsac, J., & Lockhart, A. (1989). Chrono-biological study of the relationship between dyspnoea and airway obstruction in symptomatic asthmatic subjects. *Clinical Science, 77*, 237–244.

Pennebaker, J. W. (1982). *The psychology of physical symptoms.* New York: Springer.

Pennebaker, J. W., Burnam, M. A., Schaeffer, M. A., & Harper, D. C. (1977). Lack of control as a determinant of perceived physical symptoms. *Journal of Personality and Social Psychology, 35*, 167–174.

Pennebaker, J. W., & Hoover, C. W. (1984). Visceral perception versus visceral detection: Disentangling methods and assumptions. *Biofeedback and Self-Regulation, 9*, 339–352.

Pennebaker, J. W., & Lightner, J. M. (1980). Competition of internal and external information in an exercise setting. *Journal of Personality and Social Psychology, 39*, 165–174.

Pennebaker, J. W., & Skelton, J. A. (1981). Selective monitoring of physical sensations. *Journal of Personality and Social Psychology, 41*, 213–223.

Perrin, J. M., MacLean, W. E., & Perrin, E. C. (1989). Parental perceptions of health status and psychologic adjustment of children with chronic asthma. *Pediatrics, 83*, 26–39.

Peterson, R. A., Kimmel, P. L., Sacks, C. R., Mesquita, M. L. (1991). Depression, perception of illness and mortality in patients with end-stage renal disease. *International Journal of Psychiatry in Medicine, 21*, 343–354.

Potter, P. C., & Roberts, M. C. (1984). Children's perception of chronic illness, the role of disease, symptoms, cognitive development and information. *Society of Pediatric Psychology, 50*, 13–27.

Pratter, M. R., & Barter, T. (1991). Dyspnea: Time to find the facts. *Chest, 100*, 1187.

Quirk, F. H., & Jones, P. W. (1990). Patients' perception of distress due to symptoms and effects of asthma on daily living and an investigation of possible influential factors. *Clinical Science, 79*, 17–21.

Rainville, P., Feine, J. S., Bushnell, M. C., & Duncan, G. H. (1992). A psychophysical comparison of sensory and affective responses to four modalities of experimental pain. *Somatosensory and Motor Research, 9*, 265–277.

Rietveld, S. (1996a). *Symptom perception and breathlessness in children with asthma.* Doctoral dissertation, University of Amsterdam, Amsterdam, The Netherlands.

Rietveld, S. (1996b). Breathlessness in children with and without asthma during external airflow obstruction. Manuscript submitted for publication.

Rietveld, S. (1997). Habituation to prolonged airflow obstruction. *Journal of Asthma, 34*(2), 133–140.

Rietveld, S., & Brosschot, J. (1997). Determinants of discordance between objective and subjective symptoms of asthma. *International Journal of Behavioral Medicine.*

Rietveld, S., & Dooijes, E. H. (1996). Characteristics and diagnostic significance of wheezes during exercise-induced airway obstruction in children with asthma. *Chest, 110*(3), 624–631.

Rietveld, S., Kolk, A. M. M., Colland, V. T., & Prins, P. J. M. (1996b). The influence of respiration sounds on breathlessness in children with asthma, a symptom perception approach. *Health Psychology, 16.*

Rietveld, S., Kolk, A. M. M., & Prins, P. J. M. (1996c). The influence of lung function information on self-reports of dyspnoea by children with asthma. *Journal of Pediatric Psychology, 21*, 367–377.

Rietveld, S., Kolk, A. M. M., Prins, P. J. M., & Van Beest, I. (1997). The influence of external stimulation on airflow detection by children with and without asthma. *Psychology and Health, 12*, 553–563.

Rietveld, S., & Prins, P. J. M. (1996). The relationship between negative emotions and acute objective and subjective symptoms of childhood asthma. *Psychological Medicine* (in press).

Rietveld, S., Prins, P. J. M., & Kolk, A. M. M. (1996d). The capacity of children with and without asthma to detect external resistive loads on breathing. *Journal of Asthma, 33*, 221–230.

Rubinfeld, A. R., & Pain, M. C. F. (1976). Perception of asthma. *Lancet, 2,* 882–884.

Rubinfeld, A. R., & Pain, M. C. F. (1977). Conscious perception of bronchospasm as a protective phenomenon in asthma. *Chest, 72,* 154.

Rumbak, M. J., Kelso, T. M., Arheart, K. L., & Self, T. H. (1993). Perception of anxiety as a contributing factor of asthma: Indigent versus nonindigent. *Journal of Asthma, 30,* 165–169.

Silverglade, L., Tosi, D. J., Wise, P. S., & D'Costa, A. (1993). Irrational beliefs and emotionality in adolescents with and without bronchial asthma. *Journal of General Psychology,* 199–207.

Silverman, B. A., Mayer, D., Sabinsky, R., Williams-Akita, A., Feldman, J., Schneider, A. T., & Chiaramonte, L. T. (1987). Training perception of airflow obstruction in asthmatics. *Annals of Allergy, 59,* 350–354.

Silverman, W. K., LaGreca, A. N., & Wasserstein, S. (1995). What do children worry about? Worries and their relation to anxiety. *Child Development, 66,* 671–681.

Simon, P. M., Schwartzstein, R. M., Weiss, J. W., Fencl, V., Teghtsoonian, M., & Weinberger, S. E. (1990). Distinguishable types of dyspnea in patients with shortness of breath. *American Review of Respiratory Disease, 142,* 1009–1014.

Skelton, J. A., & Croyle, R. T. (1991). *Mental representation in health and illness.* New York: Springer.

Sly, P. D., Landau, L. L., & Weymouth, R. (1985). Home-recording of peak expiratory flow rates and perception of asthma. *American Journal of Diseases of Children, 18,* 479–482.

Steiner, H., Higgs, C. M. B., Fritz, G. K., Lazlo, G., & Harvey, J. E. (1987). Defense style and the perception of asthma. *Psychosomatic Medicine, 49,* 35–44.

Steinberg, S., & Laird, J. D. (1989). Parent attributions of emotion to their children and the cues children use in perceiving their own emotions. *Motivation and Emotion, 13,* 179–191.

Sterk, P. J., & Bell, E. H. (1989). Bronchial hyperresponsiveness, the need for distinction between hypersensitivity and excessive airway narrowing. *European Respiratory Journal, 2,* 267–274.

Tack, S., Altose, M. D., & Cherniack, N. S. (1982). Effect of aging on the perception of resistive ventilatory loads. *American Review of Respiratory Disease, 126,* 463–467.

Teramoto, S. (1995). Chronic lung disease and the perception of breathlessness: Clinical perspective. *European Respiratory Journal, 8,* 338.

Tipper, S. P., Bourque, T. A., Anderson, S. H., & Brehat, J. C. (1989). Mechanisms of attention: A developmental study. *Journal of Experimental Child Psychology, 48,* 353–378.

Turcotte, H., Corbeil, F., & Boulet, L. (1990). Perceptions of dyspnoea during bronchoconstriction induced by antigen, exercise and histamine challenges. *Thorax, 45,* 914.

Vasey, M. W. (1993). Development and cognition in childhood anxiety: The example of worry. In T. H. Ollendick & R. J. Prinz (Eds.), *Advances in Clinical Child Psychology* (Vol. 15, pp. 1–39). New York: Plenum Press.

Watson, D., & Clark, L. A. (1984). Negative affectivity: The disposition to experience aversive emotional states. *Psychological Bulletin, 43,* 465–498.

Watson, D., & Pennebaker, J. W. (1989). Health complaints, stress, and distress: Exploring the central role of negative affectivity. *Psychological Review, 96,* 234–254.

Weinberger, N., & Bushnell, E. W. (1994). Young children's knowledge about their senses: Perceptions and misconceptions. *Child Study Journal, 24,* 209–235.

Weiss, J. H. (1966). Mood states associated with asthma in children. *Journal of Psychosomatic Research, 10,* 267–273.

Williams, C. W., & Lees-Haley, P. R. (1993). Perceived toxic exposure: A review of four cognitive influences on the perception of illness. *Journal of Social Behavior and Personality, 8,* 297–308.

Wilson, R. C., & Jones, P. W. (1990). Influence of prior ventilatory experience on the estimation of breathlessness during exercise. *Clinical Science, 78,* 149–153.

Wilson, R. C., & Jones, P. W. (1991). Differentiation between the intensity of breathlessness and the distress it evokes in normal subjects during exercise. *Clinical Science, 80,* 65–70.

Wolkove, N., Dajozman, E., Coalacone, A., Kriesman, H., Peiffer, C., Toumi, M., Razzouk, H., Marsac, J., & Lockkhart, J. (1992). Relationship between spontaneous dyspnoea and liability of airways obstruction in asthma. *Clinical Science, 82,* 717–724.

Yamamoto, H., Inaba, S., Nishimura, M., Kishi, F., & Kawakami, Y. (1978). Relationship between the ability to detect added resistance at rest and breathlessness during bronchoconstriction in asthmatics. *Respiration, 52,* 42–48.

Yellowlees, P. M., & Kalucy, R. S. (1990). Psychobiological aspects of asthma and the consequent research implications. *Chest, 97,* 628–634.

Yellowlees, P. M., & Ruffin, R. E. (1989). Psychological defenses and coping styles in patients following a life-threatening attack of asthma. *Chest, 95*(6), 1298–1303.

6

Common Feeding Problems in Young Children

KAREN S. BUDD AND CARY S. CHUGH

1. Introduction

Even before a baby is born, parents watch carefully for signs of their expectant child's health and development. The growing emphasis on prenatal care reflects a greater awareness of the effects of maternal health behaviors on the unborn child. However, concerns and questions about the child's developmental progress do not abate after birth. In fact, the most common questions asked of pediatricians by parents of infants and toddlers concern what is normal for a child at different ages (Reisinger & Bires, 1980; Riter, personal communication, October, 1995). Parents typically ask, "When will my child develop a stable sleep schedule?"; "When should I begin potty training my child?"; and "When will my child [reach a particular developmental milestone]?"

Feeding is no exception to this list of questions. In fact, it may be especially pertinent, as feeding is the first activity in which the parent and child work together toward a common goal, namely satiation of the neonate's hunger. Years later, parents may still recall vividly the first time they fed their baby after arriving home from the hospital, or the weary hours of trying to feed and calm their colicky infant. Disturbances in the area of feeding are likely to engender considerable parental concern, both with regard to parents' competence as caregivers and with regard to their child's well-being.

KAREN S. BUDD AND CARY S. CHUGH • Department of Psychology, DePaul University, Chicago, Illinois 60614.

Advances in Clinical Child Psychology, Volume 20, edited by Thomas H. Ollendick and Ronald J. Prinz. Plenum Press, New York, 1998.

Estimates of the prevalence of feeding problems in children vary, with some sources reporting rates around 20% (Beautrais, Fergusson, & Shannon, 1982; Lindberg, Bohlin, & Hagekull, 1991), others between 30% and 45% (Bentovim, 1970), and some as high as 62% (Reau, Senturia, Lebailly, & Christoffel, 1996). The wide discrepancy in figures across studies results in part from differing age groups sampled, sources of information (i.e., health-care professionals, parents, clinical records), and criteria for defining feeding problems. Studies also include differing subcategories of feeding concerns, such as undereating, picky or selective eating, overeating, vomiting or rumination, infant crying during or after meals, and ingesting inedible substances (pica). More stringent criteria in defining feeding problems yield a much lower estimate of prevalence, as exemplified by Dahl and Sundelin's (1986) finding of a 1–2% prevalence of persistent feeding problems in infants.

Even though many children experience feeding difficulties that are not diagnosable by the DSM-IV (American Psychiatric Association, 1994), their parents are nonetheless concerned about these problems. Feeding difficulties presumably make mealtimes more difficult and frustrating for caregivers. Suggestive of this is the finding that parents of children with feeding disorders use more negative and coercive verbalizations with their children during meals when compared to parents of children without feeding disorders (Sanders, Patel, LeGrice, & Shepherd, 1993). Additionally, parents of children with feeding problems are more likely to have negative feelings about their children (Hagekull & Dahl, 1987), presumably because of their frustration with the feeding situation. Such negative experiences associated with persistent feeding difficulties have been hypothesized to affect children's psychosocial development and their subsequent interactions with others (Hufton & Oates, 1977; Oates, Peacock, & Forrest, 1985).

Whereas much has been written about assessment and treatment of clinically significant pediatric feeding conditions (e.g., Drotar, 1985; Kedesdy & Budd, in press; Kirschenbaum, Johnson, & Stalonas, 1987; Linscheid, 1992; Woolston, 1991), writing in the area of *subclinical* feeding concerns is relatively sparse. Given the high prevalence of these less severe forms of feeding problems, it is likely that the practicing clinician will encounter children and parents struggling with feeding-related issues that do not fit the criteria for full-fledged feeding disorders. This chapter reviews the development of normal feeding practices, describes common subclinical deviations from normal feeding in otherwise healthy children, and discusses clinical assessment and management issues related to these feeding difficulties. The emphasis is on the developmental periods of infancy and early childhood, because these are the peak times for most feeding difficulties, as well as on the changing implications of overeating from infancy to latency periods.

2. Normal Feeding

Feeding mirrors other basic childhood skills in that it develops through a series of progressions over time. In the early stages of infancy, eating behaviors are a result of reflex reactions, presumably in response to the sensation of hunger and the pleasure of substances entering the mouth (Lipsitt & Behl, 1990). However, as the infant grows and develops, primitive reflexes begin to disappear, usually between 3 and 5 months of age (O'Brien, Repp, Williams, & Christophersen, 1991). It is about this time that the infant begins to acquire new oral–motor skills, including munching (5 months), tongue lateralization (7 months), biting (7 months), and the development of a mature chewing pattern (between 8 and 36 months) (Howard, 1984).

The child's increasing oral–motor capacity permits a wider range of food intake and allows for the child's participation in the feeding process. Between the ages of 4 and 6 months, bottled formula or breast milk is gradually replaced or supplemented with solid foods (e.g., pureed fruits, infant cereal) (Moss & Moss, 1980). Around 7 months of age, the infant begins to finger feed (Christophersen & Hall, 1978). As teeth appear and chewing skills improve, the child can consume more textured foods, moving from pureed to semisolid, to chopped, and then to chewy and crunchy consistencies. Self-feeding skills improve by the 12th month to the point where the use of a utensil is often possible; at around 15 months of age, the infant begins to engage in self-feeding (Christophersen & Hall, 1978).

Between the ages of 1 and 5 years, a child's appetite changes from being relatively stable to becoming more erratic and unpredictable. The child's food interests have been hypothesized to change through the effects of learning and experience (Birch, 1990), and as part of a developmental pursuit for autonomy and control (Erikson, 1950). Because of these naturally occurring shifts in the child's appetite, coupled with numerous cognitive and social developments, it is during the toddler and preschool years that issues around feeding are most likely to arise (Bentovim, 1970). Noncompliant behaviors and strong preferences during feeding as well as other child-care situations (e.g., bedtime, dressing) are normal and even necessary opportunities for the child to mature socially (Linscheid, Budd, & Rasnake, 1995). However, when feeding difficulties become exaggerated or persist over several weeks or months, they can engender considerable parental concern.

3. Deviations from Normal Feeding

Pediatric feeding problems exist on a continuum from minor disruptive behaviors at mealtimes to complete rejection of, or lack of control around, food, which may result in severe medical difficulties (Kedesdy & Budd, in press; Luiselli, 1989; Woolston, 1991). Even mild forms of feeding problems can be worrisome to parents, make mealtimes unpleasant, and have the potential, if they persist, to impair other aspects of a child's functioning. Commonly occurring subclinical feeding problems are presented in Table 1, alongside their clinical counterparts. Subclinical deviations include finicky eating habits, overeating, mouthing nonfood substances, spitting up and vomiting, and colic. Additional behaviors during mealtimes (e.g., sloppy or slow eating) that do not directly affect food intake also may concern parents. Each of these patterns will be reviewed in turn.

3.1. Finicky Eating Habits

Anyone who deals with children on a regular basis knows that their appetites, far from being constant, are quite variable over time. Foods favored one day are likely to be rejected the next. In fact, during the preschool years, mercurial feeding patterns are considered normal in young children (e.g., Bentovim, 1970).

The term *finicky eater* is used here to describe a child who refuses a wider range of foods than is considered normal for a given chronological age. This "picky eating style" is seen in 20–30% of all children at some point in their development (e.g., Bentovim, 1970; Marchi & Cohen, 1990) and is often accompanied by other feeding habits, such as eating small

TABLE 1
Deviations from Normal Childhood Feeding or Growth

Subclinical condition	Clinical counterpart
Finicky eating habits	Chronic food refusal
	Failure to thrive
	Psychosocial dwarfism
	Feeding disorder of infancy or early childhood
Overeating	Obesity
Mouthing nonfood substances	Pica
Spitting up and vomiting	Rumination
	Gastroesophageal reflux
Colic	Illness (e.g., food allergy, intestinal disease)

portions of food, eating slowly, and showing a low level of interest in eating (Marchi & Cohen, 1990). Finicky eating is distinguished from its clinical counterpart, chronic refusal of major food groups or textures (Linscheid, 1992), and also from failure to thrive (FTT), a growth deficiency that can result as a consequence of chronic undereating. FTT is characterized by weight below the 5th percentile for age, weight that is less than 80–85% of the child's ideal body weight, or a marked deceleration in the child's weight indicated by the loss of two or more percentiles in the infant's growth chart (Drotar, 1985). Woolston (1991) argued that a further distinction needs to be made between these conditions and psychosocial dwarfism. Psychosocial dwarfism is not a feeding problem per se; instead, it involves a marked deceleration in growth accompanied by disturbances in behavior (e.g., sleep disorder). These problems are thought to stem from a poor, unnurturing environment and improve upon change in the child's psychosocial environment. The DSM-IV includes a category called Feeding Disorder of Infancy or Early Childhood to denote feeding disturbances characterized by persistent failure to eat adequately, FTT symptoms, and no known medical causes (American Psychiatric Association, 1994). This diagnosis indicates a more serious problem than is implied by the term *finicky eating habits*.

Because wide variability in feeding behaviors is typical of young children, guidelines are needed for determining when such behavior transcends the boundaries of normalcy. Based on their review of the literature, Kedesdy and Budd (in press) suggest criteria for distinguishing subclinical from clinical undereating in children. Both types of feeding disturbances are characterized by parental complaints or concerns about the child's mealtime behavior. If the problem can be explained by a medical disorder, or if it interferes with the child's physical, social, or emotional development, it is considered to be of clinical significance. Alternatively, finicky eating habits without biomedical origin or negative consequences for the child fit Kedesdy and Budd's definition of subclinical feeding problems.

3.2.   Overeating

Most parents concerned with their child's overeating fear obesity as a likely consequence of this eating pattern. Obesity is assumed to result from consistently consuming more calories than the body expends during the day. In fact, Dietz (1987) asserted that excess imbalances of as little as 50 calories per day can lead to obesity over time.

In a cross-sectional study, Gortmaker, Dietz, Sobol, and Wehler (1987) examined trends in obesity for 6- to 11-year-olds over the period 1963 to 1980. They found that the prevalence of obesity and superobesity, as assessed by tricep skinfold measurements, was 27.1% and 11.7%, respectively, in the period 1976–1980. These figures represent a 54% increase for obesity and a 98% increase for superobesity from statistics collected from 1963 to 1965. The authors cite increased television viewing, changes in diet, and decreased physical activity in American youth as possible causes of this trend.

The recommended criterion for obesity is 20% above the child's ideal body weight (Israel, 1990). A child with a subclinical overeating problem falls below this level of excess weight but exhibits weight gain and/or eating habits tending toward obese status. Children with mild overeating may encounter some of the social and physical repercussions of their obese counterparts.

Although the immediate effects of mild to moderate obesity on the health of the child are not yet clear, the consequences of obesity for adults (e.g., cardiovascular disease, noninsulin-dependent diabetes) are better understood. As obese children get older and maintain their oversized physique, they are more likely to become obese adults (Epstein, Wing, & Valoski, 1985). For this reason, overeating and early signs of atypical weight gain in children are justifiable concerns. These concerns are less of an issue with infants, however, as there is a considerable rate of spontaneous remission in this group across time. Dietz (1984) reviewed several studies that followed infants who were diagnosed as being obese during the first 6 months of life. Upon reexamination at 48 months of age, a range of 25–44% of the infants remained obese. Therefore, although it is common for parents to have some concerns about the future weight status of their "chubby" babies, this research suggests that obesity in infancy it is not highly predictive of later body size.

In addition to the health-related implications of overeating, overweight children often experience social rejection and teasing, and have lower self-concepts than their lean peers, as do obese adults (Foreyt & Goodrick, 1988). In studying the perceptions of obese elementary-school children around eating and dieting, Thelen, Powell, Lawrence, and Kuhnert (1992) found that fourth- and sixth-grade girls were more concerned about becoming overweight than their second-grade counterparts and all of the male groups. When asked about their dietary habits, over one-fourth of the second-grade girls and one-third of the older girls reported dieting at some point. This research supports the notion that by middle elementary school, even nonobese children (as indicated by not weighing more than their ideal body weight) may have concerns about their body size and shape. These concerns may also be reflected in the way popularity of children in school is affected by body size, with heavier or bigger children being less well-liked than their lean classmates. Being unpopular or self-conscious about one's weight may lead to a decrease in children's participation levels in social activities and an increase in isolated, more sedentary behaviors, such as television watching. These effects may, in turn, reduce children's overall activity level and increase their opportunities to eat, thereby creating a self-perpetuating cycle.

3.3. Mouthing Nonfood Substances

Mouthing objects is one of the primary ways infants explore their environment. Mouthing, sucking, and even swallowing nonnutritive substances (e.g., dirt, paper, buttons) are relatively common occurrences in infancy. Mouthing some substances can result in serious consequences (e.g., choking, poisoning) for the infant or toddler; however, mouthing usually is not seen as reflecting physical or emotional disturbance but rather children acting on their curiosity. It has been suggested that the eating of nonnutritive substances is an imitative behavior, based on findings that young children in homes with pets and siblings of children with pica are more likely to ingest these substances (Feldman, 1986). When mouthing occurs repeatedly or involves dangerous substances, it may signal an impoverished environment or negligent care on the part of the parent.

Pica is much more severe than innocent exploration of one's environment. Rather, it is the persistent eating of nonnutritive substances that are neither age-appropriate nor culturally sanctioned (American Psychiatric Association, 1994). The prevalence of pica in the general population is unknown; however, it is associated with other disorders (e.g., mental retardation, pervasive developmental disorders) and appears to increase in prevalence with the severity of the associated disorder (American Psychiatric Association, 1994). Pica often co-occurs with lead poisoning in children, presumably due to the child's ingestion of bits of lead-based paint, particularly in areas of deteriorated housing (Madden, Russo, & Cataldo, 1980). The results of lead poisoning can be severe and lasting, including neurological damage and developmental impairment.

3.4. Spitting Up, Vomiting, and Colic

Spitting up and, to a lesser extent, vomiting during infancy are normative feeding difficulties. Forsyth, Leventhal, and McCarthy (1985) found moderate to severe levels of spitting up during feeding in 10% of breast-fed and 18% of formula-fed infants at 4 months of age. Some babies vomit occasionally after they are fed, although daily vomiting is a less common occurrence (Dahl & Sundelin, 1986). Allergies or other health problems

often are suspected when vomiting persists, but some infants vomit peri-
odically with no known cause (Satter, 1986b). One physical problem that
must be ruled out when vomiting occurs is gastroesophageal reflux, an
involuntary, spontaneous return of stomach contents into the esophagus
(Woolston, 1991).

Although spitting up or occasional vomiting is quite common among
infants, this benign pattern can be distinguished from its more severe
clinical deviation, rumination. The latter behavior is characterized by
preparatory movements followed by the voluntary bringing up of food
and rechewing or sucking that seems pleasurable to the infant (American
Psychiatric Association, 1994). Rumination disorder occurs relatively infre-
quently in the general population. It is most often seen in infancy, although
older children and adults may develop habitual rumination as well (Reis,
1994).

Typically, rumination in infancy has a high spontaneous remission
rate (American Psychiatric Association, 1994). It is believed that infants
with this disorder use rumination to provide themselves with oral stimulation. The findings that these infants are typically under- or overstimulated,
have anxious or depressed caretakers, and come from stressful environments support this hypothesis (American Psychiatric Association, 1994;
Sauvage, Leddet, Hameury, & Barthelemy, 1985).

Another common feeding-related disturbance is colic, which is characterized by inconsolable crying after feeding. Colic is diagnosed by exclusion, in that persistent crying may signal an allergic reaction to milk or
formula, intestinal pain from infection or blockage, or other medically
treatable conditions. In their review of the colic literature, Hewson, Oberklaid, and Menahem (1987) noted the prevalence of colic to be between
20% and 30%, and lasting between 13 and 16 weeks. In fact, Lindberg et al.
(1991) found colic to be the most commonly reported problem related to
feeding in early infancy. They found that the mothers of infants with colic
in their sample reported more problems with their children during meals
even after the colic had been resolved. Vomiting was rated as a problem
twice as often as colic during the latter half of infants' first year of life, and
into the beginning of the second year, although both problems declined in
frequency from early infancy.

3.5.   Other Problematic Eating Patterns

In addition to the behaviors described, some children's eating styles
may be frustrating or worrisome to parents, even if they do not impact on
food intake. These include sloppy eating, eating too fast or too slow,
packing food in the mouth, and failing to practice acquired self-feeding

skills. These patterns may raise concerns about the child's development, precipitate gagging or choking on food, or make mealtimes unpleasant for other family members. More clinically severe forms of these problems are seen mainly in children with developmental delays or oral–motor impairments (Ginsberg, 1988; Kedesdy & Budd, in press).

4. Etiology of Common Feeding Problems

There are many theories as to how feeding problems develop and are maintained. Potential etiological variables for subclinical feeding difficulties are likely to be similar to those for the more severe feeding problems. Kedesdy and Budd (in press) proposed eight major causal areas: diet, physical (i.e., oral–motor and neuromuscular) competence, appetite, illness, interaction/management problems, child constitution (e.g., temperament, developmental functioning), caregiver competence, and systemic variables (e.g., family stressors). Mild or subtle expression of these factors can contribute to the development of less severe feeding problems as well. Increasingly, research in this field is looking at the interplay of physiological, social, and behavioral factors to better understand the nature of these problems (Budd et al., 1992; Linscheid, 1992). The following discussion pertains mainly to etiological precursors of finicky eating and overeating, reflective of the greater amount of research and clinical attention to these mild feeding problems.

4.1. Biological and Conditioning Factors

Although the contribution of biological factors to overeating (to be described) is generally supported, its influence is less clear in the development of finicky eating. Kedesdy and Budd (in press), in reviewing the literature on etiological factors for finicky eating habits, found that biological factors related to physical competence and chronic illness are less frequently postulated as causes of mild selectivity but are thought to play an increasingly significant role in the emergence of extreme selectivity. Dahl and Sundelin (1992) found that children identified at 3–12 months with refusal-to-eat problems were smaller physically from birth than a matched control sample. This suggests that normal variations in health status, growth parameters, or appetite may predispose some children to mealtime problems. Likewise, subtle oral–motor weaknesses may contribute to a child's resistance to accepting textured foods or refusal of solid foods (Skuse, 1993). Mild oral–motor difficulties may be suggested by prolonged chewing, frequent drooling while eating, or occasional gagging on coarse foods.

Both biological and environmental factors influence overeating and obesity, and it is often difficult to separate the effects of these variables. For example, the connection between parents' weight and their children's weight has been well documented (e.g., Garn & Clark, 1976; Stunkard et al., 1986). Homeostatic mechanisms (e.g., set point and fat cell stores) and constitutional differences in the palatability of high-calorie foods have been hypothesized to explain individual differences in weight status. Ballard, Gipson, Guttenberg, and Ramsey (1980) stated that "obese children are more highly influenced by the relative palatability of food than their normal-weight peers" (p. 599). In their comparison of consumption trends in obese and nonobese 9- to 11-year-old children, these authors found that although all children left approximately the same amount of food on their trays when finished eating, obese children ate twice as much of their "palatable food" (i.e., main course, bread, dessert) as did the nonobese children. There was no significant difference between the two groups in the amount of "unpalatable food" (i.e., vegetable, salad, fruit). It is not clear if these differences are due to the biological makeup of the children or if these are learned behaviors.

Research also has demonstrated the similarity between infants' feeding styles and those of their parents (Agras, Berkowitz, Hammer, & Kraemer, 1988). Specifically, Agras and colleagues found that infants were most like their mothers in terms of bite frequency and most like their fathers in terms of how long they spent eating. They found that some children, whose mothers ate quickly and whose fathers spent a long time to eat, ate more calories than other children in the study. This research suggests a possible hereditary or familial determinant of overeating. It also illustrates the difficulties of separating out the roles of biology and experience in the etiology of feeding patterns.

Physiological cues can be important in determining the quality and quantity of the child's food intake. At birth, neonates have the capacity to distinguish certain tastants from one another (Desor, Maller, & Andrews, 1975). Research evidence with human infants supports the notion of an innate preference for the sweet taste (e.g., Nowlis, 1973; Steiner, 1977) and an innate aversion to bitter foods (Rozin, 1984). There is also support for the existence of neophobia, or the fear or dislike of novel tastants (Birch, 1987). This neophobia is greatest when the child has had limited exposure to the disliked food (Zajonc, 1968), again indicating the contributory influence of experience. Indeed, Birch (1979) found that familiarity with foods was the most influential factor in determining a child's preference for that food. Sweetness was the second most predictive factor.

Birch and Deysher (1986) demonstrated that children have the capacity to regulate intake of calories based on internal cues of hunger and satiety. Birch, McPhee, Shoba, Steinberg, and Krehbiel (1987) took this finding one step further by demonstrating that the methods employed by our society for determining when and how much a person should eat predispose us to having difficulty in aligning our food intake with our energy needs. Specifically, Birch and colleagues trained preschool children to focus either on their internal hunger cues when determining their food needs or on external cues (i.e., time of day, amount left on the plate, extrinsic rewards for eating). Children in the internal condition were able to vary their food intake according to the calorie level of a snack given prior to eating, whereas those in the external condition showed no such responsiveness. This research suggests that despite having the capacity to self-regulate intake of calories based on internal cues, children can easily be redirected to eat for reasons other than hunger cues (i.e., external cues), thereby making it more difficult to match energy intake with energy needs.

Another way a child's eating can be affected is through negative conditioning. It has been found that long-standing aversions to foods can be created through the association of flavor cues of the food with negative consequences (e.g., nausea, vomiting) that are brought about by its ingestion or that occur simultaneously with ingestion due to other factors (e.g., illness). Once such associations are made, they can be very resistant to change (Garb & Stunkard, 1974).

The subclinical problems of mouthing, spitting up, vomiting, and colic are usually developmentally time-limited patterns. Colic, in particular, appears briefly (albeit intensely) and typically is resolved by 4 months of age (Hewson et al., 1987). Little research has identified specific biological precipitants for mouthing nonfood substances, spitting up, or vomiting, and their usual pattern of spontaneous remission complicates the search for etiological factors. Colic has been hypothesized to be the result of the infant's reaction to various allergens in the mother's breast milk or infant formula (Hewson et al., 1987). Stifter and Braungart (1992) provide partial support for this theory. In observations of infants during colicky periods, they noted that many of these infants display behaviors indicative of gastrointestinal pain (e.g., flatulence, pained facial expressions). This theory might help explain the finding that colicky infants were found to be more irritable during meals, even after the colic had resolved (Lindberg et al., 1991).

4.2. Social and Behavioral Factors

Satter (1986a) and others conceptualize feeding disorders as being heavily influenced by social and emotional factors. She argued that in addition to the biological causes of feeding disorders, the social influence of the family plays an important role. In particular, feeding problems are likely to develop when families attempt to override the physical and physiological makeup of the child in order to fit their image of the proper body size and feeding practices for children. Several researchers have cited parent–child interactions as being important in the development of feeding difficulties, and representative findings of this research are described next. In addition, other social influences such as media and cultural practices are described.

Maladaptive patterns of parents' interactions with the child have been implicated in the development of feeding problems. Power struggles between the parent and child over feeding (Chatoor & Egan, 1983), insufficient knowledge of nutrition (Pugliese, Weyman-Daum, Moses, & Lifshitz, 1987), and lack of responsiveness to the child's behaviors during the meal (Bradley, Casey, & Wortham, 1984; Pollitt, Eichler, & Chan, 1975) are among the identified problematic behaviors that may contribute to the development and/or maintenance of the feeding problem. Christophersen and Hall (1978) suggest that the attention the child receives because of spitting up can be enough to perpetuate the behavior even after the aversive food has been removed. One etiological hypothesis of colic is that parental anxiety prestages or perpetuates infant crying, although other factors (e.g., intestinal gas and discomfort) are thought to play a complementary role (Hewson et al., 1987).

Behavioral mismanagement refers to the maladaptive practices used by a child's caregivers that strengthen problematic mealtime behaviors (Linscheid & Rasnake, 1985). Such maladaptive practices include providing an irregular or disorganized feeding environment, discouraging or responding inconsistently to the child's feeding initiatives, and failing to provide consistent consequences for undesired behaviors during meals (Drotar, 1991). In comparing mealtime interactions of mothers and children with or without persistent feeding difficulties, Sanders et al. (1993) found that the interactions of the feeding-difficulties dyads were more likely to include aversive behaviors (e.g., negative physical contact, prompts to eat, comments on eating). They further demonstrated that overall level of maternal aversive behavior was a significant predictor of child disruptive behavior during meals. These findings support the hypothesis that misplaced social contingencies in parent–child interactions play a role in maintaining problematic feeding patterns.

Parents also can influence a child's eating patterns through the dietary menu and the timing of meals and snacks. Particularly for infants and young children, parents determine the foods offered to children. The work of Birch (1990) and colleagues suggest that repeated exposure to novel foods is instrumental in shaping children's willingness to accept a variety of foods. When parents stop offering a menu item based on the child's refusal, or when they substitute a familiar food to suite the child's tastes, they may be inadvertently reinforcing picky eating habits (Skuse, 1993). Likewise, the timing of eating occasions affects appetite. Offering a child food on an inconsistent or overly frequent basis can disrupt development of a normal hunger–eating–satiety pattern that supports adaptive eating habits. Irregular meals and free access to food across the day may contribute either to overeating or finicky eating patterns in children (Pipes & Trahms, 1993).

In addition to the structure and contingencies of interactions, modeling is another means by which the social environment influences children's eating (Bandura, 1969). Observation of others accounts for an enormous amount of children's learning about appropriate behavior. Likewise, by watching poor models, children may learn to refuse nonfavored foods, that high-calorie foods are preferable to "healthy" foods, and/or that snacking throughout the day, or "grazing," is acceptable.

Parents' methods of handling mealtime situations not only affect the child's behavior during the meals, but they also have been shown to correlate with their physical growth. Klesges et al. (1983) found that young children's (aged 12–30 months) weight was positively correlated with the parents' prompts to eat, parents' offers of food, and the parents' encouragement to eat. Although these data are not sufficient to support a causal relationship among these variables, they suggest an interaction between social factors and children's eating habits.

Stein, Woolley, Cooper, and Fairburn (1994) studied mothers with eating disorders (i.e., DSM-III-R diagnoses of Bulimia Nervosa and/or Eating Disorder Not Otherwise Specified) and their mealtime interactions with their infants. They found that the amount of conflict experienced during the meal was inversely related to the weight of the child, as was the degree to which the mother was concerned about her body shape. In other words, parents who were more intrusive and interruptive with their children during meals, and had more concern about their own body weight, raised children who weighed less than those whose parents were not intrusive with their children or who did not have concerns about their body shape. Because feeding is one of the earliest forms of communication between parents and their children, and because children seem to be like their parents in terms of eating styles (Agras et al., 1988), this connection between maternal eating disorders and their children's health outcomes is an important one.

In addition to social influences of the family, children increasingly learn through other environmental contexts such as media, neighbors, and peers. With children in the United States watching an average of 4 hours of television per day (Federal Trade Commission, 1981, as cited in Dawson, Jeffrey, & Walsh, 1988), there is growing interest in exploring the effects of television viewing on children's behavior. Children see an estimated 22,000 commercials each year (Choate, 1976, as cited in Signorielli & Lears, 1992), with the majority of television commercials aired during children's shows being for highly sweetened snack foods (Condry, Bence, & Scheibe, 1988).

The viewing of television commercials for low-nutrition foods has already been found to affect children's self-reported preference for those foods (Goldberg, Gorn, & Gibson, 1978). Signorielli and Lears (1992) found a significantly positive relationship between television viewing and poor eating habits. They also found some support for a link between high levels of television viewing and poor understanding of nutrition and food. Another important aspect of television watching is that it is a sedentary behavior. As pointed out by Dietz and Gortmaker (1985), the length of time engaged in behaviors that require limited physical activity, such as television viewing, has been linked to obesity.

Prevailing cultural patterns also influence a child's eating habits. Rozin (1984) points out the importance of culture and experience in determining the child's understanding about what foods are edible, inedible, dangerous, beneficial, bad tasting, and good tasting. Indeed, several research studies support the importance of environmental context in determining eating habits by demonstrating a link between low socioeconomic status and obesity (Sobal & Stunkard, 1989). Interestingly, Siddamma (1979) found the opposite to be true for people in India; obesity is more prevalent in the upper classes, and severe obesity was non-existent in their sample for the lower classes. These findings support the importance of considering the broader cultural and social context in determining the likelihood of obesity or other feeding problems. Specifically, Siddamma speculates that the stigma attached to obesity is far less in India than in Western countries.

4.3. Behavioral Correlates of Feeding Problems

It is often the case that the child with a feeding problem exhibits concomitant behavioral deviations in other areas. In their research investigating the variables associated with feeding problems in young children, Pelchat and Pliner (1986) found that those children who were reported to have problems with acting out, toileting problems, and fearfulness had higher levels of feeding difficulties.

As discussed earlier, Sanders et al. (1993) found that interactions between mothers and children with feeding problems were more aversive than interactions between normal control dyads. In addition to displaying a greater number of direct food refusals, the children were found to exhibit higher levels of noncompliance with a parental request, verbal complaining, oppositional behavior (e.g., teasing, breaking family rules), and playing with food. These behaviors can add to the negative atmosphere of the meal and serve to perpetuate aversive interactions between the child and parent.

Research on obese individuals has tended to focus more on eating styles than on mealtime interactions. Obese people are thought to have an eating style that is different from normal-weight people. Characteristics of this eating style include taking large bites, having shorter meals, and eating quickly. Although the evidence in support of obese people taking larger bites than normal is inconsistent (e.g., Dodd, Birky, & Stalling, 1976; Marston, London, & Cooper, 1976), there is some support for the existence of a more rapid eating pace among obese people (e.g., Geller, Keane, & Scheirer, 1981; Marston et al., 1976). This finding has been shown in children as young as 1½ to 2 years of age (Drabman, Cordua, Hammer, Jarvie, & Horton, 1979).

Lindberg et al. (1991) reported that both colic and vomiting were associated with some additional behavioral difficulties in young children. Although both conditions were correlated with feeding difficulties among siblings and problems with breast-feeding, the vomiting group differed significantly in weight compared to a no-problem control group. The colic group experienced more diarrhea, and their mothers experienced more physical problems during pregnancy, including anemia, hypertonia, and sciatica.

5. Assessment of Subclinical Feeding Concerns

The previous discussion clarifies that deviations in children's feeding patterns can evolve as a result of biological, conditioning, social, and/or behavioral factors. Assessment of feeding and associated factors is needed in order to determine whether the patterns are of clinical concern and how best to respond to them.

When concerns about feeding-related behaviors arise, parents are first likely to address these issues with the child's pediatrician. In assessing the degree of severity of a feeding problem, health professionals evaluate physical growth by comparing the child's height, weight, and head circumference with a set of national norms (Hamill et al., 1979). A more detailed assessment of physical growth can include triceps skinfold measurements and arm circumference measurements. The health professional also looks for any telltale signs of specific vitamin and/or mineral deficiencies (Pipes & Trahms, 1993). Typically, the child is deemed to be growth deficient if the weight for height falls below the 5th percentile, or exceeds the 95th percentile, if the child's growth is accelerating or decelerating markedly, or if the child is showing any signs of specific nutritional deficiencies (e.g., degeneration of the retina in vitamin A deficiency) (for a review, see Walker & Hendricks, 1985).

Even when feeding problems are thought to be minor, physical or organic causes for the child's difficulties need to be ruled out through medical examination. Depending on the medical findings, the child may be referred to a variety of health-care professionals. For example, should questions arise about the child's ability to chew and swallow, a referral may be made to an occupational therapist, a speech/language pathologist, or another oral–motor feeding specialist. When dietary patterns appear inadequate, nutritionists are often consulted. When social, behavioral, or emotional aspects of the child or family environment are posited to contribute to feeding concerns, referrals may be made to psychologists or social workers.

Mental health assessment of children with mild, feeding-related problems typically entails a clinical interview, observation, and parent-collected records of relevant feeding patterns. The content and structure of feeding assessments for more serious clinical cases have been described elsewhere (e.g., Kedesdy & Budd, in press; Linscheid et al., 1995; Luiselli, 1989; Satter, 1986a), and segments from these sources are suggested here for mild problems. Although the current discussion pertains to assessment of feeding-related behavior, the clinician typically gathers information on broader aspects of the child's functioning (e.g., developmental status, behavioral adjustment at home and school, current stressful family conditions) (cf. Schroeder & Gordon, 1991).

When interviewing parents about their child's feeding difficulties, it is important to gather information about the following topics: (1) the specific nature of their child's feeding problem, (2) the factors that precede and follow the problematic behavior, (3) when the problem began and how the parents believe it developed, (4) fluctuations in the problem (e.g., "Does it vary depending on who feeds the child?"), (5) how the problem has been handled and prior professional consultation related to the problem, (6) the impact of the problem on mealtimes, (7) what typical meals include, (8) the child's food likes and dislikes, (9) the child's typical feeding schedule, and (10) who else eats with the child. With older children, many of these questions can be asked directly of the child. This can be particularly helpful when the problem is specific to settings outside of the home (e.g., school). Exploring possible peer influences can be important in these cases as well.

To supplement the interview, a written questionnaire may be helpful for gathering information about caregivers' perceptions of the child's feeding problems. The Children's Eating Behavior Inventory (CEBI) is designed to screen for mealtime problems in 2- to 12-year-old children (Archer, Rosenbaum, & Streiner, 1991). The CEBI is a relatively recent measure and thus has been subjected to limited research; however, it has been shown to differentiate clinic from nonclinic populations. A more general child behavior questionnaire, such as the Eyberg Child Behavior Inventory (Eyberg & Ross, 1978) or the Child Behavior Checklist (Achenbach, 1991, 1992) also is useful for examining the range and intensity of child difficulties perceived by the parents. These instruments are widely used and have been validated through extensive psychometric research; however, they each contain only one or two items directly related to feeding, and neither applies to children under 2 years of age.

In addition to questioning the parent about feeding practices and mealtime routines, observing a meal in the clinic setting is highly informative in learning how parent and child interact during meals and relating their interactions to the presenting concerns. If the clinical concerns relate to mouthing nonfood substances, spitting up, vomiting, or colic, it may be helpful to observe parent–child interactions outside of feedings (e.g., by simulating the conditions in which the problem is most likely to occur). Collecting sample menus and daily records of the child's food intake and other behaviors of concern (e.g., vomiting, prolonged crying) can provide insight into how often the child eats during the day, who else is present during meals, who is responsible for the child's feeding, and when problematic behaviors occur. It is also important to get a sense of other factors that might be contributing to the presenting concerns, such as the child's activity level, the parent's knowledge of an age-appropriate diet for the child, and the parent's ability to afford sufficient food.

In cases of clinical disorders, Drotar and Crawford (1987) advocate the use of home observation in assessing children, suggesting that factors that are influential in the home may not be readily observable in clinic settings. For children with persistent feeding difficulties, Budd, Chugh, and Berry (in press) describe how home observations can provide information that is different from data gleaned from clinic observations. Having parents record an audiotape or videotape sample of the problem at home can be highly useful for depicting behavioral characteristics and parental management strategies (Madison & Adubato, 1984). This information is then used to develop appropriate intervention strategies. For subclinical deviations from normal feeding, however, simple information gathering is often sufficient for helping the parent to begin addressing the presenting concerns.

6. Management Approaches

Mild feeding concerns may be handled in several different ways, depending on whether the assessment reveals that the patterns are, in fact, developmentally inappropriate and whether parents are motivated to change aspects of the child's environment or their child-related interactions. Parents may receive informal suggestions in the form of anticipatory guidance, or a mental health professional may introduce parents to specific techniques, such as those listed in Table 2. The most commonly used techniques for mild, feeding-related concerns include repeated exposure, modeling, differential attention, stimulus control, and various combinations of behavior management strategies.

6.1. Anticipatory Guidance

Anticipatory guidance, often offered by the pediatrician, is essentially a prevention effort (Brazelton, 1995). It involves providing advice and information at well-child visits about how to handle typical developmental progressions (e.g., introducing solid foods) and responding adaptively to children's ploys (e.g., insisting on having cookies for breakfast). Provid-

TABLE 2
Management Approaches to Mild Feeding Problems

Behavioral technique	Key concept
Repeated exposure	Regularly present the child with new foods and foods initially rejected, and encourage sampling of these foods.
Modeling	Provide opportunities for the child to observe others who exhibit the desired behaviors and who receive reinforcement for doing so.
Differential attention	Follow desired behaviors with praise and positive consequences, and follow undesired behaviors with the brief removal of attention.
Stimulus control	Arrange events or conditions associated with reinforcement of the desired behavior to occur regularly, and remove stimuli associated with undesired behavior.

ing parents with guidance about what to expect with the developing child is likely to assuage some fears parents might have. For example, simply reminding parents about the normal development of feeding practices, suggesting healthy foods that often are attractive to children, and emphasizing that appetites vary considerably in early childhood may prevent mealtimes from becoming a source of undue stress and worry. Primary care professionals may also ask parents about their infant's cues of satiety (i.e., spitting out the nipple, dozing off during feedings, biting or playing with nipple) and encourage them to respond to these signals to prevent problems related to overfeeding. For infant colic, pediatricians typically offer parents tips on possible ways to reduce crying, including using a pacifier, laying the infant prone, rocking, or swaddling (Hewson et al., 1987).

Unfortunately, as Reisinger and Bires (1980) found, anticipatory guidance makes up only a small fraction of the typical well-child visit (approximately 8% of the total time spent with the pediatrician). As noted previously, lack of nutritional knowledge on the part of the parent has been implicated in the poor nutrition of children (e.g., Pugliese et al., 1987). Although feeding appears to be the area of most discussion during well-child visits (Reisinger & Bires, 1980), the amount of time is still very low and appears to be insufficient for the effective prevention of problems around feeding.

To assist pediatricians in offering anticipatory guidance within this limited time frame, written guidelines have been developed for parents around typical feeding concerns. For example, Finney (1986) summarized behavior management techniques that can be used to prevent common feeding problems. Pamphlets (e.g., National Live Stock and Meat Board, 1992) illustrating recommended dietary ingredients and serving sizes for children provide useful ideas for planning meals and snacks. However, little research has examined the effects of these methods as prevention or remediation strategies for mild, feeding-related problems.

6.2. Repeated Exposure and Modeling

Of the many factors that affect a child's food preferences, exposure and modeling can be utilized as strategies for dealing with mild food selectivity in children. For instance, one method for increasing children's range of food preferences is to present new foods to them repeatedly. Several studies support the effectiveness of repeated exposure of foods in enhancing children's preference for these foods (e.g., Birch & Marlin, 1982; Pliner, 1982; Sullivan & Birch, 1990). Although it may be tempting for parents to give up presenting a food the child initially rejects, repeated exposure to that food increases the chances that the child will sample it and eventually like it. Birch and Marlin's (1982) research suggests that children's preferences for novel foods change after a mean of 10 exposures to them. However, although the logic of repeated exposure is persuasive, and research in laboratory settings suggests its effectiveness, it has yet to be studied as a clinical strategy with children who exhibit mild or severe feeding problems.

Another way to change children's feeding behavior is through modeling. Christophersen and Hall (1978) suggest that when parents want their child to eat fewer snack foods, the parents themselves should try to avoid eating these foods in front of their children. Correspondingly, arranging for the child to observe others, particularly a person valued highly by the child, eating a particular food can increase the likelihood that the child will try it as well (Greer, Dorow, Williams, McCorkle, & Asnes, 1991). Support for the notion that modeling is important in the shaping of children's consumption patterns is given by Birch (1980). This research demonstrates the effects of peers' food choices on the types of food the target children request. Specifically, 17 children in this study were asked to rate their preferences for various vegetables. During lunchtime, these children were matched with several other children who strongly disliked one of the target child's favorite foods, and who strongly liked one of the target child's least preferred foods. At each meal, all of the children were asked to select one of two vegetables for lunch that day. The two vegetables were the same for each meal. Records for each child were collected over 4 consecutive days. While 15 of the 17 target children initially chose the food they indicated they preferred most, by day 4, 10 of the 17 chose the food they originally indicated they liked least. Birch explains these shifts in food choice in terms of the modeling effect of the children's peers.

6.3. Differential Attention

Because parent–child mealtime interactions have been posited to contribute to the development and/or maintenance of feeding patterns, helping parents to alter their methods of responding to their child is a logical approach to changing their child's feeding behavior. Differential attention is based on operant conditioning and refers to the purposeful giving of attention to strengthen certain behaviors, and the purposeful removal of attention to weaken others (Bijou & Baer, 1965). For example, if the goal is to increase the number of bites of vegetables a child eats during a meal and to decrease the child's refusal of vegetables, using differential attention would involve having the parent provide positive attention (e.g., praise and approval) immediately after the child takes a bite of vegetables and to remove attention (i.e., briefly ignore the child) when refusals or food complaints occur. Social praise may be paired intermittently with tangible rewards, such as a favored drink or access to a toy, in order to strengthen the reinforcing value. Parents' ability to learn and use these techniques effectively with their children during mealtimes has been well documented (e.g., Stark, Powers, Jelalian, Rape, & Miller, 1994; Werle, Murphy, & Budd, 1993).

Differential attention also forms a core ingredient of strategies for modifying other mild, feeding-related problems. To reduce children's overeating, parents can provide social approval for eating "healthy" foods, eating at planned times and locations, and engaging in alternative behaviors such as physical exercise (Kirschenbaum et al., 1987). Finney, Russo, and Cataldo (1982) showed that pica in children with lead poisoning can be reduced by providing social reinforcement and food treats for increasing periods of time *without* any mouthing of inedible objects (i.e., differential reinforcement of other behavior—DRO). This study suggests the viability of using DRO to decrease less severe forms of mouthing as well. However, given that mouthing nonfood items appears to be a developmentally normative behavior in infants that provides oral stimulation, ensuring the child's access to safe mouthing toys and precluding access to dangerous items (as noted in section 6.4) may be more productive than social attention alone. Problematic behaviors such as sloppy eating, eating too fast or too slow, packing food in the mouth, and resisting use of utensils also can be approached through differential attention procedures. By identifying acceptable alternative responses, parents can shift their attention from disruptive or dawdling tactics to occasions of appropriate eating styles.

Behavior management techniques have less relevance to reducing behaviors such as spitting up, vomiting, or colicky crying, because these patterns are thought to be determined largely by maturational factors. Still, differential attention principles are helpful to keep in mind, mainly to avoid the parent's unintentional reinforcement of these patterns through excessive social attention.

Some controversy exists about the efficacy of differential attention techniques to modify feeding patterns in normally developing children or those with mild feeding problems. Birch (1990) has cautioned, based on her research, that preschool-aged children are able to decipher obvious praise or food rewards for eating certain foods as a "ploy," and she notes that, over time, these foods are likely to be *less*, rather than more, attractive to children. This caution implies that reinforcement should not be the primary means used to shape a child's food patterns. Because Birch's work was carried out in a laboratory, preschool setting with normal children, it is unclear whether her findings are directly applicable to the family mealtime setting with children who exhibit mild feeding problems. However, considering that children's feeding patterns are influenced by many variables, including appetite, exposure, and social contingencies, it makes sense to structure the timing of eating opportunities to take advantage of children's hunger. Likewise, it seems wise to incorporate other techniques (e.g., modeling, stimulus control) that can assist the child in developing desirable eating habits.

6.4. Stimulus Control

Arranging events or conditions that are associated with reinforcement for specific behaviors is another strategy for influencing the likelihood of these behaviors. Stimulus control involves repeatedly pairing a particular stimulus with reinforcement for engaging in the desired behavior (Bijou & Baer, 1965). For example, if a boy is routinely fed when sitting in a booster seat with his bib on at the kitchen table, he learns to associate the booster seat, bib, and table with eating occasions. Instructions to him can acquire stimulus control when they are systematically followed with praise or other positive consequences for compliance. For example, by telling him to "Blow on the soup to cool it off," and then praising him for doing so, a parent is using stimulus control tactics to teach the child how to eat hot foods safely. Another variation on this tactic is to provide a child with a choice between two alternatives (e.g., offering the child either applesauce or a banana), thereby setting the occasion for social reinforcement of the selected option.

Stimulus control also can be used to decrease problematic behaviors by removing stimuli associated with the behavior. Sucking or mouthing nonfood items is an example of a behavior that can be decreased via stimulus control. With the exception of addressing immediate health concerns based on what the child ingested (e.g., household cleaners), mouthing nonnutritive items often can be handled by "child-proofing" the environment to ensure that access to unsafe products is restricted. Alternatively, teaching the child to discriminate items that are inedible may be helpful (Finney et al., 1982).

Shaping of the environment can also be helpful with children who overeat or who eat too much "junk food." Making high-calorie snack foods less available and more healthy foods accessible can have an obvious and immediate effect on the child's consumption patterns. This would also likely impact the consumption patterns of others in the house, which would change the modeling the target child receives. Parental monitoring can help by determining the situations in which the child is likely to overeat. If it is determined, for instance, that television watching is highly associated with the eating of high-calorie snack food, a stimulus control approach might involve providing the child with low-calorie snack foods during these times, or limiting television watching during eating.

6.5. Bibliographical Strategies

The option of receiving advice and guidance in behavior management strategies from a health-care professional is not always possible for parents because of time and/or monetary considerations. In a few studies, the use of printed materials, or bibliotherapy, has been shown to produce positive results in terms of teaching behavioral techniques for altering the parents' and, as a result, the child's mealtime behaviors. McMahon and Forehand (1978) demonstrated that a brochure detailing the principles of differential attention and time-out was useful in teaching these principles to parents and in reducing inappropriate mealtime behaviors of the children. Bauman, Reiss, Rogers, and Bailey (1983) demonstrated the effectiveness of their advice package for taking children to restaurants. Their study found that parents could improve the mealtime situation simply by reading the brochure and implementing it on their own. Advice given in the package included specifying to their children the behaviors appropriate for the setting and structuring the setting in the restaurant (e.g., choosing a booth away from the crowd, separating the children, moving silverware from the children's reach, bringing toys for the children to play with prior to the beginning of the meal, removing toys when food arrives). The advice package was successful in helping the parents reduce their children's inappropriate mealtime behavior, and parents rated the package as being helpful to them.

7. Conclusions

Mild feeding difficulties, such as finicky eating habits, overeating, mouthing nonfood items, spitting up and vomiting, and colic, are quite common across childhood. A variety of biological, conditioning, social, and behavioral factors can contribute to the development, exacerbation, and maintenance of disturbances in the feeding practices of children. These disturbances can have negative effects on the child, the parents, and their interactions. In order to differentiate subclinical from clinical feeding problems and to determine if intervention is appropriate, a thorough assessment needs to be conducted. While mild feeding problems sometimes can be prevented through anticipatory guidance, behavioral strategies (e.g., repeated exposure, modeling, differential attention, and stimulus control), alone and in combination, are promising strategies for managing common feeding concerns. More attention has been paid to finicky eating and overeating; less investigation has been made into applications of behavior management to other subclinical feeding problems.

Review of the current knowledge on prevalence, etiology, and treatment of common feeding-related concerns suggests several fruitful areas for further research. First, because most research has concentrated on nonproblem samples or on clinically severe manifestations of feeding problems, relatively less is known about interventions with children who display mild feeding deviations. For example, studies with normative samples suggest that repeated exposure to novel foods results in children's increased preference for these foods (Birch, 1990). Is repeated exposure to nonpreferred foods an effective method for increasing preference and food acceptance in children with mild food selectivity, or are additional strategies (i.e., social contingencies, withholding of preferred foods) needed? Similarly, a small literature suggests that bibliographic methods are sufficient to teach parents how to increase children's cooperation during mealtimes (Bauman et al., 1983; McMahon & Forehand, 1978). Can parents of mildly overweight children learn to safely modify their children's dietary intake (and related behaviors) through a bibliographic approach? The effectiveness of such low-cost interventions would seem to be a valuable topic of study, given the prevalence of mild feeding problems in children.

A second area for further research relates to the lack of objective criteria for distinguishing clinical feeding problems from subclinical feeding problems. In order for researchers to communicate effectively about the prevalence, impact, and modification of mild, feeding-related conditions, a common set of definitions for mild feeding deviations is needed. The wide discrepancy among prevalence estimates of pediatric feeding problems underscores the need for more precise terminology and data gathering.

Although, in many cases, the subclinical problems of mouthing, spitting up, vomiting, and colic are sufficiently benign or short-lived that they do not require professional intervention, these behaviors nevertheless are worrisome and stressful for parents. A third research topic suggested by the current review entails examining how these problematic patterns are actually handled by parents. It would be informative to compare parents' methods of responding to specific subclinical feeding problems with the methods health-care professionals recommend. Such descriptive research could identify effective versus ineffective parental strategies, culturally specific practices, and caregiving practices that signal the need for professional attention (such as misinterpreting normal mouthing or spitting up as intentional child misbehavior). Research suggests that it is the accumulated, everyday stresses of child rearing, rather than extreme incidents, that frustrate parents and can escalate into child maltreatment (Wolfe, 1988). Common feeding-related problems represent one such area of vulnerability; thus, practicing clinicians need to be versed in methods of assessing and counseling parents regarding everyday feeding concerns.

ACKNOWLEDGMENT

This project was supported in part by a grant from the DePaul University Research Council to the first author.

8. *References*

Achenbach, T. M. (1991). *Manual for the Child Behavior Checklist/4-18 and 1991 Profile*. Burlington: University of Vermont, Department of Psychiatry.

Achenbach, T. M. (1992). *Manual for the Child Behavior Checklist/2-3 and 1992 Profile*. Burlington: University of Vermont, Department of Psychiatry.

Agras, W. S., Berkowitz, R. I., Hammer, L. C., & Kraemer, H. C. (1988). Relationships between the eating behaviors of parents and their 18-month-old children: A laboratory study. *International Journal of Eating Disorders, 7*, 461–468.

American Psychiatric Association. (1994). *Diagnostic and statistical manual of mental disorders* (4th ed.). Washington, DC: Author.

Archer, L. A., Rosenbaum, P. L., & Streiner, D. L. (1991). The Children's Eating Behavior Inventory: Reliability and validity results. *Journal of Pediatric Psychology, 16*, 629–642.

Ballard, B. D., Gipson, M. T., Guttenberg, W., & Ramsey, K. (1980). Palatability of food as a factor influencing obese and normal-weight children's eating habits. *Behaviour Research and Therapy, 18*, 598–600.

Bandura, A. (1969). *Principles of behavior modification* (Ch. 3). New York: Holt, Rinehart & Winston.

Bauman, K. E., Reiss, M. L., Rogers, R. W., & Bailey, J. S. (1983). Dining out with children: Effectiveness of a parent advice package on pre-meal inappropriate behavior. *Journal of Applied Behavior Analysis, 16*, 55–68.

Beautrais, A. L., Fergusson, D. M., & Shannon, F. T. (1982). Family life events and behavioral problems in preschool-aged children. *Pediatrics, 70*, 774–779.

Bentovim, A. (1970). The clinical approach to feeding disorders of childhood. *Journal of Psychosomatic Research, 14*, 267–276.

Bijou, S. W., & Baer, D. M. (1965). *Child development I: A systematic and empirical theory*. Englewood Cliffs, NJ: Prentice-Hall.

Birch, L. L. (1979). Preschool children's food preferences and consumption patterns. *Journal of Nutrition Education, 11*, 189–192.

Birch, L. L. (1980). Effects of peer models' food choices and eating behaviors on preschoolers' food preferences. *Child Development, 51*, 489–496.

Birch, L. L. (1987). Children's food preferences: Developmental patterns and environmental influences. *Annals of Child Development, 4*, 171–208.

Birch, L. L. (1990). The control of food intake by young children: The role of learning. In E. D. Capaldi & T. L. Powley (Eds.), *Taste, experience, and feeding* (pp. 116–135). Washington, DC: American Psychological Association.

Birch, L. L.., & Deysher, M. (1986). Caloric compensation and sensory-specific satiety: Evidence for self-regulation of food intake by young children. *Appetite, 7,* 323–331.

Birch, L. L., & Marlin, D. W. (1982). I don't like it; I never tried it: Effects of exposure on two-year-old children's food preferences. *Appetite, 3,* 353–360.

Birch, L. L., McPhee, L., Shoba, B. C., Steinberg, L., & Krehbiel, R. (1987). "Clean up your plate": Effects of child feeding practices on the conditioning of meal size. *Learning and Motivation, 18,* 301–317.

Bradley, R. H., Casey, P. M., & Wortham, B. (1984). Home environments of low SES nonorganic failure to thrive infants. *Merrill Palmer Quarterly, 30,* 393–402.

Brazelton, T. B. (1995). Touchpoints for anticipatory guidance in the first three years. In S. Parker & B. Zuckerman (Eds.), *Behavioral and developmental pediatrics* (pp. 10–14). Boston: Little, Brown.

Budd, K. S., Chugh, C. S., & Berry, S. L. (in press). Parents as therapists for children's food refusal problems. In C. E. Schaefer & J. M. Briesmeister (Eds.), *Handbook of parent training* (2nd ed.). New York: Wiley.

Budd, K. S., McGraw, T. E., Farbisz, R., Murphy, T. B., Hawkins, D., Heilman, N., Werle, M., & Hochstadt, N. J. (1992). Psychosocial concomitants of children's feeding disorders. *Journal of Pediatric Psychology, 17,* 81–94.

Chatoor, I., & Egan, J. (1983). Nonorganic failure to thrive and dwarfism due to food refusal: A separation disorder. *Journal of the American Academy of Child Psychiatry, 22,* 294–301.

Choate, R. B. (1976). Testimony before the Federal Trade Commission in the matter of a trade regulation rule on food nutrition advertising. Washington, DC: Council on Children, Media, and Merchandising.

Christophersen, E. R., & Hall, C. L. (1978). Eating patterns and associated problems encountered in normal children. *Issues in Comprehensive Pediatric Nursing, 3,* 1–16.

Condry, J., Bence, P., & Scheibe, C. (1988). Nonprogram content of children's television. *Journal of Broadcasting and Electronic Media, 32,* 255–270.

Dahl, M., & Sundelin, C. (1986). Early feeding problems in an affluent society: I. Categories and clinical signs. *Acta Paediatrica Scandinavica, 75,* 370–379.

Dahl, M., & Sundelin, C. (1992). Feeding problems in an affluent society. Follow-up at four years of age in children with early refusal to eat. *Acta Paediatrica, 81,* 575–579.

Dawson, B. L., Jeffrey, D. B., & Walsh, J. A. (1988). Television food commercials' effect on children's resistance to temptation. *Journal of Applied Social Psychology, 18,* 1353–1360.

Desor, J. A., Maller, O., & Andrews, K. (1973). Ingestive responses of human newborns to salty, sour, and bitter stimuli. *Journal of Comparative and Physiological Psychology, 89,* 966–970.

Dietz, W. H. (1984). Obesity in infancy. In R. B. Howard & H. S. Winter (Eds.), *Nutrition and feeding of infants and toddlers* (pp. 297–307). Boston: Little, Brown.

Dietz, W. H. (1987). Nutrition and obesity. In R. J. Grand, J. L. Sutphen, & W. H. Dietz (Eds.), *Pediatric nutrition* (pp. 525–538). Boston: Butterworths.

Dietz, W. H., & Gortmaker, S. L. (1985). Do we fatten our children at the TV set? Obesity and television viewing in children and adolescents. *Pediatrics, 75,* 807–812.

Dodd, D. K., Birky, H. J., & Stalling, R. B. (1976). Eating behavior of obese and normal weight females in a natural setting. *Addictive Behaviors, 1,* 321–325.

Drabman, R. S., Cordua, G. D., Hammer, D., Jarvie, G. J., & Horton, W. (1979). Developmental trends in eating rates of normal and overweight preschool children. *Child Development, 50,* 211–216.

Drotar, D. (Ed.). (1985). *New directions in failure to thrive: Implications for research and practice.* New York: Plenum Press.

Drotar, D. (1991). The family context of nonorganic failure to thrive. *American Journal of Orthopsychiatry, 6,* 23–34.

Drotar, D., & Crawford, P. (1987). Using home observation in the clinical assessment of children. *Journal of Clinical Child Psychology, 16,* 342–349.

Epstein, L. H., Wing, R. R., & Valoski, A. (1985). Childhood obesity. *Pediatric Clinics of North America, 32,* 363–379.

Erikson, E. (1950). *Childhood and society.* New York: W. W. Norton.

Eyberg, S. M., & Ross, A. W. (1978). Assessment of child behavior problems: The validation of a new inventory. *Journal of Clinical Child Psychology, 7,* 113–116.

Federal Trade Commission. (1981). *FTC final staff report and recommendation.* Washington, DC: Author.

Feldman, M. D. (1986). Pica: Current perspectives. *Psychomatics, 27,* 519–523.

Finney, J. W. (1986). Preventing common feeding problems in infants and young children. *Pediatric Clinics of North America, 33,* 775–788.

Finney, J. W., Russo, D. C., & Cataldo, M. F. (1982). Reduction of pica in young children with lead poisoning. *Journal of Pediatric Psychology, 7,* 197–207.

Foreyt, J. P., & Goodrick, G. K. (1988). Childhood obesity. In E. J. Mash, & L. G. Terdal (Eds.), *Behavioral assessment of childhood disorders* (2nd ed., pp. 528–551). New York: Guilford.

Forsyth, B. W. C., Leventhal, J. M., & McCarthy, P. L. (1985). Mothers' perceptions of problems of feeding and crying behaviors: A prospective study. *American Journal of Diseases of Children, 139,* 269–272.

Garb, J. L., & Stunkard, A. J. (1974). Taste aversions in man. *American Journal of Psychiatry, 131,* 1204–1207.

Garn, S. M., & Clark, D. C. (1976). Trends in fatness and the origins of obesity. *Pediatrics, 56,* 443–456.

Geller, S. E., Keane, T. M., & Scheirer, C. J. (1981). Delay of gratification, locus of control, and eating patterns in obese and nonobese children. *Addictive Behaviors, 6,* 9–14.

Ginsberg, A. J. (1988). Feeding disorders in the developmentally disabled population. In D. E. Russo & J. H. Kedesdy (Eds.), *Behavioral medicine with the developmentally disabled* (pp. 21–41). New York: Plenum Press.

Goldberg, M., Gorn, G. J., & Gibson, W. (1978). TV messages for snack and breakfast foods: Do they influence children's preferences? *Journal of Consumer Research, 5,* 73–81.

Gortmaker, S. L., Dietz, W. H., Sobol, A. M., & Wehler, C. A. (1987). Increasing pediatric obesity in the United States. *American Journal of Diseases of Children, 141,* 535–540.

Greer, R. D., Dorow, L., Williams, G., McCorkle, N., & Asnes, R. (1991). Peer-mediated procedures to induce swallowing and food acceptance in young children. *Journal of Applied Behavior Analysis, 24,* 783–790.

Hagekull, B., & Dahl, M. (1987). Infants with and without feeding difficulties: Maternal experiences. *International Journal of Eating Disorders, 6,* 83–98.

Hamill, P. V. V., Drizd, T. A., Johnson, C. L., Reed, R. B., Roche, A. F., & Moore, W. M. (1979). Physical growth: National center for health statistics percentiles. *American Journal of Clinical Nutrition, 32,* 607–629.

Hewson, P., Oberklaid, F., & Menahem, S. (1987). Infant colic, distress, and crying. *Clinical Pediatrics, 26,* 69–75.

Howard, R. B. (1984). The infant feeding experience. In R. B. Howard, & H. S. Winter (Eds.), *Nutrition and feeding of infants and toddlers* (pp. 21–39). Boston: Little, Brown.

Hufton, I. W., & Oates, R. K. (1977). Nonorganic failure to thrive: A long-term follow-up. *Pediatrics, 59,* 73–79.

Israel, A. C. (1990). Childhood obesity. In A. S. Bellack, M. Hersen, & A. E. Kazdin (Eds.), *International handbook of behavior modification and therapy* (2nd ed., pp. 819–830). New York: Plenum Press.

Kedesdy, J. H., & Budd, K. S. (in press). *Childhood feeding disorders: Biobehavioral assessment and intervention.* Baltimore: Paul M. Brookes.

Kirschenbaum, D. S., Johnson, W. G., & Stalonas, P. M., Jr. (1987). *Treating childhood and adolescent obesity.* New York: Pergamon.

Klesges, R. C., Coates, T. J., Brown, G., Sturgeon-Tillisch, J., Moldenhauer-Klesges, L. M., Holzer, B., Woolfrey, J., & Vollmer, J. (1983). Parental influences on children's eating behavior and relative weight. *Journal of Applied Behavior Analysis, 16,* 371–378.

Lindberg, L., Bohlin, G., & Hagekull, B. (1991). Early feeding problems in a normal population. *International Journal of Eating Disorders, 10,* 395–405.

Linscheid, T.R. (1992). Eating problems in children. In C. E. Walker, & M. C. Roberts (Eds.), *Handbook of clinical child psychology* (2nd ed., pp. 451–473). New York: Wiley.

Linscheid, T. R., Budd, K. S., & Rasnake, L. K. (1995). Pediatric feeding disorders. In M. C. Roberts (Ed.), *Handbook of pediatric psychology* (2nd ed., pp. 501–515). New York: Guilford.

Linscheid, T. R., & Rasnake, L. K. (1985). Behavioral approaches to the treatment of failure to thrive. In D. Drotar (Ed.), *New directions in failure to thrive: Implications for research and practice* (pp. 279–294). New York: Plenum Press.

Lipsett, L. P., & Behl, G. (1990). Taste-mediated differences in the sucking behavior of human newborns. In E. D. Capaldi & T. L. Powley (Eds.), *Taste, experience, and feeding* (pp. 75–93). Washington, DC: American Psychological Association.

Luiselli, J. K. (1989). Behavioral assessment and treatment of pediatric feeding disorders in developmental disabilities. In H. Hersen, R. K. Eisler, & P. M. Miller (Eds.), *Progress in behavior modification* (Vol. 24, pp. 91–131). Newbury Park, CA: Sage.

Madden, N. A., Russo, D. C., & Cataldo, M. F. (1980). Environmental influences on mouthing in children with lead intoxication. *Journal of Pediatric Psychology, 5,* 207–216.

Madison, L. S., & Adubato, S. A. (1984). The elimination of ruminative vomiting in a 15-month-old child with gastroesophageal reflux. *Journal of Pediatric Psychology, 9,* 231–239.

Marchi, M., & Cohen, P. (1990). Early childhood eating behaviors and adolescent eating disorders. *Journal of the American Academy of Child and Adolescent Psychiatry, 29,* 112–117.

Marston, A. R., London, P., & Cooper, L. M. (1976). A note on the eating behavior of children varying in weight. *Journal of Child Psychology and Psychiatry and Allied Disciplines, 17,* 221–224.

McMahon, R. J., & Forehand, R. (1978). Nonprescription behavior therapy: Effectiveness of a brochure in teaching mothers to correct their children's inappropriate mealtime behaviors. *Behavior Therapy, 9,* 814–820.

Moss, A. J., & Moss, T. J. (1980). *The essentials of pediatrics: The clinical core in outline.* Philadelphia: Lippincott.

National Live Stock and Meat Board. (1992). *A food guide for the first five years.* Chicago: Author.

Nowlis, G. H. (1973). Taste elicited tongue movements in human newborn infants: An approach to palatability. In J. F. Bosma (Ed.), *Fourth symposium on oral sensation and perception: Development of the fetus and infant* (DHEW Publication No. NIH 73-546). Washington, DC: U.S. Government Printing Office.

Oates, R. K., Peacock, A., & Forrest, D. (1985). Long-term effects of non-organic failure to thrive. *Pediatrics, 75,* 36–40.

O'Brien, S., Repp, A. C., Williams, G. E., & Christophersen, E. R. (1991). Pediatric feeding disorders. *Behavior Modification, 15,* 394–418.

Pelchat, M. L., & Pliner, P. (1986). Antecedents and correlates of feeding problems in young children. *Journal of Nutrition Education, 18,* 23–29.

Pipes, P. L., & Trahms, C. M. (1993). *Nutrition in infancy and childhood* (5th ed.). St. Louis: C. V. Mosby.

Pliner, P. (1982). The effects of mere exposure on liking for edible substances. *Appetite, 3,* 283–290.

Pollitt, E., Eichler, A. W., & Chan, C. K. (1975). Psychosocial development and behavior of mothers of failure-to-thrive children. *American Journal of Orthopsychiatry, 45,* 525–537.

Pugliese, M. T., Weyman-Daum, M., Moses, N., & Lifshitz, F. M. (1987). Parental health beliefs as a cause of non-organic failure to thrive. *Pediatrics, 80,* 175–181.

Reau, N. R., Senturia, Y. D., Lebailly, S. A., & Christoffel, K. K. (1996). Infant and toddler feeding patterns and problems: Normative data and a new direction. *Journal of Developmental and Behavioral Pediatrics, 17,* 149–153.

Reis, S. (1994). Rumination in two developmentally normal children: Case report and review of the literature. *Journal of Family Practice, 38,* 521–523.

Reisinger, K. S., & Bires, J. A. (1980). Anticipatory guidance in pediatric practice. *Pediatrics, 66,* 889–892.

Rozin, P. (1984). The acquisition of food habits and preferences. In J. D. Matarazzo, S. M. Weiss, J. A. Herd, & N. E. Miller (Eds.), *Behavioral health: A handbook of health enhancement and disease prevention* (pp. 599–607). New York: Wiley.

Sanders, M. R., Patel, R. K., LeGrice, B., & Shepherd, R. W. (1993). Children with persistent feeding difficulties: An observational analysis of the feeding interactions of problem and non-problem eaters. *Health Psychology, 12,* 64–73.

Satter, E. (1986a). Childhood eating disorders. *Journal of the American Dietetic Association, 86,* 357–361.

Satter, E. (1986b). *Child of mine: Feeding with love and good sense.* Palo Alto, CA: Bull.

Sauvage, D., Leddet, I., Hameury, L., & Barthelemy, C. (1985). Infantile rumination: Diagnosis and follow-up study of twenty cases. *Journal of the American Academy of Child Psychiatry, 24,* 197–203.

Schroeder, C. S., & Gordon, B. N. (1991). *Assessment and treatment of childhood problems: A clinician's guide.* New York: Guilford.

Siddamma, T. (1979). Obesity and socio-economic status among children. *Child Psychiatry Quarterly, 12,* 83–88.

Signorielli, N., & Lears, M. (1992). Television and children's conceptions of nutrition: Unhealthy messages. *Health Communication, 4,* 245–257.

Skuse, D. (1993). Identification and management of problem eaters. *Archives of Disease in Childhood, 69,* 604–608.

Sobal, J., & Stunkard, A. J. (1989). Socioeconomic status and obesity: A review of the literature. *Psychological Bulletin, 105,* 260–275.

Stark, L. J., Powers, S. W., Jelalian, E., Rape, R. N., & Miller, D. L. (1994). Modifying problematic mealtime interactions of children with cystic fibrosis and their parents via behavioral parent training. *Journal of Pediatric Psychology, 19,* 751–768.

Stein, A., Woolley, H., Cooper, S. D., & Fairburn, C. G. (1994). An observational study of mothers with eating disorders and their infants. *Journal of Child Psychology and Psychiatry and Allied Disciplines, 35,* 733–748.

Steiner, J. E. (1977). Facial expressions of the neonate infant indicating the hedonics of food, related chemical stimuli. In J. M. Weiffenbach (Ed.), *Taste and development: The genesis of sweet preference* (pp. 173–188). DHEW Publication No. NIH 77-1068. Washington, DC: U.S. Government Printing Office.

Stifter, C. A., & Braungart, J. (1992). Infant colic: A transient condition with no apparent effects. *Journal of Applied Developmental Psychology, 13,* 447–462.

Stunkard, A. J., Sorenson, T. I. A., Hanis, C., Teasdale, T. W., Chakraborty, R., Schull, W. J., & Schulsinger, F. (1986). An adoption study of human obesity. *New England Journal of Medicine, 314,* 193–198.

Sullivan, S. A., & Birch, L. L. (1990). Pass the sugar, pass the salt: Experience dictates preference. *Developmental Psychology, 26,* 546–551.

Thelen, M. H., Powell, A. L., Lawrence, C., & Kuhnert, M. E. (1992). Eating and body image concerns among children. *Journal of Clinical Child Psychology, 21,* 41–46.

Walker, W. A., & Hendricks, K. M. (1985). *Manual of pediatric nutrition*. Philadelphia: W. B. Saunders.

Werle, M. A., Murphy, T. B., & Budd, K. S. (1993). Treating chronic food refusal in young children: Home-based parent training. *Journal of Applied Behavior Analysis, 26,* 421–433.

Wolfe, D. A. (1988). Child abuse and neglect. In E. J. Mash & L. G. Terdal (Eds.), *Behavioral assessment of childhood disorders* (2nd ed., pp. 627–669). New York: Guilford.

Woolston, J. L. (1991). *Eating and growth disorders in infants and children*. Newbury Park, CA: Sage.

Zajonc, R. B. (1968). Attitudinal effects of mere exposure. *Journal of Personality and Social Psychology, 9,* 1–27.

7

New Developments in Assessing Pediatric Anxiety Disorders

JOHN S. MARCH AND ANNE MARIE ALBANO

1. Introduction

Presumably because it is associated with significant suffering, disruption in normal psychosocial and academic development and also family functioning, pathological anxiety is among the more common causes of referral to children's mental health-care providers (Black, 1995a; Simon, Ormel, VonKorff, & Barlow, 1995). From a diagnostic point of view, however, fears and anxieties are ubiquitous, so that clinicians and researchers interested in childhood anxiety disorders face the daunting task of differentiating pathological anxiety from fears occurring as a part of normal developmental processes (Costello & Angold, 1995c). Ideally, diagnostic tools designed specifically to assess anxiety in young persons should (1) provide reliable and valid ascertainment of symptoms across multiple symptom domains; (2) discriminate symptom clusters; (3) evaluate severity; (4) incorporate and reconcile multiple observations, such as parent and child ratings; and (5) be sensitive to treatment-induced change in symptoms. Other factors influencing instrument selection include the reasons for the assessment (e.g., screening, diagnosis, or monitoring treatment outcome), as well as time required for administration, level of training necessary to administer and/or interpret the instrument, reading level, and cost. With the increasing emphasis on multidisciplinary approaches to assessment and treat-

JOHN S. MARCH • Departments of Psychiatry and Psychology: Social and Health Sciences, Duke University Medical Center, Durham, North Carolina 27710.   ANNE MARIE ALBANO • Anxiety Research and Treatment Center, Department of Psychology, University of Louisville, Louisville, Kentucky 40292.

Advances in Clinical Child Psychology, Volume 20, edited by Thomas H. Ollendick and Ronald J. Prinz. Plenum Press, New York, 1998.

ment, assessment tools also must facilitate communication not only among clinicians, but also between clinicians and regulatory bodies such as utilization review committees within managed care environments.

While currently available instruments fall well short of these goals, a complex matrix of tools for assessing normal and pathological anxieties is now available, potentially making the choice of instruments for evaluating a particular child or adolescent seem daunting. In this chapter, we describe recent important developments in the assessment of anxiety in children and adolescents. Excellent reviews of pediatric anxiety disorders in general (March, 1995), and assessment issues in particular (Barrios & Hartmann, 1988; March & Albano, 1996) are available. The interested reader is referred to these general reviews and to more specific reviews for a detailed discuss of assessment tools (March & Albano, 1996; McNally, 1991; Thyer, 1991; Wolff & Wolff, 1991), neuropsychological assessment (Conners, March, Erhardt, & Butcher, 1995; Hooper & March, 1995), structured interviews (Kearney & Silverman, 1990; Silverman, 1991, 1994), developmental nosology (Rutter, Tuma, Lann, & Irma, 1988; Weiss et al., 1991), observational measures (Barrios & Hartmann, 1988), and family assessment (Dadds, Barrett, Rapee, & Ryan, 1996).

2. Background

2.1. Developmental Perspective

Since most fears occurring during childhood are developmentally appropriate to the context in which they occur, anxiety usually refers to developmentally inappropriate fears or to developmentally appropriate fears that produce excessive distress or dysfunction (Barrios & Hartman, 1988; March & Albano, 1996). Phobias are excessive and disruptive fears that are attached to specific objects and usually provide avoidance, such as the fear of snakes or heights. Anxiety is typically more diffuse than either normative fear or specific phobias, so that it is attached to myriad different situations and events. Thus, one distinguishing feature of anxiety—as in separation or generalized anxiety disorders—as contrasted to phobias, is that the latter are more sharply circumscribed. Nonetheless, the distinction is to some extent academic. For example, social phobia can be both generalized (fear or rejection or embarrassment in a variety of social situations) and narrowly defined (circumscribed public-speaking anxiety). Similarly, traumatic simple phobias grade into posttraumatic stress disorder (PTSD) insofar as anxiety is diffuse and phobias tend to generalize into an ever-widening circle of life circumstances.

Anxiety disorders are best viewed as comprised of sets of related fears or worries selected from among common fears that are present during childhood. Based on a rather large literature focused mostly on validating clusters of symptoms, the DSM-IV includes four specifically childhood-onset anxiety disorders: Generalized Anxiety Disorder, Social Phobia, Selective Mutism, Separation Anxiety Disorder (SAD; and its older age correlate, Panic Disorder [PD]) (American Psychiatric Association, 1994). Clinically, fears become pathological when excessive, unremitting, out of sequence developmentally, and/or when they are associated with maladaptive coping behaviors. In DSM-IV, fears that are normative are said to become anxiety disorders when they induce distress and dysfunction.

Despite substantial face validity, the DSM taxonomy reflects expert consensus rather than empirical findings regarding the true clustering of anxiety symptoms in the pediatric population (Shaffer, 1989); empirical support in some cases is questionable (Beidel, 1991b). Recently, in an effort to make DSM-IV more relevant to pediatric psychiatry, several DSM-III-R anxiety disorders of childhood (Overanxious and Avoidant Disorders, in particular) were collapsed into the adult categories (Generalized Anxiety Disorders and Social Phobia, respectively). However, the DSM-IV criteria sets themselves do not in general reflect a developmental perspective (Cantwell & Baker, 1988; Costello & Angold, 1995b), and it therefore falls to the clinician to translate the DSM-IV into terms that are relevant for the age, gender, and cultural background of the child.

Children with Generalized Anxiety Disorder are typically characterized as perfectionistic "worriers" who are constantly asking for reassurance (Silverman & Ginsburg, 1995). Children with Social Phobia show an exaggerated concern with self-presentation (Albano, 1995; Albano, DiBartolo, Heimberg, & Barlow, 1995). Constantly in fear of saying or doing something foolish or embarrassing, they are exquisitely sensitive to rejection and humiliation and often feel socially scrutinized, which they usually handle by avoiding social interchange, particularly where it involves public speaking (Beidel & Morris, 1995). Selective Mutism is a subset of Social Phobia, in which younger children will not talk (despite normal language) to other than "safe" friends and adults (Black & Uhde, 1995; Leonard & Dow, 1995). Separation Anxiety Disorder (SAD) is characterized by an intense fear of harm surrounding important attachment figures. While the literature on SAD is considerably less robust than the Adult Panic Disorder literature (Black, 1995b), many researchers now suspect that separation anxiety and panic disorder (PD) reflect developmentally different presentations of the same underlying diathesis, much like Selective Mutism is a youthful variant of Social Phobia (King, Ollendick, & Mattis, 1994; Ollendick & Huntzinger, 1990; Ollendick, Mattis, & King, 1994). As with PD,

SAD typically begins with somatic/autonomic complaints, with symptoms when escalating to full panic and, understandably, to activation of attachment mechanisms as a means of coping with panic. Thus, the fear of not being able to escape to a safe place in PD is not unlike the need to have a parent immediately available in SAD; both involve acute proximity seeking as a means of arousal/fear reduction (Black, 1995b; Ollendick et al., 1994). Nevertheless, despite epidemiological evidence suggesting a strong association between parental anxiety disorder, behavioral inhibition in offspring, and subsequent childhood-onset separation/panic symptoms (Rosenbaum et al., 1991, 1992), the assertion that separation is simply a youthful variant of PD remains controversial (Black & Robbins, 1990; Kearney & Silverman, 1991, 1992).

Comorbidity among the anxiety disorders, and between the anxiety disorders and other internalizing and externalizing disorders, complicates the diagnostic picture (see Albano, Chorpita, DiBartolo, & Barlow, 1996). For example, a wide variety of specific phobias commonly accompany the anxiety disorders, including fear of the dark, monsters, kidnappers, bugs, small animals, heights, and open or enclosed spaces. Nighttime fears, resistance to going to bed, difficulty falling asleep alone or sleeping through the night alone, and nightmares involving separation themes are not uncommon. These specific phobic symptoms are common triggers for panic/separation anxiety and are responsible for many of the avoidance and ritualized anxiety-reducing behaviors (Black, 1995b). Anxious children also show high rates of comorbid depression (Curry & Murphy, 1995). In younger children, SAD precedes depression in approximately two-thirds of cases and may form the nidus for recurrent affective illness and PD if left untreated (Kovacs, Feinberg, & Crouse, 1984).

Anxiety symptoms vary with developmental stage, and longitudinal comorbidity is as, if not more, important than cross-sectional comorbidity. Thus, when considering how best to inventory anxiety symptoms, it is necessary to first consider the severity and age-dependent prevalence of fears (Rutter, 1993a). For example, certain specific phobias, such as nighttime fears, are age dependent in that they are much more common in preschool and early elementary-school children (King, Tonge, & Ollendick, 1992). When present in older children, however, such fears may more reliably be seen as indicating psychopathological anxiety. Similarly, separation anxiety seems more prominent in younger children, where it is developmentally appropriate in very young children and becomes increasingly less appropriate as the child moves through middle childhood into adolescence (Black, 1992). Other fears, such as fears about self-presentation and, consequently, social phobia become more common as children mature into adolescence (Costello & Angold, 1995a). Clinically, for example, many children first present with behavioral inhibition and subsequently proceed to prepubertal separation anxiety and later to PD as adolescents (Biederman, Rosenbaum, Chaloff, & Kagan, 1995).

3. Self-Report Measures

3.1. Overview

As noted earlier, a wide variety of normal fears and worries are omnipresent among youth; pathological anxieties are less common but not rare (Costello & Angold, 1995c; Ollendick, Matson, & Helsel, 1985). Cognitive targets, such as separation fears or social anxiety, appear to undergo a developmentally sanctioned progression (Keller et al., 1992; Last, Strauss, & Francis, 1987). Some symptoms, such as refusing to attend school in the patient with PD and agoraphobia, are readily observable; other symptoms, such as interoceptive panic cues, are open only to child introspection and thus to child self-report. Unfortunately, because of a lack of acceptable measurement tools (March & Albano, 1996), the age-specific population prevalence of these childhood-onset fears, and even more, the factor structure of anxiety symptoms in community samples, has until now remained unclear, as has the relative importance of specific anxiety dimensions within gender, ethnic, or cultural groupings across time (Costello & Angold, 1995c; Last, Perrin, Hersen, & Kazdin, 1992).

Though interview techniques are necessary for diagnosis, self-report measures of anxiety, which provide an opportunity for children to reveal internal or "hidden" experience, are uniquely suited to examining the developmental epidemiology of anxiety symptoms and how they cluster together in the real world. Typically, self-report measures use a Likert-type scale format in which a child is asked to rate each questionnaire item in an ordinal format anchored to frequency or distress/impairment, or a combination of the two. For example, a child might be asked to rate "I feel tense" on a four-point frequency dimension that ranges from *Almost Never* to *Often*. Self-report measures are easy to administer, require a minimum of clinician time, and economically capture a wide range of important anxiety dimensions from the child's point of view. Taken together, these features also make self-report measures ideally suited to gathering data prior to the initial evaluation, because self-report measures used in this fashion increase clinician efficiency by facilitating accurate assessment of the prior probability that a particular child will or will not have symptoms within a specific symptom domain.

Currently published self-report pediatric anxiety scales for the most part represent age-downward extensions of adult measures (March & Albano, 1996). The Fear Survey Schedule for Children—Revised (FSSC-R; Ollendick, 1983) focuses primarily on phobic symptoms, including fear of failure and criticism, fear of the unknown, fear of injury and small animals, fear of danger and death, and medical fears. Another widely used scale, the Revised Children's Manifest Anxiety Scale (RCMAS), provides three factors: physiological manifestations of anxiety, worry and oversensitivity, and fear/concentration (Reynolds & Paget, 1981). However, the presence of mood, attentional, impulsivity, and peer-interaction items on the RCMAS clearly confounds other diagnoses, such as attention-deficit/ hyperactivity disorders (ADHD) and major depression (Perrin & Last, 1992). Another widely used measure, the State–Trait Anxiety Inventory for Children (STAIC; Spielberger, Gorsuch, & Luchene, 1976), consists of two independent, 20-item inventories that assess anxiety symptoms from a variety of domains but do not by any means exhaustively cover the symptom constellations represented in DSM-IV. The State scale purports to assess present-state and situation-linked anxiety; the Trait scale addresses temporally stable anxiety across situations. Numerous authors have questioned the validity of the state–trait distinction (Kendall, Finch, Auerbach, Hooke, & Mikulka, 1976), and the nature of item selection for the STAIC (Finch, Kendall, & Montgomery, 1976; Perrin & Last, 1992). Thus, clinicians and researchers generally agree (see, e.g., Jensen, Salzberg, Richters, & Watanabe, 1993; March & Albano, 1996) that new instruments are necessary if the field of pediatric anxiety disorders is to progress scientifically.

3.2. The Multidimensional Anxiety Scale for Children (MASC)

For these and other reasons, March and colleagues recently described the development and psychometric properties of a new pediatric self-report anxiety scale, the Multidimensional Anxiety Scale for Children (MASC; March, Parker, Sullivan, Stallings, & Conners, 1997). Table 1 summarizes differences between the MASC and other widely available instruments. Unlike older assessment tools, the MASC represents the population factor structure of anxiety and captures clinically relevant anxiety symptoms at both the factor and item level; viewed within and across factors, it approximates the DSM-IV pediatric anxiety disorders, shows excellent internal and test–retest reliability, and finally, demonstrates both convergent and divergent validity for depression and externalizing symptoms (March et al., 1997).

The MASC takes a somewhat different approach to identifying and labeling anxiety symptoms than that taken in DSM-IV (Widiger et al.,

TABLE 1
Anxiety Rating Scales

	MASC	RCMAS	FSSCR	STAI-C
Broad conceptualization	Yes	Yes	No	Yes
Specific dimensions	Yes	Three	Phobias	No
Approximates DSM-IV	Yes	No	No	No
Reliable	Yes	Yes	Yes	Trait scale
Convergent validity	Yes	Yes	Yes	Yes
Divergent validity	Yes	No	No	No

1996). In contrast to a categorical approach based on investigator's beliefs about the nature and course of fears and worries in pediatric samples, the MASC was developed to sample key anxiety symptoms from the universe of anxiety symptoms that has captured the attention of clinicians and researchers working with anxious children and adolescents (March et al., 1997). Only the most important symptoms and symptom clusters survived this process, so that the MASC can be seen as representing the population factor structure of anxiety in pediatric samples. Within each factor and subfactor, the specific items included in the MASC are those that proved to be psychometrically most robust with respect to a particular symptom domain. Stated differently, the items in the MASC were selected empirically, unlike the items in the DSM-IV, which, although validated in other ways, did not come from a "field" trial looking for the best and most important items comprising anxiety symptoms in the youth.

The MASC consists of 39 items distributed across four major factors, three of which can be parsed into two subfactors each (Table 2). Main and subfactors include (1) physical symptoms (tense/restless and somatic/autonomic), (2) social anxiety (humiliation/rejection and public performance fears), (3) harm avoidance (perfectionism and anxious coping), and

TABLE 2
MASC Factors

Physical symptoms	Social anxiety
Tense	Humiliation fears
Somatic	Performance fears
Harm avoidance	Separation/panic
Perfectionism	
Anxious coping	

(4) separation anxiety. Multisample confirmatory factor analysis demonstrates that the four-factor solution for the 39 MASC items is equivalent for males and females, as well as for younger and older children. As expected, females show greater anxiety on all factors and subfactors than males (March et al., 1997).

The empirically derived MASC factor structure to some extent validates the DSM-IV diagnostic clusters of social phobia, separation/panic and, averaged across all four factors, generalized anxiety disorder. Additionally, the hypothesized division of anxiety into physical symptoms and approach–avoidance behaviors also received empirical support. This is not particularly surprising, because social phobia and separation anxiety represent external threats; conversely, physical symptoms and harm avoidance represent physical and behavioral responses to threat, respectively. Both have received substantial support in the literature (March & Albano, 1996), but until now, no single scale has allowed their ascertainment in relationship to each other in the individual child or in subgroupings of children.

The factor structure of the MASC also is unique among extant scales in its subdivision of main factors into subfactors with considerable explanatory power in their own right. Although almost all correlations between MASC factors and subfactors are significantly correlated, the absolute magnitude of the shared variance is in the low to moderate range for most pairs (March et al., 1997). This suggests that the MASC is indeed measuring separate dimensions of anxiety, even at the subfactor level, which in turn should make it ideally suited to discriminate patterns of anxiety in subgroups of children with anxiety disorders.

Last, the MASC shows excellent internal and test–retest reliability. Internal reliability—defined as consistency between items within a group of items comprising a discrete factor (Chronbach, 1970) for the MASC—ranges from .7 to .9 for all main factors and subfactors. Thus, the individual items share factor-level variance but also contribute unique variance to the specified constructs. Stated differently, the individual items are not redundant with respect to information content, which is what one would want in a scale purporting to measure individual symptoms with unique clinical validity. In contrast to internal reliability, test–retest reliability represents consistency in a set of scores by the same rater (single case intraclass correlation coefficient; ICC) or set of raters (mean ICC) over time (Shrout & Fleiss, 1979). Test–retest reliability varies with the conditions under which the test is administered, practice or memory effects, and true change in the variable(s) of interest plus an instability component due to measurement error attributable to the instrument itself. Without adequate test–retest reliability, it is not possible to determine whether differences in scores between individuals or within-subjects' over time are due to "true" differences or to "chance" error. Using the mean ICC, which enumerates the true variance accounted for as a proportion of the total variance plus error (Shrout & Fleiss, 1979), the MASC shows good to excellent test–retest reliability at 3 weeks (ICC = .78) and 3 months (ICC = .93). Although these findings are not dissimilar to those for the RCMAS (Wisniewski, Mulick, & Coury, 1987), the FSSC-R (Ollendick, 1983) and the trait scale of the STAIC (Spielberger et al., 1976), the later studies were performed in "captive" school-based population samples, whereas this study was completed in a clinical sample of children presenting to anxiety and ADHD subspecialty clinics. Not surprisingly, stability is in part a function of symptom domain and interval, with physical symptoms, social phobia, and separation anxiety showing considerable stability, and harm avoidance showing less stability over the 3-week time interval (March et al., 1997).

Although additional research is clearly necessary, the MASC appears to be a valid and reliable tool for its intended purpose. In research settings, the MASC likely will find wide use in documenting the relationship between anxiety and other variables. For example, the MASC already has been utilized as the sole measure of self-reported anxiety in the NIMH-funded Multimodal Treatment of ADHD (MTA) study and in our studies of cognitive-behavioral psychotherapy for pediatric PTSD and OCD. Parenthetically, the latter studies demonstrate that the MASC also is change sensitive, which is one reason why the MASC has been chosen as a primary dependent measure in the randomized clinical trial of a selective serotonin reuptake inhibitor in anxiety-disordered children conducted by the NIMH-funded Research Units for Pediatric Psychopharmacology (RUPP). In clinical settings, the MASC is ideally suited to gathering data prior to the initial evaluation. Used in this fashion, the MASC should increase clinician efficiency by facilitating accurate assessment of the prior probability that a particular child will or will not have symptoms across the domains of anxiety relevant to DSM-IV (March, Mulle, Stallings, Erhardt, & Conners, 1995).

4. Diagnostic Interviews

4.1. Overview

Dimensional self-report measures such as the MASC can point clinicians toward clinically relevant symptoms and, because of their dimensionality, are better able to gauge the severity of symptoms. Conversely, establishing a DSM-IV diagnosis generally requires a clinician-administered, interview-based approach. This structured approach to diagnosis is necessary for establishing the reliability of the diagnosis, accurately defining and tracking target symptoms, and, in both clinical and research endeavors, making comparisons of results across settings (e.g., Lann, 1991; Silverman, 1994). The structured interview format provides a method for quantification of clinical data, reduces the potential for interviewer bias, and enhances diagnostic reliability (Eisen & Kearney, 1995). Semistructured interviews present diagnostic criteria and related clinical inquiries in a standardized format, while allowing the clinician a limited range of flexibility for elaboration and probing of symptoms and criteria. Thus, a clinician may adapt the wording of a particular question to meet the cognitive-developmental level and/or cultural context of the child. In contrast, there is little or no variation allowed during the structured interview format.

A number of structured and semistructured interviews are available for use with children and adolescents (see March & Albano, 1996; and Silverman, 1994). Among such interviews are the Diagnostic Interview Schedule for Children (DISC; Costello, Edelbrock, Dulcan, Kalas, & Klaric, 1984), the Children's Assessment Schedule (CAS; Hodges, Cools, & McKnew, 1989), the Kiddie Schedule for Affective Disorders and Schizophrenia (K-SADS; Puig-Antich & Chambers, 1978; Modified K-SADS; Last, 1986), Diagnostic Interview Schedule for Children and Adolescents (DICA; Herjanic & Reich, 1982), the Interview Schedule for Children (ISC; Kovacs, 1985), and the Child and Adolescent Psychiatric Assessment (CAPA; Angold, 1997).

Despite some shared features among these interviews (e.g., age range, interview of parent separate from child), the aforementioned interviews vary widely in their methods of administration, scoring, level of structure demanded by the interview, and decision rules for combining parent and child data (Silverman, 1991). Also, there is wide variability in the degree to which each of these interviews covers the anxiety disorders. Silverman (1994) presents a detailed review of currently available child interview methods, reporting that methodological differences among studies of structured interviews preclude forming any conclusions regarding their comparative reliability.

4.2. The Anxiety Disorders Interview Schedule for DSM-IV, Child Version (ADIS-IV-C)

In response to the wide variability of interview methods and relatively low reliability coefficients reported for the anxiety disorders across studies, Silverman and Nelles (1988) developed the Anxiety Disorders

Interview Schedule for Children (ADIS-C), a downward extension of the Anxiety Disorders Interview Schedule (ADIS; DiNardo, O'Brien, Barlow, Waddell, & Blanchard, 1983). Since its inception, the ADIS-C has undergone revisions to be consistent with the DSM-III-R (American Psychiatric Association, 1987), and, most recently, with DSM-IV (American Psychiatric Association, 1994). The Anxiety Disorders Interview Schedule for DSM-IV, Child Version (ADIS-IV; Silverman & Albano, 1996) is a semistructured clinical interview assessing the range of anxiety disorders, mood disorders, externalizing disorders, and related behavioral disturbances in children and adolescents. The ADIS-IV-C is appropriate for children ages 6 to 17, with developmentally appropriate wording and descriptors provided for the clinician within the interview. In structure, the ADIS-IV-C actually consists of two separate interviews, a child interview schedule and a parent interview schedule. Thus, data is first gathered separately from the child and parent(s) and then combined into an overall composite diagnosis. The authors recommend administration of the ADIS-IV-C by one evaluator. In general, administration takes upwards of 3 hours to complete both the child and parent interview schedules. Because the child is interviewed separately from the parent(s), the general rule is that data gained from one source not be used in or divulged to the second source. The authors recommend that researchers randomize the order of the interviews (parent or child seen first) in order to control for order effects (Albano & Silverman, 1996). Also, it is preferable to have both parents present for the interview.

The ADIS-IV-C allows a formal diagnosis be assigned for the following DSM-IV categories: SAD, Social Phobia, Specific Phobia, PD, Agoraphobia, Generalized Anxiety Disorder, Obsessive–Compulsive Disorder, PTSD/Acute Stress Disorder, Major Depressive Disorder, Dysthymia, and ADHD. New to the ADIS-IV-C is the inclusion of a screening section for selective mutism (SM). As previously mentioned, investigators have hypothesized the relationship between SM and social phobia (Black & Uhde, 1992), with SM being construed as an extreme variant of the latter anxiety disorder. To date, SM has been an understudied and poorly understood childhood disorder. The inclusion of a screening for SM to the ADIS-IV-C will alert investigators and clinicians to the presence of the disorder and prompt for further evaluation, if necessary. The ADIS-IV-C also includes screening questions for a range of disorders in youth, including substance abuse, somatoform disorders, eating disorders, and psychosis. The parent version of the interview also screens for enuresis, sleep terror disorder, pervasive developmental disorders, mental retardation, learning disorders, and provides full diagnostic criteria for conduct disorder and oppositional defiant disorder.

Within each disorder covered in the ADIS-IV-C are sections that guide the clinician in assessing essential DSM-IV criteria and accessing ratings of interference in functioning. The Initial Inquiry and Interference sections are required for making a DSM-IV diagnosis. Several disorders are accompanied by additional sections designed to examine the phenomenology and behavioral limits of the child. As such, the Initial Inquiry section provides questions for determining presence of specific diagnostic criteria for each individual disorder, with instructions to skip out strategically placed if threshold criteria are not met. The Interference section allows an assessment of the informant's subjective report of the degree of distress and impairment associated with each diagnosis. This section provides a quantifiable rating on a 0 to 8 scale of subjective distress from the child's perspective, or perceived distress from the parent's observation of the child. The "Feelings Thermometer," a visual prompt that accompanies the interview, can be used to assist younger children with anchoring subjective ratings of fear or distress.

Information gained from the Initial Inquiry and Interference sections are combined by the interviewer in assigning a clinician severity rating for each diagnostic category. The clinician severity rating (CSR) is assigned on a 0–8 scale, reflecting increasing distress and disability. Additional sections are provided to examine more fully the phenomenology of the disorders and degree of impairment in specific areas of functioning, and to explore relevant developmental questions pertaining to these disorders in youth. A detailed clinician's manual accompanies the instrument (Albano & Silverman, 1996). An additional packet of research questions is available from the authors.

Presently, the authors of the ADIS-IV-C are conducting reliability studies of the interview schedules (A. M. Albano, personal communication, March 1997). However, reliability of both the child and parent versions of the interview has been evaluated previously for both the DSM-III and DSM-III-R versions. For example, in a study of 51 outpatients using the interviewer–observer paradigm, Silverman and Nelles (1988) found an overall kappa coefficient of .75, with kappas ranging from .64 for overanxious disorder to 1.00 for specific phobia. Subsequently, Silverman and Eisen (1992) examined test–retest reliability in a sample of 50 outpatients presenting to the same child anxiety specialty clinic. Again, the overall kappa was .75, with kappas ranging from .64 for overanxious disorder to .84 for specific phobia. More recently, a study conducted in Australia with 161 outpatients found kappas for the composite diagnoses ranging from .59 to .82 (Rapee, Barrett, Dadds, & Evans, 1994). This study utilized an interrater reliability paradigm, involving a live interview with the child and videotaped interview with the parent. Consistent with previous findings (see Silverman, 1994, for a review), parent–child agreement was poor for most diagnostic categories, with kappa values ranging from .11 to .44 (Rapee et al., 1994). However, despite differences in parent and child reports, reliability studies of the ADIS-C and ADIS-P demonstrate that independent clinicians have little difficulty in evaluating the presence and severity of diagnoses based on the child's report, parents' report, and in formulating the composite (Silverman & Nelles, 1988; Silverman & Eisen, 1992; Rapee et al., 1994). Overall, these studies support the utility of the prior versions of the children's ADIS interview schedules. Refinements in the diagnostic criteria for most of these disorders as applied to children are expected to bolster the reliability of the ADIS-IV-C.

5. Specific Behavioral Assessment Methods

5.1. Overview

Following the diagnostic evaluation, which preferably should begin with dimensional measures and proceed to a semistructured interview, additional "pretreatment" assessments are generally required to collect additional data regarding a child's specific anxiety symptomatology. For example, much more data are required to establish a fear hierarchy, a necessary measure for implementing treatment, than is necessary for establishing a diagnosis of obsessive–compulsive disorder (OCD) or social phobia. Supplementary, largely ideographic data will serve as a basis for evaluating the progress and rate of treatment, and for identifying targets for specific interventions. At the most basic level, at least from a behavioral perspective, assessment in this sense consists of the administration of a standardized inventory for assessing the specific domain of anxiety and the construction of an individualized hierarchy of feared situations (e.g., Fear and Avoidance Hierarchy; FAH), with corresponding Subjective Units of Distress (SUDS) ratings. Patients also are sometimes given instruction in the use of a continuous, self-monitoring diary to complete during a pretreatment baseline and for the duration of treatment, and are asked to participate in behavioral observational assessments.

5.2. Behavioral Observations

Behavioral observation is the cornerstone of behavioral assessment and a vital step in developing a formal functional analysis of the child's presenting problem (Barrios & Hartmann, 1988; Dadds, Rapee, & Barrett, 1994). Yet relatively few standardized behavioral observation systems exist that have demonstrated reliability and validity. Exceptions to this trend include two standardized observation methods used to observe children in medical settings. The Behavior Profile Rating Scale (BPRS; Melamed, Yurcheson, Fleece, Hutcherson, & Hawes, 1978) assesses behaviors associated with dental anxiety, and the Observer Rating Scale of Anxiety (ORSA; Melamed & Siegel, 1975) was developed for observing anxiety behaviors in medical and dental situations. Both scales have adequate reliability and validity.

One additional standardized method is the Preschool Observation Scale of Anxiety (POSA; Glennon & Weisz, 1978). Raters note the presence of behavioral symptoms of fear and anxiety such as crying, nail-biting, whining/whimpering, physical complaints, and verbal expressions of fear or worry. The POSA is useful for evaluating a child during compulsory separation and social situations occurring during school hours. Psychometric evaluation of the POSA has revealed adequate reliability and validity (Glennon & Weisz, 1978).

In contrast to a standardized method, the most widely employed measure of behavioral observation is the behavioral avoidance task (BAT), sometimes also known simply as behavioral tests or behavioral avoidance tasks. In a typical BAT, an individual is exposed to relevant, anxiety-provoking situations while corresponding measures of approach and subjective distress are taken (Kendall et al., 1991; Ollendick & Francis, 1988). The duration of a BAT will vary according to the demands of the stimulus situation and behavioral limits of the participant. For example, in assessing the subjective discomfort of an adolescent who fears engaging in conversations, a typical BAT may involve initiating and maintaining a conversation with a confederate. In order to access an adequate sample of the adolescent's behavior, the clinician may want to observe a minimum of 10 minutes of the interaction. In this way, behaviors that may occur in any conversation would have a chance to happen (e.g., asking and answering questions). However, if an adolescent refuses to engage in the situation, or asks to prematurely terminate the interaction, then important information is gained regarding the limits of that particular adolescent's tolerance of anxiety and anxiety-provoking stimuli. In addition to the behavioral observations accessed during the BAT, following each task the participant is asked to list his/her thoughts or describe the images he/she recalled having while engaging in the BAT (or anticipating the BAT, in the case of a refusal). Thought listing is an easy method of assessing the cognitive component of anxiety. SUDS ratings are also taken during a BAT, typically at specified intervals during the ongoing task (e.g., each minute). These tasks are invaluable methods of accessing clinical information regarding individual-patient behavioral coping or escape/avoidance behaviors.

Moreover, repeating the BAT at midtreatment and posttreatment will provide the clinician with an ongoing measure of change.

5.3. Family Assessment

Until recently, investigations examining the interaction among child and family variables in the etiology and maintenance of anxiety in children and adolescents were practically nonexistent. Although an extensive literature exists promoting the utility of family evaluation in the study of externalizing disorders (cf. Dadds, 1995; Patterson, 1982; Wahler, 1976), empirical assessment studies are only beginning to appear examining the interaction patterns of anxious children and their families (e.g., Barrett, Rapee, Dadds, & Ryan, 1996; Chorpita, Albano, & Barlow, 1996).

Paper-and-pencil instruments such as the Issues Checklist (IC; Prinz, Foster, Kent, & O'Leary, 1979), Conflict Behavior Questionnaire (CBQ; Prinz et al., 1979), the Parent Expectancy Scale (PES; Eisen, Spasaro, Kearney, Albano, & Barlow, 1996), and the Family Environment Scale (FES; Moos & Moos, 1986) may be utilized to assess descriptive characteristics of families of anxious children as well as suggest areas that might benefit from intervention or further empirical examination. The IC and CBQ are measures that tap "hot" topics or issues that cause conflict between family members, and the frequency with which these issues arise in a particular family. The IC and CBQ are completed by both the parents and child. The IC and CBQ have been found to discriminate distressed from non-distressed mothers, fathers, and adolescents, and the CBQ is also sensitive to change following intervention (see Foster & Robin, 1988). The PES is a relatively new scale that measures parents' expectancies across five dimensions of the child's functioning: academic, extracurricular, household, social, and general success. This measure is completed by the parents. Preliminary studies indicate good reliability for the PES (Eisen et al., 1996), with examination of validity currently underway. Finally, the FES provides an assessment of the family climate, structure, and values, and is completed by parents and child. Norms are provided for distressed and non-distressed families, and the psychometric properties are generally good for the measure (Moos & Moos, 1986). The utility of the FES for evaluation of families dealing with anxiety disorders is currently being examined. Each of these measures can provide the clinician with information to incorporate into the case formulation and aid in treatment planning.

Only recently have investigators begun to examine molecular processes involved in the interactions between anxious children and their parents. Initial hypotheses proposed by Dadds and colleagues in Australia has prompted research in this area (Barrett et al., 1996; Dadds, 1995; Dadds et al., 1996; Dadds et al., 1994). Specifically, these investigators suggest that anxiety in children is modeled or reinforced through a series of interpersonal behaviors and interactions occurring between parents and the child. Results of a series of investigations suggest a specific interaction of cognitive processing biases for threat, combined with interpersonal interactions between family members, which set the occasion for the development and maintenance of anxiety.

Dadds and colleagues devised a family behavioral test situation in which children are presented with an ambiguous situation, asked to give a rating of their anxiety if confronted with the situation, and then provide an interpretation and action plan in response to the situation. For example, a child may be given the following situation: "You are in the school cafeteria, looking for a place to sit. You notice a table with several children, and an empty chair. You decide to go join these children. As you approach, you notice that some of the children are laughing. What do you think is happening? What would you do? How anxious would you be?" After each child provides an individual response to the situation, the parents are then called in and presented the same scenario and then asked to discuss the situation as a family. After a 5- to 10-minute discussion, the child is again asked to provide an interpretation, action plan, and subjective rating of anxiety.

Preliminary analyses at several centers have revealed that an interesting phenomenon occurs between parents and their anxious children in response to discussion of these ambiguous situations (Barrett et al., 1996; Chorpita et al., 1996; Dadds et al., 1996). Parents are observed to inadvertently reinforce avoidance or escape from these situations, as opposed to approach and problem solving. Moreover, although some anxious children initially indicate an approach plan, following the discussion with the family, these children are observed to change their plans to an avoidant or escape solution. Termed the "FEAR" effect (Family Enhancement of Anxious Responding), investigators hypothesize that the parents are attempting to protect the child from experiencing anxiety and the ensuing negative affect, but unfortunately, then, the child never gains experience with such situations, and hence the development of coping skills and process of habituation to anxiety is stalled (Barrett et al., 1996). In other words, children will encounter potentially threatening (anxiety-provoking) situations on a daily basis. During these situations, the average child will engage in particular behaviors that lead to certain outcomes. The situation itself, the child's response, and the outcome each can be accompanied by some degree of subjective anxiety. With repeated experience in such situations, the child learns certain skills and behaviors to manage the situations and any difficulties, and deal with both the anxiety response and resultant outcome. Continued exposure to these situations results in a decreased intensity of the anxiety response (habituation) and a more efficient and effective management (coping skills) of any remaining anxiety. If parents intervene and take over the management of these situations, or if they encourage avoidance of situations, the developmental process of learning skills and habituating to anxiety may not occur. The Family Anxiety Coding Schedule (see Dadds et al., 1994) provides a means to examine family interactions and quantify the data for statistical purposes. Although studies are just underway, it is expected that invaluable information will be gained regarding the complex interactions of child and family characteristics in the maintenance of childhood anxiety.

6. Neuroscience

6.1. Overview

Although not yet practical from a clinical diagnostic perspective, emerging neuropsychiatric models of the genesis and maintenance of anxiety disorders hold considerable promise for further refining our diagnostic nomenclature and for more precisely specifying psychosocial and somatic treatments (Hooper & March, 1995; March, Leonard, & Swedo, in press; Sallee & Greenawald, 1995). Here, we review some recent developments in psychophysiological assessment and introduce the topic of cognitive neuroscience as applied to developmental psychopathology (Harris, 1995; Rutter, 1993b), focusing for heuristic purposes on the overlap between anxiety and attention deficit disorders.

6.2. Psychophysiological Assessment

Anxiety is conceptualized as a complex emotion consisting of three separate yet interrelated components: cognitive, physiological, and behavioral (Lang, 1968, 1971). Studies of childhood anxiety typically focus on the cognitive and overt behavioral components, with less attention given to assessment of the physiological domain. However, the paucity of empirical attention to children's physiological functioning is not due to a lack of interest in the area. King (1994) presents a comprehensive and scholarly review of the history and current status of physiological assessment of anxious emotional states in children. As noted in this review, Mary Cover Jones (1924) described the physiological responses of young Peter in the infamous case study of the deconditioning of a child's fear. Despite an early clinical interest in the physiological changes accompanying anxious states in youth, until recently, only little empirical work was conducted examining clinically anxious children and adolescents.

Only one group of investigators has examined systematically the utility and reliability of psychophysiological assessment with anxious children (Beidel, 1988, 1991a, 1991b; Turner, Beidel, & Epstein, 1991). Preliminary data suggest that physical responses to stressful situations (e.g., heart rate) may signal the presence of an anxious biological predisposition (cf. temperament) in a subset of children (Beidel, 1989). For example, socially relevant tasks (e.g., reading aloud) have been associated with increased heart rate in socially anxious children (Beidel, 1988, 1991b). Interestingly, no baseline differences in physiological arousal were noted between socially anxious and normal control children during these assessments. However, in contrast to nonanxious children, clinical children appear to exhibit continually elevated heart rate throughout the task without evidence of habituation (Beidel, 1988, 1991b; Turner et al., 1991). Interestingly, ongoing research at the Harvard Medical School suggests that the temperamental construct of "behavioral inhibition" in children may be a precursor to, or risk factor for the development of anxiety disorders during childhood (Biederman et al., 1995; Hirshfeld et al., 1992); however, it is not clear to what extent behavioral inhibition maps reliably onto psychophysiological disturbances. Thus, while theoretically interesting, the clinical utility of these measures has yet to be demonstrated.

6.3. Cognitive Neuroscience

Despite abundant data linking impairment in specific neurocognitive processes to pediatric emotional disorders (Harris, 1995), the DSM-IV diagnostic criteria largely rely on behavioral symptoms (American Psychiatric Association, 1994). Although this approach has advanced the cause of developmental neuropsychiatry by encouraging the formation of diagnostically homogeneous groups, underlying neuropsychological constructs are not well represented (Pennington & Welsh, 1995). Recent developments in the cognitive neurosciences, which have shown a remarkable ability to correlate functional neuroanatomy with central nervous system (CNS) information processes (Gazzaniga, 1995), suggest a way out of this taxonomic conundrum (e.g., core neurocognitive processes such as attention and fear and their interrelationship, inform most behavioral/symptomatic constructs; see, e.g., Shaywitz & Shaywitz, 1991) and so may provide one explanation for the extraordinary degree of comorbidity between neuropsychiatric disorders.

Although neuropsychiatric disorders have been viewed neurocognitively as involving under- or overallocation of attentional resources

(Lorys, Hynd, & Lahey, 1990; Matthews & Margetts, 1991), it is critical to remember that allocation of CNS processing resources may be dysregulated at any of several information-processing steps, including orienting of attention, sustained attention, visual–spatial–organizational skills, cognitive and/or behavioral inhibition and/or executive dysfunction (Hooper & March, 1995), each of which shares overlapping hierarchically distributed neural networks (Posner, 1992). Note that when engaging this issue, it is also crucial to avoid confusion over level of analysis (Fletcher & Taylor, 1984). Although neurocognitive tests may both model symptomatic behavior and reflect underlying CNS function, poor test performance does not permit inference of CNS dysfunction in the absence of experimental evidence linking different levels of analysis.

From the standpoint of pediatric neuropsychiatry, the contrast between ADHD and the anxiety disorders (ANX) holds particular heuristic value. ANX and ADHD contrast sharply in risk factors, developmental course, and response to treatment. Curiously, however, these two apparently distinct psychopathological groupings, which together affect 10–15% of youths, share a high degree of comorbidity (Costello & Angold, 1995c). Indeed, it is often difficult to determine whether the symptoms of restlessness, inattention, and disorganization belong to one or the other of the disorders, which may imply that ADHD and ANX share common underlying neurocognitive processes that result in comorbidity at the symptom level while showing distinctive patterns at the neurocognitive level. For example, ADHD and ANX share inattentiveness and distractibility (cf. DSM-IV criteria), but one might hypothesize that ADHD children are distractible because their noradrenergically mediated automatic attention to sensory cues is underactivated, leading them to be underfocused, whereas pathologically anxious children are noradrenergically overactivated, causing high levels of vigilance to potentially threatening external cues. Although presenting behaviorally as "distractible," highly anxious children might show highly efficient and precise automatic responses to sensory cues at the neurocognitive level; with ADHD the opposite occurs. Behaviorally, both ADHD and ANX children are easily disinhibited and therefore impulsive, but perhaps for quite different reasons. ADHD children could have low levels of response inhibition due to underactivation of response control mechanisms, whereas ANX children under pressure might blur the distinction between target and nontarget stimuli, thus responding too often to both. In signal detection terms, ADHD children have an altered response-criterion bias, or beta-function, so that speed becomes more important than accuracy, whereas ANX children have inefficient signal discrimination, or d-prime, so that anxiety is seen to interfere with distinguishing among a range of external cue characteristics. In both disorders, the same neurocognitive systems are involved (arousal, activation, automatic and voluntary attention, vigilance), but take on different values.

Although attention is a core component in the ADHD diagnostic construct (Barkley, Grodzinsky, & DuPaul, 1992), numerous hypotheses regarding attentional dysfunction in ADHD have been proposed and later discarded (Conners et al., 1995). Current theories focus on dysregulation in short-term orienting of attention (Swanson et al., 1991) and vigilance or sustained attention. Attentional factors in anxiety-disordered adults are beginning to be explored along similar lines (see, e.g., Fox, 1994; McNally, Riemann, Louro, Lukach, & Kim, 1992); however, much less has been done in the pediatric population (Hooper & March, 1995). Only one study has focused on the issue of comorbidity from the standpoint of neurocognitive processing. In this pioneering study, Pliszka and colleagues compared children with nonanxious ADHD to children with comorbid ADHD and overanxious disorder, and found that the combination of ADHD and ANX reduced the risk of comorbid conduct disorder, decreased impulsive responding on a continuous performance task (CPT), and produced sluggish reaction times on a Memory Scanning Test (Pliszka, 1989). This study suggests that arousal level, which by itself influences a wide range of primary attentional functions (McBurnett et al., 1991), may be a critical variable when interpreting the results of neurocognitive tests across different disorders.

Impairments in visual–spatial–organizational skills also have been the subject of increasing investigation in ADHD (see, e.g., Branch, Cohen, & Hynd, 1995) and ANX (summarized in Hooper & March, 1995). Poor nonverbal reasoning skills are typically found in ADHD without hyperactivity and may partially account for the frequently observed overlap between ADHD and ANX (Lahey & Carlson, 1991). Such children often suffer from a specific academic disability characterized by slow processing speed, dysgraphia, dyscalculia, and poor written language, highlighting the overlap between neurodevelopmental and emotional disabilities (Rourke, 1989; Voeller, 1991). As yet, however, most studies in this area have not distinguished between orienting of attention, vigilance, or visuospatial skills in different diagnostic groupings, nor have they related dysregulation in these areas to behavioral symptoms.

At both the behavioral and neurocognitive levels (Conners & Wells, 1986; Zacks & Hasher, 1994), the ability to inhibit cognitions and behaviors is a cardinal feature of attentional control mechanisms. Thus, difficulty delaying impulsive responding (manifested as increased commission errors on a CPT) has proven the most reliable finding in ADHD (Conners et al., 1995). In contrast, early investigations using negative priming models suggest that cognitive inhibitory mechanisms may be dysregulated in ANX (Fox, 1994). No pediatric negative-priming studies have yet been published, but preliminary data from our laboratory suggest that negative-priming effects do not discriminate ANX from ADHD (unpublished data).

Finally, CNS imaging technologies permit researchers to link brain structure to brain function, with magnetic resonance imaging (MRI) and positron emission tomography (PET) showing more utility for structural localization and event-related potentials (ERPs) showing more utility for understanding the temporal aspects of CNS information processing (Pfefferbaum, Roth, & Ford, 1995; Rapp et al., 1989). PET studies are as yet impractical in most pediatric mental disorders, though studies in adults with childhood-onset disorders show some promise (Swedo et al., 1989; Zametkin, Nordahl, Gross, King et al., 1990). In contrast, preliminary studies using ERPs indicate that ADHD exhibits electrophysiological markers of a disturbed attentional orienting system (Klorman, 1991). No QEEG/ERP studies have yet been done in children with ANX, though QEEG studies in anxious adults suggest overfocused sustained attention (see, e.g., Towey, Tenke, Bruder, Leite, et al., 1994).

7. Conclusion

Researchers have just begun to explore methods for the comprehensive multimodal assessment of anxiety in children. Future efforts will inevitably focus on the integration of assessment methods that serve to explicate the relationship between cognitions, behaviors, and neurocognitive and neurophysiological responses associated with anxiety in youth. In addition, relatively little work has examined the utility of assessment techniques within specific diagnostic categories, yet examinations of diagnostic differences are crucial to our understanding of the nature of childhood anxiety disorders (March & Albano, 1996; Albano et al., 1995). Comprehensive and multimodal assessments that examine the interrelationship between the child's developmental level, anxiety, and related constructs (e.g., family characteristics, social skills, self-competence) are sorely needed as well. Importantly, these assessment procedures must maximize not only our understanding of the childhood-onset anxiety disorders but must also facilitate appropriate prescriptive treatment planning and outcome monitoring (Albano, Knox, & Barlow, 1995; March & Albano, 1996).

In this chapter, we reviewed a wide variety of currently available and investigational assessment methods and instruments that have been applied to pathological anxiety in pediatric populations. It should be apparent that considerable progress has been made over the past 10 years.

Self-report (e.g., MASC) and interviewer-based (e.g., ADIS) instruments now provide reliable and valid ascertainment of symptoms across multiple symptom domains. These, and construct-specific instruments (e.g., STAIC), reliably identify the major symptom clusters in anxious children, though further research is clearly necessary before discriminant validity can be claimed between specific anxiety disorders or between the anxiety disorders and other internalizing and externalizing conditions. With respect to "severity," the availability of normative data and specific criteria for assessing functional impairment are strengths of some but by no means all instruments, and much work remains to establish the clinical implications of categorical or dimensionalized ratings on available assessment tools. Moreover, our understanding of how best to incorporate and reconcile multiple observations, such as parent and child ratings, is limited, particularly since child and parent concordance is weak for some domains of anxiety, and the ascertainment of concordance is confounded by intra- and interrater reliability in any case. Finally, the development of new, empirically validated treatments (e.g., Albano, Marten, Holt, Heimberg, & Barlow, 1995; March & Mulle, 1995) is just beginning to drive the evaluation of whether newer instruments are sensitive to treatment-induced change in symptoms.

Further investigations examining the reliability and validity of these assessments with anxiety-disordered children within a developmental context are clearly warranted. Although complex assessments—whether clinically based or part of a research protocol—often are best carried out within an anxiety disorders subspecialty clinic, few children currently have access to sophisticated services outside academic centers. Thus, technology transfer from the research setting, where instruments such as the ADIS and the MASC have been developed, to everyday clinical practice is imperative if the nascent field of child and adolescent anxiety disorders is to progress.

8. References

Albano, A. M. (1995). Treatment of social anxiety in adolescents. *Cognitive and Behavioral Practice, 2*, 271–298.

Albano, A. M. Chorpita, B. F., DiBartolo, P. M., & Barlow, D. H. (1996). *Comorbidity in a clinical sample of anxious children.* Manuscript submitted for publication.

Albano, A. M., DiBartolo, P. M., Heimberg, R. G., & Barlow, D. H. (1995). Child and adolescents: Assessment and treatment. In R. G. Heimberg, M. R. Liebowitz, D. A. Hope, & F. R. Schneier (Eds.), *Social phobia: Diagnosis, assessment, and treatment* (pp. 387–425). New York: Guilford.

Albano, A. M., Knox, L. S., & Barlow, D. H. (1995). Obsessive–compulsive disorder. In A. R.

Eisen, C. A. Kearney, & C. E. Schafer (Eds.), *Clinical handbook of anxiety disorders in children and adolescents* (pp. 282–316). Northvale, NJ: Aronson.

Albano, A. M., Marten, P. A., Holt, C. S., Heimberg, R. G., & Barlow, D. H. (1995). Cognitive behavioral group treatment for social phobia in adolescents: A preliminary study. *Journal of Nervous and Mental Disease, 183,* 649–656.

Albano, A. M., & Silverman, W. K. (1996). *Clinician's guide to the use of the Anxiety Disorders Interview Schedule for DSM-IV: Child Version.* San Antonio, TX: Psychological Corporation.

American Psychiatric Association. (1987). *Diagnostic and statistical manual of mental disorders (3rd ed. Rev.).* Washington, DC: Author.

American Psychiatric Association. (1994). *Diagnostic and statistical manual of mental disorders (DSM-IV) (4th ed.).* Washington, DC: Author.

Angold, A. (1997). The Child and Adolescent Psychiatric Assessment. In C. Thoarson (Ed.), *The instruments of psychiatric research* (pp. 271–304). Chichester, UK: Wiley.

Barkley, R., Grodzinsky, G., & DuPaul, G. (1992). Frontal lobe functions in Attention Deficit Disorder With and Without Hyperactivity: A review and research report. *Journal of Abnormal Child Psychology, 20,* 163–188.

Barrett, P. M., Rapee, R. M., Dadds, M. R., & Ryan, S. M. (1996). Family enhancement of cognitive style in anxious and aggressive children. Threat bias and the FEAR effect. *Journal of Abnormal Child Psychology, 24,* 187–203.

Barrios, B. A., & Hartmann, D. P. (1988). Fears and anxieties. In E. J. Mash & L. G. Terdal (Eds.), *Behavioral assessment of childhood disorders* (2nd ed., pp. 196–262). New York: Guilford.

Beidel, D. C. (1988). Psychophysiological assessment of anxious emotional states in children. *Journal of Abnormal Psychology, 97,* 80–82.

Beidel, D.C. (1989). Assessing anxious emotion: A review of psychophysiological assessment in children. *Clinical Psychology Review, 9,* 717–736.

Beidel, D. C. (1991a). Determining the reliability of psychophysiological assessment in childhood anxiety. *Journal of Anxiety Disorders, 5,* 139–150.

Beidel, D. C. (1991b). Social phobia and overanxious disorder in school-age children. *Journal of the American Academy of Child Psychiatry, 30,* 545–552.

Beidel, D., & Morris, T. (1995). Social phobia. In J. March (Ed.), *Anxiety disorders in children and adolescents* (pp. 181–211). New York: Guilford.

Biederman, J., Rosenbaum, J., Chaloff, J., & Kagan, J. (1995). Behavioral inhibition as a risk factor. In J. March (Ed.), *Anxiety disorders in children and adolescents* (pp. 61–81). New York: Guilford.

Black, B. (1995a). Anxiety disorders in children and adolescents. *Current Opinions in Pediatrics, 7*(4), 387–391.

Black, B. (1995b). Separation anxiety disorder and panic disorder. In J. March (Ed.), *Anxiety disorders in children and adolescents* (pp. 212–234). New York: Guilford.

Black, B., & Robbins, D. (1990). Panic disorder in children and adolescents. *Journal of the American Academy of Child and Adolescent Psychiatry, 29,* 36–44.

Black, B., & Uhde, T. W. (1992). Elective mutism as a variant of social phobia. *Journal of the American Academy of Child and Adolescent Psychiatry, 31,* 1090–1094.

Black, B., & Uhde, T. W. (1995). Psychiatric characteristics of children with selective mutism: A pilot study. *Journal of the American Academy of Child and Adolescent Psychiatry, 34,* 847–856.

Branch, W. B., Cohen, M. J., & Hynd, G. W. (1995). Academic achievement and attention-deficit/hyperactivity disorder in children with left- or right-hemisphere dysfunction. *Journal of Learning Disabilities, 28*(1), 35–43.

Cantwell, D. P., & Baker, L. (1988). Issues in the classification of child and adolescent psychopathology. *Journal of the American Academy of Child and Adolescent Psychiatry, 27*(5), 521–533.

Chorpita, B. F., Albano, A. M., & Barlow, D. H. (1996). Cognitive processing in children: Relation to anxiety and family influences. *Journal of Clinical Child Psychology, 25*, 170–176.

Chronbach, L. (1970). *Essentials of psychological testing* (3rd ed.). New York: Harper & Row.

Conners, C., March, J., Erhardt, D., & Butcher, T. (1995). Assessment of attention-deficit disorders. *Journal of Psychoeducational Assessment, 28*, 186–205.

Conners, C., & Wells, K. (1986). *Hyperactive children: A neuropsychosocial approach.* Beverly Hills, CA: Sage.

Costello, E. J., & Angold, A. (1995a). Epidemiology. In J. March (Ed.), *Anxiety disorders in children and adolescents* (pp. 109–124). New York: Guilford.

Costello, E. J., & Angold, A. (1995b). *Developmental epidemiology.* New York: Wiley.

Costello, A.J., Edelbrock, C. S., Dulcan, M. K., Kalas, R., & Klaric, S. H. (1984). *Development and testing of the NIMH Diagnostic Interview Schedule for Children on a clinical population: Final report* (Contract RFP-DB-81-0027). Center for Epidemiological Studies, National Institute of Mental Health, Rockville, MD.

Curry, J., & Murphy, L. (1995). Comorbidity of anxiety disorders. In J. March (Ed.), *Anxiety disorders in children and adolescents* (pp. 301–317). New York: Guilford.

Dadds, M. R. (1995). *Families, children, and the development of dysfunction.* London: Sage.

Dadds, M. R., Barrett, P. M., Rapee, R. M., & Ryan, S. M. (1996). Family process and child psychopathology: An observational analysis of the FEAR effect. *Journal of Abnormal Child Psychology, 24*, 187–204.

Dadds, M. R., Rapee, R. M., & Barrett, P. M. (1994). Behavioral observation. In T. H. Ollendick, N. J. King, & W. Yule (Eds.), *International handbook of phobic and anxiety disorders in children and adolescents* (pp. 349–364). New York: Plenum Press.

DiNardo, P. A., O'Brien, G. T., Barlow, D. H., Waddell, M. T., & Blanchard, E. B. (1983). Reliability of DSM-III anxiety disorder categories using a new structured interview. *Archives of General Psychiatry, 40*, 1070–1074.

Eisen, A. R., & Kearney, C. A. (1995). *Practitioner's guide to the treatment of fear and anxiety in children and adolescents.* Northvale, NJ: Aronson.

Eisen, A. R., Spasaro, S. A., Kearney, C. A., Albano, A. M., & Barlow, D. H. (1996). Measuring parental expectancies in a childhood anxiety disorders sample: The Parental Expectancies Scale. *Behavior Therapist, 19*, 37–38.

Finch, A. J., Jr., Kendall, P. C., & Montgomery, L. E. (1976). Qualitative difference in the experience of state–trait anxiety in emotionally disturbed and normal children. *Journal of Personality Assessment, 40*(5), 522–530.

Fletcher, J. M., & Taylor, H. G. (1984). Neuropsychological approaches to children: Toward a developmental neuropsychology. *Journal of Clinical Neuropsychology, 6*(1), 39–56.

Foster, S. L., & Robin, A. L. (1988). Family conflict and communication in adolescence. In E. J. Mash & L. G. Terdal (Eds.), *Behavioral assessment of childhood disorders* (2nd ed., pp. 717–775). New York: Guilford.

Fox, E. (1994). Attentional bias in anxiety: A defective inhibition hypothesis. *Cognition and Emotion, 8*(2), 165–195.

Gazzaniga, M. (1995). *The cognitive neurosciences.* Cambridge, MA: MIT Press.

Glennon, B., & Weisz, J. R. (1978). An observational approach to the assessment of anxiety in young children. *Journal of Consulting and Clinical Psychology, 46*, 1246–1257.

Harris, J. (1995). *Developmental neuropsychiatry.* London: Oxford University Press.

Herjanic, B., & Reich, W. (1982). Development of a structured psychiatric interview for children: Agreement between child and parent on individual symptoms. *Journal of Abnormal Child Psychology, 10*, 307–324.

Hirschfeld, D. R., Rosenbaum, J. F., Biederman, J., Bolduc, E. A., Faraone, S. V., Snidman, N., Reznick, J. S., & Kagan, J. (1992). Stable behavioral inhibition and its association with anxiety disorder. *Journal of the American Academy of Child and Adolescent Psychiatry, 31*(1), 103–111.

Hodges, K., Cools, J., & McKnew, D. (1989). Test–retest reliability of a clinical research interview for children: The Child Assessment Schedule (CAS). *Psychological Assessment: Journal of Consulting and Clinical Psychology, 1*, 317–322.

Hooper, S. R., & March, J. S. (1995). Neuropsychology. In J. March (Ed.), *Anxiety disorders in children and adolescents* (pp. 35–60). New York: Guilford.

Jensen, P. S., Salzberg, A. D., Richters, J. E., & Watanabe, H. K. (1993). Scales, diagnoses, and child psychopathology: I. CBCL and DISC relationships. *Journal of the American Academy of Child and Adolescent Psychiatry, 32*(2), 397–406.

Jones, M. C. (1924). A laboratory study of fear: The case of Peter. *Journal of Genetic Psychology, 31*, 308–315.

Kearney, C. A., & Silverman, W. K. (1990). A preliminary analysis of a functional model of assessment and treatment for school refusal behavior. *Behavior Modification, 14*(3), 340–366.

Kearney, C. A., & Silverman, W. K. (1991). The panic disorder controversy continues. *Journal of the American Academy of Child and Adolescent Psychiatry, 30*(5), 852–853.

Kearney, C. A., & Silverman, W. K. (1992). Let's not push the "panic" button: A critical analysis of panic and panic disorder in adolescents. *Clinical Psychology Review, 12*(3), 293–305.

Keller, M. B., Lavori, P. W., Wunder, J., Beardslee, W. R., Schwartz, C. E., & Roth, J. (1992). Chronic course of anxiety disorders in children and adolescents. *Journal of the American Academy of Child and Adolescent Psychiatry, 31*(4), 595–599.

Kendall, P. C., Chansky, T. E., Freidman, M., Kim, R., Kortlander, E., Sessa, F. M., & Siqueland, L. (1991). Treating anxiety disorders in children and adolescents. In P. C. Kendall (Ed.), *Child and adolescent therapy; Cognitive-behavioral procedures* (pp. 131–164). New York: Guilford.

Kendall, P. C., Finch, A. J., Jr., Auerbach, S. M., Hooke, J. F., & Mikulka, P. J. (1976). The State–Trait Anxiety Inventory: A systematic evaluation. *Journal of Consulting and Clinical Psychology, 44*(3), 406–412.

King, N. J. (1994). Physiological assessment. In T. H. Ollendick, N. J. King, & W. Yule (Eds.), *International handbook of phobic and anxiety disorders in children and adolescents* (pp. 365–379). New York: Plenum Press.

King, N. J., Ollendick, T. H., & Mattis, S. G. (1994). Panic in children and adolescents: Normative and clinical studies. *Australian Psychologist, 29*(2), 89–93.

King, N. J., Tonge, B. J., & Ollendick, T. H. (1992). Night-time fears in children. *Journal of Paediatric Child Health, 28*(5), 347–350.

Klorman, R. (1991). Cognitive event-related potentials in attention deficit disorder. *Journal of Learning Disability, 24*(3), 130–140.

Kovacs, M. (1985). The Interview Schedule for Children (ISC). *Psychopharmacology Bulletin, 21*, 991–994.

Kovacs, M., Feinberg, T., & Crouse, N. (1984). Depressive disorders in childhood: Long-term characteristics and recovery. *Archives of General Psychiatry, 41*, 229–237.

Lahey, B. B., & Carlson, C. L. (1991). Validity of the diagnostic category of attention deficit disorder without hyperactivity: A review of the literature. *Journal of Learning Disabilities, 24*(2), 110–120.

Lang, P. J. (1968). Fear reduction and fear behavior: Problems in treating a construct. In J. M. Shlier (Ed.), *Research in psychotherapy* (Vol. 3, pp. 90–103). Washington, DC: American Psychological Association.

Lang, P. J. (1971). The application of psychophysiological methods to the study of psychotherapy and behavior modification. In A. E. Bergin & S. L. Garfield (Eds.), *Handbook of psychotherapy and behavior change* (pp. 75–125). New York: Wiley.

Lann, I. S. (1991). Introduction. *Journal of Anxiety Disorders, 5*, 101–103.

Last, C. (1986). *Modification of the K-SADS-P for use with anxiety disordered children and adolescents.* Unpublished manuscript. Nova Southeastern University, Fort Lauderdale, FL.

Last, C., Perrin, S., Hersen, M., & Kazdin, A. E. (1992). DSM-III-R anxiety disorders in children: Sociodemographic and clinical characteristics. *Journal of the American Academy of Child and Adolescent Psychiatry, 31*(6), 1070–1076.

Last, C. G., Strauss, C. C., & Francis, G. (1987). Comorbidity among childhood anxiety disorders. *Journal of Nervous and Mental Disease, 175*(12), 726–730.

Leonard, H., & Dow, S. (1995). Selective mutism. In J. March (Ed.), *Anxiety disorders in children and adolescents* (pp. 235–250). New York: Guilford.

Lorys, A. R., Hynd, G. W., & Lahey, B. B. (1990). Do neurocognitive measures differentiate Attention Deficit Disorder (ADD) with and without hyperactivity? *Archives of Clinical Neuropsychology, 5*(2), 119–135.

March, J. (Ed.). (1995). *Anxiety disorders in children and adolescents.* New York: Guilford.

March, J., & Albano, A. (1996). Assessment of anxiety in children and adolescents. In L. Dickstein, M. Riba, & M. Oldham (Eds.), *Review of Psychiatry XV* (Vol. 15, pp. 405–427). Washington, DC: American Psychiatric Association Press.

March, J., Leonard, H., & Swedo, S. (in press). Neuropsychiatry of pediatric obsessive-compulsive disorder. In E. Coffey & R. Brumback (Eds.), *Textbook of pediatric neuropsychiatry.* Washington, DC: American Psychiatric Association Press.

March, J., & Mulle, K. (1995). Manualized cognitive-behavioral psychotherapy for obsessive-compulsive disorder in childhood: A preliminary single case study. *Journal of Anxiety Disorders, 9*, 175–184.

March, J., Mulle, K., Stallings, P., Erhardt, D., & Conners, C. (1995). Organizing an anxiety disorders clinic. In J. March (Ed.), *Anxiety disorders in children and adolescents* (pp. 420–435). New York: Guilford.

March, J., Parker, J., Sullivan, K., Stallings, P., & Conners, C. (1997). The Multidimensional Anxiety Scale for Children (MASC): Factor structure, reliability and validity. *Journal of the American Academy of Child and Adolescent Psychiatry, 36*(4), 554–565.

Matthews, G., & Margetts, I. (1991). Self-report arousal and divided attention: A study of performance operating characteristics. *Human Performance, 4*(2), 107–125.

McBurnett, K., Lahey, B. B., Frick, P. J., Risch, C., Loeber, R., Hart, E. L., Christ, M. A., & Hanson, K. S. (1991). Anxiety, inhibition, and conduct disorder in children: II. Relation to salivary cortisol. *Journal of the American Academy of Child and Adolescent Psychiatry, 30*(2), 192–196.

McNally, R. J. (1991). Assessment of posttraumatic stress disorder in children. *Psychological Assessment: A Journal of Consulting and Clinical Psychology, 3*(4), 531–537.

McNally, R. J., Riemann, B. C., Louro, C. E., Lukach, B. M., & Kim, E. (1992). Cognitive processing of emotional information in panic disorder. *Behaviour Research and Therapy, 30*(2), 143–149.

Melamed, B., & Siegel, L. (1975). Reduction of anxiety in children facing hospitalization and surgery by use of a film modeling. *Journal of Consulting and Clinical Psychology, 46*, 1357–1367.

Melamed, B., Yurchison, R., Fleece, R. L., Hutcherson, S., & Hawes, R. (1978). Effects of film modeling on the reduction of anxiety-related behaviors in individuals varying in level of previous experience in the stress situation. *Journal of Consulting and Clinical Psychology, 46*, 1357–1367.

Moos, R. H., & Moos, B. S. (1986). Family Environment Scale manual. Palo Alto, CA: Consulting Psychological Press.

Ollendick, T. H. (1983). Reliability and validity of the Revised Fear Survey Schedule for Children (FSSC-R). Behaviour Research and Therapy, 21(6), 685–692.

Ollendick, T. H., & Francis, G. (1988). Behavioral assessment and treatment of childhood phobias. Behavior Modification, 12, 165–204.

Ollendick, T. H., & Huntzinger, R. M. (1990). Separation anxiety disorders in childhood. New York: Pergamon.

Ollendick, T. H., Matson, J. L., & Helsel, W. J. (1985). Fears in children and adolescents: Normative data. Behaviour Research and Therapy, 23(4), 465–467.

Ollendick. T. H., Mattis, S. G., & King, N. J. (1994). Panic in children and adolescents: A review. Journal of Child Psychology and Psychiatry, 35(1), 113–134.

Patterson, G. R. (1982). Coercive family process. Eugene, OR: Castalia.

Pennington, B. F., & Welsh, M. (1995). Neuropsychology and developmental psychopathology. New York: Wiley.

Perrin, S., & Last, C. G. (1992). Do childhood anxiety measures measure anxiety? Journal of Abnormal Child Psychology, 20(6) 567–578.

Pfefferbaum, A., Roth, W., & Ford, M. (1995). Event-related potentials in the study of psychiatric disorders. Archives of General Psychiatry, 52(7), 559–563.

Pliszka, S. (1989). Effect of anxiety on cognition, behavior, and stimulant response in ADHD. Journal of the American Academy of Child and Adolescent Psychiatry, 6, 882–887.

Posner, M. I. (1992). Attention as a cognitive and neural system. Current Directions in Psychological Science, 1(1), 11–14.

Prinz, R. J., Foster, S., Kent, R. N., & O'Leary, K. D. (1979). Multivariate assessment of conflict in distressed and nondistressed mother–adolescent dyads. Journal of Applied Behavior Analysis, 12, 691–700.

Puig-Antich, J., & Chambers, W. (1978). The Schedule for Affective Disorders and Schizophrenia for School-Age Children (Kiddie-SADS). New York: New York State Psychiatric Institute.

Rapee, R. M., Barrett, P. M., Dadds, M. R., & Evans, L. (1994). Reliability of the DSM-III-R childhood anxiety disorders using structured interview: Interrater and parent–child agreement. Journal of the American Academy of Child and Adolescent Psychiatry, 33, 984–992.

Rapp, P. E., Bashore, T. R., Martinerie, J. M., Albano, A. M., Zimmerman, A. D., & Mees, A. I. (1989). Dynamics of brain electrical activity. Brain Topography, 2(1-2), 99–118.

Reynolds, C. R., & Paget, K. D. (1981). Factor analysis of the Revised Children's Manifest Anxiety Scale for blacks, whites, males and females with a national normative sample. Journal of Consulting and Clinical Psychology, 49, 352–359.

Rosenbaum, J. F., Biederman, J., Bolduc, E. A., Hirshfeld, D. R., Faraone, S. V., & Kagan, J. (1992). Comorbidity of parental anxiety disorders as risk for childhood-onset anxiety in inhibited children. American Journal of Psychiatry, 149(4), 475–481.

Rosenbaum, J. F., Biederman, J., Hirshfeld, D. R., Bolduc, E. A., & Choloff, J. (1991). Behavioral inhibition in children: A possible precursor to panic disorder or social phobia. 11th National Conference on Anxiety Disorders: Social phobia: Advances in understanding and treatment (1991, Chicago). Journal of Clinical Psychiatry, 52 5–9.

Rourke, B. (1989). Nonverbal learning disabilities: The syndrome and the model. New York: Guilford.

Rutter, M. (1993a). Developmental psychopathology as a research perspective. Cambridge, UK: Cambridge University Press.

Rutter, M. (1993b). An overview of developmental neuropsychiatry. Educational and Child Psychology, 10(1), 4–11.

Rutter, M. E., Tuma, A., Lann, H. E., & Irma, S. E. (1988). *Assessment and diagnosis in child psychopathology*. New York: Guilford.

Sallee, R., & Greenawald, J. (1995). Neurobiology. In J. March (Ed.), *Anxiety disorders in children and adolescents* (pp. 3–34). New York: Guilford.

Shaffer, D. (1989). A participant's observations: preparing DSM-IV. *Canadian Journal of Psychiatry, 41*(6), 325–329.

Shaywitz, B., & Shaywitz, S. (1991). Comorbidity: A critical issue in attention deficit disorder. *Journal of Child Neurology, 5*, 13–20.

Shrout, P., & Fleiss, J. (1979). Intraclass correlations: Uses in assessing rater reliability. *Psychological Bulletin, 86*, 420–428.

Silverman, W. K. (1991). Diagnostic reliability of anxiety disorders in children using structured interviews [Special Issue: Assessment of childhood anxiety disorders]. *Journal of Anxiety Disorders, 5*(2), 105–124.

Silverman, W. K. (1994). Structured diagnostic interviews. In T. H. Ollendick, N. J. King, & W. Yule (Eds.), *International handbook of phobic and anxiety disorders in children and adolescents* (pp. 293–315). New York: Plenum Press.

Silverman, W. K., & Albano, A. M. (1996). *The Anxiety Disorders Interview Schedule for DSM-IV: Child Version*. San Antonio, TX: Psychological Corporation.

Silverman, W. K. & Eisen, A. R. (1992). Age differences in the reliability of parent and child reports of child anxious symptomatology using a structured interview. *Journal of the American Academy of Child and Adolescent Psychiatry, 31*(1), 117–124.

Silverman, W. K., & Ginsburg, G. S. (1995). Specific phobia and generalized anxiety disorder. In J. March (Ed.), *Anxiety disorders in children and adolescents* (pp. 151–180). New York: Guilford.

Silverman, W. K., & Nelles, W. B. (1988). The anxiety disorders interview schedule for children. *Journal of the American Academy of Child and Adolescent Psychiatry, 27*, 772–778.

Simon, G., Ormel, J., VonKorff, M., & Barlow, W. (1995). Health care costs associated with depressive and anxiety disorders in primary care. *American Journal of Psychiatry, 152*, 353–357.

Spielberger, C., Gorsuch, R., & Luchene, R. (1976). *Manual for the State–Trait Anxiety Inventory*. Palo Alto, CA: Consulting Psychologists Press.

Swanson, J. M., Posner, M., Potkin, S. G., Bonforte, S., Yourer, D., Fiore, C., Cantwell, D., & Crinella, F. (1991). Activating tasks for the study of visual–spatial attention in ADHD children: A cognitive anatomic approach. *Journal of Child Neurology, 6* S119–S127.

Swedo, S. E., Schapiro, M. B., Grady, C. L., Cheslow, D. L., Leonard, H. L., Kumar, A., Friedland, R., Rapoport, S. I., & Rapoport, J. L. (1989). Cerebral glucose metabolism in childhood-onset obsessive–compulsive disorder. *Archives of General Psychiatry, 46*(6), 518–523.

Thyer, B. A. (1991). Diagnosis and treatment of child and adolescent anxiety disorders. *Behavior Modification, 15*(3), 310–325.

Towey, J. P., Tenke, C. E., Bruder, G. E., Leite, P., Friedman, D., Liebowitz, M., & Hollander, E. (1994). Brain event-related potential correlates of overfocused attention in obsessive–compulsive disorder. *Psychophysiology, 31*(6), 535–543.

Turner, S. M., Beidel, D. C., & Epstein, L. H. (1991). Vulnerability and risk for anxiety disorders. *Journal of Anxiety Disorders, 5*, 151–166.

Voeller, K. K. (1991). What can neurological models of attention, intention, and arousal tell us about attention-deficit hyperactivity disorder? *Journal of Neuropsychiatry and Clinical Neurosciences, 3*(2), 209–216.

Wahler, R. G. (1976). Deviant child behavior within the family: Developmental speculations and behavior change strategies. In H. Leitenberg (Ed.), *Handbook of behavior modification and behavior therapy* (pp. 516–543). Englewood Cliffs, NJ: Prentice-Hall.

Weiss, B., Weisz, J., Politane, M., Carey, M., Nelson, W., & Finch, A. (1991). Developmental differences in the factor structure of the Children's Depression Inventory. *Psychological Assessment, 3*(1) 38–45.

Widiger, T., Frances, A., Pincus, H., Ross, M., First, M., & Davis, W. (1996). *DSM-IV sourcebook.* Washington, DC: American Psychiatric Association Press.

Wisniewski, J., Mulick, J. J., & Coury, D. (1987). Test–retest reliability of the Revised Children's Manifest Anxiety Scale. *Perceptual and Motor Skills, 65,* 67–70.

Wolff, R. P., & Wolff, L. S. (1991). Assessment and treatment of obsessive–compulsive disorder in children. *Behavior Modification, 15,* 372–393.

Zacks, R. T., & Hasher, L. (1994). Directed ignoring: Inhibitory regulation of working memory. In D. Dosenbach & T. Carr (Eds.), *Inhibitory processes in attention, memory and language* (pp. 241–264). San Diego: Academic Press.

Zametkin, A. J., Nordahl, T. E., Gross, M., King, A. C., Semple, W., Rumsey, J., Hamburger, S., & Cohen, R. M. (1990). Cerebral glucose metabolism in adults with hyperactivity of childhood onset. *New England Journal of Medicine, 323*(20), 1361–1366.

8

Conceptualization and Measurement of Coping in Children and Adolescents

TIM S. AYERS, IRWIN N. SANDLER, AND JOAN L. TWOHEY

1. Introduction

Recent years have seen a significant increase in the number of efforts to conceptualize and measure coping and to examine the role it plays in effecting the development of symptomatology for people in stressful situations (e.g., Billings & Moos, 1981; Carver, Scheier, & Weintraub, 1989; Endler & Parker, 1990; Folkman & Lazarus, 1980; McCrae, 1984; Miller, 1987; Pearlin & Schooler, 1978). Although the vast majority of these efforts at conceptualization, measurement, and research have involved adult populations, there has been an increase in the number of studies concerning coping by children or adolescents (e.g., Ayers, Sandler, West, & Roosa, 1996; Band & Weisz, 1988; Brodzinsky, Elias, Steiger, & Simon, 1992; Causey & Dubow, 1992; Compas, Malcarne, & Fondacaro, 1988b; Curry & Russ, 1985; Phelps & Jarvis, 1994; Rossman, 1992; Ryan-Wenger, 1990; Wertlieb, Weigel, & Feldstein, 1987; Zeitlin, 1980).

Thus, it is now timely to examine some of the conceptual, theoretical, methodological, and developmental issues related to the assessment of coping in children and adolescents (for earlier reviews of coping measures, see, Knapp, Stark, Kurkjian, & Spirito, 1991; Ryan-Wenger, 1994). This chapter begins by briefly reviewing alternative definitions and conceptual issues prerequisite to a discussion of the measures of coping, such as what

TIM S. AYERS, IRWIN N. SANDLER, AND JOAN L. TWOHEY • Program for Prevention Research, Arizona State University, Tempe, Arizona 85287.

Advances in Clinical Child Psychology, Volume 20, edited by Thomas H. Ollendick and Ronald J. Prinz. Plenum Press, New York, 1998.

represents the proper domain of coping and the dimensionality of coping. The discussion will proceed to the methods and current assessment instruments that have been used with children and adolescents, and the observed relations between these measures of coping and adjustment. Finally, the chapter discusses more general issues that are important for future research in the assessment of coping, such as theoretical versus empirical approaches to measurement development and the importance of adopting a developmental perspective in the assessment of coping during childhood and adolescence.

2. Conceptualization of Coping

A brief, although necessarily selective review (see Compas, 1997; Lazarus & Folkman, 1984; Moos & Billings, 1982; Moos & Schaefer, 1993; Skinner & Wellborn, 1994; Suls & Fletcher, 1985) of the literature and the definition of coping is presented to provide a framework for understanding recent efforts at measuring children's coping.

2.1. Definition of Coping

From a psychoanalytic perspective, coping typically has been referred to as those thoughts and behaviors that reflect the *most advanced* or *mature* ego processes. Within these formulations, *coping* is often defined as realistic and flexible thoughts and acts that *solve* problems and thereby reduce stress. As an example, Haan (1977, 1982) offers a theoretical model involving a tripartite hierarchical arrangement of coping, defending, and fragmentation. Generic ego processes can be expressed at each of these three levels. For example, sensitivity to others' thoughts and feelings can be expressed as empathy (the coping mode), projection (the defensive mode), and delusions or ideas of reference (the fragmentary mode).

The recent literature has tended to reject the psychoanalytic approach to defining coping in such hierarchical and structural terms for two primary reasons. First, to define coping as those processes that *solve* problems automatically eliminates many thoughts and behaviors that individuals utilize but which are *not* successful. Investigators in the area have pointed out that conceptualizing coping in this fashion increases the risk of confounding the measurement of the construct with the assessment of outcome, in essence creating a tautology (that which is most efficacious predicts better outcomes, and that which creates better outcomes is judged as the most adaptive; see Lazarus, 1993; Stone, Helder, & Schneider, 1988). Understanding which particular coping efforts are effective in a given situation first requires a "neutral stance" regarding the efficacy of any and all coping efforts.

The second trend in the conceptualization of coping is a change from viewing coping in more structural and dispositional terms to adopting a more transactional perspective. The most prominent description of the transactional perspective was offered by Lazarus and Folkman (1984), who take a cognitive-phenomenological approach to the problem. They define coping as "constantly changing cognitive and behavioral efforts to manage specific external and/or internal demands that are appraised as taxing or exceeding the resources of the person" (p. 141). This relational definition emphasizes that coping should be viewed as *all* cognitive and behavioral *efforts*, regardless of their outcomes, that are taken in response to *specific* external and internal demands. In this conception there is also an emphasis on the importance of understanding the specific characteristics of the situation and an individual's appraisal as to whether it is threatening, and whether a coping response is necessary.

2.2. Conceptualizing Coping as a Process versus a Trait

A significant part of a transactional perspective is that coping is seen as part of a dynamic, ongoing, and constantly changing *process* (Lazarus, 1993; Lazarus & Folkman, 1984). Lazarus and Folkman (1984) argue that there are three main features to a process approach. First, the assessment of coping needs to be concerned with *what a person actually thinks or does* in a stressful situation. This is in contrast to examining coping *dispositions*, *styles*, or *traits*, which are what a person *usually* does in a stressful situation. Second, the assessment of coping behaviors needs to be examined within a *specific context*. The coping strategies an individual chooses are, in part, dependent upon the demands of the particular situation. Finally, a process-oriented approach focuses on the *change* in coping thoughts and acts as the stressful encounter unfolds (e.g., Folkman & Lazarus, 1985).

Several authors argue that although many tout the importance of adopting a transactional perspective, the typical approach in developing and using existing coping measures has followed a dispositional or stylistic orientation (Coyne & Gottlieb, 1996; Lazarus, 1993; Stone, Kennedy-Moore, Newman, Greenberg, & Neale, 1992). Rather than arguing that the process-oriented approach is necessarily more appropriate than a dispositional- or trait-oriented approach to coping, Lazarus and Folkman (1984) note that such trait-oriented approaches tend to "grossly simplify complex patterns of coping into unidimensional schemes.... which have little explanatory and predictive value for what a person actually does in particular contexts" (p. 178). Later, Lazarus (1993) would comment that "even when multidimensional measures are employed,... environmental conditions eliciting the coping process tend to be ignored because the focus is centered on consistent coping styles" (pp. 241–242).

Lazarus (1993) recently acknowledged that the most serious weakness of conceptualizing coping as a process is that "coping process measures would be far more meaningful and useful it we knew more about the persons whose coping thoughts and actions in specific contexts are being studied" (p. 242). He notes that probably the most serious omission within such a process-oriented approach has tended to be a lack of attention to the motivational aspect of the personality, that is, the "general goals and situational intentions that mobilize and direct the choice of coping strategies employed" (p. 243). As we will discuss later in the chapter, the theoretical orientation that one adopts has implications for both the development of measures and the psychometric characteristics one can anticipate for those measures (Schwarzer & Schwarzer, 1996).

3. Dimensionalization of Coping

3.1. Classification of Coping

Coping has been classified by the *function* or purpose it is intended to serve (Billings & Moos, 1981; Lazarus & Folkman, 1984; Pearlin & Schooler, 1978). Lazarus and Folkman (1984) distinguish between coping efforts that are directed at managing or altering the stressful situation (problem-focused) and those efforts that are directed at regulating emotional responses to the situation (emotion-focused).

Rothbaum, Weisz, and Snyder (1982; Weisz, Rothbaum, & Blackburn, 1984), working within an attributional framework and emphasizing control perceptions, make a distinction between primary and secondary control. Primary control pertains to coping that is aimed at influencing objective conditions or events so as to reduce punishment or enhance reward. Secondary control is coping aimed at maximizing one's goodness of fit with the conditions as they are, thus reducing punishment and enhancing reward.[1]

In their longitudinal studies of personality development in childhood, Murphy and Moriarty (1976) identified two major types of coping techniques, which they labeled Coping I and Coping II. Coping I was defined as the "capacity to cope with opportunities, challenges, frustrations, (and)

---

[1]They also define a third category called "relinquished control," in which there is no apparent goal-directed behavior.

threats in the environment" (p. 117) and is characterized by a more active problem-solving approach to coping with the environment. Coping II is defined as the "capacity to manage one's relation to the environment so as to maintain integrated functioning (free from marked tenseness, unmanageable anxiety, deterioration of speech, disorganization of thought processes, loss of motor coordination, and so on)" (p. 117). Murphy and her colleagues (Murphy, 1974; Murphy & Moriarty, 1976) gathered an impressive array of data on the developmental and individual differences of the children they have followed longitudinally and propose that their data support the heuristic value of the Coping I and Coping II distinction for studying coping processes in children and adolescents.

Moos and colleagues (Ebata & Moos, 1991; Holahan, Moos, & Schaefer, 1996; Moos & Schaefer, 1993) maintain that two main approaches to the classification of coping efforts have predominated. The first approach emphasizes the *focus* or function of the coping efforts (i.e., the person's orientation in response to a stressor). The second approach has emphasized the *method* of coping that people employ (i.e., a response that involves primarily cognitive or behavioral efforts). They cross these two methods of classification and suggest that coping can be conceptualized based on an individual's orientation to the stressor, that is, either approach (active) versus avoidance (passive), and that both of these domains can be further subdivided into categories that reflect cognitive or behavioral coping. Therefore, they propose cognitive approach, behavioral approach, cognitive avoidance, and behavioral avoidance as four basic categories of coping processes and suggest that various subtypes of coping efforts, such as resigned acceptance or taking problem-solving action, can be categorized into these categories (in these instances, cognitive avoidance and behavioral approach).

3.2. Coping from a Motivational Perspective

Skinner and colleagues (Skinner & Wellborn, 1994, 1997) offer a conceptualization of coping using a perspective derived from a motivational theory of psychological needs. They define *coping* as "children's regulation of their behavior, emotion, and motivational orientation during psychological stress" (Skinner & Wellborn, 1994, p. 107). The motivational theory they employ posits three basic, innate psychological needs: relatedness, competence, and autonomy (Connell & Wellborn, 1991). Stressful events are those that threaten or challenge these three motivational needs. Thus, they suggest that there are three dimensions of the social context that are viewed as psychologically stressful: neglect (vs. involvement), which threatens the need for relatedness; chaos (vs. structure), which threatens competence; and coercion (vs. autonomy support), which threatens the need for autonomy.

Skinner and colleagues (Skinner & Wellborn, 1994, 1997) note that the source of the stress can be the self or the environmental context, and that the individual's appraisal of the extent to which the event or context is meeting their psychological needs determines the perceived severity (threat vs. challenge) of stress. The extent to which these basic psychological needs are met determines whether individuals will be engaged versus disaffected. Tying this notion of being engaged or disaffected together with their definition of coping as involving children's regulation of their behavior, emotion, and motivational orientation suggests that children's efforts can reflect energized versus enervated *behavior*, positive versus negative *emotion*, and committed versus alienated *orientation* to the goals of developing relatedness, competence, and autonomy.

Skinner derives a set of 36 ways of coping with problems in friendship or academic domains from this motivational theory of coping (Skinner, Altman, & Sherwood, 1991; Skinner & Wellborn, 1997) by crossing the targets of regulation (behavior, emotion, and orientation) with the motivational needs (relatedness, competence, and autonomy), and the source (self vs. context) and the perceived severity (threat vs. challenge) of stress. Skinner notes that these 36 categories of coping can also be classified by the more traditional ways of classifying coping in terms of approach versus avoidance, passive versus active, positive versus negative, but suggests that such dimensions will not go far in terms of describing the adaptiveness of these modes of coping. These authors (Skinner et al., 1991; Skinner & Wellborn, 1997) draw from the emotion-regulation literature (e.g., Eisenberg, Fabes, & Guthrie, 1997) and suggest that coping will be adaptive to the extent that it is organized (vs. disorganized), flexible (vs. rigid), and benign (vs. punitive). To illustrate how this conceptualization moves beyond an approach versus avoidance distinction in offering potentially more accurate predictions about relations to adaptation, Skinner suggests that two forms of approach coping, such as, strategizing versus perseverance, might be shown to be differentially adaptive because the first is flexible, whereas the latter reflects a more rigid approach.

Skinner and colleagues argued that there are several advantages to using this conceptualization of coping (Skinner & Wellborn, 1994, 1997). Besides being part of a larger theory of motivation, it is tied closely to the literature on self-regulation, ego resilience, and ego control; thus, one can use what is known about the development of behavioral, emotional, and motivational regulation to outline and begin to develop a theory of the epigenesis of regulated coping behaviors (Skinner & Wellborn, 1994; p. 113). It is also the only conceptualization that explicitly adds an orientation or outlook component to the conceptualization of coping (Skinner & Well-born, 1997). An additional advantage is that there is more of an emphasis on a wider range of "positive coping" in that there is a one-to-one correspondence between positive and negative modes of coping in their conceptualization. Finally, they suggest that their coping categories imply several differentiations that might be useful in other areas of research, such as help seeking, perceived control, and autonomy. As an example, helplessness due to perceived incompetence may manifest itself differently in terms of a child's behavior than helplessness due to perceived noncontingency.

4. Domain of Coping

What to include within the definition of coping responses is one of the most vexing problems in the area. Lazarus and Folkman (1984) emphasized in their definition, that it includes all responses a person shows "when demands are appraised as taxing or exceeding a person's resources" and yet in their definition of coping limited it to those efforts "which require(s) mobilization and exclude(s) automatized behaviors and thoughts which do not require effort" (pp. 141–142). Compas (1987), in his seminal review of child and adolescent coping, noted that it is "necessary to limit the use of the term to a subset of adaptational actions involving effort" (p. 399).

The decision to limit the definition of coping only to those behaviors that are "effortful" or purposeful has recently been challenged (Coyne & Gottlieb, 1996; Skinner & Wellborn, 1994). Skinner and Wellborn (1994) argue that in doing this, one excludes phenomena that are potentially very interesting aspects of coping. As an example, they note that Compas (1987) discussed learned helplessness as a form of coping, and this pattern of responding would, by most theoreticians' definitions, not reflect effortful or intentional behavior. More importantly, they argue that when one defines coping as intentional or effortful, some of the more important developmental questions such as the epigenesis of coping are more difficult to address. Many of the behaviors that infants and toddlers emit could not be considered intentional, effortful, or purposeful, yet may be important precursors to other behaviors that reflect coping by children or adolescents.

Coyne and Gottlieb (1996) take issue with the decision to exclude habitual or automatic behaviors from the domain of coping. Over time, people refine and develop routinized "coping" strategies that have proved to be effective for them in dealing with stressful circumstances. Coyne and Gottlieb ask the question: "Once a set of dependable, routine stress management behaviors have been developed, are they no longer to be considered coping?" (p. 963). At the same time, there are automatic and habitual patterns of response that are the crux of ineffective coping. As an example, automatic, negative thoughts have been implicated in exacerbating depression in individuals (e.g., Beck, 1967). Coyne and Gottlieb (1996) also question the decision to exclude behaviors that are *anticipatory* from the domain of coping. They suggest that much "effective" coping is *anticipatory*, that is, behaviors that are enacted prior to the occurrence of stressful circumstances that may actually avert the occurrence of the particular stressor entirely. Coyne and Gottlieb argue that to exclude these behaviors from the domain of coping gives one a distorted picture of the stress and coping processes.

Recently, Compas and colleagues (Compas, Connor, Harding, Saltzman, & Wadsworth, in press; Compas, Connor, Osowiecki, & Welch, 1997; Compas et al., 1997) put forth a model that places coping as a construct within a broader context of responses to stress. These authors offer a hierarchy that at the first and highest level makes a distinction between responses to stress that are effortful versus involuntary (i.e., temperamental or overlearned). They note that responses to stress vary in the degree to which the individual experiences them as under volitional or effortful control. Involuntary responses are both cognitive and behavioral response to stress that are experienced by the individual as unintentional or not under personal control. Responses to stress are not necessarily always predefined as effortful or involuntary; that is, through repeated practice, some effortful processes can be automatized or experienced as involuntary, some involuntary responses to stress can eventually be brought under personal, and therefore effortful control. In discussing this distinction, they argue that the construct of coping should be limited to those responses to stress that are effortful. In this sense, they disagree with Skinner and Wellborn's (1994) decision to conceptualize nonvolitional or noneffortful responses as coping.

At the second level of the hierarchy, the responses to stress vary in the degree to which they reflect engagement versus disengagement from the stressor. Engagement responses are oriented toward either the stressful relationship with the environment or one's emotional responses to the stressor, whereas disengagement responses are directed away from the stressful relationship with the environment or one's emotional responses. Compas and colleagues (1997) argue that this distinction can be made for both effortful or involuntary responses and is related to the basic dimension of approach–avoidance discussed elsewhere in the literature (e.g., Billings & Moos, 1981; Ebata & Moos, 1991). These authors hypothesize that both effortful and involuntary disengagement responses, and involuntary engagement responses are associated with greater symptomatology, whereas effortful engagement responses are expected to be associated with lower symptomatology. They acknowledge that there may be some differences in these associations when examining subtypes of responses within these broader categories.

Compas and colleagues (1977) suggest a number of candidates for the distinction at the third level of the hierarchy and believe that this dimension still needs to be determined empirically. They point to prominent distinctions offered in the literature: (1) those that focus on the goals of the individual (e.g., primary control vs. secondary control coping; Rothbaum et al., 1982) or problem- versus emotion-focused coping (Lazarus & Folkman, 1984); (2) self- versus externally focused responses, which is related to the work of Nolen-Hoeksema and colleagues (Nolen-Hoeksema & Morrow, 1993) on rumination (self-focused) and distraction (external focus) and Pyszczynski and colleagues' (Pyszczynski & Greenberg, 1987; Pyszczynski, Greenberg, Hamilton, & Nix, 1991) research on depressive self-focusing styles following failures; (3) the distinction between cognitive and behavioral responses (e.g., Ebata & Moos, 1991); and (4) the distinction between personal and social resources in coping. It should be noted that many of these distinctions (e.g., primary vs. secondary control coping or problem- vs. emotion-focused coping) would apply only to the effortful responses to stress (i.e., coping).

Within this hierarchy, the habitual or automatic behavior, which Coyne and Gottlieb (1996) believed should be included as part of the domain of coping, reflects important responses to stress but would not be conceptualized necessarily as reflecting coping on part of the individual because the behavior is not viewed as being effortful (Compas et al., 1997). However, within their conceptualization, Compas and colleagues (Compas et al., 1997, in press) do seem to agree with Coyne and Gottlieb (1996) about the importance of habitual, automatic behaviors, noting that involuntary processes can frequently constrain the types of coping responses that an individual can generate. Understanding the relationships between coping and involuntary, overlearned, or habitual patterns of responding to stress is therefore critically important.

5. Measurement of Coping in Children and Adolescents

In this section, we examine several efforts that attempt to measure the coping *styles* or *strategies* of children and adolescents. The review will be limited to measures that can be used in a variety of contexts and attempt to measure a range of types of coping responses or styles. We will not review measures that assess coping behaviors in response to specific stressors, which are not readily adaptable to other settings (see Miller, Sherman, Combs, & Kruus, 1992, for a review of coping assessments for children undergoing medical or dental procedures), or those that focus on one or two coping resources/strategies, for example, interpersonal problem solving (Spivack, Platt, & Shure, 1976) or social support measures (Wolchik, Beals, & Sandler, 1989).

We have organized our review of the assessment of coping measures based on whether the instruments were designed to assess the use of a variety of coping *strategies* in response to *specific* stressor(s) or whether they were intended primarily to measure general coping *styles*. This organization reflects the distinction between conceptualizing coping from a transactional perspective, in which the focus is on strategies used in *specific* situations, and from conceptualizing coping from a dispositional or stylistic perspective. Aldwin (1994) makes the point that this conceptual distinction is often overlooked in the measurement of coping. The instructions given to the respondent are key to the distinguishing between coping strategies and styles. In this review, studies that ask the respondent to report what he/she *usually* does to handle problems *without referring to a specific problem* were classified as measuring coping *styles*. Included with measures of coping style are those studies that ask children or adolescents to report their coping efforts in response to a hypothetical event (Asarnow, Carlson, & Guthrie, 1987; Danvosky, Rapoff, & Houston, 1995; Hoffner, 1993). In addition, studies that asked children to respond by "mentally aggregating" their coping efforts in response to multiple incidents of a *certain class* of problems (e.g., Causey & Dubow, 1992; Reid, Dubow, & Carey, 1995), we believe, represent a stylistic approach to assessing children's coping. Studies that asked children or adolescents to describe a *specific* stressful event and then to report their coping efforts in response to this event were classified as measuring coping strategies.

Tables 1 and 2 are included to summarize information regarding the assessment of coping strategies and styles, respectively. The tables summarize studies to assess coping in terms of the characteristics of the sample used, the methodology, coping categories, and information about the reliabilities and validity of the instruments when available. The tables are organized by type of measure, that is, interview, questionnaire and behavioral observation measures, and by author within each of these segments. Space limitations do not permit a discussion of each article included in the tables. However, several studies have been selected as illustrative examples of different approaches to the measurement of coping.

6.   Assessment of Coping Strategies

Table 1 highlights the variety of approaches that have been taken to assess coping strategies by using interview schedules (e.g., Band & Weisz, 1988; Compas et al., 1988b; Wertlieb et al., 1987), questionnaire formats (Ayers et al., 1996; Brodzinsky et al., 1992; Dise Lewis, 1988; Frydenberg & Lewis, 1991), and, occasionally, behavioral observations (Curry & Russ, 1985; Hyson, 1983).

The types of stressful experience for which respondents have been asked to report coping efforts have varied from a discrete, rather circumscribed event (e.g., dental or medical visit; Curry & Russ, 1985; Hyson, 1983; Miller, Roussi, Caputo, & Kruus, 1995) to several different domains of experience that have been suggested as potential sources of stress for children and adolescents (e.g., Band & Weisz, 1988; Wertlieb et al., 1987). Studies that have utilized primarily a self-report methodology either by semistructured interview or by use of a questionnaire will be discussed first, followed by those studies that have included an observational measure of coping behaviors.

6.1.   Interview Measures of Coping Strategies

Two studies will be discussed to illustrate the use of semistructured interviews to measure coping strategies. Compas et al. (1988b) used a structured interview format in which they asked 130 children aged 10 to 14 to describe two stressful events, one interpersonal and one academic, that happened to them in the last 3 months. They asked the children to rate the degree of control they had over the cause of the event, to generate a list of all the possible ways they could have handled or dealt with the event, and, finally, to report in their own words which strategies they actually used to cope with the stressor. The children's responses were classified by the coping *function* they served. Compas et al. (1988b) used Folkman and Lazarus's (1984) conceptual distinction between problem- and emotion-focused coping as their guide for classifying the children's responses.

Compas et al. (1988b) reported very good interrater reliabilities for categorizing children's responses into problem- versus emotion-focused coping (see Table 1) for both stressors and noted low to moderate levels of consistency in both the alternatives generated and the strategies used for the two stressors. Significant negative correlations between problem-focused coping and emotional–behavioral problems, based on child and maternal report, supported concurrent validity. The pattern of the correlations was significant but in the positive direction for emotion-focused coping and emotional–behavioral problems.

TABLE 1

Measures Assessing Coping Strategies

Development article and name of scale	Sample	Type of measure	Subscales Name (# items)	Reliability[a]	Validity
			Interviews		
Band & Weisz (1988)	73 children 6, 9, and 12 yrs. from a semirural community	Assessed coping with an event the child experienced in the past year. Events in 6 domains were sought for each child.	Primary control Direct problem solving Problem-focused crying Problem-focused aggression Problem-focused avoidance Secondary control Social/spiritual support Emotion-focused crying Emotion-focused aggression Cognitive avoidance Pure cognition Relinquished control Doing nothing	3 broad categories: *Kappas* (Range = .82–.91) M = .87 10 fine-grained categories: *Kappas* (Range = .84–.94) M = 90	—
Coletta et al. (1981)	64 teenager mothers, 14–19 yrs.	Assessed coping with three problems	Redefining the problem Avoiding the problem Taking direct action to problem Dealing with emotional effects	*Interrater* (Range = .84–.91) M = .87	Direct action was related to higher self-esteem and lower emotional stress.
Compas et al. (1988b)	130 children 10–14 yrs.	Children reported coping with interpersonal and academic events in past month.	Responses categorized as problem-focused or emotion-focused coping.	*Kappas* Academic = .88 Interpersonal = .87	Problem-focused coping negatively related to mother and child report of emotional and behavioral problems. Emotion-focused coping positively related to emotional and behavioral problems.

Sipes et al. (1985)	2,728 9th-grade students	Essays on greatest fear as a young child were coded.		—	—
		In vivo			
		Reason/age			
		People			
		Took control			
		Destroy			
		God			
		Animals			
		Escape			
		Miscellaneous			
Wertlieb et al. (1987), Child Stress Inventory (CSI)	176 children 6 and 9 yrs. upper-middle/upper class	Assessed coping with a self-identified stressor.		*Kappas[b]*	Type A behavior correlated positively with inhibited and intrapsychic coping, and negatively with direct action. Other findings not consistent with expectations.
		Categorized coping by focus, function, and mode.		Mode = .64	
		Mode categories		Focus = .53	
		Information seeking		Function = .53	
		Support seeking			
		Direct action			
		Inhibition of action			
		Intrapsychic			
Ayers et al. (1996), How I Coped under Pressure Scale (HICUPS)	303 children 9–13 yrs. M = 10.5	45 items[c] assessed coping with a stressful event that occurred in their lives during the past 3 months.	Questionnaire measures		—
		Active	.89		
		Cognitive decision making (4)	.71		
		Direct problem-solving (4)	.71		
		Seeking understanding (4)	.74		
		Positive cognitive restructuring (4)	.62		
		Distraction	.80		
		Distracting actions (5)	.65		
		Physical release of emotions (4)	.65		
		Avoidance	.73		
		Cognitive avoidance (4)	.61		
		Avoidant actions (4)	.64		
		Support seeking	.78		
		Problem-focused support (4)	.57		
		Emotion-focused support (4)	.60		

(continued)

TABLE 1 (Continued)

Development article and name of scale	Sample	Type of measure	Subscales Name (# items)	Reliability[a]	Validity
Brodzinsky et al. (1992), Coping Scale for Children and Youth (CSCY)	810 5th–8th graders, mostly white and middle-class	29 items assessed coping with a self-selected stressor of the past few months.	Assistance seeking (4)	.72	Self-efficacy positively related to cognitive-behavioral problem solving and assistance seeking, and negatively related to cognitive and behavioral avoidance. Correlated with KIDCOPE as expected.
			Cognitive-behavioral problem solving (8)	.81	
			Cognitive avoidance (11)	.80	
			Behavioral avoidance (6)	.70	
Causey & Dubow (1993), Self-Reported Coping Scale	162 7th graders, mostly white and lower middle-class	34 items assessed coping with a daily school stressor.		*Time 1/Time 2*	—
			Higher order factors found:		
			Approach	.89/.88	
			Avoidance	.82/.77	
Ebata & Moos (1991) Coping Responses Inventory—Youth Form (CRI-Y)	190 adolescents 12–18 yrs. healthy participants (38), rheumatic (45), conduct disordered (58), depressed (49)	48 items assessed coping with the most important problem faced in the past year.	Approach-cognitive		Depressed adolescents and adolescents with conduct disorder reported more avoidance coping than healthy adolescents and adolescents with rheumatic disease.
			Logical analysis (6)	.72	
			Positive reappraisal (6)	.79	
			Approach-behavioral		
			Guidance/support (6)	.71	
			Problem solving (6)	.73	
			Avoidant-cognitive		
			Cognitive avoidance (6)	.70	
			Resigned acceptance (6)	.55	
			Avoidant-behavioral		
			Alternative rewards (6)	.71	
			Emotional discharge (6)	.69	

Measure	Sample	Description	Subscales	Reliability	
Elwood (1987), Coping Response Inventory	17 children in 4th grade and 29 children in 7th grade	14 items (4th grade) and 16 items (7th grade) assessed coping with a daily hassle of past 2 weeks.	—	—[d]	—
Frydenberg & Lewis (1991), revised the Folkman & Lazarus Ways of Coping Checklist	643 11th- and 12th-grade students in Australia	66 items tapped coping with their main concern.	Problem focused Wishful thinking Detachment Seeking social support Focus on the positive Self-blame Tension-reduction Keep to self	Range: .57–.77	—
Halstead et al. (1993) modified Folkman & Lazarus Ways of Coping Checklist	306 9th–12th graders, $M = 14.8$ yrs., 60% white, 31.2% African American	35 items tapped coping with a self-identified stressful situation.	Identified 4-factors structure: Problem focused (15) Seeks social support (6) Wishful thinking (10) Avoidance (4)	.81 .79 .82 .55	—
Mooney et al. (1985), Children's Nighttime Coping Checklist	178 children 8–13 yrs.	38 items assess coping with nighttime fears.	Internal self-control (9) Social support (11) Inanimate objects (4) Prayers (2) Avoidance or escape (12)	—	—

(continued)

TABLE 1 (Continued)

Development article and name of scale	Sample	Type of measure	Subscales Name (# items)	Reliability[a]	Validity
Phelps & Jarvis (1994), Used Carver et al.'s COPE	484 adolescents 14–18 yrs. from a middle-class community	60 items assessed coping with a problem of last 2 months.	4 higher order factors identified: Active:		—
			Active coping (3)	.66	
			Planning (3)	.78	
			Suppression of competing activities (3)	.69	
			Seeking support: Instrumental reasons (3)	.72	
			Avoidant:		
			Denial (3)	.76	
			Behavioral disengagement (3)	.66	
			Alcohol-drug disengagement (3)	.75	
			Emotion focused:		
			Seeking support: Emotional reasons (3)	.83	
			Focus and venting of emotions (3)	.80	
			Acceptance:		
			Restraint (3)	.69	
			Positive reinterpretation and growth (3)	.68	
			Acceptance (3)	.74	
			Mental disengagement (3)	.51	
Ryan-Wenger (1990), Schoolagers' Coping Strategies Inventory (SCSI)[e]	250 white children 8–12 yrs., $M =$ 9.76	26 items assessed coping with a recent stressful event.		*Test–retest*	Coping distinct from measures of self-esteem. Asymptomatic children had higher coping scores than children with stress-related problems.
			Frequency	.76 .73	
			Effectiveness	.77 .82	
			Total score	.79 .81	

Measure	Sample		Categories	Reliability	Validity
Spirito et al. (1988), KIDCOPE	Pediatric patients, diabetes patients, and 4 samples of healthy children (ages 10–18 yrs., N = 437)	10 items were used to assess coping with a self-selected event.	Frequency and Efficacy scores for coping categories: Problem solving, Distraction, Social support, Social withdrawal, Cognitive restructuring, Self-criticism, Blaming others, Emotional regulation, Wishful thinking, Resignation	Test-retest: 3-day: frq: .56–.75 eff: .25–.74 7-day: frq: .07–.83 eff: .01–.50 14-day: frq: .04–.56 eff: .21–.58	KIDCOPE items correlated with like subscales of early version of Tobins's CSI and Patterson and McCubbin's ACOPE
Stern & Alvarez (1992), used the Folkman & Lazarus Ways of Coping Scale—Revised	39 teenage parents; (M = 18.08); 45 pregnant adolescents (M = 16.18); 45 nonpregnant adolescents (M = 17.06)	66 items assessed coping with a recent stressful event.	Confrontive coping, Distancing, Self-controlling, Seeking social support, Self-blame, Escape–avoidance, Planful problem solving, Postive reappraisal	Average = .72	Self-blame and escape/avoidance negatively related to psychological adjustment
Observational measures					
Hyson (1983)	48 children 6–60 mos.	Assessed coping with a doctor visit	White's (1974) 3 categories: Info. seeking, Maintaining internal equilibrium, Autonomy	Interrater (Range = .74–.92)	—

[a] Unless stated otherwise, reliabilities reported are alpha coefficients.

[b] Bull and Drotar (1991) used the CSI to assess how children with cancer coped with 5 self-selected stressful situations and reported *Kappas*: mode = .83, focus = .84, function = .61.

[c] The three-item Expressing Feelings scale was dropped because of poor internal consistency and contamination with symptomatology.

[d] The authors state that 2-week test–retest (but not necessarily on the same event) was calculated and no significant change was found. Because reliability should be calculated with respect to responses to the same event, it is not tabled here.

[e] With a sample of 59 black children, Ryan-Wagner and Copeland (1994) found an *alpha* of .80 for frequency and .73 for effectiveness.

Working from a slightly different theoretical framework, Band and Weisz (1988) investigated the coping *functions* and *strategies* of children using a semistructured self-report interview with 73 children who ranged in age from 6 to 12. They asked children to report about their coping (what they did and what they thought) in six different domains of stressful situations that occurred in the past year (e.g., separation from a friend, going to the doctor's to get a shot, getting a grade on an exam they did not like). They also probed for information about children's goals in each situation and their sense of efficacy about their coping responses.

Band and Weisz (1988) classified the children's coping strategies in two different ways. They coded each strategy generated as representing one of three broad categories (i.e., primary, secondary, or relinquished control). They also initially used Folkman and Lazarus's (1984) adult-based "ways of coping" model to classify each strategy on a more fine-grained, descriptive level. They discovered that 40% of the children's responses fell outside the "ways of coping" categories, which forced the development of new categories. The 10 categories that resulted from a content analysis and the interrater reliabilities for classifying their responses are listed in Table 1.

6.2. Questionnaire Measures of Coping Strategies

Three studies illustrate the use of a closed-ended questionnaire to assess coping strategies for a specific stressful event. Ebata and Moos (1991) developed the Coping Responses Inventory—Youth Form on which adolescents reported the coping strategies they used for the most important problem faced in the prior 12 months. Forty-eight items were developed on a rational basis to represent eight conceptually distinct dimensions that included both cognitive and behavioral methods of coping. These methods were collapsed into two broad-band dimensions of approach versus avoidance based on the focus of coping with examples of behavioral and cognitive methods within each broad-band dimension. Approach methods such as logical analysis and problem solving represent attempts to understand, resolve, or master the stressor. Avoidant methods, such as cognitive avoidance or emotional discharge, represent indirect methods to either avoid thinking about the stressor or to manage the tension created by the stressor. Internal consistency reliabilities of the eight coping scales were modest (α's .55 to .79). Evidence for concurrent validity was that adolescents who were identified as having psychological problems (depression and conduct disorder) were more likely to use avoidant than approach coping strategies. In addition, after controlling for gender, background variables, and severity of stressor, avoidant coping scales predicted higher levels of symptoms, whereas approach-oriented strategies predicted lower symptoms.

TABLE 2

Measures Assessing Coping Styles

Development article and name of scale	Sample	Type of measure	Subscales Name (# items)	Reliability[a]	Validity
			Interviews		
Asarnow et al. (1987), Coping Strategies Test (CST)	30 inpatients 8–13 yrs.	Assessed coping with 3 hypothetical situations: disciplinary crisis, father leaves home, mother dies.	Physical aggression Verbal aggression Running away Suicide Assertion Help-seeking Active cognitive coping Avoidance cognitive coping	Kappas > .88	Depression children generated more physically aggressive coping than nondepressed children. Suicidal children generated less active cognitive coping than nonsuicidal children.
Brown et al. (1986), Cognitive Questionnaire	487 children/ teenagers 8–17 yrs.	Assessed coping with 2 hypothetical and 1 real situation[b]	Different coping and catastrophizing categories were derived for each situation. Children were then judged to be copers if they used coping in at least 2 of the situations	Interrater M = .83	Children classified as copers reported less anxiety than children who used more catastrophic types of cognitions.
Hoffner (1993)	60 children 6–12 yrs., mostly white	Assessed coping responses to 4 stories: dental, medical, turbulent flight, academic	Monitoring Seeking support Blunting strategies Cognitive distraction Behavioral distraction Reappraisal of threat	89.5% agreement	—

(continued)

TABLE 2 (Continued)

Development article and name of scale	Sample	Type of measure	Subscales		Validity
			Name (# items)	Reliability[a]	
		Questionnaires			
Ayers et al. (1996); Ayers (1991), Children's Coping Strategies Checklist (CCSC)	Study 1: 217 children 9–13 yrs. M = 10.38 Study 2: 303 children 9–13 yrs. M = 10.5	45 items tapped what child does to solve a problem or feel better when faced with a problem	4-factor structure: Active:		Avoidance coping was positively related to depression and conduct problems and negatively related to self-esteem. Active coping was positively related to self-esteem and negatively related to depression. Active coping was marginally positively related to conduct problems.
			Cognitive decision making (4)	.72/.72	
			Direct problem solving (4)	.68/.67	
			Seeking understanding (4)	.72/.68	
			Positive cognitive restructuring (4)	.68/.55	
			Distraction:		
			Distracting actions (5)	.60/.59	
			Physical release of emotions (4)	.64/.53	
			Avoidance:		
			Cognitive avoidance (4)	.72/.67	
			Avoidant actions (4)	.64/.62	
			Support seeking:		
			Problem-focused support (4)	.46/.51	
			Emotion-focused support (4)	.50/.57	

Measure	Sample	Description	Subscales	Reliability	Validity
Causey & Dubow (1992), Self-Report Coping Scale	481 4th–6th graders from a mostly white, semirural, industrial community	33 items tapped what child usually does when getting a poor grade and having a peer conflict.[d]	Seeking social support (8) Self-reliance/problem solving (8) Distancing (6) Internalizing (7) Externalizing (4)	.84 .84 .69 .66 .68	In general, coping subscales positively correlated with peer ratings of corresponding subscales. Seeking social support and problem solving positively correlated with positive characteristics, such as self-worth and behavioral esteem. Distancing and externalizing were negatively related to positive characteristics, such as behavioral esteem, self-worth, and GPA.
Danovsky et al. (1995), Kansas Coping Inventory for Children (KANCOPE)	296 4th–6th graders, $M = 10.8$ yrs., mostly white	59 items assessed how child usually copes with receiving a bad grade.	Covert avoidance Passive avoidance Active behavioral avoidance Alternative demanding activity Esteem social support Substance use Spiritual support Negative emotional venting Wishful thinking Problem solving Relaxation Self-indulgent activity Resignation Reframe	First 11 alphas ranged .60–.85 Last 3 had low alphas	Measures of adjustment and social desirability correlated as expected and consistent with other studies (no details provided).

(continued)

TABLE 2 (*Continued*)

Development article and name of scale	Sample	Type of measure	Subscales Name (# items)	Reliability[a]	Validity
Dise-Lewis (1988), Life Events and Coping Inventory (LECI)	681 children/ adolescents[e] 11–14 yrs., $M = 12.6$, mostly white community	42 items assessed whether child would use each strategy in a stress situation	Aggression (7) Stress-recognition (13) Distraction (11) Self-destruction (8) Endurance (9)	.86/.85 .79/.80 .81/.89 .76/.83 .62/.68	Stress-recognition and distraction positively correlated with teacher-rated coping ability, and negatively with teacher-rated problems. Stress recognition, endurance, aggressive, and self-destructive coping positively correlated symptomology. Self-destructive coping negatively correlated with teacher-rated coping ability.
Fanshawe & Burnett (1991), Coping Inventory for Adolescents (CIA); items from Patterson's A-COPE	1699 adolescents 12–18 yrs., $M = 14.7$, in Australia	20 items assessed the extent to which child uses each strategy.	Negative avoidance (5) Anger (5) Family communication (5) Positive avoidance (5)	.74 .77 .74 .67	—
Filipp et al. (1993), Fragen-bogen zur Erfassung von Formen der Krankheitsbewaltin-gung (FEKB)	332 cancer patients 15–77 yrs. in Germany	37 items tapped the frequency of coping within given period of time[f]	Rumination (9) Search for affiliation (9) Threat minimization (8) Search for information (8) Search for meaning in religion (3)	Range: .74–.88 *Split-half:* Range .74–.90	Subjective well-being was positively related to threat minimization and search for affiliation and negatively related to rumination. Private and public self-consciousness were positively related to rumination.

Instrument	Sample	Description	Subscales (α)		Findings
Frydenberg & Lewis (1990, 1993), Adolescent Coping Scale (ACS)	673 7th–10th grade students Australia	80 items assessed coping concerns in general.	Solving the problem	.87	—
			Relax	.54	
			Work and Achieve	.68	
			Solve the problem	.72	
			Physical recreation	.64	
			Friends	.74	
			Focus on the positive	.68	
			Belong	.67	
			Reference to others	.89	
			Social Support	.80	
			Spiritual support	.85	
			Professional help	.84	
			Social action	.70	
			Nonproductive coping	.87	
			Wishful thinking	.67	
			Worry	.73	
			Belong	.67	
			Keep to self	.70	
			Self-blame	.76	
			Ignore the problem	.68	
			Tension reduction	.69	
			Not coping	.58	
Gamble (1994), Children's and Adolescent's Problem Solving Inventory (CAPSI)	146 4th–8th graders M = 11.35 yrs.; 166 college students M = 20.73 yrs.	30 items assessed coping with 3 hypothetical stressors: conflict with mother, conflict with friends, failure experience.	Emote/aggress (8)	.57–82	Perceived competence negatively associated with emote/aggress, avoid, and do nothing coping and positively associated to seek social support and direct problem-solving coping. Anxiety positively correlated with avoidant responses for failure and peer events, and emote/aggress responses for failure events.
			Avoid/do nothing (5)	.71–89	
			Problem solve (6)	.59–77	
			Independent (5)	.61–93	
			Seeking social support (6)	.66–.77 (Alphas across situation)	

(continued)

TABLE 2 (*Continued*)

Development article and name of scale	Sample	Type of measure	Subscales		Validity
			Name (# items)	Reliability[a]	
Glyshaw et al. (1989), used Will's Behavior-Based Coping Inventory	530 children at Time 1, 396 children at Time 2, 7–12 grade, mostly white	30 items tapped how child usually copes with problems	Factor analysis resulted in modified 30 item version with 5 subscales: Problem solving (9) Cognitive coping (7) Peer support (5) Social entertainment (4) Physical exercise (5)	*T1/T2* .81/.84 .75/.68 .88/.91 .74/.66 .68/.71 *Test–retest:* .44–.63	All subscales moderately correlated with corresponding mother reports of children's coping. Problem solving, peer support, and parental support were negatively related to psychological distress.
Herman-Stahl et al. (1995), revised Seiffge-Krenke and Shulman's Coping Questionnaire	603 students in grades 6–12, mostly white	18 items tapped how adolescent usually copes with problems.	Single item: Parental support (1) Approach (11) Avoidant (6)	.76 .54	Avoidant copers reported high depressive symptoms, whereas approach copers reported significantly fewer.
Lee et al. (1992), Adolescent Coping Scale (ACS)[g]	832 ethnic Chinese adolescents 14–19 yrs. in Hong Kong	25 items assessed coping with 4 problem areas: academic problems; conflict with elders; peer conflict; and concern about future.	Avoidance/blaming (# of items varies by gender and problem type) Self-reliance/rational problem solving (6) Religiosity (3) Emotional regulation (2)	.68–.74 .68–.77 .73–.89 .69–.82 (*alphas* across gender and situation)	Avoidance/blaming coping in all 4 problem areas (i.e., academic, conflicts–elders, conflicts–peers, future concerns) was associated with psychological distress.

Reference/Measure	Sample	Description	Subscales (items)	α	Findings
Patterson & McCubbin (1987b), Adolescent Coping Orientation for Problems (A-COPE)	467 adolescents, 7–12 grade, M = 15.6 yrs.[h]	54 items assessed coping used to manage difficulties and tense feelings.	Ventilating feelings (6)	.75	*For boys,* ventilating feelings and investing in close friends were positively associated with cigarette, beer, liquor, and marijuana use. Solving family problems and engaging in a demanding activity were negatively associated with substance use. *For girls,* developing social support, investing in friends, and ventilating feelings were positively associated with substance use. Solving family problems, engaging in a demanding activity, and seeking spiritual support were negatively associated with substance use.
			Seeking diversions (8)	.75	
			Developing self-reliance (6)	.69	
			Developing social support (6)	.75	
			Solving family problems (6)	.71	
			Avoiding problems (5)	.71	
			Seek spiritual help (3)	.72	
			Investing in close friends (2)	.76	
			Seeking professional help (2)	.50	
			Engaging in demanding activity (4)	.67	
			Being humorous (2)	.72	
			Relaxing (4)	.60	
Plancherel & Bolognini (1995), used Patterson & McCubbin's A-COPE, French version	353 6th graders (M = 12.5) in Switzerland	54 items assessed coping used to manage difficulties and tense feelings.	Factor analysis resulted in a different factor structure.		Solving family problems positively correlated with anxiety, and negatively correlated with depression and sleep disturbances for boys. For girls, solving family problems negatively correlated with all measures of psychological distress. Ventilation of feelings positively correlated with all measures of psychological distress for girls, but only with anxiety for boys.
			Social relationships (5)	.75	
			Solving family problems (7)	.72	
			Ventilating feelings (6)	.75	
			Developing self-reliance (5)	.67	
			Being humourous (4)	.70	
			Leisure (4)	.64	
			Schoolwork (3)	.67	
			Relaxing (3)	.52	

(continued)

TABLE 2 (Continued)

Development article and name of scale	Sample	Type of measure	Subscales Name (# items)	Reliability[a]	Validity
Reid et al. (1994) used Causey and Dubow's Self-Report Coping Scale	56 children and adolescents, 8–18 yrs. with diabetes. ($M = 13.0$)	34 items assessed how children usually cope with 3 types of diabetes situations	Higher order factor analysis: Approach: Seeking social support Problem solving Avoidance: Distance Internalizing Externalizing	Range .83–.92	Approach coping positively related to adherence to diet. Avoidance coping was negatively related to adherence to fingerpricks.
Roosa et al. (1988), used Will's Behavior-Based Coping Inventory	81 children 9–12 yrs.	24 items assessed how children typically cope with problems at home or school	Conceptual grouping resulted in modified version. Problem focused (5) Emotion focused (10) Support seeking (9)	.70 .75 .76	Problem-focused coping was negatively correlated with teacher reports of negative behavior.
Rossman et al. (1992), Child Perceived Coping Questionnaire (CPCQ)	341 children 6–12 yrs., mostly white, middle-class	33 items, method of administration not described but measure treated as dispositional	Use of caregiver (7) Distraction/avoidance (7) Distressed behaviors (3) Use of peers (7) Self-calming behaviors (6) Anger (3)	.73 .64 .29 .57 .61 .66	Distraction/avoidance coping acted as a vulnerability moderator of the relationship between stress and self-worth. None of the subscales moderated the relationship between stress and either anxiety or depression.

Reference, Instrument	Sample	Description	Coping dimensions	Reliability	Findings
Sandler et al. (1994), Children's Coping Strategies Checklist (CCSC)	258 children of divorce, 7–13 yrs., ($M = 10.1$)	44 items tapped what child does to solve a problem or feel better when faced with a problem	Factor structure replicated with divorce sample[c]	T1/T2	Avoidance coping partially mediated the relationship between negative events and each depression, anxiety, and conduct problems (all positive relations). Significant negative relations between active coping and distraction at Time 1 to internalizing symptoms at Time 2.
			Active:		
			Cognitive decision making (4)	.88	
			Direct problem-solving (4)	.66/.68	
			Seeking understanding (5)	.65/.69	
			Positive cognitive restructuring (5)	.54/.61	
				.54/.61	
			Avoidance:	.83	
			Cognitive avoidance (4)	.59/.60	
			Avoidant actions (4)	.51/.49	
			Distraction:	.76	
			Distracting actions (5)	.62/.61	
			Physical release of emotions (4)	.59/.55	
			Support:	.90	
			Problem-focused support (4)	.67/.62	
			Emotion-focused support (5)	.65/.63	
Seiffge-Krenki & Shulman (1990), Coping across Situations Questionnaire	540 adolescents 15–17 yrs. (187 from Israel and 35 from Germany)	20 items assessed coping with 8 hypothetical problem areas.		Germ./Isra.	—
			Active	.80/.72	
			Internal	.77/.71	
			Withdrawal	.73/.60	
			(factor structure differed in the two samples)		
Shulman et al. (1995), The Coping Questionnaire	25 learning-disabled adolescents 12–17 yrs.; 25 non-learning-disabled 12–17 yrs.	14 items assessed coping in 7 hypothetical problem area	Internal coping/flexible adaptive solution	.72	Learning-disabled students reported less internal coping than non-learning-disabled youth. Learning-disabled students also reported more withdrawal with problems regarding studies and problems with themselves.
			Active coping via social resources	.71	
			Withdrawal/fatalistic approach	.60	

(continued)

TABLE 2 (Continued)

Development article and name of scale	Sample	Type of measure	Subscales		Validity
			Name (# items)	Reliability[a]	
Swift et al. (1990)	224 low-income, 12–13 yr. old African-American children	Assessed coping in 2 hypothetical peer conflict situations	Palliate Adult support Agress Wonder/worry Peer support (# of items differed by situation)	—	Palliative coping was positively related to adaptation and negatively related to externalizing symptoms. Worry/wonder was negatively associated with adaptation and positively associated with externalizing symptoms.

Tolan et al. (1997), used Patterson & McCubbin's A-COPE	309 adolescents 11–16 yrs. From inner city; mostly African American and Hispanic	27 items assessed coping used to manage difficulites and tense feelings	Factor analysis—selected 7 first-order factors.
			Problem-solving factor:
			  Seeking support (5)
			  Seeking guidance (4)
			Emotion-focused factor:
			  Humor (2)
			  Venting emotton (5)
			These subscales had cross-loadings on both factors:
			  Positive thinking (3)
			  Distraction (5)
			  Avoidance by substance use (3)
				
				.73
				.64
				
				.64
				.72
				
				.63
				.69
				.73
					—

Study	Sample	Description	Subscales/Items	Reliability/Validity	Results
Tolor et al. (1987) Coping Style Questionnaire (CSQ)	174 adolescents 14–18 yrs. (male)	11 items assessed coping with hypothetical stressful situations.	Taking positive action; Seeking information; Focusing on positive; Seeking support; Altering plans; Not worrying; Withdrawing; Detaching self; Preparing for worst; Blaming others	—	Well-adjusted adolescents used more positive action and withdrawal and sought less information and support than poorly adjusted adolescents.
Whitesell et al. (1993)	355 children 11–15 yrs. (M = 12.54)	9 items assessed coping with 2 hypothetical peer problems	Expressive (3); Avoidant (3); Approach (3)	Test–retest: Range .44–.73	—
Wilson et al. (1987)	Study 1: 169 children 3–5, 6–7, 9–11 yrs. Study 2: 115 children, 4–5, 6–7, 9–11 yrs.	8 strategies in Study 1 and 5 strategies in Study 2. Pictures of coping strategies presented. Children selected whether each would be effective in reducing fear from TV movie.	Items in both studies: Hold onto a blanket or cuddly toy; Get something to drink; Leave room; Talk to Mom or Dad; Keep telling yourself it's not real. Items only in study 1: Cover face; Turn off the TV; Sit with Mom or Dad	—	

(continued)

Table 2 *(Continued)*

Development article and name of scale	Sample	Type of measure	Subscales Name (# items)	Reliability[a]	Validity
Wills (1985, 1986) Behavior-Based Inventory	4-wave longitudinal study, 1st cohort 675 children	Assessed how children typically cope with problems at home or at school	1st cohort (35 items, 8 factors): Behavioral coping Cognitive coping General social support Physical exercise Distraction Relaxation	—	Results were consistent in both cohorts and with both the behavior and intention-based inventories.
	2nd cohort 901 children 7th/8th grade		2nd cohort (54 items, 11 factors): Decision making (9) Adult social support (7) Cognitive coping (7) Peer social support (5) Substance use (3) Physical exercise (5) Aggression (5) Social entertainment (4) Individual relaxation (5) Parental support (2) Prayer (2)	—	Behavior coping, cognitive coping, adult social support, and relaxation were inversely related to substance use. Peer support, distraction, and aggressive coping were positively related to substance use.
Intention-Based Inventory			2nd cohort (8 dimensions): Behavioral coping Peer support Adult support Relaxation Entertainment Distraction Religion	(Range = .79–.93) M = .84	

Observational measures

Austin et al. (1991), Coping Health Inventory for Children (CHIC)	Data collected from parents of children 8–12 yrs. with asthma or epilepsy. Total N = 334	52-item parent report of how child copes with a chronic health problem	Competence/optimism (6) Different/withdraws (10) Irritable (13) Complies with treatment (9) Seeks support (14)	.84/.77 .80/.82 .86/.85 .72/.74 .81/.82 *2–3 week test-retest:* (Range = .57–.91)	Self-concept and attitude positively correlated with competence/optimism coping and negatively correlated with different/withdrawn and irritable coping. Behavior problems were positively correlated with different/withdrawn and irritable coping, and negatively correlated with competence/optimism, complies with treatment, and seeks support coping.
Grossman & Levy (1974), Behavior Rating Scales for Children (BRSC)	Study 1: 68 children 3–6 yrs. rated by head teachers Study 2: 62 children 3–5 yrs. rated by 2 head teachers	Teacher rating of social and task behavior	Final factor analysis: Social confidence Cooperation and control Task persistence Mobility Aggression	—	—
Kurtz (1994), used Zeitlin's Coping Inventory	61 children, 8–12 yrs. (M = 9.7)	48-item parental/teacher/caregiver report of child coping	Coping with environment, coping with self, each divided into 3 dimensions: Productive Active Flexible	(Range = .84–.98)	Children from disrupted homes were less productive, more rigid, and passive in coping with their environment and themselves.

(*continued*)

TABLE 2 (*Continued*)

Development article and name of scale	Sample	Type of measure	Subscales		Validity
			Name (# items)	Reliability[a]	
Zeitlin (1980), Coping Inventory	2 groups: nondisabled (N = 96) and disabled (N = 63) children 3–5 yrs.	48 item parental/teacher/caregiver report of child coping	Coping with environmental, coping with self, each divided into 3 bipolar dimensions: Nonproductive–productive Passive–active Rigid–flexible	*Interrater* (Range = .78–.99) *Split-half* (Range = .97–.99)	There were significant differences between handicapped and nonhandicapped children in every category and dimension of coping behavior. In general, nonhandicapped children used more coping behavior than handicapped children.

[a]Unless stated otherwise, reliabilities reported are *alpha* coefficients.

[b]Based upon our categorization scheme, this measure could have been considered a situational measure because respondents reported coping with a real situation. However, because a composite of coping with all situations was used, it was considered a measure of coping style.

[c]The three-item Expressing Feelings scale dropped in Ayers et al. (1996). It was not included due to poor internal consistency and contamination with symptomatology. Two new items were added to the scale to assess positive cognitive restructuring and emotion-focused support.

[d]One item was not included in distancing factor because of low item–total correlation.

[e]The total sample is divided into subsamples that participated in different parts of development. It's not clear which sample was used (or what combination of samples) in the PCA that resulted in the reported factor structure.

[f]The authors describe the FEKB as an measure of episodic and not dispositional coping, because patients rated the frequency of coping within a specific period of time. However, this instructional set does not ask subjects to report coping in response to a specific event and thus the FEKB is best considered a dispositional measure.

[g]The ACS is composed of translated items of Seiffge-Krenke et al.'s measure (1987) and new items the author developed.

[h]In an earlier report, McCubbin et al. (1985) used six subscales of the A-COPE with 509 families of 12 to 13-year-old children and found *alphas* ranged from .61–.76.

Brodzinsky et al. (1992) used exploratory factor analysis to develop the 44-item Coping Scale for Children and Youth (CSCY), a self-report measure of children's coping. In the development of the CSCY, the authors culled items from the existing literature that they could reliably categorize into five general strategies of coping: cognitive/affective engagement, behavioral engagement, cognitive/affective avoidance, behavioral avoidance, and passive resignation. Results from the exploratory factor analysis indicated that their preliminary conceptual structure was only partially confirmed, and four factors were identified: (1) assistance seeking, represented by items that reflected interpersonal problem solving; (2) cognitive-behavioral problem solving, reflected by both cognitive/affective and direct behavioral actions; (3) cognitive avoidance, measured by cognitive redefinition, selective attention, and minimization of the problem; and (4) behavioral avoidance, which included both direct means, such as removing oneself from the stressor, and indirect means, such as displacement of anger on to another person. The authors report a comparable factor structure across the two grades (6th and 8th) and gender of the participants. As noted in Table 1, acceptable internal consistencies were found for the four dimensions. A readministration of the CSCY 1 week later to a random subsample of 145 children responding to the same stressor identified previously yielded satisfactory test–retest correlations (.70 to .81) for the four dimensions.

Brodzinsky and colleagues (1992) addressed construct validity of the CSCY in two studies. The first study examined the relationship of the CSCY to the Kidcope (see Table 1 or Spirito, Stark, & Williams, 1988) and found the highest correlations between the CSCY and the Kidcope between the coping categories that were conceptually most similar. The second study supported construct validity of the CSCY in that assistance seeking and cognitive-behavioral problem solving were positively associated with perceived self-efficacy, whereas cognitive avoidance and behavioral avoidance were negatively associated with perceived self-efficacy.

Ayers and colleagues (1996) utilized confirmatory factor analysis to develop a 45-item, self-report measure of children's coping called How I Coped under Pressure Scale (HICUPS). The chosen confirmatory factor-analytic approach has the advantage of testing the adequacy of an *a priori* specified theoretical model of the dimensional structure of coping, and thus is more likely to yield conceptually meaningful and replicable dimensions. Instrument development for the HICUPS followed from the development of a dispositional measure of coping that will be described in more detail later. The HICUPS assesses 11 dimensions of coping that were theoretically derived through a review of the existing literature and a careful content analysis of children's coping (Ayers et al., 1989; Sandler et al., 1990). Children reported their coping efforts in response to a stressful event that occurred in the past 3 months and was selected as having the highest nomothetically based rating of "stressfulness" of all experienced events. Confirmatory factor analysis tested three theoretical models of the underlying dimensional structure of 10 coping dimensions.[2] The data collected with the HICUPS fit a four-factor theoretical model of coping better than the problem-focused versus emotion-focused model (Lazarus & Folkman, 1984) or the approach versus avoidant coping model (Ebata & Moos, 1991). The four latent constructs identified through this confirmatory factor analysis include active coping strategies, distraction strategies, avoidance strategies, and support-seeking strategies (Ayers et al., 1996). Table 1 provides a list of the dimensions that represent each latent factor and the internal consistencies for both the dimensions and factors.

The measurement and factor structure of the HICUPS was tested across age and gender and found to be invariant (Ayers et al., 1996). Relationships between these latent factors and measures of outcome based on maternal and child report were examined within structural models, and no significant relationships were found (Ayers, 1991).

6.3. Behavioral Observation Measures of Coping Strategies

A few investigators have developed coping measures that rely upon clinician/researcher, parent, and/or teacher observation of coping efforts by children or adolescents. Most efforts in this area have focused on measuring coping with a particular type of stressor, such as dental visits (Curry & Russ, 1985; Miller et al., 1995), medical procedures (Hyson, 1983), or angry interactions (Cummings, 1987; Cummings & Cummings, 1988). A few other observational measures of coping might be more accurately described as general measures of psychosocial development or competence (e.g., Hoffer & Thompson, 1986; Zeitlin, 1980). Because other reviews have examined children's coping with aversive medical or dental procedures (e.g., Miller et al., 1992; Peterson, Harbeck, Chaney, Farmer & Thomas, 1990; Rudolph, Dennig, & Weisz, 1995), we generally chose to exclude those studies from this review. However, for purposes of illustration, we will discuss one study in this section that utilized a behavioral observation strategy to assess coping in response to a particular stressor (i.e., medical visit).

Hyson (1983) developed an observational instrument to measure children's coping in response to a pediatric examination for 48 children, 6–12, 18–36, or 42–60 months old. In order to classify children's behavioral

[2]One dimension, Expressing Feelings, was dropped from all analyses due to poor internal consistencies and a concern the dimension might be contaminated with measures of symptomatology (see also Stanton, Danoff Burg, Cameron, & Ellis, 1994).

responses, Hyson operationalized White's (1974) "strategies of adaptation." White has suggested that responses to a stressful situation might include one, two, or all of the following: (1) information seeking, (2) maintaining internal equilibrium, and (3) maintaining autonomy responses. Hyson had an observer keep a continuous narrative account of all behavior that occurred during the visit. This transcript was divided into three discrete time periods that reflected preexam behavior, exam behavior, and postexam behavior. Using a behavioral coding scheme, all behaviors from each time period were coded into one of the three categories mentioned.

Hyson (1983) found that use of specific coping strategies at each time period varied with age. Not surprisingly, when the autonomy category was divided into expressive and instrumental behaviors, there were more instrumental behaviors during the preexam period and more expressive protest behaviors during the exam period. In addition, the proportion of expressive protest decreased in a linear fashion with age, whereas the number of instrumental behaviors increased proportionately. In summary, Hyson suggested that these findings emphasized the importance of understanding the adaptive context of children's coping efforts and the contribution that developmental factors play in the child's interpretation of and response to a stressful event. We will return to the discussion of these points later in the chapter.

6.4. Issues in the Assessment of Coping Strategies

There are several issues that researchers should consider in the measurement of coping strategies used by children and adolescents. These can be broadly grouped into two areas, the strategies and techniques used in the design and development of the coping measures and the methodology and design of studies that examine the relationships between coping efforts and measures of adaptation.

In the development of the coping measures, some investigators have been diligent in their efforts to sample the entire domain of coping efforts for children or adolescents within particular age ranges (e.g., Ayers et al., 1996; Band & Weisz, 1988; Brodzinsky et al., 1992; Ryan, 1988, 1989). Although this practice has been more closely followed in the development of measures for elementary and middle-school-aged children, it has not been typically the practice in measures of coping strategies developed for adolescents (Frydenberg & Lewis, 1991; Halstead, Johnson, & Cunningham, 1993; Phelps & Jarvis, 1994; Stern & Alvarez, 1992). Some authors have either modified an adult measure of coping to make it more appropriate for adolescents (Halstead et al., 1993) or initiated an investigation to determine whether the underlying factor structure of an adult measure (e.g., COPE; Carver et al., 1989) was the same when used with adolescents (Phelps & Jarvis, 1994). Checking to determine whether the measure has the same underlying factor structure (e.g., Phelps & Jarvis, 1994) represents an improvement over uncritically adopting the factor structure identified for adults (Frydenberg & Lewis, 1991; Stern & Alvarez, 1992) but still ignores the possibility that the instruments may not adequately sample the full range of coping efforts used by adolescents. This question needs to be systematically investigated so that the measures developed for middle and late adolescents adequately sample the domain of coping.

Attention needs to be paid to the scores that are created as summaries of children's coping. As an example, Ryan-Wenger (Ryan, 1988, 1989; Ryan-Wenger, 1990, 1992), in a careful series of reports, has developed taxonomies of coping strategies from children's own reports (Ryan, 1989) and from a review of the existing literature (Ryan-Wenger, 1992). This information was used to select the most commonly named strategies of the categories identified and these were used to create the Schoolagers' Coping Strategies Inventory (SCSI); see Ryan-Wenger, 1990). In this instrument, children are asked to report both their frequency of use of the coping strategies and the effectiveness of these strategies on a four-point scale. Unfortunately, Ryan-Wenger (1990) chose to create overall summary scores of frequency and effectiveness and a total of SCSI score based on these two other scales. This approach undoubtedly was taken in order to maintain high internal consistency of the scales, yet it ignores some of the potential richness the data might yield regarding the effectiveness of *different* types of coping strategies. In addition, combining the frequency and effectiveness scales confounds judgments of coping efforts and coping efficacy (Schwarzer & Schwarzer, 1996; Stone et al., 1992) and ignores the conceptual distinctions Lazarus and colleagues (Lazarus, 1991; Lazarus & Folkman, 1984) have encouraged investigators to make between primary and secondary appraisal processes, coping efforts and judgments of coping efficacy.

When discussing the methodology and design of studies in this area, Lazarus and Folkman's (1984) transactional perspective on coping is valuable. As defined here, measures that assess coping strategies (i.e., coping with a specific stressor) are most useful in exploring the relationships that might exist between a person's appraisal, coping, and efficacy judgments, and the characteristics of a stressful situation and/or context. Investigators have begun to explore issues related to the impact of situational characteristics (Compas et al., 1988b; Dubow, Roecker, & Donaldson, 1995; Reid et al., 1995; Zeidner, 1994) and appraisal and efficacy judgments (Compas, Banez, Malcarne, & Worsham, 1991; Compas, Forsythe, & Wagner, 1988a; Forsythe & Compas, 1987) on the selection of coping strategies.

Related to the design of these studies, it is important for investigators to clearly specify the time frame that respondents use when reporting on their coping efforts to a specific stressful situation. Currently, coping measures have referenced a wide range of time periods. Some investigators apparently have not specified any time frame (e.g., Bull & Drotar, 1991; Colletta, Hadler, & Gregg, 1981; Frydenberg & Lewis, 1991; Ryan, 1989; Wertlieb et al., 1987), others have been nonspecific (e.g., the last few months; Brodzinsky et al., 1992), whereas others have asked respondents to identify any events that have occurred within the past 2 weeks (Elwood, 1987) up to 1 year (Ebata & Moos, 1991). Shortening the time frame so that reports of coping are to more immediate stressful events would help alleviate concerns that investigators have voiced regarding the questionable ability of children or adolescents to recall all of their coping efforts to events that have occurred more than a month ago (Causey & Dubow, 1992; Stone & Kennedy-Moore, 1992).

Surprisingly, there has been little systematic research assessing a wide range of children's coping efforts in settings where the impact of different stressors and contextual factors can be controlled. Such studies can begin to consider the temporal aspects of coping efforts and the impact that different stages of the stressor have on coping responses (Peterson et al., 1990; Stone et al., 1992). A process-oriented approach by Cummings (1987; Cummings & Cummings, 1988), which examines child coping with adults anger, represents an excellent example for other coping investigators in that it illustrates how laboratory and field studies jointly can be used to describe systematically children's cognitive, social, emotional, and physiological responses to a stressor and how these responses change over time.

As a starting point, the literature might benefit from distinguishing coping efforts used across different stages of a stressor, from prior to the onset of the stressor, to while it is occurring and following its occurrence (Stone & Kennedy-Moore, 1992). There is a need for a greater number of studies that examine coping responses over time and across stressors. Research investigating responses to aversive medical or dental procedures (Miller et al., 1995; Peterson et al., 1990; Rudolph et al., 1995) offers some interesting leads and methodologies in this respect. Investigators in this area (Rudolph et al., 1995) have indicated a need for more sophisticated conceptual models of coping that consider children's overall coping repertories, profiles, and, importantly, the temporal sequences of their coping responses.

7. Assessing Coping Styles in Children and Adolescents

This section first addresses the degree of consistency in coping across situations and then reviews four different methods of assessing coping styles: coping in response to hypothetical situations, coping styles in specific kinds of situations, coping styles across all recent stressful situations, and coping intentions across situations.

7.1. Consistency in Coping across Situations

An assumption of a stylistic approach to coping assessment is that there is some consistency in child and adolescent use of coping strategies across stressful situations. Three studies provide empirical evidence that this assumption is quite reasonable for children and adolescents. As noted earlier, Compas et al. (1988b) used a semistructured interview to study coping strategies reported by ten 14-year-olds for two different kinds of situations: interpersonal and academic related stressors. Correlations between coping strategies reported across academic and interpersonal stressors were calculated separately for girls and boys and ranged from .25 to .43 (median r = .30). Causey and Dubow (1992) used a self-report questionnaire to assess five dimensions of coping strategies and found that the cross-stressor correlations between reported use of the same coping strategy ranged from .38 to .68 (median r = .53). These authors point out that although the correlations between use of the same coping strategies across situations were moderately high, children reported different levels of use of strategies in different situations. Gamble (1994) used a self-report questionnaire to assess the coping of fourth- through eighth-grade students across three kinds of stressors. The mean correlations for the same coping strategy across the three stressful situations were similar to that reported by Causey and Dubow (range of r = .44 to .62, median r = .55). It should be noted that the cross-situational consistency in coping reports found for children and adolescents is considerably higher than that reported for adults (see Aldwin, 1994). This may reflect either greater cross-situational consistency in coping for children, perhaps due to less differentiation of the coping requirements of different situations or less differentiation in their coping repertoire. Alternatively, it may be that children's reports of coping are more affected by common method variance than are the reports of adults.

7.2. Interview Measures of Coping Styles

As indicated earlier, we have classified all studies that have utilized hypothetically stressful situations (e.g., Asarnow et al., 1987; Brown, O'Keeffe, Sanders, & Baker, 1986; Hoffner, 1993; Krantz, Clark, Pruyn, & Usher, 1985; Mooney, Graziano, & Katz, 1985) as attempts at measuring coping styles of children or adolescents. One example is discussed as illustration of work in this area that uses a semistructured interview format. Asarnow et al. (1987) developed the Coping Strategies Test (CST) in which they have subjects imagine three different stressful situations (i.e., disciplinary crisis, parental conflict, and bereavement). These authors presented cards depicting each situation and then followed up with probes designed to assess the child's interpersonal sensitivity, expectancies, number of alternative solutions generated, and number of solutions generated after the examiner placed an obstacle in the path of one of the child's solutions. The CST was administered to a sample of 30 inpatients (age 8–13), and the content of the children's responses were classified into coping categories. These authors report good interrater reliability for the coding of all responses into the categories (all kappas > .88). Little validity data are provided for this interview schedule. However, exploratory analyses suggest that within this small sample, depressed children were more likely to generate physically aggressive coping strategies than were nondepressed children, and suicidal children were less likely to generate active, cognitive coping strategies as compared to nonsuicidal children.

7.3. Questionnaire Measures of Coping Styles

This section will review illustrative studies that have used closed-ended questionnaires for the assessment of coping styles. Three different approaches have been used in these questionnaires to assess coping styles: coping styles in specific *kinds* of situations, coping styles *across all recent* stressful situations, and the assessment of coping intentions across situations.

In the development of their coping measure for children, Causey and Dubow (1992) chose to assess coping styles in specific *kinds* of situations. They asked respondents to report their coping efforts in response to two stressors (poor grades, peer conflict) using the following type of instructional set: "When I get a bad grade in school, one worse than I normally get I usually ..." without asking students to describe a specific incident. These authors state that they chose to ask children how they usually respond to a small class of problems, because they believed it represented an improvement over the focus and scope of previous studies that referenced "problems in general" or the single, most important stressor they experienced in the past year.

Causey and Dubow's (1992) 33-item measure was designed to examine five domains of coping. Four coping domains were based on Roth and Cohen's (1986) approach–avoidance conceptualization of coping, in which two subscales assessed approach strategies (i.e., seeking social support and self-reliance/problem solving) and two subscales assessed avoidance strategies (i.e., distancing and internalizing). One added domain called "externalizing" reflected coping strategies focused outward. Principal component factor analyses with varimax rotation were conducted separately on responses to coping with a poor grade and with a peer argument, and were found to be robust with respect to gender. Internal consistencies, which are satisfactory, and evidence for concurrent validity are presented in Table 2.

Causey and Dubow (1992) also sought independent verification of the coping strategies reported. They used a peer nomination procedure in which they had children rate how likely each of their classmates might use certain strategies to cope with one of the two stressors. They found modest to moderately positive relations between the corresponding subscales of the self-report and peer-rated coping measures for the problem-solving, seeking-social-support, externalizing, and internalizing subscales. They suggested that children's self-report was at least somewhat consistent with the way in which their peers viewed their coping efforts.

In the development of one of our coping measures, the Children's Coping Strategies Checklist (CCSC; Ayers, 1991; Ayers et al., 1996; Sandler, Tein, & West, 1994), we took a stylistic approach that asked respondents to report on their coping styles across all recent stressful situations. As with the HICUPS, discussed earlier, the CCSC was developed to assess 11 dimensions of coping that were theoretically derived through a review of the existing literature and a careful content analysis of children's coping (Ayers et al., 1989; Sandler et al., 1990). A four-factor model provided an acceptable fit to the data and was more parsimonious than the originally proposed five-factor model (see Ayers, 1991). The four coping factors identified were the same as the HICUPS, namely, active coping strategies, distraction strategies, avoidance strategies, and support-seeking strategies. This four-factor structure has been cross-validated on two independent samples (Ayers et al., 1996; Sandler et al., 1994) and found to be invariant across age and gender in both samples. In cross-sectional analyses (Ayers, 1991), the use of an avoidant style of coping was positively related to depression and conduct problems, and negatively related to self-esteem. The inverse was found for active coping, which was positively related to self-esteem and negatively related to depression. Sandler et al. (1994) found that avoidance coping partially mediated the positive relationship between negative events and depression, anxiety, and conduct problems. In longitudinal analyses, they found negative significant relations between active coping and distraction coping at Time 1, and internalizing symptomatology at Time 2.

Wills (1985, 1986) developed a 54-item factorial-based coping inventory, which was refined during a four-wave, longitudinal study. Subjects for the study were two cohorts of seventh- and eight-grade, urban adolescents. The items of the inventory were presented to the subjects with the heading "When I have a problem, I _____," and subjects are asked to report the frequency with which they engage in the stated behavior on a scale of 1 to 5 with *Never* and *Usually* as anchor points. Exploratory factor analysis of the 54 items using the second cohort of adolescents resulted in an 11-factor solution. A list of the 11 factors can be found in Table 2. Wills (1985, 1986) provided no information about the internal consistency of the subscales or the test–retest reliability of the instrument. Although he does not use confirmatory factor analyses to examine the invariance of the factorial structure, he did report separate factor analyses for each measurement period and suggested that the factor structure of the measure was stable over time.

Wills (1986) found evidence of the concurrent validity of the instrument in the observed relations between adolescent reports of their coping styles and substance use, which were similar to the work of Patterson and McCubbin (1987b). They found that independent of the other predictors, four of the coping styles (behavior coping, cognitive coping, adult social support, and relaxation) were inversely related to substance use, whereas three of the coping styles (peer support, distraction coping, and aggressive coping) were positively related to substance use. Wills (1986) also found interactions consistent with stress-buffering hypotheses for the behavioral coping, cognitive coping, and adult support coping styles.

Glyshaw, Cohen, and Towbes (1989) utilized Wills' Behavior-Based Coping Inventory in a 5-month, prospective study with junior and senior high school students. They administered the scale to 396 junior and senior high school students and then conducted a series of factor analyses to examine the stability of the factors across time, gender, and grade level. Five factors consistently emerged from these factor analyses, which were identical to 5 of the 11 factors found in Will's (1985) study (i.e., problem solving, cognitive coping, peer support, social entertainment, and physical exercise). Pearson correlations between assessments at Time 1 and Time 2 ranged from .44 to .63 across all five categories for both the junior and senior high school samples supported the temporal stability of the coping styles measures.

Glyshaw and her colleagues (1989) directly addressed the issue of independent validation of child or adolescent self-reported coping styles by assessing the relation between child and parent measures of the same coping styles (cf. Causey & Dubow, 1992). They found moderate and significant correlations between mothers' reports of their adolescents' coping styles and the adolescents' own report. Since, one would *not* expect the mothers to have complete knowledge of their adolescents' coping styles (especially the strategies that reflect cognitive styles or efforts), their find-ings provide fairly strong support for the validity of the adolescents' self-reports of coping styles.

With regard to concurrent validity, Glyshaw and her colleagues (1989) found significant, negative relations between the coping styles of problem solving, peer and parental support, and psychological distress in the cross-sectional analyses, but there were no significant relations between coping styles and psychological distress in the prospective longitudinal analyses. Interestingly, they did find that initial distress was positively related to subsequent reliance on cognitive coping strategies 5 months later. This suggests that cognitive coping strategies (e.g., trying to put it out of mind) can be the effect and not the cause of maladjustment. Other studies need to be attentive to such bidirectional relationships between coping styles and mental health outcome variables (e.g., Aldwin & Revenson, 1987).

An alternative approach to assessing coping styles comes from the adult literature on coping. Due to the results of some of their initial pilot work, Stone and his colleagues (Stone, Greenberg, Kennedy-Moore, & Newman, 1991; Stone & Neale, 1984) have been critical of using a checklist or behavior-based approach when assessing coping, and eventually re-jected a checklist assessment instrument in favor of a more open-ended procedure (Stone, Kennedy-Moore, & Neale, 1995; Stone & Shiffman, 1992).

As an example of the problems they identified, Stone and Neale (1984) found that when subjects were given a sorting task and allowed the freedom to classify the coping items in as many categories as they wished, they often felt that a particular item could indeed represent more than one coping strategy. Thus, one potential problem with coping questionnaires becomes evident; subjects might interpret an item to reflect entirely differ-ent coping categories. As an example, some individuals might interpret the item "Go to a movie" as reflecting the coping strategy of relaxation, whereas others might view this as a form of distraction. The differences in the way in which individuals interpret similar coping items may be one explanation for the often low internal consistency of subscales on coping measures (e.g., A-COPE has some alphas in the .50–.60 range; Patterson & McCubbin, 1987b).[3]

---

[3]It is also the case that the subscales of the A-COPE with the lowest alpha coefficients also have the fewest items. There is an argument posed in the literature that states that internal consistencies may not be a useful form of reliability when evaluating coping inventories (Holahan & Moos, 1987; Stone & Kennedy-Moore, 1992; Stone et al., 1992). The reasoning is that the use of one behavioral or cognitive strategy from a list of several strategies that compose the coping subscale may be the only strategy that a particular individual will *need* to cope with the stressful situation. Since subjects are not endorsing other items from that subscale, the internal consistency will necessarily be attenuated.

Taking these findings into consideration, Stone and Neale (1984) offered an alternative method for assessing coping in adults that focused on assessing the *intentions* of the person who was describing his/her coping. In their daily coping scale, they allowed subjects to indicate which classes of coping behaviors they used during a specific stressful situation. They presented subjects with one-sentence descriptions of coping categories and then asked them to check whether they did or thought anything that fit into these categories. They followed up a positive response with open-ended questions asking what the specific thoughts and actions were that reflected the strategy they checked.

Wills (1986) developed a coping inventory for adolescents that uses a methodology similar to that developed by Stone and Neale (1984). In the Intention-Based Coping Inventory, Wills provided adolescents with eight coping goals (see Table 2) and asked them to indicate whether they do something with the intention of achieving a particular goal during a problem situation. Wills had adolescents report on the coping behaviors they used for five different *problem types*: school, parents, health, feeling sad, and problems with friends. High consistency in the reported use of a given coping response across the five problems was found.

One practical advantage to an intention-based approach is that the coping instruments are typically much shorter than in a behavior-based approach. This is because only one item assesses each category in the intention-based approach versus several items for each category in the behavior-based approach (for an exception, see Spirito et al., 1988). Due to the brevity of many intention-based instruments, they are ideal for assessing coping strategies or styles over multiple points in time. A relative advantage of the behavior-based approach, with its multiple items for each category of coping, is that it might capture a broader range of coping strategies when used with younger or middle-school-aged children.

In considering whether to use either a behavior-based or intention-based approach, a critical concern had to do with the age and developmental level of the respondent. Although it probably is not difficult for most adults (and some adolescents) to make the necessary abstraction that they engaged in certain coping behaviors (e.g., going to the movies) in order to avoid thinking about the problem situation or alternatively to just relax, these kinds of abstractions (or at least the verbal expression of such) become more difficult for younger children.

7.4. *Behavioral Observation Measures of Coping Strategies*

Zeitlin (1980) has developed an observational instrument called the Coping Inventory, which was based on Murphy and Moriarty's (1976) longitudinal study of children's coping behavior. It is composed of 48 items that are rated by a teacher or some other person who has a continu-ing relationship with the child. The items are rated on a scale of 1 (reflecting no or minimal competency) to 5 (behavior is effectively demonstrated). The items fall into two categories—coping with the *environment*, and coping with the *self*—which are analogous to Murphy and Moriarty's major categories of Coping I and Coping II, respectively. Within each category, items represent three bipolar dimensions that are used to de-scribe the coping style: productive–nonproductive, active–passive, and flexible–rigid. Using two different samples composed of both normal and handicapped children, Zeitlin reports high interrater reliabilities (range from .78 to .98) and split-half reliability coefficients (range from .96 to .99). Zeitlin (1980) and Kurtz (1994) provide some limited information regard-ing the concurrent validity for the scale. Zeitlin listed the types of coping behavior that most differentiated handicapped from nonhandicapped young children, and Kurtz reported that children of divorced families had a more restrictive range of coping styles than their peers with nondivorced parents (see Table 2).

8.   Guidelines for the Assessment of Coping Styles

From this review of instruments assessing coping styles a few guide-lines are offered that should aid in the revision and development of future coping inventories.

8.1.   Assessing Children's Coping: Using Hypothetical versus Actual Events

As suggested by the review of the efforts to assess coping styles, methods have included both self-reports of coping efforts in response to hypothetical event stimuli (e.g., Altshuler & Ruble, 1989; Asarnow et al., 1987; Brown et al., 1986; Egan, Linney, & Forman, 1989) and actual stressful events that have occurred in the respondent's lives (e.g., Ayers et al., 1996; Band & Weisz, 1988; Compas et al. 1988b; Ebata & Moos, 1991; Wertlieb et al., 1987). Investigators have argued that coping should be concerned with what a child *actually* thinks or does to deal with specific problems rather than rely on hypothetical situations (e.g., Compas, 1987; Compas, Wor-sham, & Ey, 1992b; Murphy & Moriarty, 1976; Zeitlin, 1980). The reasoning behind this stated preference is the questionable likelihood that the child would actually use the coping responses he/she describes in response to a hypothetical situation when confronted with a similar situation in "real" life (Lazarus, 1993; Schwarzer & Schwarzer, 1996), the external validity issue. However, one advantage of using hypothetical situations, either through written descriptions (Asarnow et al., 1987) or videotape (Egan et al., 1989) as stimuli, is that the researcher has more control over the nature of the stressful situations to which the child responds, an important internal validity issue.

The concern about the external validity of the use of hypothetical or actual events mirrors a more basic issue that deserves further investigation, which is the general relationship between child report of coping to the coping behaviors actually performed. Independent verification is obviously a difficult challenge for this area, because many coping efforts can be assumed to be cognitive in nature and not immediately accessible. As noted earlier, some investigators have tackled this problem by assessing parental report (Glyshaw et al., 1989) or peer report (Causey & Dubow, 1992) of children's coping and found moderately high correlations between the two reporters.

8.2. Assessment of Coping Styles: Theoretical and Empirical Approaches

Three approaches to the assessment of the dimensions of children's coping styles will be discussed: rational or theoretical approaches, empirical approaches using exploratory factor analysis, and the use of confirmatory factor analysis to test both the adequacy of theoretical models and to account for the empirical relations found between reports of coping styles. Rational approaches use theory to develop dimensions of coping and develop items that are derived specifically to assess those dimensions. Such scales were often readily interpretable as representing the theoretical dimensions of coping and have reasonable psychometric properties and relations with measures of children's adjustment (e.g., Herman Stahl, Stemmler, & Petersen, 1995). However, it is not known whether these dimensions are a good representation of the empirical covariation between the items on the scales.

An exploratory factor-analytic approach typically does not start with a theoretical model but identifies dimensions of coping based on the covariation between children's reports of coping on the items of the scale. Two problems with this approach are that the dimensions are often difficult to interpret and do not replicate well across populations. As an example, closer examination of Wills's Behavior-Based Inventory reveals the lack of conceptual clarity that can result with such an atheoretical approach. In the measure, the subscale Cognitive Coping appears to measure two conceptually distinct coping strategies. The majority of the items reflect what typically is referred to as positive cognitive restructuring (e.g.,

"Try to notice only the good things in life"), whereas a subset of the items on this same subscale appears to measure strategies that might be better labeled as cognitive avoidance (e.g., "Try to put it out of my mind"). These types of subscales leave considerable ambiguity in terms of what construct the subscale is actually assessing.

The second problem associated with these scales derived using exploratory factor analytic-methods has to do with the stability of the factor structure (i.e., subscales) when the instrument is used with other samples. Subscales derived by using these techniques are well known for not being replicated or cross-validated when the factor structure is tested in other samples (Horn, 1967). Often, if the new sample is different in some of the subject characteristics, the factor structure does not generalize, even when using the same method of extraction, rotation, and rules for determining the number of factors as was used in previous investigations.

As reported earlier, the development of Wills's Behavior-Based Coping Inventory (1985) provides a good illustration of a situation in which the factor structure originally derived using junior high school students was not fully replicated in a new sample (Glyshaw et al., 1989). Glyshaw and colleagues (1989) used Wills's same inventory in their prospective study of coping strategies in junior and senior high school students. Using the *same* factor-analytic technique that Wills had used, they found only 5 of the 11 factors that replicated those in Wills's original analysis.[4]

A confirmatory factor-analytic approach begins with a theoretical model of the dimensions of coping and assesses how well this model (or alternative theoretical models) accounts for the covariation between responses on the coping measure. As a reminder, Ayers et al. (1996) found that an *a priori* specified, four-dimensional model of coping provided a better fit to the empirical covariation between coping responses than alternative two-dimensional models (problem- vs. emotion-focused, or approach vs. avoidant coping). In this case, the factor structure was replicated in separate analyses on children in the general population (Ayers et al., 1996) and children of divorce (Sandler et al., 1994), reflecting the greater likelihood of cross-validating the factor structure when using confirmatory factor-analytic methods.[5]

Several researchers in the area of the assessment of adult coping

---

[4]Note that these five factors were *not* the same factors that would have resulted had Wills (1985) used the Kasier–Guttman rule or screen test in determining the number of factors to retain.

[5]As an aside, the measures of coping style (i.e., CCSC) and the measure of coping strategies used in specific situations (i.e., HICUPS) also yielded similar, although not identical factor structures (see Ayers et al., 1996).

(Aldwin & Revenson, 1987; Carver et al., 1989) and child and adolescent coping (Ayers et al., 1996) have recommended that coping instruments need to be developed using a theoretical approach. Constructing instruments that are designed to measure *a priori* the constructs identified through careful content analyses yield scales composed of items that are clearer measures of the coping dimensions of interest. This has the advantage of greatly simplifying the understanding of the relationships of each dimension to theoretically linked outcomes. These theory-based scales can be developed and refined in a number of ways. Item response theory (Waller, Tellegen, McDonald, & Lykken, 1996) and confirmatory factor analysis (Mulaik, 1988) can provide statistical methods for assuring that a scale is unidimensional and that the items measure the construct of interest. Given the successful test of an *a priori* theoretical model of the underlying dimensions of coping, the results can be expected to replicate in future samples from the same population.

In a related vein, because these measures of coping styles are intended to assess relatively stable dimensions, it is important the instruments developed have adequate psychometric properties, including but not limited to internal consistencies, test–retest reliabilities, and stable factor structures (as discussed earlier). In this respect, progress in the area of assessing child and adolescent coping has been made, yet similar to conclusions reached by other recent reviews of primarily adult measures (e.g., Parker & Endler, 1992; Schwarzer & Schwarzer, 1996), further work still needs to be done. In doing this work, investigators also need to attend to establishing the construct validity of the measures developed. Benson and Hagtvet (1996) outline traditional (e.g., correlational and multitrait–multimethod designs) and more recent methodological developments and designs (e.g., multifaceted measurement designs, generalizability theory, and structural equation modeling) that can aid coping investigators in establishing construct validity.

8.3. Assessing Coping from a Transactional Perspective

Although use of factor-analytic methods to develop coping checklists is probably the most prevalent method, it is notable that some have argued that this approach is not consistent with a transactional model of coping (e.g., Coyne & Gottlieb, 1996; Stone et al., 1988, 1991). Coyne and colleagues (1996) have argued passionately about the problems inherent in the incongruence between the checklist method and a transactional conceptualization of coping. Several different types of coping might be used by an individual during the *process* of dealing with any particular stressful situation or circumstance (Folkman & Lazarus, 1985; Stone et al., 1991). All of these different strategies would theoretically be checked by the individual responding to a coping checklist. Factor analysis as a statistical method might then create scales that combine the very different coping methods into a single factor, simply because they covary temporally. These authors (Coyne & Gottlieb, 1996; Stone et al., 1991) argue that this type of assessment procedure thus effectively obscures potentially interesting patterns that may occur during the coping *process*.

These authors highlight a limitation of the measures of coping styles in that these measures do provide a *summary* of coping efforts across multiple events, and in doing so might not assess how well coping efforts match the *demands* of specific stressful events. To the extent that this match between the demands of the situation and the coping strategies used is important, the summary measures of coping will underestimate the effects of the coping efforts. Investigations that carefully examine the *process* of coping, using the measures coping strategies, do need to be done, and these intraindividual approaches to the assessment of coping can illuminate many important issues in the area. However, many of the findings regarding significant relationships between coping and outcomes (compare evidence of validity in Tables 1 and 2) have resulted from using inventories that assess coping *styles*, that is, an interindividual approach in the assessment of coping (e.g., Causey & Dubow, 1992; Glyshaw et al., 1989; Patterson & McCubbin, 1987a; Sandler et al., 1994; Wills, 1985, 1986). Based on this progress, it seems premature at this point to abandon efforts to assess an individual's preferred coping *styles* in favor of a solely situation-specific assessment of coping behaviors.

9. Assessment of Coping from a Developmental Perspective

Assessment of children's coping necessarily requires attention to developmental issues. A number of studies have noted age differences in problem- and emotion-focused coping (e.g., Altshuler & Ruble, 1989; Band & Weisz, 1988; Brodzinsky et al., 1992; Compas et al., 1988b; Curry & Russ, 1985; Ebata & Moos, 1994; Rossman, 1992; Wertlieb et al., 1987). Specifically, the majority of studies (e.g., Altshuler & Ruble, 1989; Band & Weisz, 1988; Compas et al., 1988b; Curry & Russ, 1985; Wertlieb et al., 1987) have found that self-report of emotion-focused coping increases with age (for an exception, see Rossman, 1992). These studies have led some investigators to conclude that emotion-focused strategies increase with age (Compas, Orosan, & Grant, 1993; Compas et al., 1992b). The research on problem-focused coping is less consistent and has variously found increases (Ebata & Moos,

1994), decreases (Band & Weisz, 1988; Brodzinsky et al., 1992; Curry & Russ, 1985; Reid et al., 1995) or stability in coping with age (Altshuler & Ruble, 1989; Compas et al., 1988b; Dusek & Danko, 1994; Phelps & Jarvis, 1994; Wertlieb et al., 1987). Further research that focuses on a more fine-grained analysis of these coping strategies might help to clarify these equivocal findings.

Although some of these studies suggest that age is associated with changes in self-reported coping strategies, they do not indicate how coping strategies might change with the cognitive, social, and/or emotional development of children or adolescents. An initial distinction that needs to be made is that changes in chronological age are not necessarily equivalent to changes in developmental level. Changes in children's cognitive, social, and emotional development may have pervasive effects on the formation of various coping styles and strategies. In a reciprocal fashion, the way children cope may influence future cognitive, social, and emotional development. Although such issues are obviously complex, focusing on these relationships is critical to furthering our understanding of the development of coping behaviors in children and adolescents. Thus, a developmental perspective should guide the conceptualization and measurement of coping processes.

An extensive review of the potential developmental issues related to coping is beyond the scope of this chapter (for recent reviews, see Aldwin, 1994; Compas, Malcarne, & Banez, 1992a; Compas et al., 1992b). We will limit ourselves to several important developmental issues and their implications for *measurement* of coping processes. Some argue that individuals begin to effortfully cope with their environment from an early age (Aldwin, 1994). Aldwin notes that "infants are not passive recipients of parental care" (p. 218) and points out that babies use a number of strategies to regulate their external (e.g., they bat at blankets covering their head) and internal environments (e.g., they regulate the amount of stimulation by closing their eyes and comfort themselves by sucking their own thumb). If we adopt Compas and colleagues' (1997, in press) distinction between voluntary and involuntary responses to stress, to the extent that these are volitional attempts to deal with stress, these strategies could be considered problem- and emotion-focused coping, respectively. If we do not have confidence that these behaviors represent volitional attempts, they undoubtedly are important in the development of future coping strategies or repertoires.

As children mature, more complex strategies and cognitive strategies emerge. For example, Spivak et al. (1976) found that the ability to generate multiple solutions to interpersonal problems emerges as early as 4–5 years and that more complex means–ends thinking appears between ages 6–8.

However, even for children as old as 5 years, "simple" coping strategies such as thumb sucking and rocking are still present. In these early years, coping responses are largely behavioral. Aldwin (1994) suggests that it is possible that some children may not develop cognitive strategies to regulate emotion and may continue to rely largely upon behavioral emotion-focused strategies. This suggests the importance of continued assessment of these behavioral emotion-focused strategies.

During middle childhood and adolescence, the development and increase in metacognitive functioning (e.g., Flavell, 1985) may be an important skill that allows an older child to consider several different cognitive strategies at a time. This ability may account for the increase in cognitive coping strategies that older children report generating and utilizing during stressful problem situations (Band & Weisz, 1990; Brown et al., 1986; Curry & Russ, 1985; Wilson, Hoffner, & Cantor, 1987).

Another developmental issue relevant to coping assessment is that children's sources of support change over time, shifting from a heavy reliance on parental figures to peers. Maccoby (1983) emphasizes that for young children who lack a large repertoire of coping strategies, a primary strategy operates; that is, "In case of threat, go to attachment figures" (p. 223). She suggests that the mere presence of an attachment figure facilitates the coping of young children. However, peer support is particularly salient for adolescents. The type of coping assistance children desire (e.g., security, help solving a problem) may also change with age, and/or become more situation-specific. The measurement of children's support-seeking coping should attend to these issues, considering both the potential sources and functions of support. In addition, the presence or absence of attachment figures during stressful situations may be an important aspect of young children's coping.

Developmental changes in the appraisal of the stressor may influence children's coping. Boekaerts (1996) suggests that as children age and gain experience with different situations, they become more skilled at appraising the dimensions of a stressful situation. Specifically, their ability to ascertain the valence, controllability, changeability, ambiguity, recurrence, and familiarity of the situation develops. The ability to match the demands of the situation with appropriate coping responses may also improve with development. There is some evidence that appropriate judgment of controllability and coping matching improves with age (Blanchard-Fields, & Irion, 1988). Blanchard-Fields and Irion (1988) found that although adolescents use more emotion-focused coping regardless of controllability, older adults use more problem-focused coping for controllable stressors and more emotion-focused coping for uncontrollable stressors. This implies that the investigation of the development of children's coping would benefit from attention to developmental changes in situational appraisal processes. Finally, it is important to recognize that the function of a particular coping strategy may differ by developmental level. This could call into question the proposition that emotion-focused and problem-focused dimensionality meaningfully distinguishes coping functions across all developmental levels. Indeed, Compas and colleagues (Compas & Worsham, 1991, as cited in Compas et al., 1992b) have found that the use of complex coping strategies that serve dual purposes (emotion- and problem-focused) increases with age.

It is clear that developmental considerations should play an important role in both the conceptualization and measurement of children's coping. This is particularly important as research on children's coping turns to study of the development of children's coping strategies and styles. To embark on this line of investigation, it is crucial that instruments are sensitive to developmental issues and tap a broad range of cognitive and behavioral coping strategies. In doing so, the instruments are more likely to be socially and ecologically valid.

10. Conclusion

The assessment of coping strategies and styles in children and adolescents has benefited greatly from the adult literature. The dominant conceptualizations of the construct have moved gradually toward a more transactional perspective that recognizes the importance of both the characteristics of the situation and the appraisal processes of the individual and the significant influence these factors have upon an individual's coping response. The conceptualization and classification of coping strategies and styles is still hotly debated, yet the relative advantages and disadvantages of assessing either coping strategies and styles are becoming clearer to researchers in the area. Current work has suggested that a further understanding of coping processes might benefit from a more fine-grained analysis of coping thoughts and behaviors. In addition, little is currently known about the influence that cognitive, social, and emotional developmental processes may have on the development of children's coping styles or strategies. The investigation of the development of coping strategies and styles in children presents itself as a complex and difficult task for future researchers in this area. Such research will most likely require different measures of children's coping that are age appropriate, reliable, and valid. The review of the current literature and the suggestions offered in this chapter should help guide the development of future coping instruments that meet these standards.

ACKNOWLEDGMENTS

Work on this chapter was funded in part by the National Institute of Mental Health Grants P50-MH39246 to support a Preventive Intervention Research Center, and R01-MH49155 to evaluate a Family Bereavement Program at Arizona State University, which is gratefully acknowledged. The authors also wish to thank Mark W. Roosa, who carefully reviewed earlier drafts of this chapter and offered many helpful suggestions.

Correspondence should be directed to Tim S. Ayers, Program for Prevention Research, Arizona State University, Community Services Center, P.O. Box 871108, Tempe, AZ 85287-1108.

11. References

Aldwin, C. M. (1994). *Stress, coping, and development: An integrative perspective*. New York: Guilford.

Aldwin, C. M., & Revenson, T. A. (1987). Does coping help? A reexamination of the relation between coping and mental health. *Journal of Personality and Social Psychology, 53,* 337–348.

Altshuler, J. L., & Ruble, D. N. (1989). Developmental changes in children's awareness of strategies for coping with uncontrollable stress. *Child Development, 60,* 1337–1349.

Asarnow, J. R., Carlson, G. A., & Guthrie, D. (1987). Coping strategies, self-perceptions, hopelessness, and perceived family environments in depressed and suicidal children. *Journal of Consulting and Clinical Psychology, 55,* 361–366.

Austin, J. K., Patterson, J. M., & Huberty, T. J. (1991). Development of the Coping Health Inventory for Children. *Journal of Pediatric Nursing, 6,* 166–174.

Ayers, T. S. (1991). *A dispositional and situational assessment of children's coping: Testing alternative theoretical models*. Unpublished dissertation, Arizona State University, Tempe.

Ayers, T. S., Sandler, I. N., Bernzweig, J. A., Harrison, R. J., Wampler, T. W., & Lustig, J. L. (1989). *Handbook for the content analyses of children's coping responses*. Tempe: Program for Prevention Research, Arizona State University.

Ayers, T. S., Sandler, I. N., West, S. G., & Roosa, M. W. (1996). A dispositional and situational assessment of children's coping: Testing alternative models of coping. *Journal of Personality, 64,* 923–958.

Band, E. B., & Weisz, J. R. (1988). How to feel better when it feels bad: Children's perspectives on coping with everyday stress. *Developmental Psychology, 24,* 247–253.

Band, E. B., & Weisz, J. R. (1990). Developmental differences in primary and secondary control coping and adjustment to juvenile diabetes. *Journal of Clinical Child Psychology, 19,* 150–158.

Beck, A. T. (1967). *Depression: Clinical, experimental and theoretical aspects*. New York: Hoeber.

Benson, J., & Hagtvet, K. (1996). The interplay among design, data analysis, and theory in the measurement of coping. In N. S. E. Moshe Zeidner (Ed.), *Handbook of coping: Theory, research, applications* (pp. 83–106). New York: Wiley.

Billings, A. G., & Moos, R. H. (1981). The role of coping responses and social resources in attenuating the stress of life events. *Journal of Behavioral Medicine, 4,* 139–157.

Blanchard-Fields, F., & Irion, J. C. (1988). Coping strategies from the perspective of two developmental markers: Age and social reasoning. *Journal of Genetic Psychology, 149*, 141–151.

Boekaerts, M. (1996). Coping with stress in childhood and adolescence. In M. Zeidner & N. S. Endler (Eds.), *Handbook of coping: Theory, research, applications* (pp. 452–484). New York: Wiley.

Brodzinsky, D. M., Elias, M. J., Steiger, C., & Simon, J. (1992). Coping Scale for Children and Youth: Scale development and validation [Special Issue: Does environment really contribute to healthy, quality life?]. *Journal of Applied Developmental Psychology, 13*, 195–214.

Brown, J. M., O'Keeffe, J., Sanders, S. H., & Baker, B. (1986). Developmental changes in children's cognition to stressful and painful situations. *Journal of Pediatric Psychology, 11*, 343–357.

Bull, B. A., & Drotar, D. (1991). Coping with cancer in remission: Stressors and strategies reported by children and adolescents. *Journal of Pediatric Psychology, 16*, 767–782.

Carver, C. S., Scheier, M. F., & Weintraub, J. K. (1989). Assessing coping strategies: A theoretically based approach. *Journal of Personality and Social Psychology, 56*, 267–283.

Causey, D. L., & Dubow, E. F. (1992). Development of a self-report coping measure for elementary school children. *Journal of Clinical Child Psychology, 21*, 47–59.

Causey, D. L., & Dubow, E. F. (1993). Negotiating the transition to junior high school: The contributions of coping strategies and perceptions of the school environment. In L. A. Jason, K. E. Danner, & K. S. Kurasaki (Eds.), *Prevention and school transitions* (Vol. 10, pp. 59–81). New York: Hayworth Press.

Colletta, N. D., Hadler, S., & Gregg, C. H. (1981). How adolescents cope with the problems of early motherhood. *Adolescence, 16*, 499–512.

Compas, B. E. (1987). Coping with stress during childhood and adolescence. *Psychological Bulletin, 101*, 393–403.

Compas, B. E. (1997, January). *Placing coping in context: Effortful and involuntary responses to stress.* Paper presented at the Stress and Coping Research with Children: Strengthening the Links between Theory and Intervention meeting. Tempe, AZ.

Compas, B. E., Banez, G. A., Malcarne, V., & Worsham, N. (1991). Perceived control and coping with stress: A developmental perspective. *Journal of Social Issues, 47*, 23–34.

Compas, B. E., Conner, J. K., Harding, A., Oppedisano, G., Saltzman, H., & Wadsworth, M. (1997). *Responses to stress questionnaire: A measure of effortful and involuntary responses to stress during childhood and adolescence* (Manual). Burlington: University of Vermont Press.

Compas, B. E., Connor, J. K., Harding, A., Saltzman, H., & Wadsworth, M. (in press). Getting specific about coping: Effortful and involuntary responses to stress in development. In M. Lewis & D. Ramsey (Eds.), *Stress and soothing.* Hillsdale, NJ: Erlbaum.

Compas, B. E., Connor, J., Osowiecki, D., & Welch, A. (1997). Effortful and involuntary responses to stress: Implications for coping with chronic stress. In B. H. Gottlieb (Ed.), *Coping with chronic stress* (pp. 105–132). New York: Plenum Press.

Compas, B. E., Forsythe, C. J., & Wagner, B. M. (1988a). Consistency and variability in casual attributions and coping with stress. *Cognitive Therapy and Research, 12*, 305–320.

Compas, B. E., Malcarne, V. L., & Banez, G. A. (1992a). Coping with psychosocial stress: A developmental perspective. In B. N. Carpenter (Ed.), *Personal coping: Theory, research, and application* (pp. 47–63). Westport, CT: Praeger Publishers/Greenwood Publishing Group.

Compas, B. E., Malcarne, V. L., & Fondacaro, K. M. (1988b). Coping with stressful events in older children and young adolescents. *Journal of Consulting and Clinical Psychology, 56*, 405–411.

Compas, B. E., Orosan, P. G., & Grant, K. E. (1993). Adolescent stress and coping: Implications for psychopathology during adolescence [Special Issue: Stress and coping in adolescence]. *Journal of Adolescence, 16*, 331–349.

Compas, B. E., Worsham, N. L., & Ey, S. (1992b). Conceptual and developmental issues in children's coping with stress. In A. M. L. Greca, L. J. Siegel, J. L. Wallander, & C. E. Walker (Eds.), *Stress and coping in child health. Advances in pediatric psychology* (pp. 7–24). New York: Guilford.

Connell, J. P., & Wellborn, J. G. (1991). Competence, autonomy and relatedness: A motivational analysis of self-system processes. In M. Gunnar & L. A. Sroufe (Eds.), *Minnesota symposium on child psychology* (Vol. 23, pp. 43–77). Chicago: University of Chicago Press.

Coyne, J. C., & Gottlieb, B. H. (1996). The mismeasure of coping by checklist. *Journal of Personality, 64,* 959–991.

Cummings, E. M. (1987). Coping with background anger in early childhood. *Child Development, 58,* 976–984.

Cummings, E. M., & Cummings, J. L. (1988). A process-oriented approach to children's coping with adults' angry behavior. *Developmental Review, 8,* 296–321.

Curry, S. L., & Russ, S. W. (1985). Identifying coping strategies in children [Special Issue: Childhood vulnerability: Families and life stress: I.]. *Journal of Clinical Child Psychology, 14,* 61–69.

Danvosky, M., Rapoff, M., & Houston, K. (1995, August). *Development of Kansas Coping Inventory for Children: The Kancope.* Paper presented at the Annual Convention of the American Psychological Association, New York.

Dise Lewis, J. E. (1988). The Life Events and Coping Inventory: An assessment of stress in children. *Psychosomatic Medicine, 50,* 484–499.

Dubow, E. F., Roecker, C. E., & Donaldson, D. (1995, August). *Cross-situational patterns in children's coping with interparental conflict.* Paper presented at the Annual Convention of the American Psychological Association, New York.

Dusek, J. B., & Danko, M. (1994). Adolescent coping styles and perceptions of parental child rearing. *Journal of Adolescent Research, 9,* 412–426.

Ebata, A. T., & Moos, R. H. (1991). Coping and adjustment in distressed and healthy adolescents. *Journal of Applied Developmental Psychology, 12,* 33–54.

Ebata, A. T., & Moos, R. H. (1994). Personal, situational, and contextual correlates of coping in adolescence. *Journal of Research on Adolescence, 4,* 99–125.

Egan, M. A., Linney, J. A., & Forman, S. G. (1989, August). *Development of a measure of behavioral coping skills for adolescents.* Paper presented at the Annual Convention of the American Psychological Association, New Orleans, LA.

Eisenberg, N., Fabes, R. A., & Guthrie, I. K. (1997). Coping with stress: The roles of regulation and development. In S. A. Wolchik & I. N. Sandler (Eds.), *Handbook of children's coping with common life stressors: Linking theory, research, and interventions* (pp. 41–70). New York: Plenum Press.

Elwood, S. W. (1987). Stressor and coping responsive inventories for children. *Psychological Reports, 60,* 931–947.

Endler, N. S., & Parker, J. D. A. (1990). Multidimensional assessment of coping: A critical evaluation. *Journal of Personality and Social Psychology, 58,* 844–854.

Fanshawe, J. P., & Burnett, P. C. (1991). Assessing school-related stressors and coping mechanisms in adolescents. *British Journal of Educational Psychology, 61,* 92–98.

Filipp, S.-H., Klauer, T., & Ferring, D. (1993). Self-focused attention in the face of adversity and threat. In H. W. Krohne (Ed.), *Attention and avoidance: Strategies in coping with aversiveness* (pp. 267–295). Seattle: Hogrefe & Huber.

Flavell, J. H. (1985). *Cognitive development* (2nd ed.). Englewood Cliffs, Prentice-Hall.

Folkman, S., & Lazarus, R. S. (1980). An analysis of coping in a middle-aged community sample. *Journal of Health and Social Behavior, 21,* 219–239.

Folkman, S., & Lazarus, R. S. (1985). If it changes it must be a process: Study of emotion and coping during three stages of a college examination. *Journal of Personality and Social Psychology, 48,* 150–170.

Forsythe, C. J., & Compas, B. E. (1987). Interaction of cognitive appraisals of stressful events and coping: Testing the goodness of fit hypothesis. *Cognitive Therapy and Research, 11,* 473–485.

Frydenberg, E., & Lewis, R. (1991). Adolescent coping styles and strategies. Is there functional and dysfunctional coping? *Australian Journal of Guidance and Counseling, 1,* 35–43.

Frydenberg, E., & Lewis, R. (1993). Boys play sport and girls turn to others: Age, gender and ethnicity as determinants of coping [Special Issue: Stress and coping in adolescence]. *Journal of Adolescence, 16,* 253–266.

Gamble, W. C. (1994). Perceptions of controllability and other stressor event characteristics as determinants of coping among young adolescents and young adults. *Journal of Youth and Adolescence, 23,* 65–84.

Glyshaw, K., Cohen, L. H., & Towbes, L. C. (1989). Coping strategies and psychological distress: Prospective analyses of early and middle adolescents. *American Journal of Community Psychology, 17,* 607–623.

Grossman, B. D., & Levy, P. S. (1974). A factor analytic study of coping behavior in preschool children. *Journal of Genetic Psychology, 124,* 287–294.

Haan, N. (1977). *Coping and defending, processes of self-environment organization.* New York: Academic Press.

Haan, N. (1982). The assessment of coping, defense, and stress. In L. Goldberger & S. Breznitz (Eds.), *Handbook of stress: Theoretical and clinical aspects* (pp. 254–269). New York: Free Press.

Halstead, M., Johnson, S. B., & Cunningham, W. (1993). Measuring coping in adolescents: An application of the Ways of Coping Checklist. *Journal of Clinical Child Psychology, 22,* 337–344.

Herman Stahl, M. A., Stemmler, M., & Petersen, A. C. (1995). Approach and avoidant coping: Implications for adolescent mental health. *Journal of Youth and Adolescence, 24,* 649–665.

Hoffer, M., & Thompson, M. G. (1986). The Thompson–Patterson Scale of Psychosocial Development: II. Investigation of its use in the assessment of preschool children. *Canadian Journal of Psychiatry, 31,* 398–406.

Hoffner, C. (1993). Children's strategies for coping with stress. Blunting and monitoring. *Motivation and Emotion, 17,* 91–106.

Holahan, C. J., & Moos, R. H. (1987). Risk, resistance, and psychological distress: A longitudinal analysis with adults and children. *Journal of Abnormal Psychology, 96,* 3–13.

Holahan, C. J., Moos, R. H., & Schaefer, J. A. (1996). Coping, stress resistance, and growth: Conceptualizing adaptive functioning. In M. Zeidner & N. S. Endler (Eds.), *Handbook of coping: Theory, research, applications* (pp. 24–43). New York: Wiley.

Horn, J. (1967). On subjectivity in factor analysis. *Educational and psychological measurement, 27,* 811–820.

Hyson, M. C. (1983). Going to the doctor: A developmental study of stress and coping. *Journal of Child Psychology and Psychiatry and Allied Disciplines, 24,* 247–259.

Knapp, L. G., Stark, L. J., Kurkjian, J. A., & Spirito, A. (1991). Assessing coping in children and adolescents: Research and practice. *Educational Psychology Review, 3,* 309–334.

Krantz, S. E., Clark, J., Pruyn, J. P., & Usher, M. (1985). Cognition and adjustment among children of separated or divorced parents. *Cognitive Therapy and Research, 9,* 61–77.

Kurtz, L. (1994). Psychosocial coping resources in elementary school-age children of divorce. *American Journal of Orthopsychiatry, 64,* 554–563.

Lazarus, R. S. (1991). *Emotion and adaptation.* New York: Oxford University Press.

Lazarus, R. S. (1993). Coping theory and research: Past, present and future. *Psychosomatic Medicine, 55,* 234–247.

Lazarus, R. S., & Folkman, S. (1984). *Stress, appraisal and coping.* New York: Springer.

Maccoby, E. E. (1983). Social–emotional development and response to stressors. In N. Garmezy & M. Rutter (Eds.), *Stress, coping and development in children* (pp. 217–234). New York: McGraw-Hill.

McCrae, R. R. (1984). Situational determinants of coping responses: Loss, threat, and challenge. *Journal of Personality and Social Psychology, 46,* 919–928.

McCubbin, H. I., Needle, R. H., & Wilson, M. (1985). Adolescent health risk behaviors: Family stress and adolescent coping as critical factors [Special Issue: The family and health care]. *Family Relations Journal of Applied Family and Child Studies, 34,* 51–62.

Miller, S. M. (1987). Monitoring and blunting: Validation of a questionnaire to assess styles of information seeking under threat. *Journal of Personality and Social Psychology, 52,* 345–353.

Miller, S. M., Roussi, P., Caputo, G. C., & Kruus, L. (1995). Patterns of children's coping with an aversive dental treatment. *Health Psychology, 14,* 236–246.

Miller, S. M., Sherman, H. D., Combs, C., & Kruus, L. (1992). Patterns of children's coping with short-term medical and dental stressors: Nature, implications, and future directions. In A. M. La Greca, L. J. Siegel, J. L. Wallander, & C. E. Walker (Eds.), *Stress and coping in child health: Advances in pediatric psychology* (pp. 157–190). New York: Guilford.

Mooney, K. C., Graziano, A. M., & Katz, J. N. (1985). A factor analytic investigation of children's nighttime fear and coping responses. *Journal of Genetic Psychology, 146,* 205–215.

Moos, R. H., & Billings, A. G. (1982). Conceptualizing and measuring coping resources and processes. In L. Goldberger & S. Breznitz (Eds.), *Handbook of stress: Theoretical and clinical aspects* (2nd ed., pp. 212–230). New York: Free Press.

Moos, R. H., & Schaefer, J. A. (1993). Coping resources and processes; Current concepts and measures. In L. Goldberger & S. Breznitz (Eds.), *Handbook of stress: Theoretical and clinical aspects* (2nd ed., pp. 234–257). New York: Free Press.

Mulaik, S. A. (1988). Confirmatory factor analysis. In J. R. Nesselroade & R. B. Cattell (Eds.), *Handbook of multivariate experimental psychology* (2nd ed., pp. 259–288). New York: Plenum Press.

Murphy, L. B. (1974). Coping, vulnerability, and resilience in childhood. In G. V. Coelho, D. A. Hamburg, & J. E. Adams (Eds.), *Coping and adaptation* (pp. 69–100). New York: Basic Books.

Murphy, L. B., & Moriarty, A. E. (1976). *Vulnerability, coping and growth: From infancy to adolescence.* New Haven, CT: Yale University Press.

Nolen-Hoeksema, S., & Morrow, J. (1993). The effects of rumination and distraction on naturally occurring depressed moods. *Cognition and Emotion, 7,* 561–570.

Parker, J. D. A., & Endler, N. S. (1992). Coping with coping assessment: A critical review. *European Journal of Personality, 6,* 321–334.

Patterson, J. M., & McCubbin, H. I. (1987a). Adolescent coping style and behaviors: Conceptualization and measurement. *Journal of Adolescence, 10,* 163–186.

Patterson, J. M., & McCubbin, H. I. (1987b). A-COPE adolescent coping orientation for problem experiences. In H. I. McCubbin & A. I. Thompson (Eds.), *Family assessment inventories for research and practice* (pp. 226–243). Madison: University of Wisconsin Press.

Pearlin, L. I., & Schooler, C. (1978). The structure of coping. *Journal of Health and Social Behavior, 19,* 2–21.

Peterson, L., Harbeck, C., Chaney, J., Farmer, J., & Thomas, A. M. (1990). Children's coping with medical procedures: A conceptual overview and integration. *Behavioral Assessment, 12,* 197–212.

Phelps, S. B., & Jarvis, P. A. (1994). Coping in adolescence: Empirical evidence for a theoretically based approach to assessing coping. *Journal of Youth and Adolescence, 23,* 359–371.

Plancherel, B., & Bolognini, M. (1995). Coping and mental health in early adolescence [Special Issue: Adolescent research: A European perspective]. *Journal of Adolescence, 18,* 459–474.

Pyszczynski, T., & Greenberg, J. (1987). Self-regulatory perseveration and the depressive self-focusing style: A self-awareness theory of reactive depression. *Psychological Bulletin, 62,* 122–138.

Pyszczynski, T., Greenberg, J., Hamilton, J., & Nix, G. (1991). On the relationship between self-focused attention and psychological disorder: A critical reappraisal. *Psychological Bulletin, 110,* 538–543.

Reid, G. J., Dubow, E. F., & Carey, T. C. (1995). Developmental and situational differences in coping among children and adolescents with diabetes. *Journal of Applied Developmental Psychology, 16,* 529–554.

Reid, G. J., Dubow, E. F., Carey, T. C., & Dura, J. R. (1994). Contribution of coping to medical adjustment and treatment responsibility among children and adolescents with diabetes. *Journal of Developmental and Behavioral Pediatrics, 15,* 327–335.

Roosa, M. W., Gensheimer, L. K., Short, J., & Ayers, T. S. (1988, November). *A preventive intervention for children in alcoholic families: Results of a pilot study.* Paper presented at the National Council on Family Relations Annual Meeting, Philadelphia, PA.

Rossman, B. R. (1992). School-age children's perceptions of coping with distress: Strategies for emotion regulation and the moderation of adjustment. *Journal of Child Psychology and Psychiatry and Allied Disciplines, 33,* 1373–1397.

Roth, S., & Cohen, L. J. (1986). Approach, avoidance, and coping with stress. *American Psychologist, 41,* 813–819.

Rothbaum, F., Weisz, J. R., & Snyder, S. S. (1982). Changing the world and changing the self: A two-process model of perceived control. *Journal of Personality and Social Psychology, 42,* 5–37.

Rudolph, K. D., Dennig, M. D., & Weisz, J. R. (1995). Determinants and consequences of children's coping in the medical setting: Conceptualization, review, and critique. *Psychological Bulletin, 118,* 328–357.

Ryan, N. M. (1988). The stress–coping process in school-age children: Gaps in the knowledge needed for health promotion. *Advances in Nursing Science, 11,* 1–12.

Ryan, N. M. (1989). Stress–coping strategies identified from school age children's perspective. *Research in Nursing and Health, 12,* 111–122.

Ryan-Wenger, N. M. (1990). Development and psychometric properties of the Schoolagers Coping Strategies Inventory. *Nursing Research, 39,* 344–349.

Ryan-Wenger, N. M. (1992). A taxonomy of children's coping strategies: A step toward theory development. *American Journal of Orthopsychiatry, 62,* 256–263.

Ryan-Wenger, N. M. (1994). Coping behavior in children: Methods of measurement for research and clinical practice. *Journal of Pediatric Nursing, 9,* 183–195.

Ryan-Wenger, N. M., & Copeland, S. G. (1994). Coping strategies used by black school-age children from low-income families. *Journal of Pediatric Nursing, 9,* 33–40.

Sandler, I. N., Ayers, T. S., Bernzweig, J. A., Wampler, T. P., Harrison, R. H., & Lustig, J. L. (1990, August). *Children coping with divorce-related stressful events.* Paper presented at the annual meeting of the American Psychological Association, Boston, MA.

Sandler, I. N., Tein, J. Y., & West, S. G. (1994). Coping, stress, and the psychological symptoms of children of divorce: A cross-sectional and longitudinal study. *Child Development, 65,* 1744–1763.

Schwarzer, R., & Schwarzer, C. (1996). A critical survey of coping instruments. In M. Zeidner & N. S. Endler (Eds.), *Handbook of coping: Theory, research, applications* (pp. 107–132). New York: Wiley.

Seiffge-Krenke, I., & Shulman, S. (1990). Coping style in adolescence: A cross-cultural study. *Journal of Cross-Cultural Psychology, 21,* 351–377.

Shulman, S., Carlton Ford, S., Levian, R., & Hed, S. (1995). Coping styles of learning disabled adolescents and their parents. *Journal of Youth and Adolescence, 24,* 281–294.

Sipes, G., Rardin, M., & Fitzgerald, B. (1985). Adolescent recall of childhood fears and coping strategies. *Psychological Reports, 57,* 1215–1223.

Skinner, E. A., Altman, J., & Sherwood, H. (1991). *Coding manual for children's coping in the domains of school and friendship.* Rochester, NY: University of Rochester.

Skinner, E. A., & Wellborn, J. G. (1994). Coping during childhood and adolescence: A motivational perspective. In D. L. Featherman, R. M. Lerner, & M. Perlmutter (Eds.), *Life-span development and behavior: Vol. 12* (pp. 91–133). Hillsdale, NJ: Erlbaum.

Skinner, E. A., & Wellborn, J. G. (1977). Children's coping in the academic domain. In S. A. Wolchik & I. N. Sandler (Eds.), *Handbook of children's coping with common life stressors: Linking theory, research and interventions* (pp. 387–422). New York: Plenum Press.

Spirito, A., Stark, L. J., & Williams, C. (1988). Development of a brief coping checklist for use with pediatric populations. *Journal of Pediatric Psychology, 13,* 555–574.

Spivack, G., Platt, J. J., & Shure, M. B. (1976). *The problem-solving approach to adjustment.* San Francisco: Jossey-Bass.

Stanton, A. L., Danoff Burg, S., Cameron, C. L., & Ellis, A. P. (1994). Coping through emotional approach: Problems of conceptualization and confounding. *Journal of Personality and Social Psychology, 66,* 350–362.

Stern, M., & Alvarez, A. (1992). Pregnant and parenting adolescents: A comparative analysis of coping response and psychosocial adjustment. *Journal of Adolescent Research, 7,* 469–493.

Stone, A. A., Greenberg, M. A., Kennedy-Moore, E., & Newman, M. G. (1991). Self-report, situation-specific coping questionnaires: What are they measuring? *Journal of Personality and Social Psychology, 61,* 648–658.

Stone, A. A., Helder, L., & Schneider, M. S. (1988). Coping with stressful events: Coping, dimensions and issues. In L. H. Cohen (Ed.), *Life events and psychological functioning: Theoretical and methodological issues* (pp. 182–210). Newbury Park, CA: Sage.

Stone, A. A., & Kennedy-Moore, E. (1992). Assessing situational coping: Conceptual and methodological considerations. In H. S. Friedman (Ed.), *Hostility, coping, and health* (pp. 203–214). Washington, DC: American Psychological Association Press.

Stone, A. A., Kennedy-Moore, E., & Neale, J. M. (1995). Association between daily coping and end-of-day mood. *Health Psychology, 14,* 341–349.

Stone, A. A., Kennedy-Moore, E., Newman, M. G., Greenberg, M., & Neale, J. M. (1992). Conceptual and methodological issues in current coping assessments. In B. N. Carpenter (Ed.), *Personal coping: Theory, research and application* (pp. 15–29). Westport, CT: Praeger.

Stone, A. A., & Neale, J. M. (1984). New measure of daily coping: Development and preliminary results. *Journal of Personality and Social Psychology, 46,* 892–906.

Stone, A. A., & Shiffman, S. (1992). Reflections on the intensive measurement of stress, coping, and mood, with an emphasis on daily measures. *Psychology and Health, 7,* 115–129.

Suls, J., & Fletcher, B. (1985). The relative efficacy of avoidant and nonavoidant coping strategies: A meta-analysis. *Health Psychology, 4,* 249–288.

Swift, M., Masterpasqua, F., Cutler, P., Chapman, L., Frank, J., & Healey, K. (1990, August). *Stress, coping and adjustment among young, inner-city adolescents.* Paper presented at the annual meeting of the American Psychological Association, Boston, MA.

Tolan, P. H., Guerra, N. G., & Montaini-Klovdahl, L. R. (1997). Staying out of harm's way: Coping and the development of inner-city children. In S. A. Wolchik & I. N. Sandler (Eds.), *Handbook of children's coping with common life stressors: Linking theory, research, and interventions* (pp. 453–479). New York: Plenum Press.

Tolor, A., & Fehon, D. (1987). Coping with stress: A study of male adolescents' coping strategies as related to adjustment. *Journal of Adolescent Research, 2,* 33–42.

Waller, N. G., Tellegen, A., McDonald, R., & Lykken, D. (1996). Exploring nonlinear models in personality assessment: Development and preliminary validation of a negative emotionality scale. *Journal of Personality, 64,* 545–576.

Weisz, J. R., Rothbaum, F. M., & Blackburn, T. C. (1984). Standing out and standing in: The psychology of control in America and Japan. *American Psychologist, 39,* 955–969.

Wertlieb, D., Weigel, C., & Feldstein, M. (1987). Measuring children's coping. *American Journal of Orthopsychiatry, 57,* 548–560.

White, R. (1974). Strategies of adaptation. In G. V. Coelho, D. Hamburg, & J. E. Adams (Eds.), *Coping and adaptation* (pp. 47–68). New York: Basic Books.

Whitesell, N. R., Robinson, N. S., & Harter, S. (1993). Coping with anger-provoking situations: Young adolescents' theories of strategy use and effectiveness. *Journal of Applied Developmental Psychology, 14,* 521–545.

Wills, T. A. (1985). Stress, coping and tobacco and alcohol use in early adolescence. In S. Shiffman & T. A. Wills (Eds.), *Coping and substance use* (pp. 67–94). New York: Academic Press.

Wills, T. A. (1986). Stress and coping in early adolescence: Relationships to substance use in urban school samples. *Health Psychology, 5,* 503–529.

Wilson, B. J., Hoffner, C., & Cantor, J. (1987). Children's perceptions of the effectiveness of techniques to reduce fear from mass media. *Journal of Applied Developmental Psychology, 8,* 39–52.

Wolchik, S. A., Beals, J., & Sandler, I. N. (1989). Mapping children's support networks: Conceptual and methodological issues. In D. Belle (Ed.), *Children's social networks and social support* (pp. 191–220). New York: Wiley.

Zeidner, M. (1994). Personal and contextual determinants of coping and anxiety in an evaluative situation: A prospective study. *Personality and Individual Differences, 16,* 899–918.

Zeitlin, S. (1980). Assessing coping behavior. *American Journal of Orthopsychiatry, 50,* 139–144.

9

New Developments in Services Delivery Research for Children, Adolescents, and Their Families

ANDRES J. PUMARIEGA AND SAUNDRA GLOVER

1. Introduction

1.1. Significance of Services Research

Child and adolescent mental health services research is a relatively new field in the behavioral sciences, but one that has gained increasing attention and significance. It involves the study of the access, utilization, financing, and clinical- and cost-effectiveness of mental health services provided to children and adolescents, as well as the functioning and effectiveness of child mental health, health, and social service systems of care.

A number of recent trends have led to the increasing importance of this field. First, the increasing utilization and demonstrated need for child mental health services in the United States and other Western nations has spurred rapid growth of such services. Although child and adolescent mental illness and emotional disturbance were once thought to be relatively rare events, recent studies suggest an overall prevalence rate of 15% to 19% and 3% to 8% for serious mental illness and emotional disturbance (Knitzer, 1982; Tuma, 1989). However, at any one time less than 1% of children in the United States receive mental health treatment in hospital or

ANDRES J. PUMARIEGA • Department of Psychiatry and Behavioral Sciences, James H. Quillen College of Medicine, East Tennessee State University, Johnson City, Tennessee 36714.   SAUNDRA GLOVER • School of Public Health, University of South Carolina, Columbia, South Carolina 29208.

Advances in Clinical Child Psychology, Volume 20, edited by Thomas H. Ollendick and Ronald J. Prinz. Plenum Press, New York, 1998.

residential settings and another 5% in outpatient or community-based settings, with the majority of children in need receiving insufficient services or no mental health services whatsoever (Inouye, 1988; Tuma, 1989). In spite of this, the budgets dedicated to financing both public and private mental health services for children have grown exponentially since the 1970s, with total expenditures growing to $4.8 billion, comprising approximately 7% of the total national mental health budget (Burns, Taube, & Taube, 1990). A broad array of morbidities associated with emotional disturbances and mental illness are increasing at alarming rates among children and youth, including suicide, homicide, substance abuse, child abuse, teenage pregnancy, school dropout, youth crime, and associated institutionalization and incarceration. A number of health and human service agencies (schools, social welfare agencies, child protective agencies, juvenile justice, public health), in addition to mental health agencies, have experienced the increasing impact of these psychosocial morbidities being experienced by children and youth. Most frequently, each of these agencies addresses a piece of the service system puzzle with little or no coordination with other agencies often serving the same youth (Knitzer, 1982).

There is increasing need and utilization of mental health services by culturally diverse populations of children and adolescents. Such populations are increasing both proportionately and in overall numbers in the United States and Western Europe. This is as a result of higher birth rates and accelerating immigration. Children from these populations experience higher levels of stressors, such as poverty, discrimination, acculturation stress, and exposure to violence and trauma associated with their minority status in society, as well as the stressors involved in immigration. However, these populations traditionally have been underserved in terms of mental health, health, and human services, both in terms of overall access to services as well as the cultural competence of the services available to them. The increasing cost of serving these populations of children and adolescents is set in contrast to the cost of the high level of psychosocial morbidity they contend with, both in terms of lost potential productivity as citizens and the costs of welfare dependency and institutionalization (Cross, Bazron, Dennis, & Isaacs, 1988; Pumariega & Cross, 1997).

At the same time as these needs are recognized, there are increasingly limited resources available to fund child mental health and human services. An increasing suspicion of governmental programs and weariness over increasing taxation have led politicians and policy makers to look for ways of limiting or even cutting public budgets dedicated to health and human services. Private funding for such services has experienced similar constraints, with business and industry expressing increasing concerns about the rising costs of health and mental health care, especially the growing percentage of such spending on child and adolescent mental health. These trends have increased pressures on child mental health service providers and systems of care to demonstrate improved clinical and cost-effectiveness so as not to face the restriction or curtailment of services. The role of services research in informing providers, policy makers, and payers on clinically and cost-effective approaches is becoming progressively important (Hoagwood, Jensen, Petti, & Burns, 1996).

1.2. Emergence of Children's Mental Health Systems of Care

From its earliest origins, mental health services for children have emphasized a community orientation. These services in fact began in the United States in response to the perceived need for counseling juvenile offenders rather than incarcerating them with adult offenders. This was the case in the 1890s, when America, much as today, was undergoing rapid cultural changes due to immigration as well as rapid industrialization and urbanization. These social strains led to marked increases in crime committed by juveniles. Enlightened reformers saw the need for detaining young offenders separately from adult prisoners, adjudicating them in a separate court system (thus, the beginning of the juvenile courts) and providing rehabilitative services to them. The juvenile court clinics in Chicago and Boston gave rise to the first child mental health services in the nation. The success of these clinics led the Commonwealth Foundation to commission a study that recommended the development of child guidance clinics throughout the United States, and that these be staffed with interdisciplinary teams of professionals who could serve the child and the family. These clinics at first were primarily staffed by social workers but later attracted pediatricians, psychologists, psychoanalysts, and psychiatrists, and later served as the bases of the first child psychiatry programs in the nation. These clinics were quite removed from the specialty-driven medical system that was evolving in tertiary medical centers, and particularly apart from the practice of hospital-bound care. They provided low-cost services oriented to the needs of the child and the family, with treatment modalities evolving to include individual psychodynamic psychotherapy, family therapy, crisis intervention, and even day-treatment programs. Many have survived to this day and have served as the core for the child mental health services in many community mental health centers (Berlin, 1991).

The move toward the medicalization of psychiatry served to move child and adolescent mental health services toward a more hospital-based, tertiary-care model. This left the child guidance clinics and the community mental health centers that followed them without significant psychiatric input as well as generally understaffed and underfunded, neglecting the development of children's services. In the meantime, the United States experienced an explosion in the population of poor, minority children who needed significant mental health services but could not access them easily, leading to increasing morbidity among them. Many of these children came into the custody of child service agencies due to their parents' inability to care for them in their home environments and went on to be cared for in residential and detention facilities. In the meantime, the use of hospital-level care for the psychiatric treatment of children and adolescents increased exponentially throughout the late 1970s and 1980s, leading to spiraling costs for private and public insurers alike.

The modern era of community-based systems of care was ushered by the publication of Jane Knitzer's (1982) groundbreaking book *Unclaimed Children*, which exposed the aforementioned consequences of neglecting the provision of community-based mental health services for children and their families. Her advocacy, as well as that of others, led to the development of such services as the Child and Adolescent Service System Program (CASSP), which assisted all 50 states in the development of an infrastructure for publically funded community-based services (Lourie & Katz-Leavy, 1986). The CASSP initiative was supported by the conceptual work of Stroul and Friedman (1986), who coined the phrase "community-based system of care for seriously emotionally disturbed children" and advocated interagency coordination among all of the child service agencies in the provision of mental health services for children and related family support services. Stroul and Friedman proposed that such services be delivered as close to the child's home and community as possible to avert the use of more restrictive levels of care, which often served to separate children from natural family and community supports, and that families be involved as partners in the effective treatment for the child (Friesen & Koroloff, 1990).

The CASSP initiative set forth the initial principles inherent in community-based systems of care as developed by Stroul and Friedman (1986). The key aspects of these systems include access to a comprehensive array of services, treatment individualized to the child's needs, treatment in the least restrictive environment possible (with full utilization of the resources of the family and the community), full participation of families as partners in services planning and delivery, interagency coordination, the use of case management for services coordination, no ejection or rejection from services due to lack of "treatability" or "cooperation" with interventions, early identification and intervention, smooth transition of youth into the adult service system, effective advocacy efforts, and non-discriminating, culturally sensitive services.

This latter principle was further developed by the CASSP Minority Initiative into the principles of culturally competent systems of care for children with serious emotional disturbances (Cross, Bazron, Dennis, & Isaacs, 1988), which proposed that systems of care include practitioner guidelines for necessary attitudes, skill and knowledge base to serve minority and culturally diverse children and families in their communities, as well as policies and procedures to remove barriers for access to services. The concept of culturally competent systems of care was a natural outgrowth from that of community-based systems of care, because the latter endorses many of the traditional cultural values of ethnic minority populations in the United States. These are particularly consonant with the cultural values of ethnic minority populations, which emphasize strong extended family involvement in the life and upbringing of children and the use of natural community resources first in dealing with the emotional and physical problems of family members. These factors have been shown to be protective from some of the morbidities associated with emotional disturbance, such as substance abuse and suicidality (Pumariega, Swanson, Holzer, Linskey, & Quintero-Salinas, 1992).

Another important principle inherent in this approach is that of the targeting of services to what are termed "seriously emotionally disturbed children." The formal definition of serious emotional disturbance is listed in Table 1. This definition, though it includes the presence of an Axis I diagnosis under the *Diagnostic and Statistical Manual of Mental Disorders* (DSM-IV; American Psychiatric Association, 1994) as a criterion, places equal emphasis on the child's inability to function in at least one of his/her life domains (school, home, socially with peers, etc.). This is reflective of the difficulty that many children and their families have had in accessing necessary services when their diagnoses were not "severe enough," or when they reflected a disruptive behavior disorder. This bias still exists among many child mental health professionals, particularly psychiatrists, and ignores some key clinical and research observations. First, most clinicians have had children in treatment who have been diagnosed with serious disorders, such as schizophrenia, but have been totally able to function in their homes with treatment and some community supports, whereas other children with diagnoses reflecting disruptive behavior disorders have necessitated the most restrictive levels of care available. Some studies indicate lack of clarity and validity in clinical child diagnosis, especially in relation to the prognosis of the child, with many children with disruptive behavioral disorders having comorbid serious mental illness when evaluated systematically (Caron & Rutter, 1991). These problems are more pronounced in the diagnostic assessment of ethnic minority youth with serious emotional disturbance, with serious underestimation of com-

TABLE 1
Federal Definition of Childhood Serious Emotional Disturbance[a]

Children with a serious emotional disturbance are persons: from birth up to age 18; who currently or at any time during the past year have had a diagnosable mental, behavioral, or emotional disorder of sufficient duration to meet diagnostic criteria specified with DSM-III-R, that resulted in functional impairment which substantially interferes with or limits the child's role or functioning in family, school, or community activities.

These disorders include any mental disorder (including those of biological etiology) listed in DSM-III-R or their ICS-9-CM equivalent (and subsequent revisions), with the exception of -R "V" codes, substance use, and developmental disorders, which are excluded, unless they co-occur with another diagnosable serious emotional disturbance. All of these disorders have episodic, recurrent, or persistent features; however, they vary in terms of severity and disabling effects.

Functional impairment is defined as difficulties that substantially interfere with or limit a child or adolescent from achieving or maintaining one or more developmentally-appropriate social, behavioral, cognitive, communicative, or adaptive skills. Functional impairments of episodic, recurrent, and continuous duration are included unless they are temporary and expected responses to stressful events in the environment. Children who would have met functional impairment criteria during the referenced year without the benefit of treatment or other support services are included in this definition.

[a]Center for Mental Health Services (1993). *Federal Register, 58,* 29422–29425.

orbid affective and substance abuse disorders and overestimation of psychotic and organic disorders by clinicians (Kilgus, Pumariega, & Cuffe, 1995). Other studies indicate that the level of care received by children is only partially accounted for by their clinical diagnoses, with much of it accounted by their level of function and psychosocial stressors (Silver et al., 1992).

1.3. Emergence of Child Mental Health Services Research

The emergence of epidemiological and public health models as approaches in understanding health and disease was a necessary first step toward the development of child mental health services research. These models presented a population model for the understanding of health and disease that is consistent with the philosophy behind community-based systems of care. These approaches converge with respect to (1) an understanding of ecological factors involved in health and disease and (2) an orientation toward prevention using the natural supports found in the population.

The research methodology that has emerged to support the public health model is consistent with a systems-of-care and community-based approach. This methodology involves the use of systematic population-survey approaches using reliable and valid instruments that are acceptable and appropriate for the population being studied. It includes qualitative ethnographic and anthropological methods that place systematic, quantitative measures in an appropriate ecological context. The development of more systematic and efficient measurement and data collection methods in mental health has contributed to the feasibility and validity of mental health services research (Costello, Burns, Angold, & Leaf, 1993).

These advancements influenced the development of mental health epidemiological research. They culminated with the Epidemiologic Catchment Area (ECA) Study, funded and fielded by the National Institute of Mental Health, to assess the mental health status and needs of adults in the United States. This landmark study included the first large-scale use of standardized instrumentation for the measurement of symptomatology and psychopathology. The methodology established a community-based, household-sampling frame in multiple sites, geared to developing a regionally and nationally representative sample. The ECA study surveyed respondents on their utilization of mental health and substance abuse services, as well as on associated factors such as socioeconomic status and ethnicity. It established the first accepted prevalence rates for overall mental illness/emotional disturbance, as well as the underutilization of formal mental health services by adults, with most going untreated or partially treated by primary care practitioners. The significant findings of the ECA with adult populations spurred the development of child mental health epidemiological research and services research (Robins, 1985; Robins, Helzer, Ratcliff, & Seyfried, 1982).

2. Methodological Challenges in Child Mental Health Services Research

Child and adolescent mental health services research involves a number of special methodological challenges beyond those faced in the study of adults. Conceptual models outlined by Hoagwood et al. (1996), Pumariega, Holliday, and Holzer (1995), and Pumariega (1996) provide guides for the methodological issues that need to be addressed in conducting such research. The main areas of methodological focus in child mental health services research are outlined here, along with recent advances and current approaches used to address them.

2.1. Participant Sampling and Recruitment

The sampling and recruitment of participants involve a number of variables and limitations presented by the approaches used. In studying general populations, the two main approaches used are community/household sampling and school-based sampling. Community-based sampling has the advantage of being able to study the child's mental health status and use of services within the context of family and neighborhood/community, both of which present important facilitating and inhibitory factors toward service use. Community-based sampling facilitates the evaluation of ecological factors such as geographic location, socioeconomic status, and culture and ethnicity. It also facilitates parental involvement in studies. However, such an approach is extremely resource-intensive and expensive, given the need for a large number of field interviewers, access to extensive background data for sampling frames (census data, utility hookup data, etc.), and difficulty in obtaining sufficiently large samples.

A unique available alternative with children and adolescents is school-based sampling. The ready access to children within school settings has a number of inherent advantages. The high concentration of participants within schools and the availability of classrooms for group instrument administration (which is a familiar, structured setting for test administration for children) leads to much higher levels of efficiency and lower resource utilization. Schools offer readily available collateral databases that can be used for establishing sampling frames as well as for collateral and confirmatory data, particularly data valuable to determine the child's cognitive capacities and functional status. The availability of teachers provides access to more objective observer informants who have the built-in advantage of regular contact with large cohorts of children for comparison. Schools already provide a large proportion of the mental health services utilized by children and adolescents, particularly services to less severely disturbed children, much as primary care practitioners with adults, so they are primary sites for studying service delivery. The disadvantages of school-based sampling and administration include the lack of family and community context, the relative lack of access to parents and family respondents, and greater administrative and communication problems involved in obtaining consent and in-depth data collection. For community-based studies, a combination of these approaches, using schools for screening phases/stages, and households for more in-depth data collection and follow-up, may be the most effective approach (Pumariega et al., 1985).

A number of issues in the recruitment of subjects are important to address regardless of the sampling setting. Consent procedures with children are more complicated, because their dependent legal and intellectual status necessitates greater protection. Direct consent by parents, as well as assent from adolescents and older children, must be obtained in any study that pursues any in-depth information or involves the recording of the respondent's identity. In minimal, school-based surveys where limited, nonsensitive data are obtained, "passive" consent procedures at times can be utilized where the parent is notified of the survey and given the opportunity to review the instruments at the school, with ample time to object to the child's participation. However, these require approval from an institutional research board (IRB) and the school's administration. Family and child recruitment, however, are essential given the importance of multi-informant data collection with children's mental health data collection (see section 2.2.1). To successfully obtain community support in order to maximize recruitment and involvement, researchers must present the rationale of the study and the potential general benefits in terms of improving services to children to community leaders at various levels. Community leaders can give input on study design and implementation, which can improve acceptability of the methodology and prevent costly pitfalls. Recruiting research assistants from the community being studied can promote acceptance by that community as well as provide invaluable informal consultation on the customs, values, and concerns of the community and local culture. The latter two approaches are particularly important for longitudinal studies, where the ability to track respondents is essential (Pumariega et al., 1995; Pumariega, 1996).

Institutional sampling from clinics, treatment centers, and social service agencies is often the crux of mental health services research, because these are often the sites where services are delivered, but it presents unique challenges. The sampling frames are typically developed out of institutional databases and rosters, which have variable levels of reliability and validity (see section 2.3). However, access to clinically and functionally relevant database information, which can be contrasted with systematic data, access to the service delivery process and data, and access to service providers, can be particularly valuable. Limitations of institutional sampling include limited access to family and school collateral respondents, the interface between the clinical/intervention process and the research process (which can confound either process), complications in obtaining consent from parents or custodial agencies, and the lack of context within the community. Again, combining institutional with community-based sampling and data collection can balance the limitations and advantages of these approaches.

2.2. Measurement and Instrumentation Techniques

2.2.1. Characteristics of Instruments

A number of characteristics are essential in any instruments used in child mental health services research. Children's cognitive and emotional status lead to limitations in their serving as sole informants on their behaviors, particularly on externalizing behaviors. However, the child's perspective is equally important as that of parents and other observers, particularly in internalizing problems. Parents have limitations in their objectivity as respondents about their child's behavior, and their utilization and response to interventions. Multi-informant approaches to data collection, which use input from the child, parent(s), and other significant adult observers (such as teachers, clinicians, and mentors), are particularly important and have been shown to offer a higher level of validity (Verhulst & Koot, 1992).

Validity and reliability of instrumentation or any other data source are critical to the validity and significance of results. Increasingly, instruments have the requisite reliability and validity data, although this is not always the case across gender and ethnic groups. Another common source of confound for reliability and validity of responses that is inherent in mental health services research is that of response burden. This is particularly true for structured diagnostic interviews, although a similar risk is present in any lengthy direct data-collection procedure. A phenomenon can result in which the validity of such a lengthy instrument can greatly exceed its reliability due to respondent retest learning and fatigue, with the respondent deducing the most expeditious approach to finish the instrument regardless of validity of response. The development of brief and time-limited instrumentation and data-collection procedures, focused on critical aspects of hypothesis testing, and the development of approaches to inquiry that can maximally engage the respondent are essential. Additionally, the collection of critical data from collateral sources can help preserve informant responsiveness (Verhulst & Koot, 1992; Pumariega et al., 1995).

2.2.2. Database Data Collection

Mental health services research is frequently dependent on information from established service-based databases. These offer a number of advantages as well as containing a number of inherent limitations. Ready access to information that is already collected during the process of service delivery offers real-time data collection at the time of service delivery, which is potentially more reliable than retrospective consumer or provider data on actual service utilization. It reduces the burden on informants by using collateral sources of information. With the use of electronic databases, it is possible to pursue interlinkage of databases across multiple providers and sources as long as there are common identifiers for individual data. This allows the merging and concurrent analysis of data on different types of service utilization (mental health, social services, educational services, juvenile justice, etc.), cost and expenditures on services (form Medicaid or other third-party payers), indirect functional outcomes and associated morbidities (from service agencies listed earlier). Such data are invaluable in a comprehensive service system design, as well as in policy and cost-related service system planning.

Obviously, the ideal would be the design of databases based on systematic data collection at the time of service that integrates useful data fields and objective rating instruments, as well as outlines clear procedures for reliability in coding and data entry and data reliability checks. However, the reality is that most services research utilizes databases that were designed and implemented prior to the study, with the primary goal of administrative management. There are a number of limitations and pitfalls that need to be considered in the use of preexisting databases. Reliability of coding and entry needs to be closely examined, particularly the degree of subjective interpretation used by coders and entry personnel. Generally, the closer to service provider entry, the more confidence in the validity and reliability of the data. Data collection and inscription procedures (and associated training for such), clarity of coding, and ease of translation from paper data need to be examined. Changes in coding and data fields that may have occurred over time in the development and maintenance of the database may need to be identified and conformed. Unique identifiers for clients are necessary in order to prevent duplicate entries, as well as being able to accurately link individual clients to their unique characteristics and service utilization. There may be other technical issues involved in the compatibility of the software used in developing and collecting the database with other databases and with data-analysis packages. The combined use of information collected directly from consumers and providers, as well as from databases, lends a useful balance in any services research design (Pumariega et al., 1995).

2.3. Domains of Measurement

2.3.1. Respondent and Family Identifiers

Age, gender, socioeconomic status, ethnicity, geographic location (inner city/urban, rural, suburban, neighborhood, etc.), cognitive and educational status, parental marital status, legal status, and custodial status are only a few identifiers that are important variables in service access, utilization, and outcomes. The face validity and reliability of these data are rarely questioned, yet the source and manner in which they are collected can confound these essential characteristics. For example, respondents can withhold data out of fear of how they could be used (e.g., termination of custody, termination of benefits, or stigmatization), at times calling into question the validity of other information obtained simultaneously. When these data are presented in a categorical manner, the categorical sets may not correspond to the respondents' perspective on the variable. At times, a given respondent may not be able to respond to particular variables, such as a child often not knowing their parent(s) educational level, their parents' marital status or their own custodial status, or even whether they live in a rural or suburban setting. Careful consideration needs to be given to the appropriate source for given identifiers, the categorization used for them, assurance of confidentiality when obtaining certain information, and the importance of such variables in answering a particular research or evaluation question. The use of valid and reliable collateral sources (such as databases) and measures for these variables can help provide external validity as well as reduce respondent burden (see section 2.2.1). For example, a novel approach to determine urbanicity as well as the geographic distribution of a number of identifiers is the technique of geocoding. This technique uses mapping technology linked to various databases to identify the socioeconomic and sociocultural characteristics of various regions and neighborhoods. This technique can greatly enhance the ecological context in which identifiers are placed, as well as reduce the reliance on individual responses for certain identifiers (Pumariega, 1996; Pumariega et al., 1995).

2.3.2. Clinical Instruments: Symptomatic and Diagnostic

The development of symptomatic and diagnostic instruments have been based on three major directions within child mental health research and clinical measurement:

1. The emerging psychiatric diagnostic nosology, based on a more descriptive, nontheoretical approach, eventually led to the development of the *Diagnostic and Statistical Manual of Mental Disorders* (American Psychiatric Association, 1994). This nosology has facilitated the development of systematic diagnostic instruments, such as the Diagnostic Interview Schedule for Children (DISC; Shaffer et al., 1996) and the Diagnostic Interview for Children and Adolescents (DICA; Herjanic & Reich, 1982), which can be administered either by clinicians or trained lay interviewers to systematically evaluate the presence of diagnosed mental or emotional disorders as the presence of subdiagnostic symptomatology.

2. The development of diagnostic- or syndrome-related symptom checklists, facilitated the identification of particular disorders in at-risk individuals and the measurement of symptom reduction by focused interventions can either be self-rated by the child and significant respondents such as parents or teachers, or can be clinician-rated based on contact with the child. Included among these are the Conners Scales (Conners, 1969), the Child Depression Inventory (Kovacs, 1981), and the State–Trait Anxiety Scale (Spielberger, 1973).

3. Empirically derived instruments, which measure behavioral symptomatology and social function, have been developed as means of identifying children with significant emotional or behavioral disturbances, offering an alternative to diagnostically driven identification. Additionally, these serve as efficient means of screening populations of children, because many are directly self-administered by key informants, such as the child, parent, and teacher, without needing significant interviewer assistance. The Child Behavior Checklist and related instruments developed by Achenbach (1991) serve as the prime example of and standard for this type of instrument.

2.3.3. Functional Status of the Child and Family

The community-based systems approach has raised an important concern that has been supported by research findings (Caron & Rutter, 1991) as well as clinical experience. Quite often, the severity of a child's condition is not necessary related to his/her diagnostic or formal clinical status. It may be more clearly expressed in an inability to meet the expectations and requisite adaptive behaviors necessary to successfully negotiate roles within the family, with peers, and in school or other organized settings. This has led at times to the exclusion of children with so-called behavioral disorders that have no immediately identified biological basis, often referred as having serious emotional disturbance, from treatment settings. Another reason for exclusion is the fact that treating and caring for such children may actually be more difficult and taxing on mental health professionals than children with readily identified, biologically based disorders. Additionally, treatment plans and interventions may at times improve more formal clinical symptoms but may not address the child's function in the significant areas of life. This may in fact be explained by the focus on negative behaviors or symptoms in treatment and care planning, while the development of positive adaptive capacities receives secondary or incidental attention.

In order to more accurately reflect the true level of function in children with serious emotional disturbances, as well as to measure the outcome effectiveness of treatment interventions on children's positive functional skills, a group of children's functional rating measures have been developed over the past few years. These are generally clinician-rated, or at times parent-rated, and evaluate the child's function across different important areas of daily function. Previously, the Global Assessment of Functioning developed for the DSM and a children's adaptation titled the Children's Global Assessment Scale (C-GAS; Shaffer et al., 1983) served as the main methods of functional assessment. However, these were nonspecific to area of function and did not reflect clinical reality with children and adolescents, who can vary in their functioning across domains. These new scales address the issue of severity not only from the standpoint of overall function, but also the pervasiveness of the child's inability to function. The Child and Adolescent Functional Assessment Scale by Hodges (Hodges & Wong, 1996) is currently considered the best such measure, but many others are in development or being implemented in system-of-care studies.

Another area of functioning that has received attention from child mental health researchers in recent years has been that of family functioning. A number of reliable and valid measures have been developed that evaluate family functioning objectively, integrating the responses of multiple family members into a common score. The paradigms on which these measures are based focus increasingly on empirical and atheoretical domains such as communication, resolution of conflict, problem-solving capacity, organization, role definition, and consistency of expectations/rules. The Family Assessment Device (FAD; Epstein, Baldwin, & Bishop, 1983), the Family Adaptation and Cohesion Evaluation Scale (FACES; McCubbin & Patterson, 1981), and the Family Assessment Measure III (FAM III; Skinner, Steinhauer, & Santa-Barbara, 1984) are the most widely used family-functioning instruments in the context of evaluating children's mental health status and services outcomes.

2.3.4. Associated Psychosocial Morbidities

A negative aspect related to function is the identification of associated adverse social and behavioral morbidities in children served within systems of care. This includes such behaviors as truancy, runaway behavior, school dropout, teen pregnancy, HIV-infection rates, youth offenses, incarceration or other institutionalization, youth homicide, and youth suicide. Such morbidities are rarely the responsibility of the formal mental health system, and are more likely assigned to the child welfare, juvenile justice, educational system, courts, and public health system. However, a public health approach is most valuable and effective in influencing systems of care to address these morbidities. The measurement of such morbidities in populations of children and youth provides valuable outcome domains, especially given the high social and financial costs of their increasing prevalence. Data on such behaviors and events are most reliably found in agency databases, though the reliability of the data can vary greatly. Self-report or family-report data can be useful but may suffer from validity problems unless verified through multiple informants (Pumariega et al., 1995).

2.3.5. Consumer Attitudes/Satisfaction

With the increased emphasis on the needs and empowerment of consumers and families, child mental health services research has begun to focus on the attitudes and perceptions of consumers, how these are influenced, and, conversely, how these influence mental health service delivery and outcomes. Consumer satisfaction is perceived to be an important outcome from services, particularly because it determines the acceptability of services and, consequently, whether services are accessed and utilized. However, initial studies indicate that consumer satisfaction is a domain that is independent from level of function and symptomatic level resulting from interventions (Rosenblatt, 1996). Therefore, all three need to be considered separately and not inferred from the others in any services evaluation or research design. The degree of involvement of consumers in the treatment-planning and selection process, and the sensitivity and responsiveness to individual consumer and family developmental, functional, and cultural needs, are important process variables to be considered in conjunction with consumer satisfaction. Conversely, preexisting consumer attitudes, values, and beliefs can impact on whether accessing services is even considered in the first place. Issues of societal stigma, consumers' culturally determined values and beliefs about mental health, and the underlying value assumptions in service systems and interventions are important process variables to examine the interaction between consumer attitudes, provider attitudes, and access to services (DeChillo, Koren, & Schulte, 1994). Measures such as the Family Empowerment Scale (Singh et al., 1995) and the Family Involvement Scale (Singh et al., 1996a, 1996b) have been developed to measure the degree of family involvement, participation, and input into the treatment planning and implementation process. Garland and Besinger (1996), Young, Nicholson, and Davis (1995), and Schwab and Stone (1983) give excellent in-depth reviews of the consumer-satisfaction literature in child mental health services, as well as comprehensive discussions of current methodologies.

2.3.6. Services Access and Utilization

Two important areas of focus for services research are (1) the access that potential clients and families have to particular services or a service system as a whole, and (2) the actual degree of utilization of services in given populations. Lack of access to particularly effective services may result in the relative ineffectiveness of those services or the service system, with resultant increased disturbance and morbidity. Variables such as location of services, acceptability of the services, access procedures, socioeconomic resources, client perceptions, provider biases, and culture/ethnicity can serve as facilitating or inhibiting factors in accessing services. Perceived accessibility, actual services utilization versus need, measured attrition in the referral process or administrative procedures, such as waiting lists and registration, are important variables to consider in evaluating access to care or services. Services utilization is obviously related to access and can serve as an indirect measure of access. However, utilization of particular services and levels of care can serve as an indicator of the functioning of a system of care; for example, if more restrictive and costly services are overutilized, if lengths of stay are excessive while awaiting case management, or if community-based services are underutilized due to access barriers or limited capacity. Important measures include lengths of stay, number of visits or contacts, anticipated versus actual utilization, and service capacity at the levels of care being measured (Hoagwood et al., 1996).

2.3.7. Provider Characteristics and Attitudes

As mentioned earlier, provider attitudes and the interaction with consumer attitudes can have a significant impact as early as the point of access to services, as well as later in the treatment process. Attitudes regarding particular clinically, culturally, and socioeconomically defined populations can impact on access procedures, clinical decision making, the strength of the therapeutic alliance, and, potentially, outcomes from treatment. Degree of training and education, provider personality characteristics, provider cultural competence, provider match to consumer and family cultural background and values/beliefs, and provider or institutional orientation toward consumer-oriented, community-based treatment can be important process variables to measure. Services utilization versus need, dropout rates, clinical/functional outcomes, and consumer satisfaction can be used in determining the outcome of these factors. For example, a study by Morrisey et al. (1995) evaluated different clinician characteristics with respect to impact on hospitalization decisions with suicidal adolescents. Using 64 vignettes that systematically varied six common risk factors highly associated with suicidality, they found that proneness to hospitalization was related inversely to professional experience, and the decision to hospitalize was highly correlated to all established risk factors except gender.

2.4. Research Design

The nature of the chosen design can be a significant issue in mental health services research. Cross-sectional designs are most often used to address questions related to the current status of the level of care or service system being examined, including access, utilization, and process of care. Longitudinal designs following a cohort of clients over time are most appropriate in examining process and outcome of care. One drawback is the potential of behavioral changes, which may be specific to certain "cohort" groups that share many life experiences in common, and which make it hard to generalize results to other groups. Recruitment of a diverse sample of respondents that is well stratified for significant individual and family characteristics is important in this approach. The most difficult aspect of longitudinal designs is the problem of respondent attrition, which needs to be examined to determine the significance of findings. Studies in geographically stable populations and special procedures to track respondents can help reduce this problem. Pre–post or multiple baseline designs are often used to evaluate the effectiveness of a given treatment modality or service system. However, populations being served frequently change over time for other reasons than interventions provided, such as intervening events in their lives or in the community and cultural transition in culturally distinct populations. It is important to track such intervening changes as part of these designs. Single-case methodology, which is increasingly used in behavioral intervention studies, is useful in evaluations involving small numbers. These can serially follow rating of certain target behaviors pre- and postintervention to determine effect. Experimental designs (random assignment to different interventions) are often considered the "gold standard" scientifically. These are at times difficult to achieve in the reality of service provision, can result in ethical problems when any group is not receiving a worthwhile intervention, and thus reinforce suspicions in respondent populations. However, an increasing number of level of care studies use random assignment designs. More commonly used are control populations that are closely matched and receive different interventions or services. The degree of validity of individual identifiers (see section 2.2.2) is critical for the success of population match assumptions (Pumariega et al., 1995).

2.5. Definition of Process and Outcome Variables and Domains

As part of designing an outcome evaluation design for either a program or a system of care, population/client, process, and outcome variables or indicators need to be defined. This allows the evaluation to answer the key questions of which interventions work, for whom, and how. Program characteristics are key in developing an evaluation design. The philosophy of the program or system determines the service model/ modalities delivered (how it expects to facilitate change) and the associated process (performance) variables or indicators to be examined. Process indicators can include referral processes, access procedures and portals of entry, type and frequency of interventions, length of stay or number of visits, the degree to which individual treatment goals on care plans are met, staff involved in interventions, and demonstration of precursor changes or behaviors as a result of applying interventions. Outcome indicators in evaluation usually involve domains of symptom change, functional change, safety, cost, community tenure and level of restrictiveness, and consumer/family burden and satisfaction (Windle, Jacobs, & Sherman, 1986).

2.6. Impact of Culture, Ethnicity, and Social Class

Sampling of culturally diverse groups must assure that the racial/ ethnic, socioeconomic status, age, and gender composition of any sample reflects the service population. However, sampling within a given region or cultural group/subgroup leads to limited applicability of the results to that group. Sampling across different regions or subgroups often requires a much larger sample. Oversampling or "stratification" of samples may be necessary if the samples of culturally diverse individuals are too few in number to be representative (Pumariega, 1996).

Instrumentation and measurement strategies require many cultural considerations. Very few instruments are appropriate for use across different cultural groups, and some have subtle but distinct cross-cultural biases and require significant adaptation and testing to establish operational equivalence (Guillermin, Bombardier, & Beaton, 1993; Pumariega, 1996). A common issue that arises is that of using monocultural instruments versus cross-cultural instruments. Monocultural instruments may be necessary when specific aspects of a culture are being evaluated as a variable in the impact of a program, such as ethnic pride/ethnic identification in a particular culture or particular cultural beliefs/practices. Such instruments should be normed for the particular group or subgroup studied. Cross-cultural instruments, or instruments that theoretically can measure constructs cross-culturally, are necessary when making comparisons across cultural/ethnic groups. It may be necessary to develop parallel versions of instruments that are specific for different groups, or even to pilot-test instruments with community populations to obtain normative data and to identify problems in acceptability and response (Flaherty et al., 1988; Pumariega et al., 1995).

Qualitative or ethnographic approaches may be useful in obtaining information about culturally related variables, eliciting important perceptions or attitudes without the stringent categorical limits of rating instruments (Thornton & Garret, 1995). These approaches are often consonant with cultural values and means of transmission of information in many communities, which include differences in traditions of oral versus written language and what types of information are to be shared with whom and when. Such methods include open-ended questions, questionnaires, interviews, or observational data. Focus groups of community members or leaders can discuss certain problems to be addressed by intervention and develop associated themes. These can be compared to similar groups postintervention. Ethnographic measures can be used in combination with standardized instruments or to develop culturally sensitive standardized measures (Pumariega, 1996).

There are special issues to be considered around the measurement of specific, culturally related variables. The measurement of cultural identification and cultural value orientation presents particular challenges. The construct that is most commonly endorsed in the cross-cultural mental health field is that of biculturality or multiculturality (i.e., that culturally diverse individuals by necessity are bicultural or multicultural in order to adapt successfully). The domain of cultural/ethnic identification must allow for this construct and take into account a number of domains, such as self-identification, relational patterns, culturally related traditions and preferences (clothing, foods, traditions, language, media), and cultural value orientation. In order to measure the latter, one must decide on a model for value orientation and on which dimensions to measure (e.g., attitudes vs. behaviors). For children and for many families, the measure of concrete behaviors or activity orientations (culturally related activities of daily living) are a valuable means of assessing cultural identification. These include simple activities such as the amount of time spent with family, religious activity, and time spent exposed to the media (Pumariega et al., 1992). As mentioned previously, the measure of functional status needs to differ ecologically according to cultural expectations for role functioning. Measures of socioeconomic status need to be nonintrusive so as to assure cooperation and valid responses. The implementation of traditional cultural healing methods requires special measures and methods for certification of the appropriate application of the intervention by a healer/practitioner, as well as for the expected behavioral or attitudinal responses. The collaboration of spiritual healers in developing such measures may be crucial, so that they are relevant as well as acceptable (Pumariega, 1996; Robbins, 1994).

3. Approaches to Children's Mental Health Services Research and Literature Review

3.1. General Service Need, Utilization, and Access Studies

A number of studies have been devoted to examining the factors that lead to access to and utilization of child mental health services. Barber, Rosenblatt, Harris, and Attkisson (1992) reported high levels of family dysfunction as well as physical and sexual abuse and neglect in their population in San Francisco. Furthermore, they found that age, race, history of physical and sexual abuse, and history of psychiatric diagnosis were correlated to previous out-of-home placements. In an epidemiological survey of Puerto Rico, Staghezza-Jaramillo, Bird, Gould, and Canino (1995) evaluated the utilization of mental health services and barriers to access in 777 children and adolescents recruited from a probability sample. They found the overall service use was 6%, compared to 26% of children who had definite emotional disturbances and 5% who had probable disturbances. Services were provided for the most part by psychologists and social workers in school settings and general medical facilities. In 60% of the children who did not receive services, parents saw their problems as "not serious," with children more likely to use services if teachers perceived the need or if the rated high levels of parental criticism and hostility. Cullinan, Epstein, and Quinn (1996) examined individual identifying variables and their relationship to personal and family service utilization and level of placement in a suburban Chicago area system of care. They generated five "placement clusters": Cluster 1 (few placements), Cluster 2 (psychiatric hospital), Cluster 3 (correctional), Cluster 4 (relative/friend and psychiatric hospital), Cluster 5 (foster care in combination with moderate extent of psychiatric hospital, group home, and residential placement). Clusters did not differ significantly by age group, diagnostic group, IQ, parental marital status, maternal employment, mental illness risk, substance abuse risk, criminal convictions risk, within-family violence risk, or total risks. However, they differed by sex, DSM status, medication usage, adjudications, living arrangements, and public assistance. Pavuluri, Luk, and McGee (1996) evaluated barriers to help seeking of preschool children with behavioral problems using a screening and evaluation study of 320 preschool children. Only 19% of children with behavioral disturbances had parents who crossed all filters in the screens for help seeking. Major blocks to help seeking were parental recognition of problems and overcoming perceived barriers to care. Parents sought help more frequently from informal sources and sought less help when they were separated, had a lower income, and faced multiple adversities, which are themselves risk factors for childhood behavioral disturbances. Leaf et al. (1996) reported on the mental health service utilization data from the Methodological Epidemiological Catchment Area (MECA) study, which is the methodological precursor to the national mental health epidemiological and services study of children and adolescents, titled UNO-CAP (Utilization, Need, and Outcomes for Child and Adolescent Psychopathology). In this study, an instrument called the SURF (Services Utilization and Risk Factor Interview) was administered along with the DISC 2.3 diagnostic interview. It contained items on services utilization, barriers to access, demographic factors, functional impairment, and risk and protective factors to over 1,000 respondents selected through community probability sampling at four sites (New York suburban, San Juan, New Haven, and Atlanta). Different patterns emerged in the four communities, with youth in New York being more likely to receive mental health services (18%), whereas youth in San Juan had the lowest utilization (7.4%); youth in New Haven were 3–3.5 times as likely to have services delivered in general medical settings as youth in New York and San Juan. Overall service use differed little in the three U.S. mainland sites, approximately 23% when parent and child reports (which were often divergent) were combined. About 38–44% of youth with psychiatric diagnoses received services in the last year, with youth with both psychiatric diagnoses and low levels of function as measured by the C-GAS being 6.8 times as likely to receive services as youth with neither condition. Both diagnostic status and level of function were found to contribute to service use equally in this study.

3.2. Level-of-Care Studies

3.2.1. Inpatient and Residential Treatment

Psychiatric hospitalization and residential treatment for children and adolescents was relatively rare until the 1970s and 1980s, when there was explosive growth in frequency and utilization as a result of higher levels of third-party reimbursement (England & Cole, 1992). More recently, it has been viewed with greater skepticism given its high cost as well as limited documentation of outcome. Some studies have supported the role of psychiatric hospitalization as only one component of the continuum of services. They point to predictors of positive outcome from hospitalization, such as child and family characteristics, diagnostic features, length of stay, and aftercare (Blotcky, Dimperio, & Gossett, 1984; Curry, 1991; Dalton, Muller, & Forman, 1989; Parmalee et al., 1995; Pfeiffer & Strzelecki, 1990). However, the child's adjustment within the hospital setting failed to predict long-term subsequent adjustment, with family support being a more significant predictor (Curry, 1991). The few studies that have compared inpatient treatment with nonresidential alternatives in children have not examined comparability of outcomes, but studies with adults have indicated that alternatives to hospitalization had better outcomes, particularly in terms of clinical status, subsequent employment, independent living, expense of treatment, and readmission (Braun et al., 1981; Kiesler, 1993). Hoagwood and Cunningham (1992) studied outcomes of all children and adolescents (n = 114) with serious emotional disturbances placed by school districts for educational purposes over a 3-year period. Total expenditures in treating these children totaled $5 million, averaging $80,000 per child. Only 25% of the children had a positive outcome, defined as return to school of a vocational placement, whereas another 11% made substantial progress, and 63% made minimal to no progress. There was no correlation between cost and outcomes, although positive outcomes were associated with shorter lengths of stay. Students with positive outcomes had more severe emotional disturbances at the outset. Again, family involvement and the availability of community-based services at discharge were the most likely reasons for positive outcomes.

3.2.2. Community-Based Residential Services

A number of innovative, community-based residential programs have been piloted, which offer an intermediate level of care with some of the advantages of traditional residential treatments without the degree of restrictiveness, cost, stigma, or disruption of family and community support usually associated with these. Few of these have been subjected to systematic evaluation in terms of outcomes and the process of care. For example, Chamberlain (1990, 1996), and Chamberlain and Weinrott (1990) reported on studies in which children were assigned to therapeutic foster care or regular care, with symptoms, function, and system outcomes being measured. Results indicated that children receiving this intervention could be better maintained in their communities with substantially lower costs than for control group homes. On 2-year follow-up data, fewer youth in the experimental group were rearrested (50% vs. 94%). In the only other control study of therapeutic foster care (Lee, Clark, & Boyd, 1994), fewer aggressive behaviors and fewer general behavioral problems were reported by children treated in therapeutic foster care compared to group homes. Friman, Toner, Soper, Sinclair, and Shanahan (1996) evaluated a program to protect the placements of 23 highly disruptive youth in voluntary residential care. They found that reduced client-to-staff ratios helped to reduce incidents of program restrictiveness and increased program success to a level comparable to that of a much less disruptive cohort. Teare, Authier, and Peterson (1994) studied the transition of youth from community shelters to formal treatment settings in 154 youth departing a homeless and runaway shelter. They found that youth at higher risk of suicide, and who came from more dysfunctional families, departed to more restrictive environments.

3.2.3. Community-Based Nonresidential Services

A number of innovative approaches that go far beyond traditional outpatient services in providing more intensive and individualized services have been developed recently and are undergoing initial evaluation studies. Kiser, Culhane, and Hadley (1995) documented the increasing utilization of day treatment programs for the treatment of children and adolescents in their national survey of day-treatment programs. Out of 560 programs nationally, 95 indicated that at least 50% of their clients were children and youth, with 29% of the programs providing acute care (under 30 days), 29% providing intermediate care (30–90 days), and 50% providing long-term care (over 91 days). For-profit programs had lower mean lengths of stay, treated more youth with affective disorders and substance abuse, provided more hours of psychological assessment per week, and charged more per day. Not-for-profit programs had longer lengths of stay, served more youth with conduct disorders, and reported lower costs. Bandoroff and Scherer (1994) evaluated a treatment program that combined a wilderness intervention with an intensive family-therapy intervention. A group of 66 youth initially underwent the wilderness intervention, with 27 of them having families who also underwent the family-therapy intervention. There was a high level of family satisfaction with both interventions (92%), with FAM III scores showing reductions from clinical levels to normal levels for families who underwent both interventions. Youth who underwent both interventions, as well as those who only received the wilderness intervention, experienced significant improvements in self-concept and decreased reports of delinquency. These interventions are aided by the increasing effectiveness of cognitive, behavioral, family-based, and psychopharmacological therapies. Behavioral and cognitive interventions have demonstrated effectiveness in depressive disorders, anxiety disorders, psychosomatic disorders, and conduct disorders (Van Hasselt & Hersen, 1993). Diamond, Serrano, Dickey, and Sonis (1996) reviewed selected studies in family-based treatment as well as several process and outcome meta-analytic studies. They found that family-based therapies have demonstrated effectiveness in the treatment of schizophrenia, conduct disorders, and substance abuse, and some effectiveness in the treatment of eating disorders, with family-based therapies being as effective as other modalities. Pharmacological effectiveness was demonstrated in the treatment of attention deficit disorders, conduct disorders with aggression, schizophrenia, obsessive–compulsive disorder and other anxiety disorders, and beginning evidence of treatment effectiveness in the treatment of depressive disorders, eating disorders, and bipolar disorders (Campbell & Cueva, 1995).

Model programs that consist of multiple, coordinated, community-based interventions based on an interdisciplinary approach have been successfully implemented and tested. For example, Moore (1990) reported on a Children's Mobile Outreach service that provides stabilization of the child in his/her present location at times of crisis. Their evaluation examined children who received evaluation services only, as well as children who also received mobile outreach services. The children mostly lived in natural or adoptive homes; some lived in shelters, group homes, and other nontherapeutic residential settings. The most common problems involved aggression, oppositional behavior, depression with suicidal ideation, and extreme agitation. At 1-year follow-up, the program had successfully stabilized 77% of its clients within their current residence, while only 42% of clients who received evaluation averted hospitalization. Pastore, Thomas, and Newman (1990) reported on the Therapeutic In-Home Emergency Services program, which provides a 6-week, home-based crisis intervention and family therapy to youth at risk. In their evaluation of 50 youth served in their program, 45 of them remained in their home for over a year after discharge. Increases in family activities and extent of family participation were correlated with reduction in internalizing symptoms and improved self-control, and improved individual functioning was correlated overall to family functioning. Doherty, Manderson, and Carter-Ake (1987) evaluated a program that offers time-limited hospitalization and an array of comprehensive services in the community for children with acute psychotic symptoms. They tracked 212 youth over a 3-year period and found an average length of stay of 28 hospital days, only 4% failing to comply with follow-up, and only 15% needing long-term residential services, with 67% discharged to less-intensive outpatient care. Evans et al. (1994) randomly assigned children to receive either intensive case management or family-based treatment foster care and assessed symptoms, functioning, parental skills, and placement rates. Outcome data at 6-month follow-up show no difference between groups in all variables except for parent skills, where greater improvement is seen in the family-based treatment group. Another randomized trial of intensive case management associated with the Robert Woods Johnson model demonstration program (Burns, Farmer, Angold, Costello, & Behar, 1997) found that adding a trained case manager to the child's treatment team resulted in longer participation in services, use of a wider array of services, use of fewer inpatient days, and increased child and family satisfaction, but no improvements in symptoms or functional level. Family support services are increasingly utilized in systems of care, but only a study by Reis, Bennett, Orme, and Herz (1989) has evaluated these services using a controlled design. In that study, no relationship was found between support services and improvements in symptoms, function, or family characteristics, though these need to be evaluated more appropriately from a consumer perspective.

The wraparound model of care embodies this approach toward multimodal, community-based interventions. This model emphasizes aggressive outreach, use of least restrictive treatment options, and individualized, flexible, and unconditional child- and family-centered services for children imminently at risk or already in out-of-home placements. A number of studies of model wraparound programs in different communities across the nation with diverse populations of at-risk children and families have reported positive outcomes in terms of reduction of externalizing behavioral problems, level of function, reduction in out-of-home placement, improved family management skills and function, and consumer/family satisfaction (Clark, Lee, Prange, & McDonald, 1996; Eber, Osuch, & Redditt, 1996; Evans, Armstrong, & Kuppinger, 1996; Hyde, Burchard, & Woodworth, 1996).

A similar approach that has attracted much attention recently is the Multisystemic Therapy (MST) model. This model has been applied with youth at risk of detention and incarceration, with significant results in reducing out-of-home placement, externalizing criminal problem behaviors, and rates of incarceration, particularly with rural minority youth in a randomized clinical trial (Scherer, Brondino, Henggeler, Melton, & Hanley, 1994). As a follow-up to this randomized trial, Henggeler, Melton, Smith, Schoenwald, and Hanley (1993) examined the archival juvenile justice in the state to evaluate rearrest rates an average of 2.4 years later, and they found significantly lower rearrest rates in youth who received MST. Schoenwald, Ward, Henggeler, Pickerel, and Patel (1996) demonstrated that MST resulted in sufficient cost offsets in terms of reduction of utilization of other more restrictive services (inpatient, residential, and incarceration) by youth offenders with substance-abuse disorders. In the short term, it offsets the incremental cost of its implementation and potentially could result in longer term cost savings in service utilization.

3.3. Evaluation of State and Regional Systems of Care

The demographic, clinical, social, educational, and family functioning of children and adolescents served in system of care programs located in California (Barber, Rosenblatt, Harris, & Attkisson, 1992; Rosenblatt & Attkisson, 1992), Illinois (Epstein, Cullinan, Quinn, & Cumblad, 1994), and Virginia (Landrum, Singh, Nemil, Ellis, & Best, 1995) has been reported. The individuals served in such systems tend to be older adolescent males of average intelligence, who exhibit primarily externalizing disorders of a severe nature that are chronic in nature. They have received services from multiple agencies, with a high percentage having histories of out-of-home placement and being on psychotropic agents for behavioral control. However, there are few outcome data on the overall service system in these states or on the levels of care offered to children within them. In one of the few state level studies, Evans, Banks, Huz, and McNulty (1994) evaluated the state of New York's Children and Youth Intensive Case Management Program, whose goal is to maintain children in the least restrictive environment appropriate to treatment needs. They reported on outcomes on 1,700 children served by this program since 1988. Participation in the program was associated with fewer hospital admissions and fewer hospital days 2 years after intervention as compared to prior to enrollment.

The Vermont system of care took a particularly innovative approach in developing the Wraparound Care Initiative for seriously emotionally disturbed children, which formally adopted the wraparound model of care. They have recently reported a number of outcome findings from their experience with this model. Pandiani, Maynard, and Schacht (1994) reported on a study of service utilization and movement between residential options in the Vermont system and used data on 504 children and youth served over 3 years to develop a Markov mathematical model for the operation of the system in terms of its transition across levels of care. They then modeled the impact of home-based services and/or step-down procedures, and found that both of these incrementally improved the operation of the system, with decreasing out-of-home placement and less restrictive placements when these were made. Bruns, Burchard, and Yoe (1995) evaluated outcomes for 27 youth with serious emotional disturbances served in the Vermont system using their wraparound model for over a year. They found a significantly lower incidence of negative behaviors placing them at risk out-of-home placement, increased compliance behaviors, and decreases in Child Behavior Checklist (CBCL) Total Problem T-scores. Whereas 70% of the youth previously required inpatient or residential care, 89% were maintained in the community after a year, with lower total costs of care. Yoe, Santarcangelo, Atkins, and Burchard (1996) reported that after 12 months, 40 youth being served in this program were in significantly less restrictive community-based placements and had significantly fewer problem behaviors than at intake.

3.4. Evaluation of Model Demonstration Systems

The emerging community-based, systems-of-care model was introduced and tested over the past 5 years by a number of funding programs and in a number of sites. Over 20 pilot community programs were funded by the Center for Mental Health Services in the past 5 years and based in states and communities with strong child mental health services infrastructures. The Robert Woods Johnson Foundation (England & Cole, 1992) developed and funded eight community-based systems-model demonstration sites that utilized existing community-based services and agencies, organized them into networks with access to flexible funding for services for seriously emotionally disturbed children, and used actuarial models to develop capitation rates for the covered population of children as well as subcapitation rates for children with serious emotional disturbances. In North Carolina, the state's Division of Mental Health not only successfully obtained a model Robert Woods Johnson site in the Asheville/ Buncombe County area but was also responsible for the implementation of the Ft. Bragg Demonstration Project, the largest totally developed system of care and continuum of services project in the United States.

3.4.1. Ventura Demonstration Project

The Ventura Demonstration Project was one of the early children's system-of-care demonstrations, implemented in Ventura County, California. It piloted the integration of school-based and community-based residential services in combination with blended multiagency funding and services coordination. Jordan and Hernandez (1990) reported that the program offset two-thirds of its cost by reducing other public agency costs and improved a variety of client-related outcomes. These included reduced out-of-home placements, reduced recidivism of juvenile offenders, improved school attendance, and improved academic performance. As part of their evaluation, Jordan and Hernandez performed a cost–outcome analysis of their service planning. They found that treatment outcome was not directly related to its cost, suggesting that lower cost alternatives may be as effective as more costly traditional services. Ichnose, Kingdon, and Hernandez (1994) evaluated the Ventura interagency resource and planning approach as applied to special education students with emotional disturbances, including developing day-treatment and school-based services with blended mental health and school funding. They reported an average of 3.5 fewer youth per month placed in group homes, total savings of $290,000 in expected placement costs, and total revenues of $280,000 from their community alternative programs.

3.4.2. Fort Bragg Demonstration Project

The Fort Bragg Demonstration Project is one of the largest systems-of-care demonstration projects attempted so far. The project developed a comprehensive continuum of care for the children of military dependents at Fort Bragg, North Carolina, with ready access to outpatient and intermediate levels of care, and relatively restricted utilization of residential and inpatient services. The outcomes from this system was compared to the usual CHAMPUS-funded services accessed by military dependents at various military installations nationally. Multiple process, quality, and outcome indicators (including clinical indicators, level of function, cost of care, etc.) were evaluated and compared across the experimental site and the usual service sites.

The initial results from the evaluation of this project have been widely debated in the mental health services literature. They suggest that the demonstration project did achieve significantly lower restrictiveness of care, higher consumer satisfaction, greatly increased access to services (5.9% of children covered by the project were treated, as compared to 1.8% at the comparison sites), and greater funding spent in less restrictive services (27% spent on inpatient and residential services in the project, compared to 84% at the comparison sites). However, clinical and functional outcomes were not significantly different overall, with split differences in different diagnostic subgroups favoring either the project or the comparison sites, and overall outcomes being no different. Additionally, costs were not significantly different and possibly were even somewhat higher in the demonstration site (Bickman, Heflinger, Lambert, & Summerfeldt, 1996). A number of arguments have been raised regarding the lack of outcome effects found in the study, including the timing of the project's implementation (during Desert Storm and the Gulf War, which artificially drove up utilization); the design of benefits (no copayment), and relative lack of utilization review, provider accountability, and intensive case management to mobilize children across levels of care, at a time when the implementation of managed care technologies was in full swing in private, third-party managers of CHAMPUS benefits; the choice of multiple narrow-band measures of psychopathology, which may have inflated nonsignificant results, and the lack of long-term comparisons (which are yet to be performed, but are forthcoming); and possible problems with the interventions themselves, which some believed were not sufficiently embedded in the community (Burchard, 1996; Evans & Banks, 1996; Friedman, 1996; Henggeler, Schoenwald, & Munger, 1996).

3.5. Minority/Cross-Cultural Services Research

Services research literature on underserved minority youth has been sparse and had initially focused on documenting racial differences in services provided. Comprehensive services studies require analyses of the relationship between race and service delivery across a range of services to include mental health, child welfare, and juvenile justice. However, studies to date usually have been limited to one service area. For example, African-American children tend to remain in foster care for longer periods of time and have more foster-care placements than European–American children (Finch & Fanshel, 1985; Mech, 1983; Seaberg & Tolley, 1986; Shyne, 1980; Shyne & Shroeder, 1978). Longres and Torrecilha (1992) examined the effect of race on the delivery of mental health and found a significant relationship between race and the service needs of racial ethnic minorities. Another similar finding was established by Hawkins and Salisbury (1983), who found that minority juvenile offenders in delinquency prevention programs were more likely to receive academic and employment skills in comparison to white youth, who were more likely to be given family services and affective skills training.

Studies have shown culturally diverse children to be underrepresented in mental health institutions and overrepresented in child welfare and juvenile justice settings and placements (Gruber, 1980). Studies have shown that even when the two groups are equally psychiatrically impaired, African-American adolescents are more likely to be incarcerated, and white adolescents are likely to be psychiatrically hospitalized (Cohen et al., 1990; Lewis, Balla, & Shanok, 1979; Lewis, Shanok, Cohen, Klingfield, & Frisone, 1980; Westendorp, Brink, Robertson, & Ortiz, 1986). In a large study of incarcerated youth in South Carolina (Pumariega et al., 1996a, 1996b), incarcerated youth, comprised of over 70% African Americans, had higher levels of psychopathology than youth treated in community treatment settings, but previously utilized lower levels of mental health services. Cuffe, Waller, Cuccaro, Pumariega, and Garrison (1995) found significantly lower rates for treatment of depression among African-American youth as compared to white youth in their community-based longitudinal epidemiological study. Pumariega, Glover, Holzer, and Nguyen (in press) reported on results from a large school-based study of adolescent psychopathology and found that lower rates of mental health services utilization by Hispanic youth in Texas were related to ethnicity as well as to regional service accessibility, socioeconomic status, and family characteristics, confirming a more complex picture of factors determining mental health service use by underserved minority youth.

Some studies have focused on biases in diagnostic assessment that may lead to different service utilization outcomes for minority youth. Kilgus et al. (1995) examined racial differences in the final discharge diagnoses of psychiatrically hospitalized adolescents. Mood and anxiety disorders, as well as substance abuse, were more often diagnosed in whites than African Americans. They found that African-American adolescents were more likely involuntarily committed than white adolescents and had significantly more organic/psychotic diagnoses. Fabrega, Ulrich, and Mezzich (1993) found that African-American youth were overdiagnosed with conduct disorders and disruptive behavior disorders in their clinic population. Some authors (Cervantes & Arroyo, 1994) have indicated the need for caution in the utilization of the standard psychiatric diagnostic nosology across different ethnic groups, where symptom expression and clustering may differ.

4. Future of Child Mental Health Services Research

4.1. Anticipated Developments and Advances

4.1.1. Large System Studies

The immediate future of child mental health services research looks extremely promising, especially given emerging and newly initiated studies. The evaluations of the systems of care model demonstration programs funded by the Robert Woods Johnson Foundation, the Casey Foundation, and the Center for Mental Health Services are soon to be available, enriching the knowledge base about the operational characteristics of community-based systems of care for children and adolescents as well as the methodological basis for such research and evaluation. The diversity of sites, populations being served, service system structures, levels of care and interventions, and degree of interagency involvement will provide much data on the effectiveness of different systems of care approaches and interventions with diverse populations of children and families.

The implementation and completion of the study on Utilization, Needs, and Outcomes for Child and Adolescent Populations (UNO-CAP), the national multisite child and adolescent study on the epidemiology, services utilization, and outcomes for children with mental/emotional disturbances in the United States, will be completed within the next 3–4 years. This study will provide data that should help us understand the extent of need for child mental health services on a national scale, as well as provide information on the effectiveness of our current service systems and our evaluation and research methods. The results of UNO-CAP will certainly fuel the national debate on the extent of resources that should be allocated for child mental health services given both the need for such services and their current effectiveness and efficiency (Jensen, Hoagwood, & Petti, 1996).

4.1.2. Methodological Advances

In addition to the advances in design and instrumentation that the aforementioned studies will provide, other developments in the mental health services field will impact our capacity to study systems of care and their components. The push toward financing and management of costs through managed care technologies is contributing to the development of more complete and reliable electronic clinical records and databases, which include not only client characteristics but also provider characteristics and service provision data. These management-of-information systems are critical for the calculation of financing formulas, for the measure of clinical outcomes, and for quality assurance and improvement. Additionally, managed care networks are promoting the development of systemwide measures of process and outcome variables for the evaluation of contract performance and of quality and cost assessment. For example, some state-level public mental health managed care contracts as well as model requests for proposals such as that developed by the American Academy of Child and Adolescent Psychiatry (Pumariega et al., 1996; Pumariega, 1997) call for the development of clear process and outcome measures and extensive management of information systems to support their measurement and analysis. The advent of electronic clinical records, with direct data input by the clinician and including the use of systematic clinical and functional rating instruments, could revolutionize the field of child mental health services research, making critical data on most of these systems readily analyzable (Pumariega et al., 1997b).

4.2. Future Needs in Services Research

In spite of research activity currently underway, there are still areas where significant deficits exist in our knowledge base on children's mental health services and systems of care. The areas listed are identified by a number of authors (Hoagwood & Hohmann, 1993; Jensen et al., 1996; Kupermine & Cohen, 1995; Pumariega, 1996).

4.2.1.   Hospitalization and Residential Treatment

Although these are the most restrictive and costly levels of care in any system, there is still a paucity of well-designed studies that document their relative effectiveness and appropriateness. Randomized collaborative studies with sufficiently large cohorts that examine the relative benefits of these interventions in different clinical populations and more clearly define their role within the service system are still needed.

4.2.2.   Studies of Community-Based Systems of Care Models

The impact of parent, family, and consumer involvement in systems of care has yet to receive much formal attention in spite of data that point to the importance of these variables. The system outcomes of increased utilization of alternative interventions at less restrictive levels of care, interventions and services with preventive value at the most accessible levels (such as school and home-based interventions), and the integration of these different services using management of information systems based on electronic database technologies to facilitate seamless level of care transition and continual case management are additional areas of focus for future research.

4.2.3.   Culturally Competent and Appropriate Services

Studies that examine factors impacting on the service need/utilization, barriers to access to care, bias in clinical assessment, bias in service system triage and referral (mental health vs. juvenile justice or child welfare), and comparable effectiveness of child mental health services for underserved minority populations are urgently needed. The impact of cultural competence training for providers, culturally competent services, and access to professionals of color need to be studied given the rapidly rising population of children of color in the United States without a comparable increase in professionals of color. These studies should help establish comparability of outcomes for children of color, who require different treatment approaches and different concepts and measures of functional and clinical outcomes (Pumariega, 1996).

4.2.4.   School–Mental Health Interface

The settings where children are most readily accessible, with the greatest potential for preventive impact on the largest number of children, are school settings. However, relatively few studies have evaluated the impact of school-based mental health services or preventive interventions, nor the role of school-based services within a wider system of care.

4.2.5. Interface with Juvenile Justice and Child Welfare

The community-based-systems perspective has allowed us to recognize children and youth within these two systems as being highly at risk, or already having a high percentage with serious emotional disturbances. Given the foreseeable levels of psychosocial morbidity and resulting societal costs, much attention still needs to be devoted to interventions and systems approaches to address their needs. With the juvenile justice population, early access to mental health services as a means of diversion from incarceration, the impact of court decisions, and access and effectiveness of mental health services in preventing recidivism need to be studied. The impact of mental health services on children under child welfare custody, particularly on permanency planning and reunification for children in foster care, deserve continued emphasis.

4.2.6. Innovative Treatment/Service Approaches

The effectiveness of such innovative treatment and service approaches as family preservation, therapeutic foster homes, wraparound services, and other alternative interventions deserve further systematic evaluation that both establishes their longer-term effectiveness and appropriateness with different populations of seriously emotionally disturbed children and demonstrates their cost-effectiveness.

4.2.7. Cost-Containment and Reimbursement Mechanisms

The current movement toward managed care should serve as the ultimate incentive for right-sizing systems of care, with an inverted pyramid of greatest access and funding to less costly, preventive services and least access and funding to more restrictive, costly services. However, there is a danger of these changes resulting in services restrictions based purely on financial and political pressures and not related to the clinical and functional needs of children and families. Research in this area should evaluate the application of systems of care principles in children's mental health managed care (American Academy of Child and Adolescent Psychiatry, 1996). Studies of state-managed Medicaid waivers need to use epidemiological field methods to study their impact on access to care, quality of care, patterns of utilization, and outcomes. Studies should evaluate capitated financing in children's systems of care, including subcapitation for seriously emotionally disturbed, the relative merits of psychosocial versus medical necessity in establishing service need, and the use of blended funding from multiple service agencies while assuming comprehensive shared risk for psychosocial morbidities.

4.2.8. Interagency Collaboration and Coordination

An increasing trend toward multiagency programs for the coordination of services to children involved with multiple agencies opens opportunities for studies of services coordination and planning approaches, the use of blended flexible funding, and integrated cross-agency case management.

4.2.9. Consultation–Liaison Psychiatry and Behavioral Medicine

This area has traditionally involved the delivery of mental health services for acutely and chronically ill children and their integration with their specialty medical care. With the increasing primary care emphasis in medicine, new areas of focus have emerged. These include services interface with family practice and pediatrics, evaluation of mental health services delivered by primary care physicians, and effectiveness of integrated service delivery models. The effectiveness of services for children with medical illnesses and disabilities in reducing their overall health-care utilization and improving their individual and family functional status deserve further attention.

4.3. Application of Research Findings in Policy and Service Systems Planning

The ultimate value of child mental health services research is in providing an objective basis for rational policy decisions about the organization and financing of needed services and the service system as a whole. The potential impact of this research on state Medicaid waivers and managed care programs, as well as the design of local systems of care, is invaluable. The methods that have been developed within a relatively short time in child mental health services research make it feasible to incorporate ongoing evaluation into systems of care for continual improvement and midcourse corrections as the nature of our populations of children and youth and the types of problems faced change over time. Additionally, such research methods should help us focus increasing attention on preventive strategies that would ultimately benefit society the most.

5. References

Achenbach, T. (1991). *Integrative Guide for the CBCL 4-18, YSR, and TRF Profiles.* Burlington: University of Vermont Department of Psychiatry.

American Psychiatric Association. (1994). *Diagnostic and statistical manual of mental disorders* (4th ed.). Washington, DC: Author.

Bandoroff, S., & Scherer, D. (1994). Wilderness family therapy: An innovative treatment approach for problem youth. *Journal of Child and Family Studies, 3,* 175–191.

Barber, C., Rosenblatt, A., Harris, L., & Attkisson, C. (1992). Use of mental health services among severely emotionally disturbed children and adolescents in San Francisco. *Journal of Child and Family Studies, 1*(2), 183–207.

Berlin, I. (1991). Development of the subspecialty of children and adolescent psychiatry. In J. Weiner (Ed.), *Textbook of child and adolescent psychiatry* (pp. 8–15). Washington, DC: American Psychiatric Press.

Bickman, L., Heflinger, C., Lambert, E., & Summerfeldt, W. (1996). The Fort Bragg Managed Care Experiment: Short-term impact on psychopathology. *Journal of Child and Family Studies, 5,* 137–160.

Blotcky, M., Dimperio, T., & Gossett, J. (1984). Follow-up of children treated in psychiatric hospitals: A review of studies. *American Journal of Psychiatry, 141,* 1499–1507.

Braun, P., Kochansky, G., Shapiro, R., Greenberg, S., Gudeman, J., Johnson, S., & Shore, M. (1981). Overview: Deinstitutionalization of psychiatric inpatients, a critical review of outcome studies. *American Journal of Psychiatry, 138,* 736–749.

Bruns, E., Burchard, J., & Yoe, J. (1995). Evaluating the Vermont system of care: Outcomes associated with community-based wraparound services. *Journal of Child and Family Studies, 4,* 321–339.

Burchard, J. (1996). Evaluation of the Fort Bragg managed care experiment. *Journal of Child and Family Studies, 5,* 173–176.

Burns, B., Farmer, E., Angold, A., Costello, E., & Behar, L. (1997). A randomized trial of case management for youths with serious emotional disturbance. *Journal of Child Clinical Psychology, 25*(4), 476–486.

Burns, B., Taube, C., & Taube, J. (1990). Mental health services for adolescents. Contract paper prepared by the Office of Technology Assessment, U.S. Congress. Cited in U.S. Congress, Office of Technology Assessment (November, 1991) *Adolescent Health, Volume II: Background and Effectiveness of Selected Prevention and Treatment Services* (OTA-H-466). Washington, DC: U.S. Government Printing Office.

Campbell, M., & Cueva, J. (1995). Psychopharmacology in child and adolescent psychiatry: Part II. A review of the past seven years. *Journal of American Academy of Child Psychiatry, 34,* 1262–1272.

Caron, C., & Rutter, M. (1991). Co-morbidity in child psychopathology: Concept, issues, and research strategies. *Journal of Child Psychology and Psychiatry, 32,* 1063–1080.

Cervantes, R., & Arroyo, W. (1994). DSM-IV: Implications for Hispanic children and adolescents. *Hispanic Journal of Behavioral Sciences, 16,* 8–27.

Chamberlain, P. (1990). Comparative evaluation of specialized foster care for seriously delinquent youths: A first step. *International Journal of Family Care, 2,* 1–36.

Chamberlain, P. (1996). Community-based residential treatment for adolescents with conduct disorder. In T. H. Ollendick & R. J. Prinz (Eds.), *Advances in clinical child psychology* (Vol. 18, pp. 63–90). New York: Plenum Press.

Chamberlain, P., & Weinrott, M. (1990). Specialized foster care: Treating seriously emotionally disturbed children. *Children Today, 19,* 24–27.

Clark, H., Lee, B., Prange, M., & McDonald, B. (1996). Children lost within the foster care system: Can wraparound service strategies improve placement outcome? *Journal of Child and Family Studies, 5,* 39–54.

Cohen, R., Parmalee, D., Irwin, L., Weisz, J., Howard, P., Purcell, P., & Best, A. (1990). Characteristics of children and adolescents in a psychiatric hospital and a correctional facility. *Journal of American Academy of Child Psychiatry, 29,* 909–913.

Conners, C. K. (1969). A teacher rating scale for use in drug studies with children. *American Journal of Psychiatry, 126,* 884–888.

Costello, E. J., Burns, B., Angold, A., & Leaf, P. (1993). How can epidemiology improve mental health services for children and adolescents? *Journal of American Academy of Child Psychiatry, 32,* 1106–1113.

Cross, T., Bazron, B., Dennis, K., & Isaacs, M. (1989). *Towards a culturally competent system of care.* Washington, DC: CASSP Technical Assistance Center, Georgetown University Child Development Center.

Cuffe, S., Waller, J., Cuccaro, M., Pumariega, A., & Garrison, C. (1995). Race and gender differences in the treatment of psychiatric disorders in young adolescents. *Journal of American Academy of Child and Adolescent Psychiatry, 34,* 1536–1543.

Cullinan, D., Epstein, M., & Quinn, K. (1996). Patterns of correlates of personal, family and prior placement variables in an interagency community-based system of care. *Journal of Child and Family Studies, 5*(3), 299–321.

Curry, J. (1991). Outcome research on residential treatment: Applications and suggested directions. *American Journal of Orthopsychiatry, 61,* 348–357.

Dalton, R., Muller, B., & Forman, M. (1989). The psychiatric hospitalization of children: An overview. *Child Psychiatry and Human Development, 19,* 231–245.

DeChillo, N., Koren, P., & Schultze, K. (1994). From paternalism to partnership: Family and professional collaboration in children's mental health. *American Journal of Orthopsychiatry, 64,* 564–576.

Diamond, G., Serrano, A., Dickey, D., & Sonis, W. (1996). Current status of family-based outcome and process research. *Journal of American Academy of Child and Adolescent Psychiatry, 35,* 6–16.

Doherty, M., Manderson, M., & Carter-Ake, L. (1987). Time-limited psychiatric hospitalization of children: A model and three year outcome. *Hospital and Community Psychiatry, 38,* 643–647.

Eber, L., Osuch, R., & Redditt, C. (1996). School-based applications of the wraparound process: Early results on service provision and student outcomes. *Journal of Child and Family Studies, 5,* 83–99.

England, M. J., & Cole, R. (1992). Building systems of care for youth with serious mental illness. *Hospital and Community Psychiatry, 43,* 630–633.

Epstein, M., Cullinan, D., Quinn, K., & Cumblad, C. (1994). Characteristics of children with emotional and behavioral disorders in community-based programs designed to prevent placement in residential facilities. *Journal of Emotional and Behavioral Disorders, 2,* 51–57.

Epstein, N., Baldwin, L., & Bishop, D. (1983). The McMaster Family Assessment Device. *Journal of Marital and Family Therapy, 9,* 171–180.

Evans, M., Armstrong, M., Dollard, N., Kuppinger, A., Huz, S., & Wood, V. (1994). Development and evaluation of treatment foster care and family centered intensive case management in New York. *Journal of Emotional and Behavioral Disorders, 2,* 228–239.

Evans, M., Armstrong, M., & Kuppinger, A. (1996). Family-centered intensive case management: A step towards understanding individualized care. *Journal of Child and Family Studies, 5,* 55–65.

Evans, M., & Banks, S. (1996). The Fort Bragg managed care experiment. *Journal of Child and Family Studies, 5,* 169–172.

Evans, M., Banks, S., Huz, S., & McNulty, T. (1994). Initial hospitalization and community tenure outcomes of intensive case management for children and youth with serious emotional disturbances. *Journal of Child and Family Studies, 3,* 225–234.

Fabrega, H., Ulrich, R., & Mezzich, J. (1993). Do Caucasian and black adolescents differ at psychiatric intake? *Journal of the Academy of Child and Adolescent Psychiatry, 32,* 407–413.

Finch, S., & Fanshel, D. (1985). Testing the equality of discharge patterns in foster care. *Social Work Research and Abstracts, 21,* 3–10.

Flaherty, J., Gaviria, F., Pathak, D., Mitchell, T., Wintrob, R., Richman, J., & Birz, S. (1988). Developing instruments for cross-cultural psychiatric research. *Journal of Nervous and Mental Disease, 176,* 257–263.

Friedman, R. (1996). The Fort Bragg study: What can we conclude? *Journal of Child and Family Studies, 5,* 161–168.

Friesen, B., & Koroloff, N. (1990). Family-centered services: Implications for mental health administration and research. *Journal of Mental Health Administration, 17,* 13–25.

Friman, P., Toner, C., Soper, S., Sinclair, J., & Shanahan, D. (1996). Maintaining placement for troubled and disruptive adolescents in voluntary residential care: The role of reduced youth-to-staff ratios. *Journal of Child and Family Studies, 5,* 337–347.

Garland, A., & Besinger, B. (1996). Adolescents' perceptions of outpatient mental health services. *Journal of Child and Family Studies, 5,* 355–375.

Gruber, M. (1980). Inequality in the social services. *Social Service Review, 54,* 59–75.

Guillermin, F., Bombardier, C., & Beaton, D. (1993). Cross-cultural adaptation of health related quality of life measures: Literature review and proposed guidelines. *Journal of Clinical Epidemiology, 46,* 1417–1432.

Hawkins, J., & Salisbury, G. (1983). Delinquency prevention programs for minorities of color. *Social Work Research and Abstracts, 19,* 246–267.

Henggeler, S., Melton, G., Smith, L., Schoenwald, S., & Hanley, J. (1993). Family preservation using multisystemic therapy: Long-term follow-up to a clinical trial with serious juvenile offenders. *Journal of Child and Family Studies, 2,* 283–293.

Henggeler, S., Schoenwald, S., & Munger, R. (1996). Families and therapists achieve clinical outcomes, systems of care mediate the process. *Journal of Child and Family Studies, 5,* 177–183.

Herjanic, B., & Reich, W. (1982). Development of a structured psychiatric interview for children: Agreement between child and parent on individual symptoms. *Journal of Abnormal Child Psychology, 3,* 41–48.

Hoagwood, K., & Cunningham, M. (1992). Outcomes of children with emotional disturbance in residential settings for educational purposes. *Journal of Child and Family Studies, 1,* 129–140.

Hoagwood, K., & Hohmann, A. (1993). Child and adolescent services research at the National Institute of Mental Health: Research opportunities in an emerging field. *Journal of Child and Family Studies, 2,* 259–268.

Hoagwood, K., Jensen, P., Petti, T., & Burns, B. (1996). Outcomes of mental health care for children and adolescents: I. A comprehensive conceptual model. *Journal of the Academy of Child and Adolescent Psychiatry, 35,* 1055–1063.

Hodges, K., & Wong, M. (1996). Psychometric characteristics of a multidimensional measure to assess impairment: The Child and Adolescent Functional Assessment Scale. *Journal of Child and Family Studies, 5,* 445–467.

Hyde, K., Burchard, J., & Woodworth, K. (1996). Wrapping services in an urban setting. *Journal of Child and Family Studies, 5,* 67–82.

Ichnose, C., Kingdon, D., & Hernandez, M. (1994). Developing community alternatives to group home placement for seriously emotionally disturbed special education students in the Ventura County system of care. *Journal of Child and Family Studies, 3,* 193–210.

Inouye, D. K. (1988). Children's mental health issues. *American Psychologist, 43*, 813–816.

Jensen, P., Hoagwood, K., & Petti, T. (1996). Outcomes of mental health care for children and adolescents: II. Literature review and application of a comprehensive model. *Journal of the Academy of Child and Adolescent Psychiatry, 35*, 1055–1063.

Jordan, D., & Hernandez, M. (1990). The Ventura Planning Model: A proposal for mental health reform. *Journal of Mental Health Administration, 17*, 26–47.

Kiesler, C. (1993). Mental health policy and mental hospitalization. *Current Directions in Psychological Science, 2*, 93–95.

Kilgus, M., Pumariega, A., & Cuffe, S. (1995). Influence of race on diagnosis in adolescent psychiatric inpatients. *Journal of American Academy of Child and Adolescent Psychiatry, 35*, 167–172.

Kiser, L., Culhane, D., & Hadley, T. (1995). The current practice of child and adolescent partial hospitalization: Results of a national survey. *Journal of American Academy of Child and Adolescent Psychiatry, 34*, 1336–1342.

Knitzer, J. (1982). *Unclaimed children: The failure of public responsibility to children and adolescents in need of mental health services.* Washington, DC: Children's Defense Fund.

Kovacs, M. (1981). Rating scales to assess depression in school-aged children. *Acta Paedopsychiatrica, 46*, 305–315.

Kupermine, G., & Cohen, R. (1995). Building a research base for community services for children and families: What we know and what we need to learn. *Journal of Child and Family Studies, 4*, 147–175.

Landrum, T., Singh, N., Nemil, M., Ellis, C., & Best, A. (1995). Characteristics of children and adolescents with serious emotional disturbance in systems of care. Part II: Community-based services. *Journal of Emotional and Behavioral Disorders, 3*, 141–149.

Leaf, P., Alegria, M., Cohen, P., Goodman, S., Horwitz, S., Hoven, C., Narrow, W., Vaden-Kiernan, M., & Regier, D. (1996). Mental health use in the community and schools: Results from the four community MECA study. *Journal of American Academy of Child and Adolescent Psychiatry, 35*, 89–897.

Lee, B., Clark, H., & Boyd, L. (1994). An individualized system of care for foster children with behavioral and emotional disabilities: Effects on juvenile delinquency. In C. Liberton, R. Friedman, & K. Kutash (Eds.), *Sixth Annual Research Conference Proceedings on Children's Mental Health Services and Policy: Expanding the Research Base.* Tampa: Florida Mental Health Institute, University of South Florida.

Lewis, D., Balla, D., & Shanok, S. (1979). Some evidence of race bias in the diagnosis and treatment of the juvenile offender. *American Journal of Orthopsychiatry, 49*, 53–61.

Lewis, D., Shanok, S., Cohen, R., Klingfield, M., & Frisone, G. (1980). Race bias in the diagnosis and disposition of violent adolescent offenders. *American Journal of Psychiatry, 137*, 1211–1216.

Longres, J., & Torrecilha, R. (1992). Race and the diagnosis, placement and exit status of children and youth in a mental health and disability system. *Journal of Social Services Research, 15*, 43–63.

Lourie, I., & Katz-Leavy, J. (1986). Severely emotionally disturbed children and adolescents. In W. Menninger (Ed.), *The chronically mentally ill* (pp. 159–185). Washington, DC: American Psychiatric Association.

McCubbin, H., & Patterson, J. (1981). *Systematic assessment of family stress, resources, and coping: Tools for research, education, and clinical intervention.* St. Paul: Family Social Service.

Mech, E. (1983). Out-of-home placement rates. *Social Services Review, 75*, 659–667.

Moore, J. (1990). Children's mobile outreach: An alternative approach to the treatment of emotionally disturbed children and youth. In A. Algarin & R. Friedman (Eds.), *A system of care for children's mental health: Building a research base* (pp. 299–312). Tampa: Florida Mental Health Institute, University of South Florida.

Morrisey, R., Dicker, R., Abikoff, H., Avir, J., DiMarco, A., & Koplewicz, H. (1995). Hospitalizing the suicidal adolescent: An empirical investigation of decision-making criteria. *Journal of American Academy of Child and Adolescent Psychiatry, 34,* 902–911.

Pandiani, J., Maynard, A., & Schacht, L. (1994). Modeling of movement between residential placements: A systems analytic approach to understanding systems of care. *Journal of Child and Family Studies, 3,* 41–53.

Parmelee, D., Cohen, R., Nemil, M., Best, A., Cassell, R., & Dyson, F. (1995). Children and adolescents discharged from public psychiatric hospitals: Evaluation of outcome in a continuum of care. *Journal of Child and Family Studies, 4,* 43–55.

Pastore, C., Thomas, J., & Newman, I. (1990). Therapeutic in-home emergency services. In A. Algarin & R. Friedman (Eds.), *A system of care for children's mental health: Building a research base* (pp. 291–298). Tampa: Florida Mental Health Institute, University of South Florida.

Pavuluri, M., Luk, S., & McGee, R. (1996). Help-seeking for behavior problems by parents of preschool children: A community study. *Journal of American Academy of Child and Adolescent Psychiatry, 35,* 215–222.

Pfeiffer, S., & Strzelecki, S. (1990). Inpatient psychiatric treatment of children and adolescents: A review of outcome studies. *Journal of American Academy of Child and Adolescent Psychiatry, 29,* 847–853.

Pumariega, A. (1996). Culturally competent outcome evaluation in systems of care for children's mental health. *Journal of Child and Family Studies, 5,* 389–397.

Pumariega, A., Atkins, L., Montgomery, L., Appenzeller, S., Caesar, R., & Millus, D. (1996a). Service utilization in incarcerated youth. *1996 Annual Meeting New Research Programs and Abstracts* (Abstract NR 230, p. 130). Washington, DC: American Psychiatric Association.

Pumariega, A., Atkins, L., Montgomery, L., Rogers, K., Sease, F., & Jeffers, G. (1996b). Psychopathology in incarcerated youth. *1996 Annual Meeting New Research Programs and Abstracts* (Abstract NR 229, p. 130). Washington, DC: American Psychiatric Association.

Pumariega, A., & Cross, T. (1997). Cultural competence in child psychiatry. In J. Noshpitz & N. Alessi (Eds.), *Basic handbook of child and adolescent psychiatry* (Vol. IV). New York: Wiley.

Pumariega, A., Glover, S., Holzer, C., & Nguyen, H. (in press). Utilization of mental health services in a tri-ethnic sample of adolescents. *Community Mental Health Journal.*

Pumariega, A., Holliday, B., & Holzer, C. (1995). *Conceptual paradigms in support of mental health research on immigrant and ethnic minority populations.* Alexandria, VA: NASMHPD Research Institute.

Pumariega, A., Nace, D., England, M. J., Diamond, J., Mattson, A., Fallon, T., Hanson, G., Lourie, I., Marx, L., Thurber, D., Winters, N., Graham, M., & Wiegand, D. (1997). Community-based systems approach to children's managed mental health services. *Journal of Child and Family Studies, 6*(2), 149–164.

Pumariega, A., Swanson, J., Holzer, C., Linskey, A., & Quintero-Salinas, R. (1992). Cultural context and substance abuse in Hispanic adolescents. *Journal of Child and Family Studies, 1,* 75–92.

Quinn, K., Epstein, M., Dennis, K., Potter, K., Sharma, J., McKelvey, J., & Cumblad, C. (1996). Personal, family, and service utilization characteristics of children served in an urban family preservation environment. *Journal of Child and Family Studies, 5,* 469–486.

Reis, J., Bennett, S., Orme, J., & Herz, E. (1989). Family support programs: A quasi-experimental evaluation. *Children and Youth Services Review, 11,* 239–262.

Robbins, M. L. (1994). Native American perspective. In J. Gorden (Ed.), *Managing multiculturalism in substance abuse services* (pp. 148–176). Thousand Oaks, CA: Sage.

Robins, L., Helzer, J., Ratcliff, K., & Seyfried, W. (1982). Validity of the Diagnostic Interview Schedule, Version II: DSM-III diagnoses. *Psychological Medicine, 12,* 855–870.

Robins, L. (1985). Epidemiology: Reflections on testing the validity of psychiatric interviews. *Archives of General Psychiatry, 42,* 918–924.

Rosenblatt, A. (1996, February). *Using the CAFAS in systems of care in California.* Presentation at the 9th Annual Research Conference: A system of care for children's mental health: Expanding the research base. Sponsored by the Research and Training Center for Children's Mental Health, Florida Mental Health Institute, University of South Florida.

Rosenblatt, A., & Attkisson, C. (1992). Integrating systems of care in California for youth with severe emotional disturbance. I: A descriptive overview of the California AB377 Evaluation Project. *Journal of Child and Family Studies, 1*(1), 93–113.

Scherer, D., Brondino, M., Henggeler, S., Melton, G., & Hanley, J. (1994). Multisystemic family preservation therapy: Preliminary findings from a study of rural and minority serious adolescent offenders. *Journal of Emotional and Behavioral Disorders, 2,* 198–206.

Schoenwald, S., Ward, D., Henggeler, S., Pickerel, S., & Patel, H. (1996). Multisystemic therapy treatment of substance abusing or dependent adolescent offenders: Costs of reducing incarceration, inpatient, and residential placement. *Journal of Child and Family Studies, 5,* 431–444.

Schwab, M., & Stone, K. (1983). Conceptual and methodological issues in the evaluation of children's satisfaction with their mental health care. *Evaluation and Program Planning, 6,* 283–289.

Seaberg, J., & Tolley, E. (1986). Predictors of the length of stay in foster care. *Social Work Research and Abstracts, 22,* 11–17.

Shaffer, D., Fisher, P., Dulcan, M., Davies, M., Piacentini, J., Schwab-Stone, M., Lahey, B., Bourdon, K., Jansen, P., Bird, H., Canino, G., & Regier, D. (1996). The NIMH Diagnostic Interview Schedule for Children Version 2.3 (DISC 2.3): Description, acceptability, prevalence rates, and performance in the MECA study. *Journal of American Academy of Child and Adolescent Psychiatry, 35,* 865–877.

Shaffer, D., Gould, M., Brasic, J., Ambrosini, P., Fisher, P., Bird, H., & Aluwahlia, S. (1983). A children's global assessment scale (CGAS). *Archives of General Psychiatry, 40,* 1228–1231.

Shyne, A. (1980). Who are the children? A national overview. *Social Work Research and Abstracts, 16,* 26–33.

Shyne, A., & Schroeder, A. (1978). *National study of social services in children and their families.* Rockville, MD: Westat, Inc.

Silver, S., Duchnowski, A., Kutash, K., Friedman, R., Eisen, M., Prange, M., Brandenburg, N., & Greenbaum, P. (1992). A comparison of children with serious emotional disturbance served in residential and school settings. *Journal of Child and Family Studies, 1*(1), 43–59.

Singh, N., Curtis, W., Cohen, R., Nicholson, M., Villani, T., & Wechsler, Z. (1996a). *Measuring perception of family involvement. I: The Family Involvement Scale—Family Version.* Richmond, VA: Commonwealth Institute for Child and Family Studies.

Singh, N., Curtis, W., Cohen, R., Nicholson, M., Villani, T., & Wechsler, Z. (1996b). *Measuring perception of family involvement. I: The Family Involvement Scale—Professional Version.* Richmond, VA: Commonwealth Institute for Child and Family Studies.

Singh, N., Curtis, W., Ellis, C., Nicholson, M., Villani, T., & Wechsler, H. (1995). Psychometric analysis of the Family Empowerment Scale. *Journal of Emotional and Behavioral Disorders, 3,* 85–91.

Skinner, H., Steinhauer, P., & Santa-Barbara, J. (1984). *The Family Assessment Measure: Administration and interpretation guide.* Toronto, Ontario: Addictions Research Foundation.

Spielberger, C. (1973). *Preliminary Test Manual for the State–Trait Anxiety Inventory for Children* Palo Alto, CA: Consulting Psychologists Press.

Staghezza-Jaramillo, B., Bird, H., Gould, M., & Canino, G. (1995). Mental health services utilization among Puerto Rican children ages 4 to 16. *Journal of Child and Family Studies, 4,* 399–418.

Stroul, B., & Friedman, R. (1986). *A system of care for severely emotionally disturbed children and youth.* Washington, DC: Georgetown University Child Development Center, CASSP Technical Assistance Center.

Teare, J., Authier, K., & Peterson, R. (1994). Differential patterns of post-shelter placement as a function of problem type and severity. *Journal of Child and Family Studies, 3*(1), 7–22.

Thornton, S., & Garret, K. (1995). Ethnography as a bridge to multicultural practice. *Journal of Social Work Education, 31,* 67–74.

Tuma, J. (1989). Mental health services for children: The state of the art. *American Psychologist, 44,* 188–199.

Van Hasselt, V. B., & Hersen, M. (1991). *Handbook of behavior therapy and pharmacotherapy for children.* Needham Heights, MA: Allyn & Bacon.

Verhulst, F., & Koot, H. (1992). *Child psychiatric epidemiology: Concepts, methods, and findings.* In A. Kazdin (Ed.), *Developmental clinical psychology and psychiatry* (Vol. 23, pp. 20–41). Newbury Park, CA: Sage.

Westendorp, F., Brink, K., Roberson, M., & Ortiz, I. (1986). Variables which differentiate placement of adolescents into juvenile justice or mental health systems. *Adolescence, 21,* 23–35.

Windle, C., Jacobs, J., & Sherman, P. (1986). *Mental Health Program Performance Measurement.* Rockville, MD: Division of Biometry and Applied Sciences, National Institute on Mental Health, Alcohol and Drug Abuse and Mental Health Administration.

Yoe, J., Santarcangelo, S., Atkins, M., & Burchard, J. (1996). Wraparound care in Vermont: Program development, implementation, and evaluation of a statewide system of individualized services. *Journal of Child and Family Studies, 5*(1), 23–39.

Young, S., Nicholson, J., & Davis, M. (1995). An overview of issues in research on consumer satisfaction with child and adolescent mental health services. *Journal of Child and Family Studies, 4,* 219–238.

Index